# Digital Russia

I0008962

*Digital Russia* provides a comprehensive analysis of the ways in which new media technologies have shaped language and communication in contemporary Russia. It traces the development of the Russian-language internet, explores the evolution of web-based communication practices, showing how they have shaped and been reshaped by social, political, linguistic and literary realities, and examines online features and trends that are characteristic of, and in some cases specific to, the Russian-language internet.

**Michael S. Gorham** is an Associate Professor of Russian Studies at the University of Florida, USA.

**Ingunn Lunde** is Professor of Russian at the University of Bergen, Norway.

**Martin Paulsen** is a Postdoctoral Fellow at the University of Bergen, Norway.

## Routledge Contemporary Russia and Eastern Europe Series

1 **Liberal Nationalism in Central Europe**
*Stefan Auer*

2 **Civil-Military Relations in Russia and Eastern Europe**
*David J. Betz*

3 **The Extreme Nationalist Threat in Russia**
The growing influence of Western Rightist ideas
*Thomas Parland*

4 **Economic Development in Tatarstan**
Global markets and a Russian region
*Leo McCann*

5 **Adapting to Russia's New LabourMarket**
Gender and employment strategy
*Edited by Sarah Ashwin*

6 **Building Democracy and Civil Society East of the Elbe**
Essays in honour of Edmund Mokrzycki
*Edited by Sven Eliaeson*

7 **The Telengits of Southern Siberia**
Landscape, religion and knowledge in motion
*Agnieszka Halemba*

8 **The Development of Capitalism in Russia**
*Simon Clarke*

9 **Russian Television Today**
Primetime drama and comedy
*David MacFadyen*

10 **The Rebuilding of Greater Russia**
Putin's foreign policy towards the CIS countries
*Bertil Nygren*

11 **A Russian Factory Enters the Market Economy**
*Claudio Morrison*

12 **Democracy Building and Civil Society in Post-Soviet Armenia**
*Armine Ishkanian*

13 **NATO-Russia Relations in the Twenty-First Century**
*Aurel Braun*

**14 Russian Military Reform**
A failed exercise in defence decision making
*Carolina Vendil Pallin*

**15 The Multilateral Dimension in Russian Foreign Policy**
*Edited by Elana Wilson Rowe and Stina Torjesen*

**16 Russian Nationalism and the National Reassertion of Russia**
*Edited by Marlène Laruelle*

**17 The Caucasus – An Introduction**
*Frederik Coene*

**18 Radical Islam in the Former Soviet Union**
*Edited by Galina M. Yemelianova*

**19 Russia's European Agenda and the Baltic States**
*Janina Šleivytė*

**20 Regional Development in Central and Eastern Europe**
Development processes and policy challenges
*Edited by Grzegorz Gorzelak, John Bachtler and Maciej Smętkowski*

**21 Russia and Europe**
Reaching agreements, digging trenches
*Kjell Engelbrekt and Bertil Nygren*

**22 Russia's Skinheads**
Exploring and rethinking subcultural lives
*Hilary Pilkington, Elena Omel'chenko and Al'bina Garifzianova*

**23 The Colour Revolutions in the Former Soviet Republics**
Successes and failures
*Edited by Donnacha Ó Beacháin and Abel Polese*

**24 Russian Mass Media and Changing Values**
*Edited by Arja Rosenholm, Kaarle Nordenstreng and Elena Trubina*

**25 The Heritage of Soviet Oriental Studies**
*Edited by Michael Kemper and Stephan Conermann*

**26 Religion and Language in Post-Soviet Russia**
*Brian P. Bennett*

**27 Jewish Women Writers in the Soviet Union**
*Rina Lapidus*

**28 Chinese Migrants in Russia, Central Asia and Eastern Europe**
*Edited by Felix B. Chang and Sunnie T. Rucker-Chang*

**29 Poland's EU Accession**
*Sergiusz Trzeciak*

**30 The Russian Armed Forces in Transition**
Economic, geopolitical and institutional uncertainties
*Edited by Roger N. McDermott, Bertil Nygren and Carolina Vendil Pallin*

**31 The Religious Factor in Russia's Foreign Policy**
*Alicja Curanović*

**32 Postcommunist Film – Russia, Eastern Europe and World Culture**
Moving images of postcommunism
*Edited by Lars Kristensen*

**33 Russian Multinationals**
From regional supremacy to global lead
*Andrei Panibratov*

**34 Russian Anthropology After the Collapse of Communism**
*Edited by Albert Baiburin, Catriona Kelly and Nikolai Vakhtin*

**35 The Post-Soviet Russian Orthodox Church**
Politics, culture and Greater Russia
*Katja Richters*

**36 Lenin's Terror**
The ideological origins of early Soviet State violence
*James Ryan*

**37 Life in Post-Communist Eastern Europe after EU Membership**
*Edited by Donnacha Ó Beacháin, Vera Sheridan and Sabina Stan*

**38 EU-Border Security**
Challenges, (mis)perceptions, and responses
*Serghei Golunov*

**39 Power and Legitimacy – Challenges from Russia**
*Edited by Per-Arne Bodin, Stefan Hedlund and Elena Namli*

**40 Managing Ethnic Diversity in Russia**
*Edited by Oleh Protsyk and Benedikt Harzl*

**41 Believing in Russia – Religious Policy After Communism**
*Geraldine Fagan*

**42 The Changing Russian University**
From state to market
*Tatiana Maximova-Mentzoni*

**43 The Transition to National Armies in the Former Soviet Republics, 1988–2005**
*Jesse Paul Lehrke*

**44 The Fall of the Iron Curtain and the Culture of Europe**
*Peter I. Barta*

**45 Russia After 2012**
From Putin to Medvedev to Putin – continuity, change, or revolution?
*Edited by J.L. Black and Michael Johns*

**46 Business in Post-Communist Russia**
Privatisation and the limits of transformation
*Mikhail Glazunov*

**47 Rural Inequality in Divided Russia**
*Stephen K. Wegren*

**48 Business Leaders and New Varieties of Capitalism in Post-Communist Europe**
*Edited by Katharina Bluhm, Bernd Martens and Vera Trappmann*

**49 Russian Energy and Security up to 2030**
*Edited by Susanne Oxenstierna and Veli-Pekka Tynkkynen*

**50 The Informal Post-Socialist Economy**
Embedded practices and livelihoods
*Edited by Jeremy Morris and Abel Polese*

**51 Russia and East Asia**
Informal and gradual integration
*Edited by Tsuneo Akaha and Anna Vassilieva*

**52 The Making of Modern Georgia, 1918–2012**
The first Georgian Republic and its successors
*Edited by Stephen F. Jones*

**53 Digital Russia**
The language, culture and politics of new media communication
*Edited by Michael S. Gorham, Ingunn Lunde and Martin Paulsen*

# Digital Russia

## The language, culture and politics of new media communication

**Edited by Michael S. Gorham, Ingunn Lunde and Martin Paulsen**

Routledge
Taylor & Francis Group
LONDON AND NEW YORK

First published 2014 by Routledge

2 Park Square, Milton Park, Abingdon, Oxon OX14 4RN
711 Third Avenue, New York, NY 10017, USA

*Routledge is an imprint of the Taylor & Francis Group, an informa business*

First issued in paperback 2016

Copyright © 2014 selection and editorial material, Michael S. Gorham, Ingunn Lunde and Martin Paulsen; individual chapters, the contributors.

The right of Michael S. Gorham, Ingunn Lunde and Martin Paulsen to be identified as authors of the editorial material, and of the individual contributors as authors of their chapters, has been asserted by them in accordance with sections 77 and 78 of the Copyright, Designs and Patents Act 1988.

All rights reserved. No part of this book may be reprinted or reproduced or utilised in any form or by any electronic, mechanical, or other means, now known or hereafter invented, including photocopying and recording, or in any information storage or retrieval system, without permission in writing from the publishers.

Notice:
Product or corporate names may be trademarks or registered trademarks, and are used only for identification and explanation without intent to infringe.

*British Library Cataloguing in Publication Data*
A catalogue record for this book is available from the British Library

*Library of Congress Cataloging in Publication Data*
Digital Russia : the culture, language and politics of new media communication / edited by Michael Gorham, Ingunn Lunde, and Martin Paulsen.
pages cm. — (Routledge contemporary Russia and Eastern Europe series)
Includes bibliographical references and index.
1. Internet—Social aspects—Russia (Federation) 2. Information technology—Russia (Federation) 3. Russian language. I. Gorham, Michael. II. Lunde, Ingunn, 1969– III. Paulsen, Martin.
HM851.D544 2014
320.23'1–dc23
2013032729

ISBN: 978-0-415-70704-6 (hbk)
ISBN: 978-1-138-20600-7 (pbk)

Typeset in Baskerville MT
by RefineCatch Limited, Bungay, Suffolk

**In loving memory of Daniela S. Hristova (1962–2010), who graced us with her love for life and language.**

# Contents

# Illustrations

## Figures



## Tables

# Notes on contributors

**Aleksandrs Berdicevskis** is a Postdoctoral Fellow in Russian linguistics at the University of Tromsø. As a member of the "Future of Russian" project, he was a PhD student at the University of Bergen, writing a dissertation on linguistic innovations in Russian induced by computer-mediated communication.

**Michael S. Gorham** is an Associate Professor of Russian Studies at the University of Florida, Associate Editor of *The Russian Review* and *Russian Language Journal*, and author of *Speaking in Soviet Tongues: Language Culture and the Politics of Voice in Revolutionary Russia* (Northern Illinois UP 2003) and *After Newspeak: Language Culture and Politics in Russia from Gorbachev to Putin* (Cornell UP, 2014).

**Gasan Gusejnov**, PhD in Classics, Dr.phil.habil in Russian Studies, is a Professor at the Higher School of Economics in Moscow. He teaches classical philology, Russian political rhetoric and Digital Humanities at the HSE's Faculty of Media.

**Natalya Konradova** is a writer and a journalist at Radio Liberty in Moscow. She co-authored and co-edited the book *Control + Shift: Public and Private Usages of the Russian Internet* (with Henrike Schmidt and Katy Teubener, 2006).

**Roman Leibov** is an Associate Professor in the Department of Russian Literature, University of Tartu (Estonia). His main research interests are Tiutchev's poetry, the Russian literary canon, new media and creative writing. His main online project is Ruthenia.ru.

**Ingunn Lunde** is Professor of Russian at the University of Bergen and Professor of Russian Literature and Culture at the University of Tromsø. She is the author of *Verbal Celebrations: Kirill of Turov's Homiletic Rhetoric and its Byzantine Sources* (Harrassowitz 2001) and the General Editor of Slavica Bergensia.

**Kåre Johan Mjør** is a Postdoctoral Research Fellow at the Uppsala Centre for Russian and Eurasian Studies (Uppsala University). He is the author of *Reformulating Russia: The Cultural and Intellectual Historiography of Russian First-Wave Emigré Writers* (Brill 2011).

**Martin Paulsen** is a Postdoctoral Fellow at the University of Bergen, where he received his PhD in Russian language studies in 2009. With Ingunn Lunde, he co-edited *From Poets to Padonki: Linguistic Authority and Norm Negotiation in Modern Russian Culture* (University of Bergen 2009).

**Tine Roesen** is an Associate Professor of Russian Literature at the University of Copenhagen, Denmark. She is the co-editor (with Ingunn Lunde) of *Landslide of the Norm: Language Culture in Post-Soviet Russia* (2006) and (with Dirk Uffelmann) of *Sorokin's Languages* (2013).

**Ellen Rutten** is a Professor of Slavonic Studies at the University of Amsterdam and the leader of the digital memory research project "Web Wars" (www.web-wars.org). She is also the editor of the new media journal *Digital Icons* and author of *Unattainable Bride Russia* (Northwestern UP, 2010).

**Henrike Schmidt** is a Private Lecturer at the Peter Szondi Institute for Comparative Literature, Freie Universität Berlin. Her research interests include digital and networked culture in East and Central Europe, and Russian and Bulgarian literature. Her recent publications include *Russische Literatur im Internet: Zwischen digitaler Folklore und politischer Propaganda* (transkript Verlag).

**Vlad Strukov** is an Associate Professor in Russian Cultural Studies and World Cinemas, University of Leeds. He is the founding director of the Leeds Russian Centre and the editor of a journal entitled *Digital Icons: Studies in Russian, Eurasian and Central European New Media.*

**Dirk Uffelmann** is a Professor of Slavic Literatures and Cultures and the Vice President for Academic and Student Affairs at the University of Passau, Germany. His research interests are Russian, Polish, Czech, Slovak and Central Asian literature, philosophy, religion, migration and internet studies.

**Vera Zvereva** is a Research Fellow and Manager at the Princess Dashkova Russian Centre, University of Edinburgh, and Associate Professor in the Department of Art History at the Russian State University of the Humanities. A member of the "Future of Russian" (Bergen 2008–12) and "Memory at War" (Cambridge 2010–12) projects, she has published extensively on media culture.

# Acknowledgments

This book is the result of a four-year research project "The Future of Russian: Language Culture in the Era of New Technology," based at the University of Bergen, 2008–12. The chapters were commissioned from the international group of project partners and their extended networks. We thank the Research Council of Norway for its generous funding of a wide range of project events, including five international conferences in Bergen, Berlin, Passau, and St Petersburg, 2008–12.

First drafts were vetted at a workshop in Solstrand near Bergen in June 2012. We thank our invited discussants, Stephen Hutchings, Ilya Kukulin, Lara Ryazanova-Clarke, Sali Tagliamonte, and Alexei Yurchak, for their creative criticism. We are also grateful to the international network of scholars who have contributed to the collected efforts of the Future of Russian project over its four-year duration, including Jannis Androutsopoulos, Sandra Birzer, Helge Blakkisrud, Ewa Callahan, Helene Dounaevsky, Eugene Gorny, Susan Herring, Maksim Krongauz, Sergei Kuznetsov, Maria Maiofis, Nina Mechkovskaia, Galina Miazhevich, Natalia Moen, Elena Morenkova-Perrier, Daniel Müller, Alla Nedashkivska, Catharine Nepomnyashchy, Vladimir Plungyan, Oleg Reut, Sean P. Roberts, Marie-Laure Ryan, Natalia Sokolova, Victor Sonkin, Tatiana Teterevleva, and Espen Aarseth.

We thank Kyrill Dissanayake for his careful editing of our non-native English, Alexander Burak and Kyrill Dissanayake for translating two chapters, and Peter Sowden and Helena Hurd of Routledge for their enthusiasm and efficiency.

Finally, our warmest thanks to all contributors for their wonderful cooperation at all stages of the making of this book.

# A note on transliteration and translation

Russian has been transliterated according to the Library of Congress system. Where established English spellings of names and place names exist, these have been given preference (e.g., Yeltsin rather than E'ltsin, Dostoevsky rather than Dostoevskii).

All translations are ours unless otherwise stated. The contribution by Roman Leibov was translated by Alexander Burak; the contribution by Gasan Gusejnov was translated by Kyrill Dissanayake.

# Introduction

*Michael S. Gorham, Ingunn Lunde and Martin Paulsen*

За правдой ходим к интернету—#спасибопутинузаэто
(To get the truth, we seek out the internet, thanks to Putin for that.)

On 7 October 2011, the blogger and United Russia Party member Vladimir Burmatov wanted to congratulate Prime Minister Vladimir Putin on the occasion of his 59th birthday. He posted a rhyming couplet on Twitter—"Moscow is warm and sunny. Summer! #thankstoputinforthat" (*V Moskve teplo i solntse. Leto! #spasiboputinuzaeto*)—and encouraged others to follow up with their own tweets using the #thankstoputinforthat hashtag. The invitation was quickly accepted, but not in the way Burmatov had anticipated. The growing anti-Putin sentiment on the Russian-language internet, commonly known as the *Runet*, meant that the majority of tweets were critical of Putin's rule, and this critique was voiced in playful, satirical verses directed at the ruling tandem (i.e. the joint rule of Putin and Medvedev), the upcoming elections, or the general state of affairs in Russian politics and society.

Есть выборы и как бы нету, #спасибопутинузаэто
Elections exist, and yet they don't, #thankstoputinforthat

Свобода слова лишь в инете #спасибопутинузаэто
Freedom of speech exists only on the web #thankstoputinforthat

Тандем – восьмое чудо света #спасибопутинузаэто
The Tandem is the eighth wonder of the world! #thankstoputinforthat

Over the rest of the day, more than 10,000 similar tweets were sent, with the result that *#spasiboputinuzaeto* became the top trending hashtag globally on that day, the first Cyrillic hashtag to achieve this level of popularity.[1] This led to news headlines such as *The Wall Street Journal*'s "Putin Becomes a Twitter Sensation." The event illustrates that the Runet is a highly politicized domain, and is generally critical of the incumbent regime, as is obvious from tweets such as "I watch TV, but there's no truth #thankstoputinforthat" (*Smotriu TV, a pravdy netu #spasiboputinuzaeto*).

To understand the hashtag's popularity, we also need to take Russian cultural traditions into consideration, including the particular aesthetics of Soviet and post-Soviet linguistic and political humor. In inventing the hashtag, Burmatov had taken inspiration from a well-known and ironic Soviet couplet: "Winter is gone, summer's here, thanks to the Party for that" (*Ushla zima, nastalo leto, spasibo Partii za eto*). Many tweets responded playfully with similar rhymes, as in the following example: "No money and no flat #thankstoputinforthat" (*Khochu kvartiru—deneg netu #spasiboputinuzaeto*). In the #thankstoputinforthat example, then, we see how cultural traditions combine with the specific stylistic, rhetorical, and technological dynamics of new media usage in Russia today.

It is the intersections of the technological with the creative, the political with the cultural, and the global with the local that provide the focal point for this volume. *Digital Russia* provides the most comprehensive analysis to date of the manner in which new media technologies have shaped language and communication in contemporary Russia. As importantly, it integrates a variety of analytical perspectives—including conceptual histories, genre studies, and disciplinary case studies—to explore how web-based language practices (broadly defined) themselves give shape to social, political, linguistic, and literary events and reality. In some cases, the processes resemble trends in other national or transnational internet cultures; in other cases, distinctively Russian features emerge. As a result, the book as a whole offers insight into two main issues simultaneously: (1) the nature of and tension between web-based language practices and broader social contexts—and more specifically the mutual determination of the two; and (2) features and trends characteristic of, and in some cases specific to, the Russian-language internet.

The internet became a mass phenomenon in Russia only after the turn of the millennium. If, in 2003, 9 percent of the Russian population accessed the internet on a monthly basis, the ensuing decade has seen a dramatic increase in the use of internet users in the country, with 43 percent of the population accessing web-based resources on a *daily* basis by February 2013 (Redaktsiia FOM 2013). This makes Russia the European country with the highest number of internet users—now over 50 million daily—even if the relative numbers are far lower than in Western Europe (Internet World Stats 2012).

Over half of Russia's internet users reside in and around the major metropolitan hubs of Moscow and St Petersburg. In 2013, two-thirds of the population in Moscow and St Petersburg had regular access to the internet, but the same is true only for one out of three villagers (Redaktsiia FOM 2012a). Yet when examined according to growth rate, internet use in Russia currently owes its strong growth to increased usage in regional cities and in small towns and villages (Redaktsiia FOM 2013). Part of this recent growth, especially in the countryside, is related to the spread of mobile phones with internet connections. In 2011, the number of mobile phone subscriptions far exceeded the population (ITU n.d.), and a third of Russia's internet users accessed the net via mobile phones at least once a month. After a slow start, third- and fourth-generation mobile phone infrastructure is spreading rapidly (Freedom House 2012).

Internet use is still stratified according to age. In 2012, 82 percent of those aged between 25 and 34 accessed the internet on a regular basis, while pensioners are only starting to engage with the internet, with only 16 percent using the internet regularly in 2012 (Duzhnikova 2012). And yet here, too, much of the most recent growth in web connectivity has come as a result of these previously underrepresented groups. So even though the overwhelming majority of Russians still consider television to be their main source of information, the internet is gaining influence: already dominant among urban youth, and growing in importance among older Russians, as well as in the regions (N.n. 2011; Redaktsiia FOM 2012b). In fact, by early 2013, the leading Russian search engine, Yandex, had surpassed Russia's most widely watched television station, *Pervyi kanal*, in daily traffic, and had drawn even with it in advertising revenue generated (N.n. 2013).

Official Russian response to this rapid growth has varied. Particularly during the presidency of Dmitry Medvedev, himself a self-professed new technophile, the Russian government has invested money and prestige in the development of a competitive IT industry, most prominently through the establishment of the special economic zone in Skolkovo, the Russian "Silicon Valley." Early in his presidency, Medvedev even established his own video blog to communicate with the Russian population, encouraging his fellow bureaucrats to do the same. His predecessor and successor, in contrast, has been markedly less enthusiastic. In 2010, in a reaction to criticism in internet publications, Putin declared that half of the internet is pornography (Lastochkin 2010). And since being sworn in for a third presidential term in May 2012, he has overseen a string of legislative initiatives that can only be interpreted as an attempt to rein in the Runet as a space for opposition discourse. In the summer of 2012, he signed a new federal law that ostensibly seeks to protect children from harmful information and regulate access to illegal information on the internet (Zakon N 139-F3 2012). The law has been criticized for introducing new opportunities for censorship, especially through the creation of a "Unified Registry of illegal sites," quickly rebranded as an internet "blacklist" by its many opponents.[2] Laws designed to combat extremism have already been used to shut down sites and block or remove information, while more covert efforts to shut down independent news sites through denial of service (DDoS) attacks and harass opposition bloggers through trolling, smear campaigns, and trumped-up legal proceedings are clearly on the rise (Freedom House 2012).[3]

Whether the Russian-language internet is merely going through growing pains typical of most revolutionary technologies or heading toward a twenty-first-century "cyber curtain" is too early to determine. It is clear, however, that neither the technologies, nor the tensions to which they have given rise, are disappearing anytime soon, and more thoughtful, well-informed study and analysis are acutely needed to better understand the nature of their origins and evolution. The present volume provides a significant step in that direction, focusing on the global features and national particularities of web-based public communication in Russia.

Although the study of the internet and communication is a young discipline, several stages and trends can already be discerned. Linguist and new media scholar Jannis Androutsopoulos (2006, 2011) has identified two "waves" in the various linguistic approaches to digital culture. The "first wave" focused on features and strategies that were assumed to be specific to linguistic practices in the new media, seeking to determine the "effects" of digital technology on language (e.g. Baron 1984; Ferrara, Brunner, and Whittemore 1991; Crystal 2006, 2008). Partly as a reaction to this trend, the "second wave," informed by sociolinguistics, discourse studies and pragmatics, moved from media-related to user-related approaches, with a focus on contextual uses of language and linguistic diversity (e.g. Herring 1996; Androutsopoulos 2006; Georgakopolou 2006). Since then, we have seen a great amount of research ranging from quantitative studies with large corpora (e.g. Tagliamonte and Denis 2008) to studies grounded in qualitative and ethnographic methods (e.g. Androutsopoulos 2008). A related recent trend is the heightened awareness of the Web 2.0 as a multimodal entity incorporating text, image, audio, and video—often in playful combination—in an environment characterized by social interaction and cultural diversity. Attempts to develop new analytical tools to assess how discourses emerge and develop in Web 2.0 environments can be seen in publications such as the comprehensive *Discourse 2.0: Language and New Media* (Tannen and Trester 2013).

One of the consequences of the reorientation from media-focused to user-focused studies is the "multilingual turn" in CMC (computer-mediated communication) research. English is no longer the one and only dominant language used on the internet, and in recent years researchers have turned their attention to the fact that "communication technologies with a 'global' reach [are also] situated in very local cultures of use" (Goggin and McLelland 2009b: 4). The multilingual turn in CMC, or, more generally, internet studies, has been recorded by publications such as *The Multilingual Internet: Language, Culture, and Communication Online* (Danet and Herring 2007), *Internationalizing Internet Studies: Beyond Anglophone Paradigms* (Goggin and McLelland 2009a) and *Digital Discourse: Language in the New Media* (Thurlow and Mroczek 2011). As yet, Russian and other Slavic languages are virtually absent in such collections.[4]

Meanwhile, Russian internet studies have flourished in their own particular way. A rich amount of research has carved out an understanding of Runet culture and politics, Russian digital literature, and Russian online language culture (e.g. Trofimova 2004; Schmidt, Teubener, and Konradova 2006; Sidorova 2006; Gorny 2009; Mechkovskaia 2009; Deibert et al. 2010; Toepfl 2012; Oates 2013).[5] While theoretically sophisticated and rich in original empirical material, this research is generally less informed by recent developments in international CMC studies.

This book fills that gap by integrating current CMC research with Runet studies and thus contributing to the internationalization of both sub-disciplines. In addition to offering a basic introduction to key subsectors of Russian internet culture, it also seeks answers to broader questions: How do new technologies influence the ways we communicate, interact, and create? How are linguistic practices shaped by the tension between social context and new technologies? How are offline events represented, recreated, and transformed in online contexts? How do linguistic practices online shape and transform political, social, and cultural reality? To what extent are the features and trends discussed in these pages specific to Russia, Russian, and the Russian internet, and to what extent do they reflect more global lingustic and social practices?

Part I of *Digital Russia* features two interpretive histories critical to understanding Russia-specific new media phenomena today: the first tracing the evolution of the personal computer as both technology and ideology (Chapter 1 by Strukov), the second examining the rise of the Russian-language internet, or Runet, itself as both virtual and imagined space (Chapter 2 by Konradova and Schmidt). Part II focuses more generically on key platforms or spaces of new media communication: the blogosphere (Chapter 3 by Gusejnov), social networking sites (Chapter 4 by Roesen and Zvereva), and more recent trends in microblogging, primarily through the use of Twitter (Chapter 5 by Paulsen and Zvereva). In addition to discussing some of the main communicative and linguistic characteristics, these chapters also take up more specific case studies that provide concrete examples of some of the broader discursive trends at work.

The analyses in Parts I and II provide a critical historical, descriptive, and interpretive framework for better understanding and contextualizing the remaining chapters of the book. Parts III–V concentrate on three different spheres where language and communication have been significantly transformed as a result of the emergence of new media technologies. Part III focuses on the language itself and features analyses of three different levels of language: structural and lexical (Chapter 6 by Berdicevskis and Chapter 7 by Berdicevskis and Zvereva), metalinguistic (Chapter 8 by Lunde), and orthographic (Chapter 9 by Paulsen). Issues of non-standard and innovative language, of discourse on language itself, and of orthography and scripts, have long been territories ripe for contestation and debate: new media technologies have raised issues both old and new in all of these areas, some specific to Russia and Russian media, others of a more global nature. The authors in Part IV train their gaze on the impact of new media technologies in the literary realm, Chapter 10 (Schmidt) discussing some of the main trends in web-based literary culture, Chapter 11 (Leibov) looking at the rebirth of old poetic genres in new media contexts, and Chapter 12 (Mjør) discussing how online libraries have influenced the general perception and consumption of books. Finally, Part V forges into the realm of politics, looking at the challenges and opportunities new media technologies present for projects of political self-fashioning (Chapter 13 by Gorham), historical memory (Chapter 14 by Rutten), and virtual colonization in a post-colonial world (Chapter 15 by Uffelmann).

Runet is a lively, rapidly-growing and contested part of the global web which offers rich ground for research on linguistic, cultural, and politic developments. This book aims to further the understanding of both the peculiarities and the global trends of Russian digital media in the multifaceted and truly international internet.

## Notes

1 See the Wikireality entry (wikireality.ru/wiki/спасибопутинузаэто).
2 Edinyi reestr (zapret-info.gov.ru).
3 This volume went to press just prior to the start of the Russian government's court case against opposition blogger and anti-corruption advocate Aleksei Navalny, for allegedly illegal business dealings in the Kirovskaia oblast' while serving as an advisor to Oblast' Governor Nikita Belykh.
4 There is an excellent article by Eugene Gorny in Goggin and McLelland (2009a), telling the story of the immensely popular Russian site Anekdot.ru (Russian jokes). However, it stands somewhat isolated in the collection and Russian internet research is not taken into account in the bibliographical survey of the book.
5 The path-breaking online journal *Digital Icons: Studies in Russian, Eurasian and Central European New Media* (digitalicons.org) has made important contributions to all of these areas since its inception in 2009.

## References


Androutsopoulos, Jannis. 2006. "Introduction: Sociolinguistics and Computer-Mediated Communication." *Journal of Sociolinguistics* 10(4): 419–38.

—— 2008. "Potentials and Limitations of Discourse-Centered Online Ethnography." Language@Internet 5. Available at: http://www.languageatinternet.org/articles/2008/1610 (accessed 29 March 2013).

—— 2011. "Language Change and Digital Media: A Review of Conceptions and Evidence." In *Standard Languages and Language Standards in a Changing Europe*, edited by Nikolas Coupland and Tore Kristiansen, 145–60. Oslo: Novus.

Baron, Naomi, S. 1984. "Computer-Mediated Communication as a Force in Language Change." *Visible Language* 18(2): 118–41.

Crystal, David. 2006. *Language and the Internet.* Cambridge: Cambridge University Press.

—— 2008. *Txtng: the gr8 db8.* Oxford: Oxford University Press.

Danet, Brenda and Susan Herring. 2007. *The Multilingual Internet: Language, Culture, and Communication Online.* New York: Oxford University Press.

Deibert, Ronald, John Palfrey, Rafal Rohozinski, and Jonathan Zittrain, eds. 2010. *Access Controlled: The Shaping of Power, Rights, and Rule in Cyberspace.* Cambridge, MA: MIT Press.

Duzhnikova, Anna. 2012. "Internet segodnya." *VTsIOM.* Available at: http://www.old.wciom.ru/fileadmin/news/2012/Duzhnikova_internet-2012_wciom.pdf (accessed 29 April 2013).

Ferrara, Kathleen, Hans Brunner, and Greg Whittemore. 1991. "Interactive Written Discourse as an Emergent Register." *Written Communication* 8(1): 8–34.

Freedom House. 2012. "Freedom of the Net 2012." *Freedom House.* Available at: http://www.freedomhouse.org/sites/default/files/resources/FOTN%202012%20-%20Full%20Report_0.pdf (accessed 29 April 2013).

Georgakopolou, Alexandra. 2006. "Postscript: Computer-mediated Communication in Sociolinguistics." *Journal of Sociolinguistics* 10(4): 548–57.

Goggin, Gerard, and Mark McLelland, eds. 2009a. *Internationalizing Internet Studies: Beyond Anglophone Paradigms.* New York: Routledge.

—— 2009b. "Introduction: Internationalizing Internet Studies." In *Internationalizing Internet Studies: Beyond Anglophone Paradigms*, edited by Gerard Goggin and Mark McLelland, 3–17. New York: Routledge.

Gorny, Eugene. 2009. *A Creative History of the Russian Internet: Studies in Internet Creativity*. Saarbrücken: VMD Verlag.

Herring, Susan. 1996. *Computer-Mediated Communication: Linguistic, Social and Cross-Cultural Perspectives*. Amsterdam: John Benjamins.

Internet World Stats. 2012. "Internet and Facebook Usage in Europe." *Internet World Stats*, 30 June. Available at: http://www.internetworldstats.com/stats4.htm (accessed 29 April 2013).

ITU. N.d. "Mobile-Cellular Telephone Subscriptions." *International Telecommunications Union*. Available at: http://tinyurl.com/cperfvj (accessed 29 April 2013).

Lastochkin, Viktor. 2010. "Putin skazal vsiiu pravdu ob Internet: 50%—eto pornografiia." *UralDaily.ru*, 25 January. Available at: http://uraldaily.ru/node/381 (accessed 29 April 2013).

Mechkovskaia, Nina. 2009. *Istoriia iazyka i istoriia kommunikatsii: ot klinopisi do interneta*. Moscow: Flinta/Nauka.

N.n. 2011. "98% rossiian ispol'zuiut kak osnovnoi istochnik informatsii tsentral'noe televidenie, no ne doveriaiut emu—oprosy VTsIOM." *Tass telecom*, 2 November. Available at: http://tasstelecom.ru/news/one/5729 (accessed 29 April 2013).

N.n. 2013. "'Iandex' dognal Pervyi kanal po reklamnym dokhodam." *Lenta*, 16 April 2013. Available at: http://lenta.ru/news/2013/04/16/yafirst/ (accessed 29 April 2013).

Oates, Sarah. 2013. *The Political Limits of the Internet in the Post-Soviet Sphere.* Oxford: Oxford University Press.

Redaktsiia FOM. 2012a. "Internet v Rossii: dinamika proniknoveniia. Osen' 2012." *Fond Obshchestvennoe Mnenie*, 18 December. Available at: http://runet.fom.ru/Proniknovenie-interneta/10738 (accessed 29 April 2013).

Redaktsiia FOM. 2012b. "Osobennosti potrebleniia informatsii: stolitsy vs drugie goroda Rossii." *Fond Obshchestvennoe Mnenie*, 29 November. Available at: http://runet.fom.ru/Proniknovenie-interneta/10712 (accessed 29 April 2013).

Redaktsiia FOM. 2013. "Internet v Rossii: dinamika proniknoveniia. Zima 2012–2013." *Fond Obshchestvennoe Mnenie*, 13 March. Available at: http://runet.fom.ru/posts/10853 (accessed 29 April 2013).

Schmidt, Henrike, Katy Teubener, and Natalja Konradova, eds. 2006. *Control + Shift: Public and Private Uses of the Russian Internet*. Norderstedt: Books on Demand GmbH. Available at: http://www.katy-teubener.de/joomla/images/stories/texts/publikationen/control_shift_01.pdf (accessed 29 March 2013).

Sidorova, Marina. 2006. *Internet-lingvistika: russkii iazyk: mezhlichnostnoe obshchenie*. Moskva: 1989.ru. Available at: http://www.philol.msu.ru/~sidorova/files/blogs.pdf (accessed 29 March 2013).

Tagliamonte, Sali A., and Derek Denis. 2008. "Linguistic Ruin? Lol!: Instant Messaging and Teen Language." *American Speech* 83(1): 4–34.

Tannen, Deborah, and Anna Maria Trester, eds. 2013. *Discourse 2.0: Language and New Media*. Washington, DC: Georgetown University Press.

Thurlow, Crispin, and Kristine Mroczek, eds. 2011. *Digital Discourse: Language in the New Media.* Oxford: Oxford University Press.

Toepfl, Florian. 2012. "Blogging for the Sake of the President: The Online-Diaries of Russian Governors," *Europe-Asia Studies* 64(8): 1435–59.

Trofimova, Galina. 2004. "Funktsionirovanie russkogo iazyka v Internete: kontseptual'no-sushchnostnye dominanty." PhD thesis, Peoples' Friendship University of Russia, Moscow.

Zakon N 139-F3. 2012. "Federal'nyi zakon Rossiiskoi Federatsii ot 28 iuliia 2012 g. N 139-F3 'O vnesenii izmenenii v Federal'nyi zakon "O zashchite detei ot informatsii, prichiniaiushchei vred ikh zdorov'iu i razvitiu" i otdel'nye zakonodatel'nye akty Rossiiskoi Federatsii'." *Rossiiskaia gazeta*, 30 July. Available at: http://www.rg.ru/2012/07/30/zakon-dok.html (accessed 29 April 2013).

# Part I

# Contexts

# 1 The (im)personal connection

## Computational systems and (post-) Soviet cultural history

*Vlad Strukov*

This is the cherished computer
That even Stanislaw Lem could not dream of,
That is the subject of poems and odes,
That is the pain in the neck of IBM.[1]
*That is the House that Jack Built.*
(Humorous sketch, Jubilee celebrations, the Institute of Precision Mechanics and Computer Engineering, Moscow, 14 December 1973)

## Introduction

The word "computer" (*komp'iuter*) is a recent addition to the Russian language. In the late 1980s it entered into use alongside the Russian term "EVM," an acronym that stands for "electronic calculating machine" (*elektronno-vychislitel'naia mashina*). The new term was introduced deliberately to designate a personal computing machine, and, in the early 1990s, following the dissolution of the USSR and the collapse of the Soviet computer industry, it gained the additional meaning of a Western-made computing device. The change from "EVM" to "computer" signifies a change in the methods of consumption; as the title of the chapter suggests, Soviet computers were never intended for personal, individual use—the (im)personal connection—and, therefore, the contemporary collaborative practice on the Russian internet is grounded in the early collective use of computers in the USSR. In fact, even when personal computers became available, in the official discourse the use of the term "personal" was carefully avoided; ideologically correct euphemisms were used instead, such as *EVM massovogo primeneniia* ("electronic calculating machine for use by the masses"; see Naumov 1987). Ironically, these Soviet ideologemes correctly defined the future of computing—the move from specialized use by experts to mass use everywhere in the world.

In this chapter I aim to put forward a theoretical framework for the analysis of late Soviet and post-Soviet computational practice in relation to ideologies of consumption and digital subjectivities in both historical and cultural perspective. The focus of the chapter is on the personal computer conceived simultaneously as a utilitarian object, social practice, means of communication, type of organization of labor and an element in the ideological apparatus of the state. I interrogate the relationship among three nodes of enquiry—computer technology, ideology and subjectivity—both as modes of production and consumption, as well as their transformation over the period of transition to a market economy. I reposition the technologically-enhanced subjectivity by contrasting it with types of technological use. The term "impersonal" means "not having personality" and refers normally to the "impersonalizing" effect of computers (for example, see Walther and Carr 2010; Bolin 2012); in this chapter, however, the term denotes the lack of personal, private consumption of computer technologies in the USSR, presenting the Soviet computer as a collective, collaborative practice. In addition, the personal computer is regarded as a key component in Soviet and Russian systems of knowledge formation (*informatika*), which evolved from being a technical tool to a system of "immaterial labor" (Lazzarato 1996). The history of the relationship between computers and ideology has been explored in Slava Gerovitch's (2002) detailed study of Soviet cybernetics, where he argues for the emergence of a whole discourse, what he calls "cyberspeak," that shifted the boundaries between knowledge and ideology in the 1950s–1970s. In my study, I focus on the later Soviet period and Gorbachev's perestroika, and I analyze Soviet technological ideologemes in relation to Soviet ideologies and practices of consumption, thus extending and refining the theoretical framework of the "technology versus ideology" debate.

Research presented in this chapter is multidisciplinary, and it includes archival work that traces digital history in Russia and the USSR, oral histories collected in the form of interviews with engineers who worked at Soviet computer manufacturing plants,[2] and digital memoirs of early practitioners of the Runet.[3] I combine digital anthropology with analysis of Soviet and post-Soviet media in order to reconstruct the official and popular discourses surrounding computer technology.[4] The chapter consists of three sections. The first provides a critical overview of early Soviet experiments with computer technologies, and it situates the computer in relation to the Soviet ideological machine. The second and third sections focus on two periods, 1985–95 and 1995–2005. These periods are designated *historically* (the transition from the USSR to post-Soviet Russia), *technologically* (the release of the first Soviet personal computers in 1985; the launch of Microsoft Windows Cyrillic in 1995, enabling coding in Russian; and the emergence of social networking sites in the mid-2000s), *socially* (the transition from elite to mass use of computers), and *culturally* (from collective to collaborative use). While the overall development of the Soviet-Russian computer industry is similar to those of other countries, it differs in that there has been a complete overhaul of the production system and a seismic shift in the understanding of the role of computation technologies over the past 25 years. These technological and cultural differences inform the discussion in the second and third sections concerning the transformation of the ideological system as well as social and cultural practice. As the Soviet-Russian tradition of computer manufacturing was interrupted in the early 1990s, my analysis begins with both the production of the hardware and the consumption of computer technologies in the USSR, and then in its latter stages focuses on consumption and artistic, commercial and other uses of computers. I demonstrate how the ideological "cyberspeak" of the Soviet era is transformed into the technological and cultural "double-speak" of the post-Soviet period and later into social and political "counter-speak" in the new millennium. The chapter concludes by considering the use of computers in Russia in the new globalized context of the Putin era.

## Ideologies of computation and consumption (the pre-Gorbachev period)

In the USSR, as in the UK, the USA, France and other countries, computers appeared as part of the military-industrial complex at the start of the Cold War. In fact, a research facility for applied mathematics and computer technology was established in 1947 to run calculations for ballistic missiles and anti-missile defenses. The first analogue computational device was built in Kiev in 1951, and an automatic computing machine was assembled in Moscow in 1953. Both were designed by engineer-enthusiasts who had managed to overcome ideological hurdles.[5] The development of the Soviet computer program was initially hindered for ideological reasons. In 1953, *Voprosy Filosofii* published an anonymous article entitled "Whom Cybernetics Serves," which denounced cybernetics as a reactionary bourgeois science that was at odds with dialectical and historical materialism. Cybernetics was rehabilitated as part of de-Stalinization, leading to the establishment of a Scientific Council of the USSR Academy of Science on Cybernetics in 1958. The original ideological conflict was resolved by accepting cybernetics as a science of rationality that fostered and advanced the teaching of Marxism-Leninism. This provided scholars and engineers with the boost needed for the creation of a competitive computer industry. In fact, Loren A. Graham (1973: 324) observed that in the 1960s cybernetics enjoyed more prestige in the USSR than in any other country in the world.

If, during the Thaw,[6] cybernetics and, by extension, computers, were at the center of the ideological debate, in the 1970s, there were firm moves to integrate computer systems into the Soviet industrial complex. In his speech at the 24th Party Congress in April 1971, Leonid Brezhnev argued for the improvement of management in the USSR:

> Science has substantially enriched the theoretical arsenal of planning [. . .] We should use these methods more widely and establish automated management systems more quickly, bearing in mind that in the long run we should establish a state-wide automated system of information collection and processing.
>
> ("Materialy" 1971: 67–8)

In the long-standing tradition of Soviet economic development, Brezhnev favored a country-wide, centrally-controlled, top-down system of collecting and processing information. As V.F. Sirenko documents, the system was necessitated by the rising complexity of industrial production, a greater variety of products and the speed of technological change (1976: 6–8). The computer and other types of automation were conceived of as means to improve the Soviet planning system. A nation-wide system for collection, storage and processing of data for economic planning, management and accounting, known by its acronym OGAS, was established in order to facilitate the work of the state central planning department, Gosplan. With its automated systems for the control of technological processes, the management of enterprise, planning calculations, state statistics and other systems, OGAS was meant to emerge as a super-system of management and control that would supersede and normalize inefficient structures inherited from the pre-war period of rampant industrialization. Therefore the Party's ideologists fostered the use of the computer as an administrative, managerial tool rather than as a means of production, a key component in a new electronic industry.

Instead of utilizing available technologies, the Party officials prescribed the very development of computer systems, thus making the process unnecessarily complicated and unwittingly jeopardizing the whole computer industry. For example, in 1974, Gosplan adjusted its own targets, aiming to install 1,583 computers (417 in construction, 129 in agriculture, 129 in transport, etc.) (Samborskii and Simchera 1974). In reality, there were far fewer computers available, and the technological system was forced to rely on the second generation of computers at a time when the third generation had already appeared. As a result, the ideological system supported the production of computers that had already become outdated, thus severing the link between innovation and production, as well as widening the technological gap between the USSR and the West. Furthermore, dizzied by the rivalry with the USA, the Soviet authorities financed computer projects that would surpass American equivalents in terms of speed of automation or any other easily quantifiable feature that they could use for their own ideological aims. This approach gave birth to the world's fastest computer and the computer with the largest memory, but rarely to a technology that could provide users with a reliable service in mundane circumstances.[7] Such a distortion of the computer industry occurred at the level of technological implementation but not at the level of ideas. Finally, computers had been integrated into the Soviet system of what Martin Cave, following on Soviet scientists, calls meta-planning—"the selection of and, where necessary, the transfer to a new planning and management system" (1980: 24–5). In other words, computers became—at least at the level of discourse—part of the state super-structure, overseeing and servicing all of society and industry. As a result, the Soviet state had major stakes in the computer industry, which were military—as in the USA and other countries—but also structural and ideological. To reiterate, unlike in the USA, computers in the USSR were expected to reconfigure the structure of the Soviet economy and the state itself and, as a result, diffusion of authority occurred at the level of political and economic leadership. For instance, the Academy of Sciences was responsible for research, Minpribor for the production of the hardware, and Gosplan for various enterprises. In turn, this gave rise to technological, administrative and political incompatibilities, while at the same time creating a large class of workers trained in information management. This class—the authority at the middle level—would be instrumental in dismantling the Soviet political system in the late 1980s and privatizing industrial property in the 1990s.

It is estimated that in 1970 the USSR had about 5,000 computers, or about 20 per million inhabitants. By comparison, the USA had a stock of 344 per million, and the UK and Japan—91 and 96, respectively (Cave 1980: 190). The statistics demonstrate that personal computers were not a mass phenomenon in either the USSR or the West in the 1970s; there is, however, a clear indication that work was being carried out in this direction. The comparison also reveals that, unlike in the West and Japan, the Soviet computer was never intended for personal consumption. It was firmly rooted in the Soviet industrial complex and it was framed as an ideological phenomenon, encouraging continuous exercise in computer discourse rather than actual application. The figures also reveal that the USSR was lagging behind other countries, something that was well known to the Soviet leadership. In the late 1970s, the Soviet authorities attempted to counteract what they assumed was the technological backwardness of the computer industry by encouraging engineers to copy legally and illegally obtained Western computers.[8] As the engineers were unable to imitate foreign computers fully, they often had to come up with their own solutions, which would result in the development of a hybrid, Western-Soviet computer system. For example, El'brus, one of the components of the Soviet defense system, used original programming languages; however, it contained an analytical system of tagging used in machines produced by the American Burroughs Corporation.[9] In Russia today, some people in the industry view the political/technological moves of the late Brezhnev era as catastrophic for the Soviet computer industry (see, for example, Losenkov 2012; Nedobezhkin 2012, Sosnovskii and Orlov 2002). On one level, it destroyed the indigenous computer industry, but, arguably, paradoxically it enabled the fast integration of Soviet engineers into the Western computer industry, something from which it has benefited greatly (see, for example, the case of Pentkovskii discussed below). On another level, it helped establish a culture of state-sponsored theft of computer technologies, to such an extent that even nowadays copyright laws are hard to enforce in the Russian Federation, and the discussion of free exchange of information and cultural products via computerized networks dominates the Russian blogosphere and social media.

## From the "perestroika machine" to the computer "kooperativ" (1985–95)

Soviet computers became "personal" as part of the process of gradual privatization introduced by Mikhail Gorbachev. Gorbachev placed computers at the center of his political and social reform. The comprehensive strategic vision adopted in Moscow in 1985 identified several areas where accelerated development was required. One of them was "informatization" of the economy.[10] While the focus of "informatization" was on the Soviet economy, it was closely linked to the other two main policies of perestroika—*uskorenie* (acceleration) and *glasnost'* (transparency)—in that it was believed that the computer would enable free circulation of information and more efficient and rapid development of the economy and society. In other words, the computer was conceived as a perfect "perestroika machine" that would enable the transition of Soviet society into a new era of prosperity. As part of this political vision, the USSR Academy of Sciences was charged with the task of developing new supercomputers for military and research purposes, as well as building computers for Soviet industry. For instance, the vector-conveyor supercomputer was to be developed in 1987 and a super mini-computer was to be built in 1988 (Adirim 1991: 651–4). Adirim notes that one-third of the measures and investment were directed at computer production (1991: 660), and such measures introduced a reorganization of labor as research institutes and industrial concerns were merged into laboratories.

My analysis of publications in *Iunyi tekhnik* in 1985 indicates that, at the start of perestroika, the computer was perceived as part of the greater Soviet industrial project. The following example illustrates the point. Published in issue seven, collages—the prevailing form for visual representation of new technologies in the USSR—show the usual paraphernalia of Soviet technological interest: aviation, space exploration, mining natural resources, agriculture, etc.; the imagery of computers is injected alongside the images of airplanes and industrial control stations. In addition, the theme of the computer and computation is highlighted in the editorial, entitled "Welcome to Moscow." It is a typical address to visitors to Moscow, which, in this instance, is aimed at internal consumption, i.e. branding the capital and with it the wider Soviet Union as the center for cutting-edge technologies. The editorial is written in the form of a mathematical equation; it explicates the complexity of the problem and calls on computers to solve it. The second image shows a laboratory with the computers that provide such services. In this case, we are witnessing an instance of the Soviet tradition of introducing technical innovation as part of the utilitarian agenda, i.e. aiming to achieve greater efficiency and precision but not to sell a technological marvel.

Soviet technological utilitarianism dominated the discourse over new technologies in 1985–88. For example, *Iunyi tekhnik* (1985, issue 10) boasts a new Soviet computer EC 1066; in an interview, the senior technician, O.B. Kalmykov, claims that "similar computers are available in virtually all computer centers in the country," and goes on to suggest that a future specialist would almost certainly work on one of them. The computer here is used as a means to attract the new generation into the Soviet industrial complex—a difficult task indeed, since, as we know from the feature films of the period (for example, Karen Shakhnazarov's 1986 *The Courier*), young Soviet people were disenchanted with and disconnected from the ideals of Soviet industry, which in turn found it harder and harder to recruit new workers. The consumer aspect of the computer is virtually non-existent in this discussion and can only be found in a description of the new machine's user-friendly interface.[11]

Gorbachev's political vision also relied on the recent successes of the Soviet computer industry. In 1985, in Zelenograd, the Soviet "Silicon Valley" in the suburbs of Moscow, the first personal computer was launched—BK0010. The original model consisted of one element—the keyboard—which had to be connected to a television set, that was used as a screen, and the keyboard could also be connected to a stereo if the user wanted to record any information. The design of the first Soviet personal computer was clunky; in fact, it epitomized the general Soviet attitude to the design of consumer goods, in that the product had to be assembled, adapted, remodeled or reshaped by the users in order to meet their needs and expectations. BK0010 required extensive knowledge of programming and engineering in order to be operated. In spite of these challenges, the computer was so loved by the Soviet people that they fondly christened it "Bukashka" (little bug), a name derived from the Cyrillic characters used in the official name. Bukashka came to symbolize the Soviet personal computer of the 1980s: on the one hand, it was an odd item in the Soviet DIY-style consumer economy; on the other, as current developments in digital media demonstrate (e-book readers, smart phones, etc.), it was an ingenious gadget since it enabled adaptive, on-the-go use of the computer technology that otherwise became widespread only in the mid-2000s.[12] The emphasis on the keyboard also signaled the perceived primacy of writing,[13] highlighting the Soviet obsession with the printed word. While in previous decades the Soviet state had regulated the use of typewriters by compelling all owners to register their devices with the KGB, no such policy was implemented in relation to either tape recorders or personal computers, thus freeing the PC from Soviet ideological controls over the means of production of information and knowledge. This practice had a long-lasting effect on Russian networked technologies in that they remained unregulated until Putin's government in the early 2000s.

The Bukashka boasted 32kb of memory and a 3MHz CPU which was astonishingly good for the time. The actual keyboard was of the membrane type: the user had to press on plastic covers rather than key caps.[14] In this regard, Bukashka foreshadowed the haptic screens of iPads and other tablets. This design revealed the intended use of the computer—as an educational tool in Soviet schools—and displayed the logic of many Soviet consumer products: it was dust- and spill-proof but, as a result, was quite hard to operate, as pressing plastic buttons was tricky and required a certain degree of skill. Eventually, the plastic keyboard was replaced with a more conventional one and, while BK0010 became commonplace in Soviet schools, its original "portable" design was lost. In education, the computer was seen as a means of propagating physics and mathematics as the two schools of thought in which the USSR had been leading the world. My analysis of school textbooks of the time (see, for example, Maksimov 1992; Martuzian 1991; Miachev 1992; Mironov 1994; Valov 1993) reveals that the emphasis was on teaching logic and advanced mathematics—defined in terms of subject area as *informatika* (informatics), or computational processes—rather than teaching pupils how to use computers.

The importance of creating a new class of workers was highlighted in the September 1986 issue of *Rabotnitsa*; its front cover featured a computer classroom in a Soviet school (see Figure 1.1). The photograph portrays a young male teacher showing a little girl how to use a personal computer. Although the readership of the journal was predominantly female, the use of the male teacher symbolizes Soviet engineering dominated by men,[15] with the little girl representing the workforce of the future. His formal attire—a white military-style shirt and a

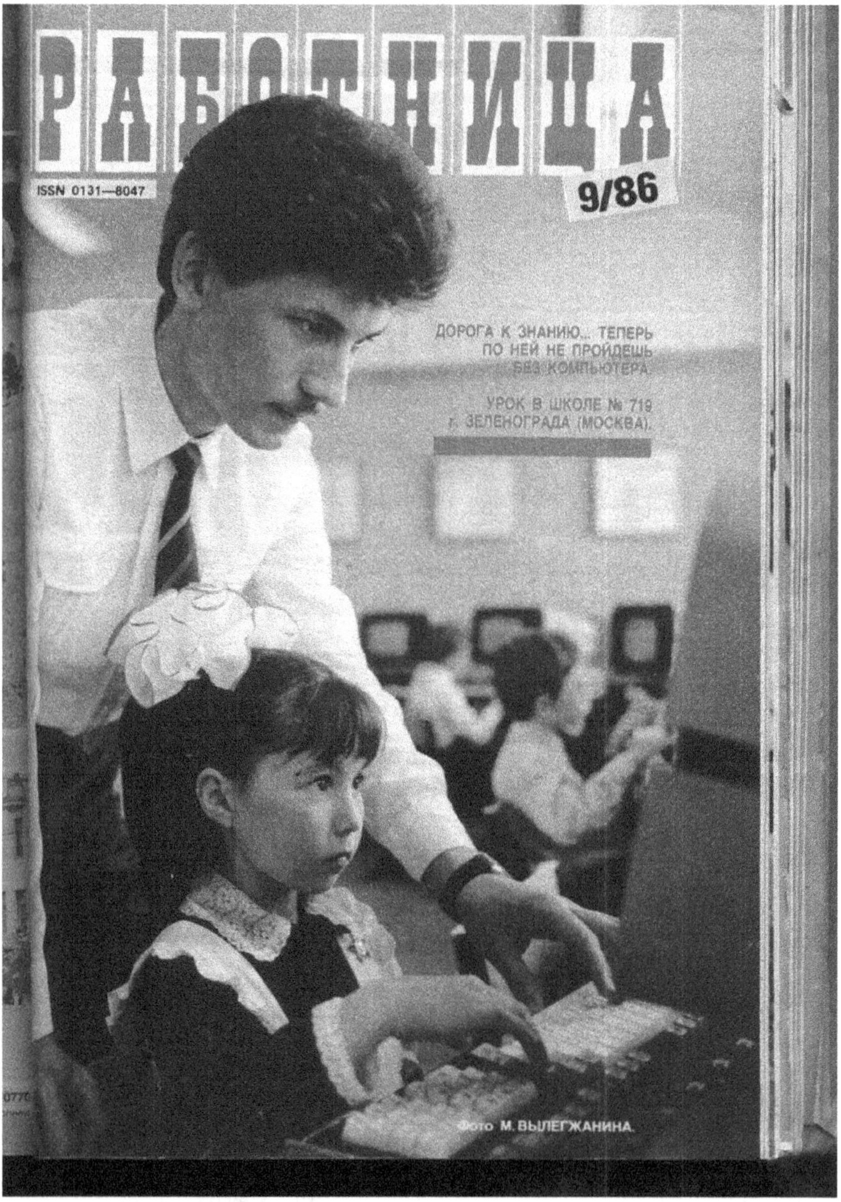


*Figure 1.1* Scan of the cover of *Rabotnitsa* magazine (1986, issue 9). The caption in Russian reads, "A path to knowledge . . . now you cannot walk it without a computer. A lesson in school 719 in Zelenograd (Moscow)."

striped tie—emphasizes the connection between the Soviet military complex and the emerging post-industrial base. The image focuses on one part of the computer—the keyboard—because of its symbolic capacity to represent labor, unlike the computer screen, which was linked to television and leisure. Although the image centers on the man and the girl, it shows other users in the room, thus putting forward the idea of the availability of technology in the USSR, as well as stressing the collective aspect of computer use. As is demonstrated in this and many other images that circulated in Soviet media, the computer was perceived as something occupying the professional and not domestic space, as a tool of learning and production and not entertainment or self-expression. Furthermore, the visual materials published in the press at that time documented the collective, shared use of computers and rarely hinted at the possibility of an individual, personal connection between man and machine.

In the true spirit of perestroika, Soviet industry produced competing makes of personal computers: "Mikrosha" was released at the Lianozovskii electromechanical factory in 1987. Like Bukashka, the machine relied on the use of a black-and-white television as its screen and a home cassette player as its storage device. With their very specific designs, the release of both Bukashka and Mikrosha signified the position of electronics as gadgets in the USSR: these were seen as parts of the same family of domestic electronic equipment, with significant emphasis on entertainment. Mikrosha came with a set of games, for example, chess, and other useful applications, such as file editing and programs enabling use of simple graphics. The producers of Mikrosha appealed to the family market by providing Mikrosha with programs that made it possible to catalogue the home library and create a database of cooking recipes (Matveev 1992). The design of Mikrosha and Bukashka also projected official views on the class structure of Soviet society, defined in its relation to consumer commodities. It was assumed that a user buying a Bukashka would already own a television set and a tape recorder; indeed, both were common household items in the 1980s and yet were not possessed by everyone. For example, Soviet nuclear industry specialists would bring tape recorders from Cuba and other countries in the Eastern Bloc at the end of their business trips. Thus, the first personal computers were deliberately aimed at the Soviet technological elite, and this intention marked the digression of conservative Soviet ideological views on class, commodity and private ownership.

The first Soviet computer fully intended for personal use by the mass user was the Elektronnika MK-85, produced at the Voronezh Protsessor plant. It was a modification of a personal computer previously released by the Digital Equipment Corporation and, like its American predecessor, was positioned as an affordable computing device for personal use. Unfortunately the Elektronnika MK-85 had a few significant drawbacks. When it was released, it had fewer than 40 programs to run and was therefore used chiefly as an advanced calculating machine. Although it provided the user with the opportunity to create and edit texts, it was not equipped with a printer, and Epson printers were used instead, which at times were not entirely compatible. This meant that it could not be efficiently used for editing, or general word-processing purposes. In true Soviet fashion, the computer did not come with a manual, and therefore required in-depth knowledge of computation, including the knowledge of programming languages such as Basic (Khmeliuk 1992).

In addition to Bukashka, Mikrosha and Elektronnika, the Soviet industry produced another type of personal computer, known as "ES" type (*edinaia sistema*). Designed to provide a modular link between Soviet and foreign computers such as IBM PCs, it served as a technological bridge and cultural adaptor between different types of machines, computer systems and cultures of computing. As such, it symbolized the Soviet computer industry's position as a global bridge, linking local, indigenous computing systems with mass-produced Western products. In the USSR, the industry aimed to adapt and translate information and technological flows for local use; it also engaged in more radical, semi-legal forms of localization and customization. As part of the process of personalization of computers, Elektronnika produced a handheld video game that was an almost exact replica of Nintendo's Game and Watch Consoles. For example, it featured a local character, the famous Wolf from the *Nu pogodi!* (You Just Wait!) animation series.[16] Adopted from Western technology and design, Elektronnika was one of the first computerized gadgets in the USSR that was designed to provide absolutely individual enjoyment. The Elektronnika craze seemed to contradict the Soviet ideals of shared, communal life, as it placed emphasis on electronic forms of communication in the private realm.

In general, however, the Soviet industry failed to respond to the demands of consumers: not enough video games and personal computers were available in Soviet shops, giving a boost to the unofficial, black market for electronic devices. At first, illegally obtained Elektronnikas would be offered for sale on street markets: sellers and buyers would congregate outside official electronic stores and would exchange spare parts, programs, devices, etc. This practice reinforced the culture of sharing technologies and software in the 1990s and, later, in the 2000s, on social networks. After Gorbachev's government allowed private entrepreneurship in the form of "cooperatives" in May 1987, many companies trading electronics—including computers and spare parts—appeared almost instantaneously. As has been claimed on many occasions (see, for example, Kuz'michev 2010; Sitnikov 2012), these cooperatives paved the way for private ownership in the USSR and created the first Russian millionaires, while at the same time having a negative effect on the economy and society by providing hubs for illegal trade, fraud and other forms of corruption. In Russian digital culture, the cooperatives cemented a culture of theft of intellectual property, illegal exchange of copyrighted material and unauthorized use of public resources. As a result, the personal computer was transformed from its status as "perestroika machine" into a symbol of a new era of rampant privatization, modernization and personal success.

## From computer boutiques to "digital masses" (1995–2005)

As a political entity the Soviet Union came to an end in 1991; however, the former Soviet republics continued to rely on the Soviet technological infrastructure until the late 1990s, and in some areas have even continued to do so right up to the present day. Production of the EVM 5E26, designed by Lebedev and Burtsev in

1978, was discontinued only in 1994; 1,500 devices were produced in 16 years (Burtsev 2002: 274). On one level, this example highlights post-Soviet technological inertia. On another level, it demonstrates the "double-speak" of the first decade of transition, whereby different, often contradictory systems of production, management and consumption were in use. In relation to Soviet modernity, Gerovitch defines "cyberspeak" as a monolithic "grand narrative" of the Soviet regime; my analysis shows that "cyberspeak" splits at the end of the Soviet period, thus stressing the fragmentation of the Soviet project and associated cultural practice. On the one hand, the state drew on Soviet technology for its own purposes, military in this case as the Russian defense system relied on the Soviet infrastructure, and so computers used in the Russian army had to be replaced with their counterparts. On the other hand, the private sector and ordinary consumers had started using what they perceived as Western technology and, in actual fact, was a product of global capitalism, when technology had been developed and built by international corporations. Therefore, "cyberspeak" identified by Gerovitch in relation to the Soviet period tells part of the story of the computer industry and consumption of PCs in the USSR; moreover, my analysis demonstrates that "cyberspeak" transforms into the "double-speak" of the late Soviet era and informs the technological and cultural divides in contemporary Russia. For example, Medvedev's call for modernization (2008–9) was aimed at the state itself rather than ordinary citizens, as it required the modernization of outdated, Soviet-made and Soviet-style technologies still in use. In other words, Medvedev's government felt threatened not only by global capitalism but also by its own more technologically advanced citizens. Medvedev's call for modernization, or what I would call the "counter-speak" of the Russian government, is an extension of the Soviet "cyber-speak" and post-Soviet "double-speak," which raises new concerns that I address in the final part of the chapter.

Overall, in the newly formed Russian Federation, production of personal computers went into total decline in the early 1990s. Factories specializing in building computers were closed down or had undergone special "conversion" programs (*konversiia*), that is, switched to produce, for example, coffee-makers, plastic bowls and other low-tech consumer goods. The gap in the market was almost immediately filled with imported computers; the former "cooperatives," now transformed into private companies, continued to thrive as they carried on selling foreign-made computers and/or computers assembled in Russia from imported parts. From a country producing its own computers and even exporting some technologies abroad, Russia turned into a country fully reliant on technological imports. At the same time, US-made computers such as IBM PCs became symbols of de-Sovietization, commercial enterprise and individual success. While in the USSR the computer was perceived as an extension of the Soviet industrial complex, in the early 1990s it came to symbolize the commercial sector, which had replaced outdated Soviet heavy industry. By 1995, Soviet personal computers were obsolete, a distant memory of socialist electronic modernity. At the same time, imported personal computers were expensive—they cost more than a Russian car—and therefore remained out of reach for the majority of Russian citizens until the late 1990s. The major shift occurred in the mid-1990s when the economy was reignited and there was an increase in wages, and also when Microsoft released its Windows 95 operating system, with a consumer-oriented graphical user interface and built-in Cyrillic, allowing programming and encoding in Russian. Since this product did not require any knowledge of English, it marked the arrival of a new computer era in Russia.

While new technologies traveled East, from the USA and Europe to Russia, Russian computer scientists and engineers migrated in the opposite direction. It is hard to estimate the damage to the Russian economy and society from the brain drain of the 1990s. In 2005, Vladimir Zernov, the President of Independent Universities of Russia, put it at 1 trillion roubles (Zernov 2005). The case of Vladimir Pentkovskii exemplifies the losses and the gains of the new Russia. Pentkovskii graduated from the Radio Technology and Cybernetics Department of the Moscow Physics-Mathematical Institute and belonged to the school of thought established by Lebedev in the 1950s. In the early 1990s, Pentkovskii emigrated to the USA, and secured employment with the Intel Corporation in 1993. While in the Soviet Union he was involved in the development of the El'brus superscalar computer; the project was completed in 1978, some 15 years before similar computers emerged in the West. After joining Intel, Pentkovskii was in charge of the team that developed the Pentium Pro, introduced by Intel in 1995. The architecture of the new processor relied on the structure of the Soviet supercomputer (Fatkullin 1999). In 2010, Pentkovskii returned to Russia, where he became Chair of the newly founded Super Computer Applications Laboratory for Advanced Research (i-SCALARE 2010). Pentkovskii's story is proof of the afterlife of the Soviet computer project: it survived—albeit in a completely transformed form—in spite of ideological pressures, the dissolution of the USSR and the financial collapse in post-Soviet Russia. It also demonstrates that the boundaries between different technological systems were largely ideological, and that the Soviet and American computer traditions merged in their global search for a new generation of personal computers after the Cold War.[17]

Nationally, the development of computer systems in the Russian Federation had three main sources: (1) the state, which continued to invest in super-fast computers; (2) private enterprise, which required new technologies in order to meet rising consumer demand; and (3) philanthropists, who believed in the ability of the computer to change societies and political regimes. George Soros was one such generous patron; he played a key role in the development of Russian computer and internet systems. In 1995, he founded the Open Society Institute (the Soros Foundation) and began to provide financial support for the creation of computer centers in Russian universities and non-governmental organizations. Over six years 33 centers emerged in major urban centers in Russia, linking together academics and students across the country and also enabling access to information centers around the world. By focusing on humanities, the Soros Foundation upended Russian academia's assumption that computers were research tools for the hard sciences and engineering, thus fostering a new generation of computer-savvy researchers in humanities. The Foundation was likewise responsible for changing the focus of the first internet pages to appear on the Russian-language internet, from mostly technology-oriented content to content related to social activity and personal expression. By supporting academics in the 1990s, especially after the financial crisis of 1998, which for many made the purchase of new technologies prohibitively expensive, the Soros Foundation helped develop the Russian intellectual elite, with its traditionally liberal orientation towards society. Along with Soviet technologists, post-Soviet entrepreneurs and the finance sector, Russian academics were the first users of internet technologies in the country, and formed its "digital intelligentsia" (Strukov 2006).

One of the tasks facing the "digital intelligentsia" in this period was transgressing technological, national and cultural boundaries. They aimed to build a new democratic world using personal computers and a newly available internet. By personalizing technology they wished to "technologize" and democratize society, i.e. they believed in technological determinism, and new computer practices occurred in environments sponsored by private business or non-governmental organizations. In this regard, the technological utopia of Russian digital intelligentsia was unique, because it envisaged public discourse in the private realm. That was because, after perestroika, "private" was based on technological innovation and was charged with the new democratizing potential that had been curtailed in the USSR. The personal computer facilitated the peculiar inversion of private and public, official and unofficial that occurred in the late 1990s as part of the process of de-Sovietization. The creative work of Olia Lialina exemplifies these tendencies.

Lialina belongs to a group of artists—Vuk Ćosić, Jodi.org, Alexei Shulgin and Heath Bunting—who have been working in the medium of internet-enabled art since 1994. Their first collaborative projects appeared in 1995 and included works that queried the role of computer technology, the status of art and national boundaries. They engaged in a critique of official art by curating their own exhibitions on the internet, and they problematized the existing notions of space and communication by staging digital performances online. Their art occupied post-national zones in the cyber world, and they utilized the computer as a means for the production, display and consumption of art. For example, Lialina's *My Boyfriend Came Back from the War* (1996) explores the notions of private and public space by using an interactive, non-linear narrative, which signifies the break-up of a relationship, and graphic frames that had been used in the construction of early web pages; frames signal boundaries that are imposed on individuals as well as imagined by them.[18] By engaging with the artwork, the user constructs their own unique experience of computer culture and also violates the privacy of other individuals, and the characters in the story, eventually disavowing their own privacy and subjectivity. Thus, Lialina's work advances collaborative use of the internet by problematizing the relationship between private and public and renegotiating the (im)personal connection of the computer as a communication machine. Her work demonstrates a departure from the collective use of computers as represented in Soviet media and discussed above.

If Lialina's net.art exemplifies the first artistic experiments with computer and internet technologies, Artemii Lebedev's career epitomizes the commercial successes of Russian early computer enthusiasts. Born into the family of the writer, Tatiana Tolstaya, and literary scholar, Andrei Lebedev, Artemii was educated in Russia and the USA. In 1995, he founded a computer studio called "WebDesign," which was one of the first web development studios in Russia and on the Runet. In 1998, it was renamed "Artemii Lebedev's Studio," which signified the emergence of Lebedev's personal brand. The studio produced computer designs for major international corporations, such as General Motors, and internet projects such as the Russophone search engine Yandex (Popel' 2012). The studio drew on the work of talented graphic artists and web designers such as Roma Voronezhskii and Il'ia Mikhailov. The studio grew to include over 50 developers by 2005, and it was responsible for the actual "look" of the Runet in its early days. Artemii Lebedev's—perhaps slightly offensive—brand "Abiding, Expensive, and Fucking Brilliant" (*Dolgo. Dorogo. Okhuenno.*) symbolized the dominant position of the studio on the Russian web design market, and also highlighted the experience of early internet users, who found the technology irresistibly exhilarating, albeit expensive and time-consuming, as they had to rely on dial-up connections and dilapidated telephone lines (Strukov 2009). The success of Artemii Lebedev showcases the importance of personal contacts and entrepreneurship in the early days of the Russian digital economy. In fact, up to 2005, the Russian computer and internet industry was characterized by the proliferation of personalities and personal brands that created and cemented a specific culture of computer-enabled communication. In my 2010 study of the culture of celebrity and glamour (2010; co-edited with Helena Goscilo), I argued that the Russian internet was dominated by internet stars whose popularity and authority were grounded in their involvement in the construction of the medium (also see Idlis 2010; and Gorbachev and Krasil'shchik 2011). Olia Lialina, Artemii Lebedev, Roma Voronezhskii, Anton Nosik, Linor Goralik and many other producers of digital content constituted the Russian digital intelligentsia before the arrival of the mass user circa 2000.

While in the 1990s the personal computer was a prestigious sign of personal success and a mark of belonging to Russia's digital intelligentsia, in the 2000s it turned into a standard commodity and quotidian means of communication. Although emerging much later than in other industrially developed countries, the speed of proliferation of computer technologies was astounding, at times reaching 25 percent per annum, with the result that, by 2010, half of Russia's population were regular users of the internet (FOM 2010). In an echo of the USSR, the average Russian of the Putin era became a computer user both thanks to, and in spite of, the regime. On the one hand, the Russian government facilitated access to computers and the internet for its citizens even in the most remote parts of the country, by equipping schools, education centers, libraries and post offices with computers. On the other hand, Russians turned to new media due to their dissatisfaction with the mainstream, "old," media, particularly television, because it had been stifled by Putin's "remote control" (Hutchings and Rulyova 2009). In other words, the Russian government was instrumental in supplying computer technology to Russia's internal and external peripheries. Yet it was the private sector and the appeal of the internet as a free, uncontrolled environment that have boosted the rapid growth of new media since 2000.

While the computer provided users with a personal connection during the period 1995–2005, the use of technology remained largely collective, i.e. a group activity, and for a number of reasons. First of all, the majority of users had access to the technology only at work.[19] As the Moscow journalist Lilia Iashchenko recalls of her work in the late 1990s,

> The computer was shared by 2–3 editors as well as another 3–4 freelancers . . . We used to call it jokingly the "agregat" [power module]. "Is the 'agregat' free?" was the most popular question in our everyday conversations. If someone was late for work and did not manage to secure a place in front of the "agregat," he or she would have to spend the day having cigarette breaks and doing other exciting things.
>
> (Iashchenko 2011: 117)

Iashchenko's digital memoirs make an ironic reference to the computer as the Soviet industrial machine, and she also documents the Soviet type of organization of labor—frequent breaks, the need to wait to use the technology, the constant negotiation of access and procedure—that prevailed even a decade after the dissolution of the USSR.[20]

Those who did not have access to computers at work would make use of cyber cafés—the second example of the collective use of computers. In 1998–2005, these included computer salons (*komp'iuternye salony*), where a number of services would be provided, including word processing, printing, photocopying and translation. See, for example, Figure 1.2 which shows just such a salon in Voronezh. The salon was in the city center in close proximity to governmental institutions, major transportation links and shopping centers. Decorated in smart plastic, the salon served as a communication hub and a business center for those who either did not own a computer or were away from their office. The second type of cyber cafés—gaming salons (*igrovye salony*)—served a different set of clients. Normally located in suburban areas (*spal'nye raiony*), these salons targeted Russian youth, particularly males aged 15–25, who were avid players of computer games. Often very dark and smoky, these salons provided gamers with an opportunity to play online games, engage in team competitions and socialize.[21] These salons were closed down across the country after the government clamped down on gambling and closed casinos in 2009 on the basis of legislation passed in 2006.

Whether providing space for engaging in a business activity, or a hobby, the salons, as well as Soros's computer centers, exemplify the collective use of the computer and the internet among Russian users. This use is based on the idea of sharing the cost of technology, especially if it is semi-legal or its immediate economic gain cannot be identified. It is also rooted in the long-standing tradition of public festivities and activities, sponsored by the Soviet state, such as *subbotniki*,

*Figure 1.2* Computer salon in Voronezh. Note the expensive double-glazed windows and doors and individual computer stations with flat-screen displays.

Source: Photograph by Vlad Strukov.

*kruzhki*, and *utrenniki*. The monthly journal, *Iunyi tekhnik*, for example, targeted technologically-minded youth attending semi-professional youth associations, or *kruzhki*. In the 1980s, video salons, showing films that had been unavailable in the USSR, became extremely popular, displacing *utrenniki*—officially organized celebrations and/or activities imposed on Soviet young people—and developed into centers of alternative consumer culture. Finally, *subbotniki*—the practice of using unpaid labor over a weekend in honor of the Communist Party and its Leadership—were carried forward into the post-Soviet era in the form of "free immaterial labor" (Lazzarato 1996).

Finally, the collective use of computers prevails even in personal environments such as the private home. In his study of working-class families in Russian provincial towns, Jeremy Morris demonstrates that the shared, collective use of new media mimics the practice of the shared use of old media, such as television. He notes that "in the Russian context 'productive' modes of internet use are no less economically determined . . . and reflect unchanging imperatives of small town life—self-provisioning, the maintenance of the home and updating of skills and knowledge relating to economic priorities" (Morris 2012: 1561). In other words, in the period 2000–5, the mass user conceived of the computer in Soviet terms as a tool that required and enabled "assembling, adapting, remodeling or reshaping." Thus, over the course of the decade running from 1995 to 2005, a two-tiered computer society emerged in Russia: one dominated by the digital intelligentsia, who had embraced modernity and neo-liberal economics, with its emphasis on post-industrial production, and who operated from the safety of their "digital boutiques," and the other featuring the mass user, who, while owning the technology of "personal connection," continued to rely on traditions of collective use and free labor carried over from the Soviet times.

## Conclusions, or digital "happy ever after" (2005–12)

This juxtaposition of users, with its social boundaries and distinctions, became largely irrelevant after 2005 because of the rise of new media, including social networks (VKontakte, Odnoklassniki and others). Indeed, the use of smart phones and portable computer devices and the greater proliferation of stationary desktops across all sectors of the Russian economy and society enhanced economic activity, communication and opportunities for self-expression. New forms of communication "untethered" Russian users both literally and metaphorically. For example, according to Romir Monitoring, the number of Russians using cellphones grew from 25 percent in February 2004 to 53 percent in September 2005 (Romir Monitoring 2005). With the number of users doubling in less than a year, the handset market grew exponentially: in 2004, the value of cellphones sold on the Russian market was worth 4.5 billion dollars (Koshkina 2005), with almost 27 million new phones being sold and Moscow leading the trend (35 percent of new sales were registered in the Moscow region) (MMTs "Moskva" 2005). The computer and the cellphone became symbols of the new, highly individualized, increasingly customized economy of cultural exchange and formation of subjectivity. In this regard, since 2005 the adaptation of new computer technologies has followed exactly the same pattern as in other industrialized countries, with Russia, especially Moscow, becoming a global center of consumption, with a virtually non-existent domestic system for the production of computer technologies. The new technologies enabled the emergence of a digital economy that thrives on media, gaming and file-sharing sites. The users—and in 2012, that meant half the Russian population (eMarketer 2013)—were liberated thanks to the internet: the technology transformed the economic, cultural and social outlook for all, and this volume explores the profound impact the internet has had on all aspects of Russian life. In spite of this change, the digital divide remains in the Russian Federation. There are people who would like to connect to the internet but lack the technological or financial opportunity (11.5 percent of all respondents, summer, 2011); there are also those who are not motivated at all (46 percent, summer 2011). The Public Opinion Foundation (FOM) has called the second group *otkazniki*, or refuseniks (FOM 2011a). They are predominantly women aged 55 and over, residing in rural areas, with a low level of education and income. While Soviet refuseniks were denied access to the global economy and culture because the authorities would not grant them permission to emigrate, Russian refuseniks are deprived of the opportunity to migrate into the digital economy, continuing to occupy Russian internal and external peripheries. By disabling their access to the digital realm, the Russian authorities maintain the Soviet practice of technological control and sponsor the elite type of access to resources, thus disempowering these people and putting them in a cache of the impersonal technological hiatus. As a result, while some users belong to the deterritorialized transnational realm of the Runet, others occupy extremely narrow spaces of cultural exchange.

The Soviet practices concerning the development of computing technologies and use have been preserved in a transformed way. For example, the earlier practices of sharing and collective use have been translated into the practice of file-sharing and collaborative creative projects on the internet, especially in terms of online networked communities fostered by social media and predicated on the collaborative artistic practice of Olia Lialina and net.art discussed above. At the same time the disruption of the production line, that is, the discontinuation of the Soviet computer as an industrial enterprise, has produced an impediment to cultural memory. For example, there are no museums of Soviet computing technologies in Russia, with an online museum filling the gap.[22] In December 2012, Manezh, a large exhibition space a stone's throw away from the Kremlin, organized a retrospective exhibition of Soviet design of the 1950–80s (curated by Alena Sokol'nikova). It displayed watches, cameras, vacuum cleaners, cars, television sets, radios and other paraphernalia of everyday life, with the Soviet computer being conspicuous by its absence. By contrast, US-made computers featured prominently at the "Cold War: Modern Design 1945–1970" exhibition at the Victoria and Albert Museum in London (2008, curated by David Crawley and Jane Pavitt).[23] On the one hand, the omission at the Manezh exhibition highlights Russian techno-cultural amnesia. On the other, it situates the computer ideologically: it no longer represents the totalitarian past but rather the neo-liberal future, with its emphasis on consumption, the free circulation of information and "attention economy" (Davenport and Beck 2001). In spite of the discontinuation of the technological tradition, the foundations of contemporary Russian digital modernity were laid in the 1980s through the use of computers in the Soviet educational system and the techno-intellectual merger between Soviet industry and Soviet education in the same period. Gorbachev's perestroika lent additional impetus to the development of computer technologies and, at the same time, relied on Soviet industry to deliver the necessary technological power base. In many respects, the mismatch between these two components caused the technological and social upheaval of the early 1990s, resulting in the collapse of the Soviet Union. The government failed to liberalize Soviet industry and, as a result, the industrial complex fell short of providing technologies that would enable the USSR to enter the post-industrial phase. The Soviet computer challenged the ideological discourse by problematizing the relationship between the individual and technology, whereby the double-speak of the Soviet era was transformed into the digital divide of post-Soviet Russia. The Soviet computer, with its emphasis on "the impersonal connection," is an objectified grand narrative of the Soviet project of modernity; and its technological demise in the early 1990s produced new subjectivities, new forms of organization of labor and entrepreneurship, and new social organizations.

## Notes

1 А вот—желанная ЦВМ,/которую не выдумает сам Лем,/которая—тема для од и поэм,/которая шпилька в заду Ай-Би-Эм.

2 The first round of interviews was conducted in Voronezh in March 2012. I am grateful to Viacheslav Strukov for organizing these interviews for me. The second round of interviews was conducted in Yekaterinburg in November 2012. I acknowledge the financial support of the Ural Federal University which enabled my field work in Yekaterinburg.

3 Some of these interviews were published in *Digital Icons: Studies in Russian, Eurasian and Central European New Media* (*Digital Memoirs* special project; www.digitalicons.org); others are available in publications such as Kuznetsov (2004).

4 In my media analysis, I examined the representation of computers in the *Pravda* newspaper and the *Iunyi tekhnik*, *Smena*, *Rabotnitsa* and *Ogonek* magazines. The choice of the media outlets was determined by the need to consider the issue across a wide range of publications in terms of age (*Smena*, targeted at young Soviet people), gender (*Rabotnitsa* was a Soviet magazine for working women), and occupation/leisure activities (*Iunyi tekhnik* was a Soviet magazine for children and young people who were interested in new technologies and science). *Pravda* and *Ogonek* present the official view on technological development and its mediation in the high-quality popular press, respectively. Media were sampled at specific intervals. *Pravda* was examined using a thematic search. The issues of the magazines from 1985–86 and 1990–91 were scrutinized for their mediation of computer technologies. The mediation of computer technologies in the post-Soviet period was analyzed using cinematic and televisual representations as well as extensive materials from online collections.

5 Professor Sergei Alekseevich Lebedev (1902–74) was responsible for the construction of the first Soviet computer; he was in charge of the laboratories that developed the most significant technologies and machines in the 1950s and 1960s. He started as an engineer in the 1930s and very quickly developed a research portfolio. Although he built the early Soviet computer industry, his initial theoretical concerns related to the Soviet Union's national electricity grid (30 electrical stations were completed in 1931 as part of the GOELRO plan), thus connecting different stages of Soviet technological modernity. His long-lasting technological impetus is evident in the construction of the most significant Soviet computers (BESM-1, EVM M-40, MVK El'brus, Elektronnika BIS, and others).

6 The Thaw (*ottepel'*) refers to the period of de-Stalinization and liberalization introduced by Nikita Khrushchev in the late 1950s.

7 During his visit to Japan in 1965, Lebedev, the father of the Soviet computer industry, noted that the majority of Japanese computers in use were computers of medium capacity; however, they came equipped with reliable input devices, tape recorders and printers (Burtsev 2002: 224). In other words, computers in Japan formed part of an integrated technological package, something that was not achieved in the Soviet Union in the 1960s and 1970s.

8 For example, Lebedev, along with a group of Soviet scientists and computer engineers, spent a month in Japan (at the University of Kyoto) in 1965 researching Japanese computer technologies.

9 It would be a misapprehension to consider the evolution of computer technologies in the post-World War II period as a basic binary opposition between the USSR and the West (largely the USA). In actual fact, the history of computer technologies is characterized by mutual rivalry and polycentric developments. First, the USSR,

and especially the Russian Federation and the Ukrainian Republic, were at the center of a wider Eastern European network of computer engineering, with Bulgaria playing an important role as a supplier of computer hardware. Second, illegal trade and technological espionage dictated computer developments not only in the USSR but also in other countries. Finally, the USSR was an exporter of computer technologies to developing countries, such as China, where BESM-2, developed by Lebedev in Moscow, was adopted in 1958.

10 *Informatizatsiia* is sometimes translated as "electronization" (see, for example, Kneen 1989) and sometimes as "automation" (see, for example, Battle 1988); the Russian term refers to the use of information theories on the platform of computers in the economy and social practice.

11 Third generation personal computers are not only fast and reliable but also easy to operate (cf. *Iunyi tekhnik* 1985, issue 10, p. 5).

12 The PC consisted of only one item; it was not very heavy and could be carried around and plugged in whenever appropriate.

13 Here writing is understood in symbolic terms as a form of embodiment explored by Jacques Derrida in his *Of Grammatology* (1976).

14 Plastic packaging, for example, plastic carrier bags, was used extremely rarely in the USSR, and so Soviet consumers perceived the use of plastic in the design of this computer not as something cheap and unattractive but, on the contrary, as something quite innovative and "cool." I am grateful to Thea Pitman for pointing out this cultural difference in comparison with the countries of South America.

15 *Rabotnitsa* concerned itself with the issue of the gender divide in relation to new technologies as early as 1986. In its June issue, the magazine addressed this concern by emphasizing the role of knowledge of technologies in the new industrial age; however, the gender polemic was resolved in typically Soviet fashion, that is, by showcasing the achievements of Soviet women elsewhere—in arts, education and science—and not by suggesting that more women learn how to use computers. In fact, the image used in the publication shows a woman dressed in trousers and a man's shirt, thus accentuating male dominance in the arena of information technologies.

16 Directed by Viacheslav Kotenochkin and Aleksei Kotenochkin; in existence 1969–2002. Arguably, the Soviet animation series was itself an adaptation of the American cartoon, *Tom and Jerry*.

17 See, for example, the American register of technological innovations authored and patented by Pentkovskii at: patent.ipexl.com/inventor/Vladimir_Pentkovski_1.html (accessed 15 January 2013).

18 The artwork may be viewed on the internet: teleportacia.org/war/ (accessed 10 January 2013).

19 It has been noted that the trend began to change in 2004, i.e. access to the internet from home began to increase (FOM 2012). In 2011, only 22 percent of internet users could access the network at work only (FOM 2011b).

20 For a humorous exploration of Soviet office culture, see the films of El'dar Riazanov.

21 A similar description can be found in literature, for example, see Pecheikin (2008). For a cinematic depiction of such gaming salons, see Oleh Sentsov's (2011) *Gamer*. Although the film shows a gaming salon in Ukraine, the general environment and culture are similar to those in Russia.

22 Virtual'nyi komp'iuternyi muzei (computer-museum.ru/index.php).

23 The catalogue of the exhibition includes John Harwood's article "Imagining the Computer: Eliot Noyes, the Eames and the IBM Pavilion," in which he analyzes the computer as "a novel means of communication through design" (Harwood 2008: 195). He notes that the original pavilion featured a number of technical innovations, including a demonstration of automatic Russian language translation by character recognition software and hardware. I argue this demonstration represented the

USA–USSR technological rivalry and the need to "translate" ideology using an ideologically-neutral machine code.

## References

Adirim, I. 1991. "Current Development and Dissemination of Computer Technology in the Soviet Economy." *Soviet Studies* 43(4): 651–67.

Battle, John M. 1988. "Uskorenie, Glasnost' and Perestroika: The Pattern of Reform under Gorbachev." *Soviet Studies* 40(3): 367–84.

Bolin, Goran. 2012. "Personal Media in the Digital Economy." In *Moving Data: The iPhone and the Future of Media*, edited by Pelle Snickars and Patrick Vonderau, 91–103. New York: Columbia University Press.

Burtsev, V.S. ed. 2002. *Sergei Alekseevich Lebedev (k 100-letiiu so dnia rozhdeniia osnovopolozhnika otechestvennoi elektronnoi vychislitel'noi tekhniki)*. Moscow: Fizmatlit.

Cave, Martin. 1980. *Computers and Economic Planning: The Soviet Experience.* Cambridge: Cambridge University Press.

Davenport, Thomas, and John Beck. 2001. *The Attention Economy: Understanding the New Currency of Business.* Cambridge, MA: Harvard Business School Press.

Derrida, Jacques. 1976. *Of Grammatology*. Baltimore, MD: The Johns Hopkins University Press.

eMarketer. 2013. "Russia: Usage Patterns." Available at: http://www.newmediatrend-watch.com/markets-by-country/10-europe/81-russia (accessed 15 January 2013).

Fatkullin, Andrei. 1999. "Intel Uses Russian Military Technologies: Russian Designer Could Have Been Inspiration for Pentium Name." *Business*, 7 June. Available at: http://www.theregister.co.uk/1999/06/07/intel_uses_russia_military_technologies/ (accessed 15 January 2013).

FOM (Fond obshchestvennoe mnenie). 2010. "Proniknovenie interneta." Available at: http://runet.fom.ru/Proniknovenie-interneta (accessed 25 November 2010).

FOM (Fond obshchestvennoe mnenie). 2011a. "Rossiia–oflain." Available at: http://fom.ru/SMI-i-internet/10254 (accessed 18 January 2013).

FOM (Fond obshchestvennoe mnenie). 2011b. "Internet ukhodit domoi." Available at: http://runet.fom.ru/Proniknovenie-interneta/10217 (accessed 18 January 2013).

FOM (Fond obshchestvennoe mnenie). 2012. "Proniknovenie interneta." Available at: http://runet.fom.ru/Proniknovenie-interneta/10249 (accessed 13 January 2013).

Gerovitch, Slava. 2002. *From Newspeak to Cyberspeak: A History of Soviet Cybernetics*. Cambridge, MA: MIT Press.

Goscilo, Helena, and Vlad Strukov, eds. 2010. *Celebrity and Glamour in Contemporary Russia: Shocking Chic*. London: Routledge.

Graham, Loren A. 1973. *Science and Philosophy in the Soviet Union.* London: Heinemann.

Gorbachev, Aleksandr, and Il'ia Krasilshchik, eds. 2011. *Istoriia russkikh media 1989–2011: Versiia Afishy*. Moscow: Afisha indastriz.

Harwood, John. 2008. "Imagining the Computer: Eliot Noyes, the Eames and the IBM Pavilion." In *Cold War Modern Design 1945–1970*, edited by David Crowley and Jane Pavitt, 192–7. London: V&A Publishing.

Hutchings, Stephen, and Natalya Rulyova. 2009. *Television and Culture in Putin's Russia: Remote Control.* London: Routledge.

Iashchenko, Lilia. 2011. "From the Typewriter to the Computer." *Digital Icons* 6: 113–19.

Idlis, Iuliia. 2010. *Runet: Sotvorennye kumiry*. Moscow: ANF.

i-SCALARE. 2010. "O nas." Available at: http://iscalare.mipt.ru/about.html (accessed 15 January 2013).

Khmeliuk, V.A. 1992. "Samyi malen'kii i samyi personalnyi." *Vychislitel'naia tekhnika i ee primenenie* 2: 3–15.

Kneen, Peter. 1989. "Soviet Science Policy under Gorbachev." *Soviet Studies* 41(1): 67–87.

Koshkina, El'vira. 2005. "IDC: v 2004 gody ob'em rossiiskogo rynka mobil'nykh telefonov pochti udvoilsia," *Compulenta*, 12 May. Available at: http://telecom.compulenta.ru/182969 (accessed 3 April 2010).

Kuz'michev, Andrei. 2010. "Kooperativy." *Forbes*, 20 October. http://www.forbes.ru/svoi-biznes/58499-kooperativy (accessed 10 January 2013).

Kuznetsov, Sergei. 2004. *Oshchupyvaia slona: zametki po istorii russkogo interneta*. Moscow: Novoe Literaturnoe Obozrenie.

Lazzarato, Maurizio. 1996. "Immaterial Labour." Available at: http://www.generation-online.org/c/fcimmateriallabour3.htm (accessed 19 January 2013).

Losenkov, Viktor Ivanovich. 2012. [Interview], former chief engineer of the Protsessor computer manufacturing plant, USSR, 26 March, Voronezh.

Maksimov, S.N. 1992. *Perestroika i problemy khoziaistvennykh reform*. St Petersburg: University of St Petersburg Press.

Martuzian, B.Ia. 1991. *Podruzhis' so mnoi komp'iuter! Kniga dlia uchashchikhsia*, Moscow: Prosveshchenie.

"Materialy XXIV S"ezda KPSS." 1971. Available at: http://publ.lib.ru/ARCHIVES/K/KPSS/_KPSS.html (accessed 6 January 2013).

Matveev, A.A. 1992. "Personal'naia elektronnaia vychislitel'naia machine 'Mikrosha'." *Vychislitel'naia tekhnika i ee primenenie* 1: 3–9.

Miachev, A.A. 1992. *Personal'nye EVM: kratkii entsiklopedicheskii spravochnik*. Moscow: Finansy i statistika.

Mironov, Iu.P., ed. 1994. *Otechestvennye i zarubezhnye sredstva vychislitel'noi tekhniki*. Moscow: Vserossiiskii nauchno-issledovatel'skii institut mezhotraslevoi informatsii.

MMTs "Moskva." 2005. "Obzor rossiiskogo rynka mobil'nykh telefonov." Available at: http://www.marketcenter.ru/content/doc-2-10295.html (accessed 3 April 2010).

Morris, Jeremy. 2012. "Learning How to Shoot Fish on the Internet: New Media in the Russian Margins as Facilitating Immediate and Parochial Social Needs." *Europe-Asia Studies* 64(8): 1546–64.

Naumov, B.N., ed. 1987. *EVM massovogo primeneniia*. Moscow: Nauka.

Nedobezhkin, Mitrofan Il'ich. 2012. [Interview], former mechanic at the Protsessor computer manufacturing plant, USSR, 27 March, Voronezh.

Pecheikin, Valerii. 2008. "ICQ." *Ural* 9. Available at: http://magazines.russ.ru/ural/2008/9/pe14.html (accessed 10 January 2013).

Popel', Anatolii. 2012. "Istoriia Studii Artemiia Lebedeva." Available at: http://popel.com.ua/blog/article/istorija-studii-artemija-lebedeva-2.html (accessed 18 January 2013).

Romir Monitoring. 2005. "Tsifry i fakty: Rossiiane aktivno eksperimentiruiut s SIM-kartami." Available at: http://www.romir.ru/news/res_results/176.html (accessed 3 April 2010).

Samborskii, G., and V. Simchera. 1974. "Put' povysheniia effektivnosti vychislitel'noi tekhniki." *Voprosy ekonomiki* 7: 79–89.

Sirenko, V.F. 1976. *Organizatsionno-pravovye voprosy deiatel'nosti vychislitel'nykh tsentrov, funktsioniruiushchikh v usloviiakh ASU*. Kiev: Naukova dumka.

Sitnikov, Aleksandr. 2012. "Ot kooperatsii Gorbacheva k vertikale Putina." *Svobodnaia pressa*, 26 May. Available at: http://svpressa.ru/society/article/55682/ (accessed 10 January 2013).

Sosnovskii, Vladimir, and Anton Orlov. 2002. "Sovetskie komp'iutery: predannye i zabyty." Available at: http://nnm.ru/blogs/dusty74/istoriya_razvitiya_otechestvennogo_kompyuterostoroeniya_2/ (accessed 10 October 2012).

Strukov, Vlad. 2006. "Actors and Agents: Russian Internet and Civil Society." Lecture presented at St Anthony's College, University of Oxford, 9 June.

—— 2009. "Russia's Internet Media Policies: Open Space and Ideological Closure." In *The Post-Soviet Media: Conflicting Signals*, edited by Birgit Beumers, Stephen Hutchings, and Natalya Rulyova, 208–23. New York: Routledge.

Valov, A.S. 1993. "Esli by u Marianny byla EVM. . . ." *Vychislitel'naia tehnika i ee primenenie* 1:4–6. Moscow: Znanie.

Walther, Joseph B., and Caleb T. Carr. 2010. "Internet Interaction and Intergroup Dynamics: Problems and Solutions in Computer-Mediated Communication." In *The Dynamics of Intergroup Communication*, edited by Jake Harwood, Scott Reid, and Howard Giles, 209–20. New York: Peter Lang.

Zernov, Vladimir. 2005. "Ushcherb Rossii ot 'utechki mozgov' sostavliaet svyshe 1 trl rublei." *Newsru.com*, 30 June. Available at: http://www.newsru.com/russia/30jun2005/mozg.html (accessed 15 January 2013).

## Films

Sentsov, Oleh (dir.) 2011, *Gamer*, Ukraine, 2011; script by Oleh Sentsov, cinematography by Ievheniia Vradii, Iehor Petryk, Hennadii Veselkov; music by Volodymyr Kozlov.

Shakhnazarov, Karen, dir. 1986. *The Courier*. Mosfil'm; script by Aleksandr Borodianskii, cinematography by Nikolai Nemoliaev and Valerii Shuvalov; music by Eduard Artem'ev.

# 2 From the utopia of autonomy to a political battlefield

## Towards a history of the "Russian internet"

*Natalya Konradova and Henrike Schmidt*

### The "country Runet" and its history as an object of research

РУНЕТ
Больше нет страны РФ на свете,
нет России—есть страна Рунет. . . .
Власть географическая пала,
мы переселились по хостам,
где средь исторического бала
мир переместился на экран, . . .

RUNET
There's no country called the Russian Federation any longer,
No Russia,—there's just a country called Runet, . . .
The power of geography has been broken,
We've moved to live with our [IP] hosts,
When in the midst of a historic ball
the world moved onto the screens, . . .

(Shcherbina [2001] 2008)

In her poem dedicated to the *Runet*, the popular acronymic abbreviation for the Russian Internet, the poet Tatiana Shcherbina describes the "country Runet" (*strana Runet*) as a virtual space beyond geography, where life has moved onto the screens. The "country Runet" is a *contradiction in adjecto*, as it projects the idea of an existent, delimited geographic space onto the networked spaces of the internet. And as such it highlights the problematic status of the Runet as an object of research, defined by different approaches and scholars either with regard to geography ("the internet in the Russian Federation"—*rossiiskii internet*) or language ("the Russian-speaking internet"—*russkoiazychnyi internet*) or culture and tradition ("the Russian internet"—*russkii internet*) (see, for example, Bruchhaus 2001: 12; Alexanyan and Koltsova 2009).

Shcherbina's poem is noteworthy in another sense, as it combines utopian and dystopian visions, which characterize the emergence of the internet in general, and in Russia specifically, from its very beginnings: the hope that in "cyberspace" the power of "geography has been broken," on the one hand, and the fear that the idea of society and commonality has faded away in a world where the individual is trapped behind a monitor. Last but not least, the emphatic salutation of the Runet highlights the considerable potential for individual and collective identification in terms of something as volatile and abstract as a nationally or culturally defined segment of the global information and communication networks.

The strong potential for identification of the Runet has been a topic of analysis ever since research in the field got under way. From an external point of view, Bruchhaus (2001: 31) explains this particular emotional attachment by referring to the coincidence of political and media revolution in the early 1990s. It is rooted in the biographical experience of the early protagonists, who perceived the fall of the Iron Curtain and the discovery of cyberspace as being intimately linked. The intensity of the engagement of early Russian users with the new communication environment, which after decades of informational patrimony by the totalitarian State was experienced as deliberative, manifests itself not least through the common practice of referring to the Russian or Russian-language segment of the internet as the Runet. Such emotive labeling is not common in other national segments of global networks.[1] The abbreviation, sometimes supplemented by the collectivizing possessive pronoun "our Runet" (*nash Runet*), has established itself throughout the last decade even within academia (Schmidt and Teubener 2006a). It is used by politicians such as the former Russian President and current Prime Minister Dmitry Medvedev. And it has been included in dictionaries and encyclopedias, which even specify which syllable has to be stressed—"Runét" (*Russkii orfograficheskii slovar'*). For this reason, the term "Runet" is also used in this chapter, with the caveat that it does not signify a distinct and set entity, but functions rather as a heuristic construct designating a social and cultural phenomenon of post-Soviet online communication in Russian, with neither fixed geographical nor technological parameters.

While the Runet has thus entered colloquial speech and professional discourses, and has become a topic for poetic reflection and indeed a dictionary entry, no scientific monograph on the historic development of the internet in Russia, or even the history of information and communications technology (ITC) and computer-mediated communication (CMC) in the country, has been written.[2] This is, in fact, true for most of the national or language segments of the global internet (e.g. there exists no history of the German internet or the internet in Germany either); existing "histories" of the internet in a more general sense are concerned mostly—and quite logically—with its origins in the military and academic sphere of the United States (e.g. Salus 1995; Hafner and Lyon 1996; Naughton 2000). One could even go so far as to argue that the construction of national histories of a global communication technology such as the internet is anachronistic and runs the risk of inventing rather than describing its object of study. Nevertheless, if we acknowledge that technology and its usages interact with local cultures, some historical "facts" seem to be necessary in order to compare the dynamics in different segments of the internet and understand the emergence of specific, culturally encoded phenomena.[3] Much research, for example, has been devoted to the emergence and impact of the internet in China (e.g. Goldenstein 2007; Tai 2012; Zheng 2008), as well as to cross-cultural comparisons of Russian and Chinese internet cultures (e.g. Saunders and Ding 2006; Deibert et al. 2008; Fossato, Lloyd, and Verkhovskii 2009: 9–11), given their semiotic (non-Latin alphabets), geographic (vast territory, huge diaspora), and political (State-controlled public sphere, censorship) similarities.

What we propose to do here, then, is to sketch out some relevant historical storylines in the development of the internet in Russia (and, to a lesser extent, in Russian-speaking transnational communication environments), to provide a "history of content" (Kuznetsov 2004: 7) by examining how major trends and phenomena have inscribed themselves, both semiotically and discursively, into Russian culture. We focus on the early period of 1991–2000, in part because its history is less well known and is difficult to reconstruct, in part in order to lay a conceptual foundation for the more recent trends witnessed in the new millennium, which are covered in greater detail in subsequent chapters in this book.

## From history into mythology: narratives of self-historicization

While there does not (yet) exist an academic history of the internet in Russia, the protagonists of the early Runet showed a high degree of historical awareness, even a tendency toward self-historicization, from the very beginning. As one such protagonist, Sergei Kuznetsov (2004: 6), put it, "I often thought that what we were doing would first turn into history, and then into mythology." (This historical, sometimes even revolutionary mission and consciousness can also be seen in the reflections of American pioneers of computer engineering and network technologies, such as Steve Jobs ["Think different!"].)

It is not surprising that attempts of (self-)historicization were made at the turn of the twenty-first century, when the first, "romantic," period in the development of the Runet was coming to an end and the second, "pragmatic," one was just beginning. As the Runet changed from a free space of creative articulation into a fully-fledged mass medium of national significance, its founders cast their first glance back to its history. Two projects are among the most popular of these endeavors: the chronicle, "Annals of the Russian Internet" (*Letopis' russkogo interneta*), compiled by the journalist, editor and academic Eugene Gorny, and the research platform "History of the Internet in Russia" (*Istoriia Interneta v Rossii*),[4] initiated by the historian and media manager Dmitrii Ivanov. The titles alone illustrate how differently the projects position themselves (another testimony to the uncertainties of historicizing the Runet). While Gorny's "chronicle"—by its genre definition already opening up a historical perspective—uses the adjective "Russian" and thus focuses on the cultural and linguistic dimensions (including phenomena taking place in the Russian-speaking diaspora), Ivanov clearly defines the aim of his project as investigating the development of CMC and the internet on the national-geographic territory of the Russian Federation. While these two facets of the term Runet partly overlap, especially for the early period of its development, we will for practical reasons assume the latter approach, taking into account, where necessary, the significance and influence of the Russian-speaking diaspora.

Given the Russian internet's marginal status from 1991 to approximately 1995–96—not only in terms of user numbers, but also in terms of its political and economic significance—it was easy to become a pioneer. The first electronic library, the first online journal, the first search engine—almost any activity had the potential to make history. Guided by this "first-of" principle, Gorny thus employs chronology in his "Annals" to document what to date is still the most valuable source of facts and data for the early history of the Runet. The chronological principle results in a mixture of eclectic facts and technological, economic, cultural and biographic events, all with little context provided. It assumes the form of a neutral collection of data, the narrative frame for which must be reconstructed by taking into account Gorny's later work on the Russian blogosphere, where the principle of creativity emerges as the driving force behind technological and cultural innovation (very much in line with technological evangelists such as the aforementioned Steve Jobs). Lurking beneath the surface of his "Annals" is the idea that creative individuals revolutionize technology and cultural communication as a result of their enthusiasm and free spirit. The pathos of the individual creative innovator as the agent of historical progress sometimes leads to hyperbolic distortions, which Roman Leibov—himself among the undisputed "pioneers" of the Runet and an incessant innovator—wittily unmasked when in an interview he refused to name "legendary personalities of the Runet," dismissing such efforts as "petty histories for petty people" (*malen'kaia istoriia dlia malen'kikh liudei*) (Travin n.d.).

"The History of the Internet in Russia" strives to overcome such elevated discourses. Its initiator, Dmitrii Ivanov, describes it as a "simple and functional project, with the main aim of being an instrument for the compilation of the history of the internet in the Russian Federation (*istoriia rossiiskoi seti*)" (Webplaneta 2003). The functional approach is reflected in the site's Modernist design, with Ivanov relying heavily on biographical and scientific contextualization—as seen from navigation rubrics such as "Historic encounters" (*Istoricheskie besedy*), "Chronology," "Books and Articles," and "Editorial board." The "Chronology" in fact represents an extended and interactively co-authored version of Gorny's earlier "Annals," but, tellingly, given a more neutral title. The site likewise embeds the development of the Runet within global contexts, using a photograph of Marshall McLuhan as a placeholder, for example, where gaps in Russian national web history have yet to be filled.

In the history of digital culture, it is typical, rather than paradoxical, that most of the (self-)historicizing projects, in their very attempt to preserve the past, have either disappeared from the web altogether (Nethistory), or been constantly relocated from one virtual home to the next.[5] In our sketch of the history of the Runet, we nevertheless rely to a large extent on the material collected in both of these projects, but structure them around thematic clusters and along distinct timelines.

## The birth of the Runet in the 1990s: between digital colonization and virtual Russification

The internet in Russia in the early 1990s was regarded as a "Western technology," and a "Western import," and as such was viewed in a positive light for its "foreignness" and "exoticness" (Leibov 2003; see also Kuznetsov 2004). But prejudices concerning Russia's technological "backwardness" were largely unfounded, as Höller (1998) notes:

> Regarding the key technological developments in the field of information technology, Russia has always been, especially in the 19th century and to a lesser extent in Soviet times, at the pulse of the time. Russian scientists were among the pioneers in this field.

The Soviet Union lost the race for cyberspace not so much because of a lack of scientific competence as because of an excess of ideology. In 1949, Western powers initiated the so-called CoCom initiative, imposing a highly efficient embargo on the import of high technology into the countries of the Warsaw Pact. The embargo was designed to hamper the economic and military development of the Eastern bloc, and information technologies were viewed as particularly crucial assets, without which an efficient communicative infrastructure for any state—let alone the entire political alliance—would be impossible to implement. In this sense, the CoCom initiative is among the very few examples of a politically motivated embargo that was successfully implemented and that achieved its goals: the computer industry in the Soviet Union and the countries of the Warsaw Pact suffered severely from the import restrictions.[6] The discrepancy in the development of ICTs in the United States and the Soviet Union was thus grounded in an identical political situation, but caused effects that were diametrically opposed: while in the USA the Cold War inspired the development of non-hierarchical computer networks which could circumvent a total knockout of the communication infrastructure in case of a nuclear attack, the Soviet Union deprived itself of efficient ICTs and computer networks, as their horizontal structures potentially endangered the system's political hierarchies.

The prominent sociologist Manuel Castells (1997: 10) goes so far as to claim that the Soviet Union collapsed in 1991 as a result of the centralized system's inability to react to the challenges of the information era. But for Russian/Soviet scientists, deprived for decades of scientific exchange, the breakdown of the Soviet Union opened up new opportunities for professional and commercial (self-) realization. According to Valerii Bardin (cited in Gagin 1999), a co-founder of the academic cooperative Demos, in its early years the internet in Russia was introduced almost without any assistance from State institutions, which were too busy managing political turmoil. The development was driven by two different forces: one internal, the other foreign. Domestically, the technical elite and its scientific institutions urgently sought to close the gap in international developments and standards; externally, programmers and scientists from the Russian émigré community—along with foreign, mostly US-based foundations—sought to promote democratic transition via new information technology.

One of the breeding grounds for the nascent Russian ITC and internet sector within the country was the Kurchatov Institute of Atomic Energy, which played a role similar to that of CERN (the European Organization for Nuclear Research/ Conseil Européen pour la Recherche Nucléaire) in the West, where Tim Berners-Lee developed the HTML (Hypertext Markup Language) and HTTP (Hyper-Text Transfer Protocol) technologies used to create web pages and lay the foundation for the World Wide Web as we know it today. Some of the scientists from the Kurchatov Institute had begun experimenting with computer networks back in the early 1980s. The economic liberalizations of early perestroika finally allowed Soviet academics to engage directly on the global stage. So-called "creative collectives" that had been introduced and promptly quashed by Khrushchev in the 1960s were revived and eventually superseded by private economic "co-operatives." The technological *intelligentsiia* of the Eastern bloc was highly professional, showed extraordinary mathematical faculties, and displayed a high degree of creative inspiration. The American "internet-guru" and initiator of the *Cyberspace Independence Declaration* (1996), John Perry Barlow, after attending a meeting with programmers and software engineers from the East in Budapest in 1990, remarked that, "despite its bureaucratic gloom, [the] environment was ideal for the construction of elegant code. Their machines were primitive, . . . and their mathematical skills the best the Soviet system could produce, which is to say superb" (Barlow n.d.). No less astonishing to Barlow was the wish of these Soviet computer pioneers to make money from their skills and products, their "desire to convert those talents into globally credible currency" (ibid.).

Among the first notable achievements of this new type of socialist economics was the Russification of the operating system (OS) UNIX, its adaptation "to the severe Russian hardware-iron" (*surovoe russkoe zhelezo*, Maslov 1996). UNAS was the abbreviation for this innovation, a creative and geographically sensitive word-play from the Russian "at our place/we have" (У НАС)—as juxtaposed to "at their place/they have" (У НИХ), which, with some linguistic inventiveness, could be rendered as "U NIX," or UNIX. Based on the operating system UNAS, which was soon to be renamed DEMOS (*Dialogovaia Edinaia Mobil'naia Operatsionnaia Sistema*), in 1990, the cooperative of the same name founded the first computer network in the Soviet Union. The name of the network—Relkom—was also symbolic, an abbreviation for "Russian electronic communications" or "reliable electronic communications" (*Rel*iable *com*munications instead of *real com*munism, joked some of the Demos staff). Relkom soon included more than 30, primarily scientific, institutions from Dubna to Novosibirsk. And on 19 September 1990, representatives of the cooperative Demos registered the first Soviet internet domain, *.su*.

Thus, the internet in Russia, then still part of the Soviet Union, was born. On 28 August of the same year, Relkom established its first international data connection via the global networks, with Finland. "Our entry into the world has taken place" (*Sostoialsia nash vykhod v Mir!*), the Relkom homepage reads to this day. This entrance, at least as seen from inside by the Soviet protagonists, should not be compared to the arrival of the "poor relative" (Bardin, cited in Gagin 1999: 22): the Relkom network developed with remarkable speed and soon turned into one of the biggest computer networks in Europe. In 1992, it officially became part of the European networks' EUnet. A report by one of the prominent eyewitnesses to these events, Demos founder Valerii Bardin, captures the unique status of the Relkom group on the international stage:

> We came from a still socialist state . . ., but as representatives of a network, existing exclusively through its own money. And we were confronted with the fact that most of the other 22 countries participating were represented by semi-governmental institutions . . . And we always had to explain that we were voting on behalf of a computer network situated on the territory of some of the countries of the former Soviet Union.
>
> (Gagin 1999: 22)

Relkom was soon transformed into a joint-stock company, with shares held by the Kurchatov Institute (Demos), a couple of banks and the Moscow Commodities Exchange. On Relkom's initiative, the technological standards of data transfer were standardized by implementing the world-wide operating IP-protocol. The Russian internet turned into an integral part of the global networks.

Two years later, on 7 April 1994, the domain *.ru* was officially registered, providing a virtual reflection of the new geopolitical reality that had come to pass. To this day, Russian internet users, ICT companies, mass media and state institutions remember and celebrate that date in the most enthusiastic terms (Vesti 2011). The Soviet *.su* domain was closed, but then resurrected in 2003, becoming a source of pride for patriotic users from "the only country which has two national domains" (1stat.ru n.d.). Both domains commemorate their anniversary with publications, glamorous internet awards and a range of other activities (Reg.ru n.d.a and n.d.b).

In the late 2000s, this specific duality of domain names, deeply implanted in Russian contemporary history and reflecting both Russia's political background and the nature of social communication there,[7] was further amplified into a triadic system. In 2009, a new, third national top-level domain for the Russian Federation, *.рф* (*.rf*), was opened, and its introduction was actively supported by then President Dmitry Medvedev.

It was not only Russian computer engineers and network technicians who expressed a euphoric, romantic vision of the politically deliberative and economically promising prospects for network technology in the countries of the ex-Soviet bloc. Internet pioneers from the West shared their utopia by turning Eastern Europe or Russia, not for the first time in history, into a *tabula rasa*, whose vast expanse could be newly colonized, without repeating the mistakes already committed in the "old" world. "There are reasons to think," John Perry Barlow told a conference of computer engineers in Budapest,

> that the whole of Eastern Europe is about to look at a promising future, because you can leapfrog by virtue of never really having built much of an

industrial infrastructure under the previous system. You can leapfrog the tail-end of the industrial period and go directly into the informational period . . . So I think it is very promising here.

(Barlow 1996)[8]

Besides such utopian hopes and visions, one could also witness a very pragmatic engagement from foreign institutions, especially the USA, in the promotion of computer technology and the internet in the region. As early as 1990, the non-profit initiative *Glasnet* started to promote the creation of a computer network for the intellectual elite and human rights groups, as mediators of techno-social progress and democratization. Financed by the American Association for Progressive Communication, the network went by a highly symbolic name, a stump-compound fusing "glasnost" and "network"—Glasnet. The Hungarian-American George Soros likewise engaged in Russia's computerization and internetization through his Open Society Foundation, which in these early years provided critical support in the form of computer and network technologies in academic institutions and especially in the humanities (Leibov 2003).[9] From Relkom to Glasnet, as witnesses of the abundance of telling acronyms, the implementation of CMC and internet technologies in Russia can thus be read not only as dynamic technological progress, but as a process of symbolic or even ideological change in national communication culture between digital colonization and virtual Russification.

## Demographics and media elites

Most of the early Runet adopters entered the digital sphere by professional qualification, because access to the internet could be obtained primarily by people working at academic organizations such as the Kurchatov Institute. Any activity on the early internet also required special technical skills. For that reason, the first web generation consisted mainly of programmers, while the first noticeable projects appeared on the borders of disciplines. These pioneers or "founding fathers"[10] of the Runet, as they are often referred to (only slightly ironically) by their followers, developed new models of economics, interactive literature and online journalism, which at least partly would set the standards for the coming decade.

Throughout 1992, the first content projects emerged.[11] In most cases these early sites were at the time still hosted on American servers and/or initiated by representatives of the Russian émigré community in the USA. Thus, the astrophysicist Sergei Naumov started his site, Dazhdbog's Grandchildren, while working at an American university,[12] the title being a mythological reference to ancient pagan gods as the ancestors of modern Russians. The server offered information in English on Russia's early history. SovInformbiuro—initiated by Vadim Maslov, and the first fully Russian-language resource abroad—focused more on contemporary challenges.[13] Maslov offered information on issues such as how to emigrate or how to Russify a computer, an eclectic information mix topped off with some typical Russian anecdotes. In the same year Evgenii Peskin, a member of Demos and a manager of the Relkom network, founded the first electronic library.[14] As these examples suggest, the protagonists of the early period were mostly members of the scientific elite, to a large extent living in the Russian-speaking diaspora, who not only technologically advanced Russian computer and network technologies, for example, with regard to the Russification of encoding and software, but were also eager to fill them with their own content. Some of the characteristics and intentions of these early resources proved significant in the years that followed: a fascination with mythological, esoteric and mystical thinking, a great love for humoresque genres, and an ardent concern for the free distribution and circulation of (literary) texts via the internet.

Who were these pioneers of the Runet? The years from 1992 to 1996 were years of "firsts." The first social and political project appeared in 1994 (Moscow Libertarium),[15] the first advertisement was sold in 1996 (on the Simplex and SovInformBiuro sites), in the same year the first literary online contest was organized (*Teneta*—"Fishnet"), the first political party created its website (Yabloko Party), the first Russian search engine was launched (Rambler), and the first e-magazine dedicated to the internet was established (*Vechernii internet*—"Evening internet" by Anton Nosik).[16]

Despite the rapid growth of the Runet in the mid-1990s, almost all the content was produced by several dozens of users who lived mainly in Moscow and St Petersburg (Bowles 2006) and were most likely acquainted with each other. In 1995, Anton Nosik published on his homepage a list of 30 external links, which he claimed "described almost the whole Russian internet." In 1996, he would invite all 193[17] subscribers to his magazine *Evening Internet* to a birthday party for Norvezhskii Lesnoi (Norwegian Forest, pseudonym of Nikolai Danilov), another Runet pioneer. The digital elite of this time resembled a *tusovka*, a club of friends and personal acquaintances.

Some of the pioneers belonged to the youngest generation of students of the renowned professor and founder of Russian cultural semiotics, Iurii Lotman, at Tartu University (Estonia). Young scholars such as Roman Leibov, Dmitrii Itskovich, and Eugene Gorny, with their interest in cultural history and the semiotics of communication, promoted all kinds of experimentation in the emerging digital culture and literature. Other early adopters came from Moscow schools for gifted children (*spets-shkoly*), specializing in mathematics and physics. Along with scores of engineers, programmers, writers, literary translators and others, they joined the community that would later come to view themselves as "the Runet elite."

As a repatriate who returned from Israel to Russia in 1998, Anton Nosik was the first *runetchik* who addressed the issue of Russian users abroad and targeted their needs and interests. Emigrants were among the most active users on the Runet, because it enabled them to connect with their home country and Russian-speakers worldwide. Maksim Moshkov established a special rubric called "Abroad" (*Zagranitsa*) in his online library, specifically devoted to Russians living outside Russia proper. Russians in different countries around the world shared their impressions with Russian residents. Sometimes "holy wars" flared up over ideologies and patriotism (Konradova 2006). This was a new experience for post-

Soviet Russian society, which had for decades been divided into two isolated parts—those residing in Russia and those living abroad.

Meanwhile, the Runet was being settled by tens of thousands of new users every year. Penetration grew from 2 percent of the Russian population in 2000, to 10 percent in 2003 (FOM 2004). Geographically, the degree of connectedness within the country varied hugely: while European Russia and the Urals showed online activity above the national average Siberia and the Far East still found themselves on the wrong side of the digital divide. At this point the profile of the average Runet user was that of a young male, well educated and fairly well off, living in one of Russia's largest cities and accessing the internet from his office or home.

Over time, in the course of the early 2000s, the elite community of early pioneers was replaced by a mass of users with neither special software skills nor ambitions to change the world. They wrote blogs devoid of literary quality—"ordinary" people penning "ordinary" diaries and provoking, as a consequence, the wrath of the early adopters. This is how Anna Bowles analyzed the changes in the Runet elites over time:

> Not all early adopters of Internet technology could belong to the elite, but the concept of such an online class—implying as it does hierarchy, definition and finitude, a subculture with leaders and a pecking order rather than a limitless expanse—is key to an understanding of the Runet atmosphere of the 1990s . . . However, the changing nature of the Russian Internet elite had as much to do with the social advancement of individual Runet elite members as with the arrival of a wave of financial thugs who shoved the old guard aside.
>
> (Bowles 2006: 26)

Discussions about the Runet elite were characteristic of the online community as much during the early years as later on. The Celebrities of the Russian Internet award (*Znamenitosti russkogo interneta*, see Shilov 2000) triggered a strong response from users in the late 1990s. Ten years later the topic still evoked significant interest among users, although few could agree over who qualified as a "founding father of the Runet" (Polit.ru 2008). And while some have disappeared from the virtual map, others, such as Anton Nosik (as a journalist and media manager), Artemii Lebedev (as a web designer), and Roman Leibov (as a literary scholar and poetic innovator), continue to maintain an active and popular presence in the new Runet of the masses.

By the late 2000s, the population of the Runet was continuing to grow, while the dynamics reduced. In 2007, 22 percent of the Russian population were connected to the internet. In 2010 the percentage of online users in Russia had risen to 46.5 percent—as compared to approximately 70 percent in the United States or Germany (FOM 2010). Moscow and St Petersburg still dominate the picture, but the regions are catching up (25 percent of users live in towns with fewer than 100,000 inhabitants). Sociologists predict an average level of connectedness in Russia of 75 percent by 2015 (TassTelekom 2011).

With growing internet penetration, a new generation of young adults came to the internet, and changed it profoundly. The first post-Soviet generation consisting of consumerists "by birth" (Voikova 2010), they envision Russia as an affluent society and show little empathy for the previous generation's traumatic experience of perpetual shortage—in the late Soviet years as well as the 1990s. They are drawn in their online activities not so much to the written word as to photography and photo editing, fashion and design. They attend numerous courses, lectures, master classes and workshops dedicated to art and fashion photography. Almost all have their own portfolios, websites and photo-blogs. As a result, new modes of online activities have appeared to appeal to this new mindset—such as posting one's own pictures in different fashion looks, with "mixed and mashed" clothes, as one can do at the website Lookatme.[18] The poet and critic Dmitrii Golynko describes such digital consumerism as a kind of pragmatic cynicism, when social media networking is enjoyed for hedonistic goals in a society such as Russia's, which is for historical reasons characterized by a lack of social networks in the real world (Golynko 2009).

## Economic significance

The economic growth and significance of the internet in Russia in the different fields of computer technology and software, internet access and content services are, of course, closely tied to the expansion of users. Commodification of the Russian internet, even among the younger generation, is, as mentioned above, a comparatively late phenomenon. While the first computer networks on Russian (Soviet) territory were initiated as private commercial initiatives by members of the technical *intelligentsia* (Bardin, cited in Gagin 1999), the Runet as a whole did not play an important economic role in the early 1990s or even right up to the turn of the century. Moreover, a significant proportion of the early Runet elite was rather skeptical with regard to the economic potential of the web. As Gorny (2009) put it, "While in the 1990s the Western segments of the web started to bow under the pressure of economic interests and growing commercialization, the Runet—due to its comparatively slow implementation in the country—still remained . . . an 'other place'." This is specifically true with regard to online content and its distribution free of charge, which subsequently led to battles over data piracy and hacking, of which Russia had its fair share (see Gornyi 1999).

Serious investment in Russian internet business thus started only in the early 2000s, paradoxically just as the global dotcom bubble was bursting. Concurrently, existing players in the field merged into large internet companies and holdings, while players and institutions from the offline economy engaged as investors in online business. The relative dearth of Runet users offered significant opportunities for growth, which had already been exhausted in digitally more developed countries.

In May 2011, the Boston Consulting Group presented a report commissioned by the Russian branch of Google on the significance of the Runet for the country's economic development. The report found that, in 2009, the internet contributed

$19.3 billion to the Russian economy, amounting to 1.6 percent of GDP (or 2.1 percent, excluding income from oil and gas, see Boston Consulting Group 2011)—a figure which puts Russia on the same level as Italy or Spain, and slightly behind European IT leaders Great Britain (7.2 percent), Sweden (6.6 percent) and Denmark (5.8 percent). Private consumption accounts for the biggest share of the Russian internet economy: in 2009, Russian users acquired IT products and services amounting to $13 billion. The second largest share comes in the form of investments by private companies ($10.5 billion), followed by State investments, which amount to only $1.5 billion. The report's authors attribute the relatively high level of investment to the still underdeveloped IT infrastructure, especially in the Russian regions. Despite a number of negative indicators, including underdeveloped e-commerce and e-government infrastructures, and a persistent digital divide between the major cities and the regions with regard to online usage and the economy, the report takes a positive view of the Runet's future economic prospects.

As far as State investment is concerned, the Federal Target Program "Electronic Russia" (*Federal'naia Tselevaia Programma "Elektronnaia Rossiia"* 2002–10) has been the first serious endeavor to bring public agencies and services into the digital age. The initiative focused mainly on implementing e-government strategies and tools to foster an "information society," seen as a prerogative for economic growth and wealth in the future. The program's aim was to enhance electronic communication between government institutions, on the one hand, and the government and its citizens on the other (Elektronnaia Rossiia 2010). Of investments of 77 billion roubles originally planned, however, only 21 billion roubles was actually spent. Furthermore, the effectiveness of the program was questioned by Russian as well as by foreign experts. According to reports from the World Bank, the effectiveness of Russian government structures did not improve within the eight-year funding period (Oleinik 2010; Tumanov and Faliakhov 2010), and corruption further impeded progress (Interfaks 2011). The "Electronic Russia" program has more recently been followed by the State program "Information society" (*Gosudarstvennaia programma "Informatsionnoe obshchestvo"*), scheduled for the period 2011–20. Yearly investments of approximately 100 billion roubles are planned, supplemented by additional budgetary means from the regions (Konsultant plius 2011).

While the government has obviously responded to the call to promote IT and digital business, it has also clearly encountered serious problems in its realization. Private-sector investments show greater global growth, in contrast, with Russian IT companies not only attracting considerable foreign investment, but also positioning themselves as potent investors on the global markets. In February 2011, *Forbes* Russia (Babitskii 2011) listed the 30 most influential Russian IT businessmen and investors, with the leading positions occupied by Iurii Milner (DST Global, Mail.ru Group), Arkadii Volosh (Yandex) and Pavel Durov (VKontakte). All three of the internet companies represented by these leaders of the Russian IT market are reported to be worth more than $1 billion and are actively participating in the global digital market, with Mail.ru buying shares in Facebook, and Yandex trading its shares on the American NASDAQ stock exchange. To round off the picture, prominent investors such as Vladimir Potanin, Mikhail Prokhorov,

Alexander Mamut and Alisher Usmanov, who top lists of the wealthiest Russians, have made serious investments in the IT and internet sector, which has political implications for the influence of the state and media policy (see, for example, Igumenov and Dorokhov 2010).

## Politics on the Runet

In the early period of internet usage in Russia, new technologies were used more for communication needs and aesthetic experiments than for politics. First, there were no proper social forces to engage in politics online and, second, following the Soviet period, with its almost completely politicized private and public spheres, the pure communication environment of the emerging internet seemed especially appealing for decidedly apolitical self-expression (see Gorny 2009). When digital and networked communication acquired a broader status and significance in the mid-1990s, the first politicians, political initiatives and activities appeared on the web. In 1998, the first website of a politician, then Deputy Prime Minister Boris Nemtsov, was launched. Throughout the following years politicians, civic groups and user communities would explore the whole range of political usages for web technology, including information policies (websites of politicians and political parties), communication (the first interactive online conferences with politicians), campaigning (support for electoral campaigns, election polls), and various forms of "black PR." As politicians themselves lacked the technological and communicative skills, they turned to IT professionals to realize these projects. These experts in political online communication sometimes had their intellectual roots in samizdat and underground culture. This conversion of parts of the digital elite—such as the programmer and journalist Maksim Kononenko (aka Mr Parker) or the media manager and politician Konstantin Rykov (aka Jason Foris)—into service providers for political content marked the transition from the romantic to the pragmatic or cynical period of the Runet (see Schmidt and Teubener 2006b).

As television media came increasingly under state control after 2000 and the implementation of Putin's "power vertical" (Zasurskii 2000; Brunmeier 2005; Fossato, Lloyd, and Verkhovskii 2009), the Runet provided a space for diverse opposition movements, ranging from small, Western-style liberal parties (such as Yabloko) to radical, partly nationalist movements such as the National-Bolshevik Party, led by the writer and journalist Eduard Limonov. The panoply of digital technologies and formats practiced by oppositional forces was broad and encompassed news websites, personal blogs and Twitter accounts, as well as Facebook profiles and community accounts. Opposition politicians and candidates who had been excluded from the traditional media by being blacklisted could convey their political programs and opinions freely on the internet.

Opposition activities on the Russian internet have evolved over time and varied in effectiveness depending on the conceptual and technological skills of their instigators. The liberal wing of the opposition, as well as human rights movements, experienced significant problems in applying effective mobilization tools to propagate their views (Fossato, Lloyd, and Verkhovskii 2009), in part due to their over-reliance on the idea of a rational discourse, in the sense of Jürgen Habermas, and their lack of inclination to mobilize the emotional effects of digital and networked communication (see Lovink 2007). Much more efficient in this respect were the radical youth movements, who used the Runet early as a tactical medium, relying on viral communication modes and memes (see Konradova 2006; Fossato, Lloyd, and Verkhovskii 2009). Generally speaking, Russian online politics in the 2000s followed the universal Web 2.0 move away from static information and communication policies towards more mobile tactical usages (Boler 2008), on both sides—official and opposition.

As the Russian internet became, starting in the late 1990s, a growing factor in the political life and consciousness of society, concerns over control of the new medium also took on a new urgency. The first widely and controversially discussed attempt at technological control came in the late 1990s with the so-called SORM initiative—"System for Operational-Investigative Activities" (*Sistema teknicheskikh sredstv dlia obespecheniia funktsii operativno-rozysknykh meropriiatii*). Internet service providers were obliged to install hardware enabling the Federal Security Service to monitor web content (see Bruchhaus 2001; Alexander 2003: 10; Brunmeier 2005). In subsequent years a wide range of measures of control were tested, including technological and legislative initiatives and, later, in the second half of the 2000s, hacking and denial of service (DDOS) attacks. A more recent initiative of this kind is the law "On Protecting Children from Information Harmful to Their Health and Development" (*O zashchite detei ot informatsii, prichiniaiushchei vred ikh zdorov'iu i razvitiu*). The new law took effect on 1 November 2012 and was intended to protect children from the dangers of pornography, pedophilia and drug abuse on the internet, by blacklisting the respective web resources. Critics assume that the law opens up opportunities for misuse—such as censoring politically disagreeable content (Bovt 2012; Ekho Moskvy 2012).

Since the early 2000s, the authorities have been trying to "assimilate" and control the internet symbolically and ideologically as well. They created a positive buzz by introducing glamorous internet awards, throwing a special "birthday party" for the new, Cyrillic-alphabet top-level domain ".rf" and promoting the brand of Dmitry Medvedev as State blogger No. 1. Concurrently, the authorities attempted to generate negative associations with the internet, describing it as a place for terrorists and foreign political spin-doctors.

While discussions on censorship issues have accompanied the development of the internet in Russia and the Runet in a more global sense, practitioners and researchers agree that, up to 2012 at least, despite individual incidents, no global control or censorship had been enacted (Fossato, Lloyd, and Verkhovskii 2009: 15, 53). This stunning absence of effective web censorship in a politically controlled media system has been interpreted in different ways: (1) as a result of the technological inability of the State institutions to enact effective control; or (2) as a strategy to use the Runet as a kind of safety zone or safety valve, where users can freely articulate their discontent without transforming it into "real," offline political action (Guseinov 2008; Dubin, in Fossato, Lloyd, and Verkhovskii

2009).[19] Alexander (2003) argued that Russia occupied an intermittent place between "Western-type" democracies, which enhanced communicative freedom on the web, and the Chinese (or Iranian or Cuban) model, which relied on strict technological and political censorship. In Russia, by comparison, the internet would be controlled from the inside with the help of political technology, State-generated content and tactical propaganda. Later, in 2010, the OpenNet Initiative (ONI) posited a tripartite model which argued that the Russian authorities preferred sophisticated methods of "second-" and "third-generation controls," which focus "less on denying access than successfully competing with potential threats through effective counter-information campaigns that overwhelm[ed], discredit[ed], or demoralize[d] opponents" (Deibert et al. 2010).[20]

The events of the so-called "Russian winter," with its political protests against electoral fraud and pro-Putin resolve spreading from the blogs onto the streets, are still too recent an event to be subjected to historical judgment. Against the sketched history of the Runet and its political usages, it becomes clear, though, that some of the prominent premises of both internal and external discourses have been challenged by those events, for example, the often subsumed apathy of Russia as a non-networked society or the dissociation of a politically active new media sphere and a passive offline society (Fossato, Lloyd, and Verkhovskii 2009; Golynko 2009).

## From the utopia of autonomy to a political battlefield: the Runet as a medium of crisis

Existing historical narratives about the Runet, as proposed by "embedded researchers" like Eugene Gorny and Sergei Kuznetsov, focus on the aspect of creativity and personal freedom as the main driving forces for the emergence of a networked and digital culture in both Russia and the Russian language. This is not, of course, unique to the Russian case, as historical accounts of the development of ICT and internet technologies in the USA, for example, show, with the technological elites being rooted in the alternative culture of the 1960s. The romantic period of the early Runet, however, is specifically inspired by the experience of the Soviet past, by the totalitarian domination of private and public spheres and the excessively politicized field of art and literature, with the web offering an autonomous place of free and unrestricted articulation. Internet creativity in the pragmatic or cynical period that followed then has turned into the central raw material for political mobilization on both sides—official and opposition—as witnessed in such popular novels as Viktor Pelevin's *Generation P* or Sergei Minaev's *Dukhless* (*Soulless*).

Without denying the decisive impact of individual and collective creativity and the striving for personal and communicative freedom, we propose a complementary narrative centered on the phenomenon of crisis. Communication technology from the outset has been closely tied to moments of crisis and war. No crisis can be solved and no war can be won without a functioning information and communication infrastructure. In times of new media, this complex relationship has to be complemented by another facet: social networks, with their rapid mobilization potential, can arouse or foster a crisis by themselves. As a consequence, the progress in communication technologies and their usages is generally closely linked to tragedies in human lives and societies. The latest illustrations of this complex relationship between the internet and political crisis are the so-called Facebook revolutions in the Arab world, which in turn played an important role as a framing for the Russian "Snow Revolution" of 2011–12.

The development of both the Runet and its political significance can be described in terms of a history of crisis. In a certain sense, the internet is a child of the Cold War, and its decisive periods of development are characterized as much by crisis and conflict as by the private and collective needs for communication (and consumption). The Runet emerges as a consequence of the political breakdown of the Soviet Union. It first showed its effectiveness as a medium for political resistance during the attempted coup of August 1991, when part of the communist leadership rebelled against the perestroika politics by Gorbachev and put him under arrest, while Boris Yeltsin, at that time President of the Russian Soviet Federative Socialist Republic, defended the reforms together with Russian citizens in the White House in Moscow. It first attracted mass interest in 1998, when the financial crisis hit Russia and the Runet was the only reliable source on the exploding exchange rates. The political changes in 2000, when Boris Yeltsin was succeeded by Vladimir Putin, was the starting point for what is called virtual political technology in Russia, the manipulation of public opinion by fake information. The war between Georgia and Russia in 2008 turned the Runet for the first time into a public battlefield for competing political opinions.[21] Most recently, the Russian "Snow Revolution" of 2011–12 illustrates once again the involvement of the Runet with moments of political crisis.

Against the background of the dubious tendency to prove the specificity of Russia and Russian culture—a beloved occupation for analysts both inside and outside Russia—it might appear anachronistic and even questionable to construct a distinct historical narrative for the Russian internet or the internet in Russia. Nevertheless, Soviet historical experience and post-Soviet political practices do lay the groundwork for particular developmental trends and symbolical and ideological interpretations of digital and networked culture in Russia. If, for the early Runet elite, who possessed biographical experience of Soviet times, the internet was a technology and a communication environment offering individual freedom, not only in a direct political, but in a broader cultural context, for younger generations the internet made Russian culture truly global for perhaps the first time. At the same time, as Putin has gradually re-established a hierarchical structure in the social and media systems,[22] the once autonomous Runet has turned into a strategic field of action for both sides—official authorities and opposition forces. To sum up both tendencies in a nutshell: while the early romantic Runet, in its marginality, is presented as a utopia of hypertrophic cultural autonomy, the later pragmatic or cynical Runet is subject to a no less excessive politicization. Both trends foster an especially emotional and/or ideological attitude toward the internet. It is precisely this specific interplay between the historical circumstances of the post-Soviet period, the politics of the Putin–Medvedev era and the integration of Russia into truly global contexts, which make "the Runet" a unique and intriguing object of historic and cultural research.

## Notes

1 With the telling exception of other national web segments in the post-Soviet region, which are modeled according to the Runet-prototype, such as Kaznet for the Kazakh internet (see Chapter 15 by Uffelmann, in this volume).
2 Gorny (2009) constitutes a first important step in this direction, but is concerned primarily with just one mode of Russian online communication—blogging. Kuznetsov (2004) offers valuable insights and materials concerning the first few years following the Internet's emergence, but, as the author himself underlines, he does not intend to construct a proper historical narrative.
3 See the conference and publication series, "Cultural Attitudes Towards Technology," http://www.catacconference.org.
4 Nethistory (nethistory.ru). The site is no longer online. A copy is available at http://web.archive.org/web/20110721203236/http://www.nethistory.ru/.
5 "The Annals," for example, have been republished in a fourth "reprint" in the digital literary journal *Net Literature* (*Setevaia slovesnost'*). For methodological questions on web history as a new emerging discipline, see Brügger (2010) and Cohen and Rosenzweig (2006).
6 For more on the history of the computer in Russia, see Revich (2000) as well as Trogemann, Nitussov, and Ernst (2001) and Chapter 1 by Vlad Strukov, in this volume.
7 The "binarity" of Russian culture is an important topic for Russian philosophers and historians such as Nikolai Berdiaev, Iurii Lotman and others, see Kondakov (1998).
8 For a critical account of the democratizing potential of new media in Eastern Europe, see Kovats (1999) and lately especially Morozov (2011).
9 To this day, the activities of foreign institutions and foundations aiming to promote the spread of the Internet/CMC as a means of "liberation technology" remain a contentious issue for the Russian authorities, who often view such initiatives as interference in Russia's domestic affairs or even as an effort to promote regime change. For a critical account of the activities of Soros as a patron in Eastern Europe, see *Süddeutsche Zeitung* (2008).
10 The term is used both by the "historians" of the Runet and the pioneers themselves, see Leibov (2008).
11 Here and in the following examples in this section, we rely on the information collected by Gorny (2000).
12 Dazhdbog's Grandchildren (ibiblio.org/sergei/).
13 Sovinformbiuro (kovrik.com/sib).
14 Publichnaia elektronnaia biblioteka (public-library.narod.ru).
15 Moskovskii libertarium (libertarium.ru).
16 Vechernii internet (vi.bhost.ru/shtml).
17 The number of subscribers increased exponentially: 193, 277 and 333 on 16, 18 and 20 January, respectively.
18 Look at me (lookatme.ru).
19 The most prominent critic of "cyber utopianism" is Evgeny Morozov in *The Net Delusion* (2011), where he dismantles what he sees to be an illusion of the Internet and ICT as a *per se* deliberating technology, both in Russia and world-wide.
20 For a critical review, see Strukov (2010).
21 We are indebted to Ilya Kukulin for this thought.
22 See Ivan Zasurskii (2000).

## References

1stat.ru. N.d. "Statistika Runeta." http://1stat.ru/ (accessed 30 October 2012).

Alexander, Marcus. 2003. *The Internet in Putin's Russia: Reinventing a Technology of Authoritarianism.* Oxford: Department of Politics and International Relations University of Oxford. Available at: http://www.psa.ac.uk/cps/2003/marcus%20alexander.pdf (accessed 31 October 2012).

Alexanyan, Karina, and Olessia Koltsova. 2009. "Blogging in Russia Is Not Russian Blogging." In *International Blogging: Identity, Politics and Networked Publics*, edited by Adrieene Russell, 65–84. New York: Lang.

Babitskii, Andrei. 2011. "Khoziaeva virtual'noi real'nosti." *Forbes.ru.* 28 February. Available at: http://www.forbes.ru/tehno-slideshow/internet-i-telekommunikatsii/63930-hozyaeva-virtualnoi-realnosti (accessed 31 October 2012).

Barlow, John Perry. 1996. "Re-Experimentalizing Information." Talk presented at the conference, *The Moment before Discovery*, Mucsarnok, 22–4 January. Available at: http://www.c3.hu/scca/butterfly/themomen.html (accessed 31 October 2012).

—— N.d. "Through Many Panes of Shattered Glass: Random Scenes from The Capitalist Fool Tour of Eastern Europe." *Electronic Frontier Foundation Website.* Available at: http://w2.eff.org/Misc/Publications/John_Perry_Barlow/HTML/many_panes.html (accessed 30 October 2012).

Boler, Megan, ed. 2008. *Digital Media and Democracy: Tactics in Hard Times.* Cambridge, MA: MIT Press.

Boston Consulting Group. 2011. "Rossiia onlain: vliianie Interneta na rossiiskuiu ekonomiku." Available at: http://statistic.su/blogfiles/it/bsg.pdf (accessed 31 October 2012).

Bovt, Georgy. 2012. "A Harmful Law Against the Internet." *The Moscow Times.* 12 July. Available at: http://www.themoscowtimes.com/opinion/article/a-harmful-law-against-the-internet/462234.html (accessed 31 October 2012).

Bowles, Anna. 2006. "The Changing Face of the Runet." In *Control + Shift: Public and Private Usages of the Russian Internet*, edited by Natalja Konradova, Henrike Schmidt and Katy Teubener, 21–33. Norderstedt: Books on Demand. Available at: http://www.katy-teubener.de/joomla/images/stories/texts/publikationen/control_shift.01.pdf (accessed 30 October 2012).

Bruchhaus, Jürgen. 2001. "Runet 2000: Die politische Regulierung des russischen Internet." *Arbeitspapiere des Osteuropa-Instituts der Freien Universität Berlin: Arbeitsbereich Politik und Gesellschaft* 31. Available at: http://www.segbers.eu/dateien/working-paper-arbeitspapiere/AP31.pdf (accessed 30 October 2012).

Brügger, Niels, ed. 2010. *Web History.* New York: Lang.

Brunmeier, Victoria. 2005. *Das Internet in Russland: Eine Untersuchung zum spannungsreichen Verhältnis von Politik und Runet.* Munich: Verlag Reinhard Fischer.

Castells, Manuel. 1997. *The Information Age: Economy, Society and Culture.* Malden, MA: Blackwell.

Cohen, Daniel J., and Roy Rosenzweig. 2006. *Digital History: A Guide to Gathering, Preserving, and Presenting the Past on the Web.* Philadelphia, PA: University of Pennsylvania Press.

Deibert, Ronald, John Palfrey, Rafal Rohozinski, and Jonathan Zittrain. 2008. *Access Denied: The Practice and Policy of Global Internet Filtering.* Cambridge, MA: MIT Press.

—— 2010. *Access Controlled: The Shaping of Power, Rights, and Rule in Cyberspace.* Cambridge, MA: MIT Press.

Ekho Moskvy. 2012. "Runet po novym pravilam: kogo i otchego zashchishaet gosudarstvo?" Available at: http://echo.msk.ru/programs/tochka/909039-echo/≤ement-text (accessed 31 October 2012).

Elektronnaia Rossiia. N.d. "Federal'naia Tselevaia Programma (2000–2010 gody)." Available at: http://minsvyaz.ru/ru/doc/index.php?id_4=59 (accessed 30 October 2012).

FOM Fond "Obshchestvennoe Mnenie." 2004. Internet v Rossii. Polls. Issue 6, Winter 2003–2004. 22 March. Available at: http://bd.fom.ru/report/map/o040322 (accessed 30 October 2012).

—— 2010. Internet v Rossii. Fall 2010. December 15, 2010. Available at: http://bd.fom.ru/report/cat/smi/smi_int/pressr_151210 (accessed 30 October 2012).

Fossato, Floriana, John Lloyd, and Aleksandr Verkhovskii. 2009. "The Web that Failed: How Opposition Politics and Independent Initiatives Are Failing on the Internet." *RISJ Challenges*. Oxford: Reuters Institute for the Study of Journalism of the University of Oxford. Available at: http://reutersinstitute.politics.ox.ac.uk/fileadmin/documents/Publications/The_Web_that_Failed.pdf (accessed 30 October 2012).

Gagin, Aleksandr. 1999. " 'V ptichem polete': S V. Bardinym besedoval Aleksandr Gagin." *InterNet magazine* 14. Available at: http://www.gagin.ru/internet/14/6.html (accessed 30 October 2012).

Goldenstein, Jan. 2007. *Das Internet in der Volksrepublik China: Regionale Ausprägung eines globalen Mediums*. Saarbrücken: VDM.

Golynko, Dmitrii. 2009. "Sotsial'nye seti v nesetevom sotsiume." *Digital Icons: Studies in Russian, Eurasian and Central European New Media* 2: 101–13. Available at: http://www.digitalicons.org/wp-content/uploads/2009/12/Dmitry-Golynko-DI-2.7.pdf (accessed 31 October 2012).

Gorny, Eugene. 2009. *A Creative History of the Russian Internet: Studies in Internet Creativity*. Saarbrücken: VDM.

Gornyi, Evgenii. 1999. "Problema kopiraita v russkoi seti: bitva za 'Goluboe salo'." *Zhurnal.ru*. September. Available at: http://www.zhurnal.ru/staff/gorny/texts/salo.html (accessed 31 October 2012).

—— 2000. *Letopis russkogo interneta 1990–1999*. Versiia 3.0. 25 December, 2000. Available at: http://www.zhurnal.ru/staff/gorny/texts/ru_let/index.html. Versiia 4.0. 14 March, 2007. http://www.netslova.ru/gorny/rulet/ (accessed 31 October 2012).

Guseinov, Gasan. 2008. "Liberty's Autistic Face: Challenges and Frustrations of the Russian Blogosphere." Unpublished manuscript.

Hafner, Katie, and Matthew Lyon. 1996. *Where Wizards Stay Up Late: The Origins of the Internet*. New York: Simon & Schuster.

Höller, Herwig G. 1998. "12 Russische Netzideen: Über künstlerische und nicht-künstlerische Projekte im postsowjetischen Cyberspace." *Springerin: Hefte für Gegenwartskunst* 4. Available at: http://www.springerin.at/dyn/heft_text.php?textid=297&lang=de (accessed 30 October 2012).

Igumenov, Valerii, and Roman Dorokhov. 2010. "Ruka Moskvy." *Forbes.ru*. 15 September. Available at: http://www.forbes.ru/svoi-biznes/predprinimateli/56771-ruka-moskvy (accessed 31 October 2012).

Interfaks. 2011. " 'Elektronnaia Rossia' v tsentre skandala." 30 August. Available at: http://www.interfax.ru/business/txt.asp?id=205752 (accessed 31 October 2012).

Kondakov, Igor'. 1998. *Russkaia kultura: kratkii ocherk istorii i teorii*. Moscow. Available at: http://www.kultu-rolog.ru/library/culturology/i-v-kondakov-russkaya-kultura-kratkij-ocherk-istorii-i-teorii/ (accessed 31 October 2012).

Konradova, Natalja. 2006. "Formation of Identity on the Russian-Speaking Internet: Based on the Literary Website Zagranica." In *Control + Shift: Public and Private Usages of the Russian Internet*, edited by Natalja Konradova, Henrike Schmidt and Katy Teubener, 147–55. Norderstedt: Books on Demand. Available at: http://www.katy-teubener.de/

joomla/images/stories/texts/publikationen/control_shift_01.pdf (accessed 16 December 2013).

Konsultant plius. 2011. "Realizatsiia gosudarstvennoi programmy 'Informatsionnoe obshchestvo' i puti ee razvitia." 31 October. Available at: http://www.consultant.ru/law/interview/popovau.html (accessed 30 October 2012).

Kovats, Stephen, ed. 1999. *Ost-West-Internet: Elektronische Medien im Transformationsprozess Ost- und Mitteleuropas*. Frankfurt: Campus Verlag.

Kuznetsov, Sergei. 2004. *Oshchupyvaia slona: zametki po istorii russkogo interneta*. Moskva: Novoe Literaturnoe Obozrenie.

Leibov, Roman. 2003. "Konets starogo interneta uzhe proizoshel—ego ostatki eshche mozhno nabliudat', no oni vpolne marginal'ny." *Nethistory.ru*, 27 March. Available at: http://www.nethistory.ru/memories/1040595042.html (accessed 12 December 2008).

—— 2008. "Pochemu moia monetka tak legla." *Polit.ru*, 20 February. Available at: http://www.polit.ru/article/2008/02/20/r_l/ (accessed 30 October 2008).

Lovink, Geert. 2007. *Zero Comments: Elemente einer kritischen Internetkultur*. Bielefeld: Transcript.

Maslov, Vadim. 1996. "Russkaia Set': istorii." *Zhurnal.ru: vestnik setevoi kultury*. Available at: http://www.zhurnal.ru/1/maslov.htm (accessed 30 October 2012).

Morozov, Evgeny. 2011. *The Net Delusion: How Not to Liberate the World*. London: Allen Lane.

Naughton, John. 2000. *A Brief History of the Future: The Origins of the Internet*. London: Phoenix.

Oleinik, Anton. 2010. "Chas iks: asotsial'naia set." *Vedomosti* 226 (2744), 30 November 2010. Available at: http://www.vedomosti.ru/newspaper/article/250727/asocialnaya_set (accessed 30 November 2010).

Polit.ru. 2008. "Ottsy-osnovateli: vstrechi s pionerami Runeta." 10 April. Available at: http://www.polit.ru/article/2008/04/10/alebedev/ (accessed 30 October 2012).

Reg.ru. N.d.a. "Domenu .SU i rossijskomu segmentu internet ispolnilos' 20 let!" Available at: http://www.reg.ru/announce/20let_su (accessed 30 October 2012).

—— N.d.b. "S dnem rozhdenia .rf." Available at: http://с-днем-рождения.рф/логотип (accessed 30 October 2012).

Revich, Iurii. 2000. "Neizvestnye EWM." *Izvestiia*, 11 July: 7.

Russkii orfograficheskii slovar' Rossiiskoi akademii nauk. "Runet." Ed. V.V. Lopatin. Electronic version at Gramota.ru 2001–2007. Available at: http://www.gramota.ru/slovari/info/lop/ (accessed 30 October 2012).

Salus, Peter H. 1995. *Casting the Net: From ARPANET to INTERNET and beyond* . . . Reading, MA: Addison-Wesley.

Saunders, Robert A., and Sheng Ding. 2006. "Digital Dragons and Cybernetic Bears: Comparing the Overseas Chinese and Near Abroad Russian Web Communities." *Nationalism and Ethnic Politics* 12(2): 255–90.

Schmidt, Henrike, and Katy Teubener. 2006a. " 'Our RuNet'? Cultural Identity and Media Usage." In *Control + Shift: Public and Private Usages of the Russian Internet*, edited by Natalja Konradova, Henrike Schmidt, and Katy Teubener, 14–20. Norderstedt: Books on Demand. Available at: http://www.katy-teubener.de/joomla/images/stories/texts/publikationen/control_shift_01.pdf (accessed 16 December 2012).

—— 2006b. "(Counter-)Public Spheres on the Russian Internet." In *Control + Shift: Public and Private Usages of the Russian Internet*, edited by Natalja Konradova, Henrike Schmidt, and Katy Teubener, 51–72. Norderstedt: Books on Demand. Available at: http://www.katy-teubener.de/joomla/images/stories/texts/publikationen/control_shift_01.pdf (accessed 16 December 2013).

Shcherbina, Tatiana. 2008 [2001]. "RUNET." In *Pobeg smysla: izbrannye stichi. 1979–2008.* Moscow: Argo-Risk. Available at: http://www.vavilon.ru/texts/shcherbina1.html#63 (accessed 30 October 2012).

Shilov. 2000. "Pervyi den'." *Ezhe.* Available at: http://ezhe.ru/zri/history/2000/2.html (accessed 30 October 2012).

Strukov, Vlad. 2010. Review of *Access Controlled: The Shaping of Power, Rights, and Rule in Cyberspace*, by Ronald Deibert. *Digital Icons: Studies in Russian, Eurasian and Central European New Media* 3: 151–4. Available at: http://www.digitalicons.org/wp-content/uploads/2010/07/Review-3.8.2.pdf (accessed 31 October 2012).

*Süddeutsche Zeitung.* 2008. "Der Milliardenzocker, dem der Kapitalismus zu kalt ist," 13 February. Available at: http://www.sueddeutsche.de/finanzen/418/300416/text/3 (accessed 30 October 2012).

Tai, Zixue. 2012. *The Internet in China: Cyberspace and Civil Society.* London: Routledge.

TassTelekom. 2011. "Reiting samykh populiarnykh saitov Runeta." 3 October. Available at: http://tasstelecom.ru/ratings/one/3009#ixzz1pwt1SOlP (accessed 30 October 2012).

Travin, Andrei. N.d. "Komu nuzhna Istoriia.Ru?" Personal website. Available at: http://travin.msk.ru/arc/nethistory.html (accessed 30 October 2012).

Trogemann, Georg, Alexander Y. Nitussov, and Wolfgang Ernst, eds. 2001. *Computing in Russia: The History of Computer Devices and Information Technology Revealed.* Braunschweig: Vieweg.

Tumanov, Grigorii, and Rustem Faliakhov. 2010. "Elektronnaia Rossia oflain." *Gazeta.ru*, 1 March. Available at: http://www.gazeta.ru/social/2010/03/01/3331850.shtml (accessed 30 October 2012).

Vesti. 2011. "Istoriia Runeta." 25 November. Available at: http://www.vesti.ru/doc.html?id=409127&tid=85255 (accessed 30 October 2012).

Voikova, Natalia. 2010. "Mezhdu Tvitterom i Lobsterom." *Russkii Zhurnal*, 30 September. Available at: http://www.russ.ru/pole/Mezhdu-tvitterom-i-lobsterom (accessed 30 October 2012).

Webplaneta. 2003. "NetHistory.Ru zaimetsia istoriei interneta v Rossii." 27 March. http://www.webplanet.ru/news/internet/2003/3/27/nethistory.html. Copy in Archive.org. Available at: http://web.archive.org/web/20031127225222/http://webplanet.ru/news/internet/2003/3/27/nethistory.html (accessed 30 October 2012).

Zasurskii, Ivan. 2000. *Re-konstruktsiia Rossii: mass-media i politika v Rossii devianostykh* (Ispravlennaia i znachitel'no dopolnennaia versiia knigi "Mass-media vtoroi respubliki"). *Russkii zhurnal*, 14 December. Available at: http://old.russ.ru/politics/20001114_II.html (accessed 30 October 2012).

Zheng, Yongnian. 2008. *Technological Empowerment: The Internet, State, and Society in China.* Stanford, CA: Stanford University Press.

# Part II

# New media spaces

# 3 Divided by a common web

## Some characteristics of the Russian blogosphere*

*Gasan Gusejnov*

As a technology, the blogosphere emerged at roughly the same time in every part of the world, and is supported by technologies that spread at great speed, as a rule, irrespectively of national borders. Nonetheless, as with all new technological resources (such as the telephone and the car), their adaptation across the globe can be culturally specific. For example, in certain areas of post-socialist society, having your own motor vehicle is considered more a source of prestige than a means of transport. Similarly, access to virtual communication (a LiveJournal account, an email address) can enable a user to take up social roles that are not available to them in their life outside the internet. Not only have linguistic communities within the global blogosphere developed distinctive traits. But the internet itself continues to be organized in territorial terms, with IP addresses and web-hosting platforms traceable to physical locations. In this chapter, I will analyze the sociolinguistic aspect of the internet and its divisions, usually described by the word blogosphere. My main case study is the Russian-language segment of the blogosphere, with its national, regional, and global diaspora elements, which set it apart from blogospheres in other languages.

Before we can get to the peculiarities of the Russian case, some preliminary remarks on the general characteristics of the blogosphere and its users will be helpful. According to Lev Manovich's pioneering social theory of the internet, the virtual space of new media has created several types of users: the flâneur, the dandy, the online vagabond, the natural scientist, the surfer, and the navigator (Manovich 2001: 268–73). Thanks to the rise of the internet, the closely knit community of a small-scale traditional society (*Gemeinschaft*, in Ferdinand Tönnies' terms) is being replaced by the anonymous association of modern society (*Gesellschaft*, according to Tönnies ([1887] 1957)) (Manovich 2001: 269). Subsequent interpreters have corrected this view, by stressing the function of the blogosphere in creating a "society of experience" (*Erlebnisgesellschaft*) (Schulze 1992). According to Simanowski (2008), its users commonly exhibit two often contradictory tendencies: fighting to attract attention, on the one hand, and, on the other, taking part in mass production "under the influence of group pressure," in an "internet democracy," in the role of "mercenary (purchased) bloggers," "paid storytellers" or "free amateur advertisers."

The technological basis for the internet gives rise to a situation in which institutional boundaries in the offline world (the "real" world) are erased, and the space thus cleansed provides a potential communications platform capable of connecting, in one and the same place, communication between a multitude of people who, in an Internet-free world, would not have had the chance to meet. Until blogs appeared, this potential had only partially been realized. Websites were created en masse by technical specialists familiar with the intricacies of domain delegation and HTML. The few mechanisms for feedback included chat forums, guest books and email. However, the content of chats was ephemeral, and could be saved only on a local computer, while email remained a form of correspondence, and guest books were not intended for communication as such, but instead were designed purely to convey the views of visitors to site administrators, without making any provision for a response. Moreover, guest books could not be combined into a single network similar to what would later become the blogosphere, because each guest book belonged to a separate website and was exclusively tailored towards that website.

This situation changed when creators of websites started following a new blueprint for populating the internet with content. Now all they did was to provide the technical infrastructure for users to publish, declaring that the users themselves were now responsible for textual content. Without needing to possess special technical skills, each internet user could play his part in creating the look of the internet. The opportunity for comment turned a communications space into a communications environment (the blogosphere), where restrictions were imposed not by external factors, but by the limitations of human ability.

As one of the media and, at the same time, genres in which social interaction occurs, the blog denotes a public, web-based media platform, which takes the form of a collection of entries (text or video), displayed in reverse chronological order, united around the identity of the author (a personal blog) or the common interests of a team of authors or a specific topic (collective blogs, a blog community), and offering readers the opportunity to post comments. A blog (irrespective of whether it is personal or collective) may be a personal diary, a news feed, a platform for comment on current affairs or a collection of recreational, educational or other material (Rettberg 2008). On occasion, blogs are conceived as a form of media, although from the legal standpoint a blog only acquires this status once it has been officially registered.

## Historical overview of the Russian blogosphere

By the end of the 2000s, three main blog formats had clearly established themselves in Russia: (1) the text-based blog (sometimes accompanied by illustrations or embedded video and audio, usually hosted on platforms such as LiveJournal, LiveInternet, Diary.ru and others); (2) the video-blog (each post consisting of a video address to readers; recordings are normally stored on the YouTube and RuTube video-sharing websites and then exported to traditional blogging platforms by embedding); and (3) the micro-blog (a blog with limited functionality, including a restriction on the number of characters in each entry, such as Twitter). A group of blogs located on one blogging platform usually forms a relatively closed community (see LiveJournal, for example). The blogosphere is, in essence, the sum total of all blogs. From the beginning, the Russian internet was highly regionalized, with Internet provisions focusing overwhelmingly in Moscow, and only then spreading through its large cities further to the periphery.[1]

It was not too long ago that the blogosphere carried an air of the exotic; its name is itself a loan from English, regarded with a certain degree of irony. As the author of these lines defined it in 2009:

> The blogosphere (from the Greek, English and American, literally "universe of blogs") is a term which brings together all social networking sites and clusters of online diaries, which are understood to be potentially interlinked. In paronymous and semantic terms, the word brings together the concepts of *blagodat'* ["grace"] and *noosphere*, although stripped of all religious and particularly philosophical content, in the meantime planting in the user a pleasant feeling that they are not simply wasting time and money in fruitless conversation with unknown individuals, but are among the first inhabitants of this new universe.
>
> (Lenta n.d.)

But in the years since, it has found new ways to integrate into both the internet and the offline socio-political environments. As social networks have expanded rapidly, we have witnessed a global "devirtualization" of users in those regions where for many years the internet space was controlled by the state. The moment when bloggers transformed into *public figures*, they also became *humorous mascots*, e.g. *khomiachok* ("hamster"). This became apparent in slogans such as *khomiak raspravil plechi* ("the hamster has squared its shoulders"), which appeared at public protests in Moscow and other Russian cities in 2011. These protests themselves were partly organized through social networking sites (Dragunskaia 2012).

To what extent can we use the Russian blogosphere as an example of either a society of detached flâneurs, or as a "community of experience"? In order to answer this question, we need to map out the external offline boundaries of our subject matter, or, to be more precise, its border posts—those issues in public and political life which are actively depicted in both environments but which are most passionately discussed in the blogosphere and on social networking sites. Among the more prominent of such issues: the political campaigns against Russian bloggers, primarily Aleksei Navalny, and representatives of the opposition; Ukraine's democratic revolution in 2004; the "Arab Spring"; the web-based organization in Russia of public protest events; and the attempt to use the blogosphere and social networking sites to draw up an "alternative diplomatic agenda," focusing on developments such as the Pussy Riot case and global online campaigns in support of the "Magnitsky list." The list would also include more local online campaigns against corrupt officials who flout traffic regulations, or for the preservation of local hospitals and schools.

## From affective community to an economy of attention-seeking

In the modern economy of attention-seeking, the internet plays a central role. But paradoxically, while the lag with which the Russian sector of the global blogosphere has stayed behind its Anglo-American counterpart by approximately a decade, closed by the mid-2000s, the differences in character between the Russian and the English-speaking internet became more apparent. This has to do as much with the role of individual Russian users, who influenced their community by becoming its gurus (Anton Nosik aka *dolboeb*, Roman Leibov aka *r_l* and several dozen other leading bloggers with thousands of followers), but also with the development of the blogosphere in its sociopolitical context. In this respect, the Russian blogosphere has acquired new and unexpected properties, which can be described not so much in terms of "lagging behind" the Western blogosphere as in terms of "creating an idiosyncratic and on occasion very strange identity."

As an intellectual system that displays self-awareness and seeks to be as expressive as possible, the blogosphere revolves around the relentless fluctuations of its users—as individuals, groups or herds—between complete openness and demands for privacy. This is how the blogger *sherman* describes this contradiction:

> Life online
> 12 May 2011
>
> We devise new forms of communication, we develop old ones, we walk around in large groups, lots of people are our "friends" on social networking sites, and YET we feel lonely. We say that we live the way we want to, but at the same time we don't know what it is that we want. We are a new generation who are devaluing words and feelings and creating a new God. And we ourselves are trying to control that God, but ultimately we remain under his control. We refer to this God by various names: dollars, rubles, euros, there are thousands of different names. But is that really what we want? . . . We are a generation of people who are free. We are free to express our thoughts, share our vision of the world and try o be individual, and yet we forget that we are individuals. We freely make our own choices, freely moving forward, seeking assistance and resorting to various means, some of them unlawful, in order to achieve our aims.
> Yes, we are free. Emotionally, we are not dependent on other people. But when we find ourselves alone, why do we feel sorry for ourselves, why do we regret our actions, why do we want to change the past? Why, then, do we look for more and more friends and people to love, if we are independent? Why is it so painful for us to be ourselves?
>
> (*sherman* 2011, orthography and punctuation as in the original)

## The blogosphere and the history of counterculture in Russia

In the early 2000s, the predominantly private space represented by blogs started to enter the global media landscape alongside traditional media. On the one hand, on their websites, major traditional publications began to create pages where both the publication's employees and ordinary users could launch their own blogs. Between 2000 and 2005, as an employee of the Deutsche Welle radio station, I was involved in numerous debates within the journalistic community about the relationship between the blogosphere and professional journalism. These debates petered out of their own accord in the mid-2000s, when it became clear that amateur journalism, on the one hand, and professional news dissemination, on the other, did not in any way hinder one another. On the contrary, they contributed to the creation of new genres. The blogosphere rapidly defined itself as an arena for citizen and/or amateur journalism and everyday communication and self-representation (see also Timchenko 2012).

Meanwhile, having closely studied the balance of power between professional media and blogging (including micro-blogging) for many years, some specialists have come to the conclusion that "the media are working to popularize social networking sites, rather than social networking sites popularizing the media." As an example, Timchenko cites statistics from the RIA Novosti news agency, which has "more than 200,000 subscribers on VKontakte, but barely 10,000 people accessing its website from social networking sites" (Timchenko 2012).

If one looks back on the history of the blogosphere in Russia from the perspective of the early 2010s, two stages stand out, the first of which, measured by many parameters, coincides with the international blogosphere. During the first stage, by the end of 1990s and the very beginning of 2000s, blogging platforms constituted a materialized private-public space, with no managers or supervisors to provide access to the resource as a showcase for the diversity of individual and communal life. However, the most popular blogging platform of the early 2000s, LiveJournal, fairly quickly found itself at loggerheads with some in its community over the attempts by its management (and principally its abuse team) to monitor bloggers' use of politically incorrect phrases.[2] This was a crucial moment in the history of the Russian blogosphere, since the early Russian blogosphere's most advanced users immediately began to position themselves as a counter-culture.[3]

On the internet, this anarchic subculture turned out to constitute the mainstream of textual production, acquiring its own leaders, including Dmitrii Gal'kovskii, Aleksandr Dugin and Mikhail Verbitskii. Verbitskii, indignant at attempts to exert the pressure of censorship on LiveJournal, set up his own blogging platform, Lj.russia, as an alternative to LiveJournal where there would be absolute freedom (an Abbaye de Thélème for our time, also known as Tifaretnik, based on Verbitskii's own nickname, *tiphareth*).

It is worthy of note that the most active of these pioneers who started with LiveJournal and ended with their own "underworld" of Tifaretnik, became involved with the internet during lengthy stays (for study or work) in the USA or in European countries, and then brought this media to Russia at a time when strong anti-Western feelings were on the rise. The LiveJournal abuse team ganged up on Verbitskii over a campaign bearing the slogan "Kill NATO!"

The Lurkmore portal is an archive of the sort of politically incorrect and, at the same time, socially and politically edgy material that has been deposited in the blogosphere and its neighbors on the internet. In late 2012, facing the threat of closure owing to the generous use of bad language, Lurkmore moved to the .to domain. Lurkmore is assembling an archive of all the notable activists involved in the Russian blogosphere in its early years. Despite Lurkmore's language and style, the blogosphere archive under construction at this counter-cultural portal possesses additional merits. For example, the archive does not contain dead links, and, like the best articles on Wikipedia, backs all its facts and artifacts up with citations. In addition, Lurkmore places portraits of the main protagonists in the wider offline historical and cultural context. In particular, it is of historical and literary interest that the protagonists of the early Russian blogosphere are mentioned in the works of the most famous Russian writers of the 1990s and 2000s, Viktor Pelevin and Vladimir Sorokin (*Day of the Oprichnik*).

In the opinion of Aleksandr Dugin, a proponent of the ideology of a new Eurasia and a radical critic of liberalism in Russia, the blogosphere is "a crowd of degenerate teenagers who are gradually decomposing":

> They create a virtual dialogue that never goes anywhere. Living in LiveJournal is something that people who have no chance of leading a real life can afford. It's about the retelling of distorted stock phrases that reflect the late autumn of the young soul. It's about systematically subsiding into nothing. It's a cemetery. Among the people sitting there are wanker managers who pretend to be Beowulf. It's the illusion of an artificial life (*protezirovannaia zhizn'*). It's the shameless exposure of total nonsense. There are no critical or apologetic meanings. It's a brutal, half-demented atmosphere. Archetypes of decomposed spirits. It's a dictatorship of two or three formulae that are passed between one another in a senseless relay.[4]

The first Russians to use the blogosphere thus turned out to be radical critics of this new "system," emerging out of the new medium, which was understood simultaneously as a focal point of Western liberalism and an institution resembling a totalitarian Soviet kindergarten or a pioneer camp for children with learning difficulties. The combination of hatred and contempt with enthusiasm and admiration, of complete assimilation and profound Russification, with a radical rejection of one's existence in the "blogosphere," as if in an alien and hostile space—that is what provides the cornerstone for the habitat occupied by Russian-language bloggers. It is possible that both the subculture nature of the Russian blogosphere as a whole, and the marked counter-culture nature of LiveJournal in particular, as the most popular Russian-language blogging platform, would have led to the blogosphere's gradual transformation into a peripheral environment, located adjacent to the various new media of the "Web 2.0 generation." But in the mid-2000s, a new stage opened in the development of the Russian blogosphere, in some respects different from what was taking place at the same time in the West.

## The citizen platform and Russia's media landscape since the mid-2000s

Since the mid-2000s, the Russian blogosphere and the Russian media environment have witnessed processes that have moved in a variety of directions. On the one hand, advanced hybrid media have emerged, including within their ranks more blogs maintained by representatives of the so-called expert community. Publishing projects such as Slon, Forbes, Grani.ru and Snob have either launched blogging communities on their own platforms, or turned in their entirety into semi-closed (expert) blogging platforms.[5] At the same time, professional writers and journalists have found themselves in a community of authors who may have been specially selected, but are nevertheless far from professional. As a result, the material published by these hybrid media does not differ greatly from what can be found in LiveJournal's blogs and blogging communities. Moreover, even these media outlets' most popular bloggers and columnists cannot compete in terms of the size of their subscriber base with the former editor-in-chief of Stolitsa, Andrei Malgin (*avmalgin*), internet guru Anton Nosik (*dolboeb*) or photoblogger Rustem Adagamov (*drugoi*).

As citizen journalism has developed technologically and substantively—along with the prominence of online video and audio material, censorship has gradually returned to the domain of registered media. Towards the end of the 2000s, the publishing policy of state television channels and internet publications, as well as the majority of their privately-owned mass-audience counterparts, began to experience such strong pressure from censorship that the blogosphere increasingly came to assume the function of "grown-up" media outlets. Indicative of this is the role that web-based sources served in providing reliable reporting on one of the major man-made disasters of the 2000s—the accident at the Saiano-Shushenskaia hydroelectric power station in August 2009. Initially covered up at the order of then emergencies minister, Sergei Shoigu, the true extent of the damage quickly became clear once internet publications used the blogosphere to post photographs and primary textual material telling the story of the accident. On 17 August 2009, on its homepage, the Lenta.ru news website published a photo taken by a semi-anonymous blogger, because the official news agencies had failed to post any images from the scene. That same day, Shoigu said there was absolutely no threat to the safety of people living in towns and villages near the hydroelectric power station, and that the dam had not been damaged. "In situations such as these, people can always be found who will spread panic," he said (Mil'man 2009). But it was too late—the panic was already under way. A photo report from a road jammed with cars was published not on news websites, but on LiveJournal. To the majority of LiveJournal users, the photographs of a queue at a petrol station in Abakan, posted by someone living in Khakassia and still available on their blog (*rukhakasia* 2009), and a photo report on attempts by several local people to withstand possible flooding on a mountain, were only some of the blog-based evidence that demonstrated the importance of maintaining this medium not so much as a private space but as a social space. By the second and third day after the accident, even official television channels were using material from bloggers.[6]

By the start of the 2010s, the blogosphere had turned into an alternative source of information on the most important low-level events in public life in various regions around the country. The precise nature of the material and the rapid verifiability of reports made LiveJournal an archive for micro-blogs such as Twitter. For many bloggers, the automatic reposting of LiveJournal updates to Twitter and Facebook accounts counter-balanced both platforms' like tags on the organizer—the daily diary (LiveJournal), hour notes (Facebook) and minute signals (Twitter) of a clock. Different ways of visualizing memes appeared, along with demotivating caricatures, summarizing the behavior of users in the blogosphere and on social networking sites, or providing users with stylistic recommendations. The more censorship and deviation from fidelity users find in the media, the more active and aggressive bloggers become in their world. The spread of swear words and other forms of mutual humiliation provokes new censorship. Any new attempt to jam free expression provokes the expansion of obscene speech acts in the blogosphere.

The spread of social networking sites that provide users with new technological opportunities has not led to the abandonment of the blogosphere. It may be that the blogosphere's direct social effectiveness across post-Soviet space did not manifest itself until 2004, during the elections in Ukraine, when several Russian- and Ukrainian-language LiveJournal communities played a significant part in mobilizing society and helping to organize civil society.[7] In Russia, the blogosphere and social networking sites could be seen performing a similar function from the winter of 2011–12 through to the winter of 2012–13.

During this period, the blogosphere assumed several useful functions normally performed by institutions of civil society, serving as a virtual surrogate for micro-group, street and parliamentary democracy. Particularly influential was the LiveJournal blog of Aleksei Navalny, where daily posts appeared documenting a multitude of high-profile criminal and civil cases—posts that inevitably spread through social networking sites through reposting. One recent exposé featured a scheme used on state procurement websites to rig the supposedly public procurement process. Officials maintaining the site mixed Latin letters inconspicuously into the Cyrillic script, making the tender pages inaccessible through ordinary searches. Only those provided with the specific algorithm could access and bid for the tenders. Within a day after being exposed on Navalny's blog, the scheme became common knowledge to several tens of thousands of people. As of 24 January 2013, 164 people reposted the information elsewhere on LiveJournal, 1,500 reposted it on Facebook, 1,279 reposted it on Twitter, 2,261 reposted it on VKontakte and 317 reposted it on Google Plus (Naval'nyi 2013).

At the same time as it was republished on social networking sites, the event was reported by major online publishers, so the text of the post authored by Navalny comfortably reached a circulation of more than 100,000. Since the inception of Navalny's blog in 2006, this sort of citizen journalism has turned the account into a serious media outlet with more than 70,000 subscribers, justifiably reinforcing the presumption that Navalny's subscriber and support base will become a factor of national political significance. Over the course of six years, some 3,000 posts on LiveJournal have attracted more than 1.5m comments. On Twitter, Navalny has 320,000 followers.

Since late 2012, state prosecutors have been leveling increasingly serious allegations at Navalny and his brother. Tens of thousands of Navalny's subscribers are following the confrontation between the lawyer and the Russian state in real time. Since December 2011, some of these subscribers have been attending actual political rallies and marches. Official electronic media (primarily the television channels owned by state media conglomerate VGTRK) have been smearing Navalny with terms such as "troublemaker," "nationalist," and "populist." Each such accusation boosts the lawyer-blogger's support base. And yet, despite all the quantitative measures mentioned above, even the tens of thousands of subscribers and "friends," none of this in any way signifies that all these people, or even the majority of them, are active or even passive supporters of the blogger. The pejorative classification of bloggers as "office plankton" is reinforced in practice by the fact that the online political and cultural efforts of bloggers, as well as of people who do not have their own blogs but are registered on social networking sites, remain marginalized. Even popular bloggers do not find much demand for their blogging from larger media outlets—official, semi-official and actively dissident (anti-government). The social stratum of "television viewers," the passive majority of Russia's population, continue to view the avant-garde segment of the blogosphere as alien, and even less influential than the official Soviet "intelligentsia" was during the Soviet era.[8]

Researchers studying the Russian internet tend to exaggerate the extent of the integration that has taken place between offline and online environments during the political protests of 2011–2012, which took place primarily in Moscow and St Petersburg. In his article, "The End of Virtuality," Sam Greene refers, in particular, to the "mobilization segment" as being the most intriguing, in the context of the collaboration between blogs and social networking sites, on the one hand, and "normal," "offline" citizens, on the other:

> Of all of those who participated on December 24th, some 56% had taken part in the December 10th protest on Bolotnaia Square, and 21.5% were at the unsanctioned rally at Chistye Prudy on December 5th. But those active in online debates were significantly more likely to have been at each of those earlier protests: 25.3% of on-liners took part in the December 5th protest, versus 16.5% of off-liners, and 67.2% of on-liners came out on December 10th, versus 47.5% of off-liners.
>
> (Grin 2012)

Greene interprets the chasm between "on-liners" and "off-liners" as follows:

> On-liners were 53% more likely to have participated in the December 5th protest, but only 41% more likely than off-liners to have come out on December 10th. Tentatively, at least, this suggests a mainstreaming of the protests, as they gain more attention in the off-line media and more prominence in public debate. Moreover, it appears that solidarity is increasingly being generated not in the media, but on the streets themselves.
>
> (ibid.)

And yet, in exposing the corrupt nature of Russian society "from the top down," Navalny also serves as a negative example for the frightened inhabitant: the Russian Prosecutor-General's Office openly and mockingly declares him to be under investigation. Even if the majority of the population does sympathize with Navalny, there is no way in which he can be described as a trendsetter (at least at the time of this writing), neither for the offline majority, nor for the "office plankton."

The vulnerability of critical voices in the blogosphere was also exposed by the media campaigns waged in the late 2000s and early 2010s, such as those against Navalny and Adagamov, which spread across to the television channels, which enjoy far larger audiences than the Russian blogosphere. The art of using dirty tricks to "troll" or "extinguish" an opponent is acquiring ever newer forms. In 2012, public accusations that Adagamov had abused children were placed at the heart of the political campaign against the opposition. Signs that the security services and organizations of uncertain origin (Nashi, etc.) had apparently "developed" this case divided the protest movement: for some, the campaign was a sign of the mendacity and weakness of the country's leaders, while, for others (988 2012), it was a sign that the authorities were right to say that the whole of the opposition blogosphere is sustained by an amoral and impure group of people (Belokurova 2012).

## The "thick journal" in the blogosphere

In Russia and the USSR, the "thick literary journal" was considered to be one of the main cultural institutions of the pre-computer and pre-internet era (Martinsen 1997).This is despite the fact that, historically, Russia and the USSR are far from being the only countries in which this sociocultural genre has played an important role,[9] it was specifically in the era of Web 2.0 that almost the whole of Russia's thick-journal environment was packed into one mega-website, called the "Russkii Zhurnal," the Periodicals Room.[10] This online publication represents a special form of co-existence between the personal blogosphere—the diaries and blogging communities of writers and readers—and the collective blog environment of the editorial offices of the "thick journals," "linked" to one another via social networking sites and/or broadcast to LiveJournal.

When, in 2000, I proposed comparing the "population" of the blogosphere's prototypes with the "nation" in Stalin's sense of the word, which, for example, populated the "archipelago GULag," that "nation" was yet to acquire its own history (Guseinov 2000). Over the past few years, that history has emerged. The self-perception of bloggers as a very special and even elite part of the population, with its own codex of norms and values since then has widely referred to the traditions of the Russian intelligentsia subscribing to the same thick journals, watching the same performances, reading the same books, and sharing very similar points of view on how things should be organized in Russia (*rokina* 2007). The controversial co-existence of encapsulated "solid" communities and fragments of the still non-existent open civil society is thus making virulent the historical pattern of the intelligentsia situated between people (*narod*) and a monarch (*vlast'*) as we know it at the end of the nineteenth century and throughout the Soviet era.

The historicization of a blogger's user experience can be illustrated by referring to certain comments on posts on Tatiana Tolstaya's blog, which has more than 25,000 regular readers/subscribers ("friends"). Since Tolstaya's blog is a literary project, she positions some of her entries as drafts or sketches for possible scripts. In a 12 March 2012 comment on one of those drafts, which contained alternative scenarios for "annual inaugurations of President Putin" (Tolstaia 2012a), one of the users said that Tolstoya's sketch reminded him of an earlier joke by the same author. At the request of another user, he readily provided a link to an entry posted by Tolstaya on 17 September 2011.

> *tanyant*:
> "Prokhorov
> We finally have someone who fits the saying: "Give an idiot a dick made out of glass—he'll break his dick and cut his hands."
>
> (Tolstaia 2011)

Written following billionaire Mikhail Prokhorov's refusal to become leader of a liberal party, the post triggered an immediate response from those who felt they had been offended. A comment on Tolstaya's post contained a link to Andrei Mal'gin's blog, in which Mal'gin, quoting Prokhorov's former deputy in the Union of Right Forces party (Right Cause), said that Tolstaya had offended Prokhorov personally (Mal'gin 2011). Under the guise of exposing an anti-Medvedev conspiracy on the part of the billionaire, Mal'gin performed some so-called "mudslinging."

The volume alone of the literary texts which pass through this sort of discussion is becoming an existential challenge for users of the blogosphere. Some discussions continue for years, like chess matches conducted by correspondence. Others turn into promotional events for forthcoming book launches, consisting of posts from LiveJournal being effectively recycled. In this way, the literary blogosphere forms communities of many thousands of people around a wide range of authors who constitute an alternative "Periodicals Room." To a certain extent, this "room" overlaps with the "Russkii Zhurnal" Periodicals Room, and the points of overlap consist of reactions (likes) and comments on Facebook.

The blogosphere is developing into a synergetic advertising resource that allows an author not only to be open about the purpose of a post as advertising, but indeed to stress that purpose. After all, the goods that are on offer are of very high quality, and the reader will not be disappointed. For example, *tanyant* publishes a detailed account of her new personal series "Tatiana Tolstaya recommends," published by the Eksmo publishing house. Lavishing praise on a collection of stories by Lora Beloivan, Tolstaya reminds her readers that Beloivan blogs as *tosainu* and has 9,000 followers, as well as pointing out that the hard copy of the book will be on sale at shops run by the Artemy Lebedev Studio (Tolstaia 2012b).

The openness and lack of subtext in Tolstaya's blog create a favorable environment for authors, editors and publishers to keep an eye on one another. The existence of an objective indicator such as the time at which entries and comments were posted makes it possible to establish that maintaining this sort of writer's blog can take up a significant proportion of someone's so-called spare time—not just the writer's, but also that of some of their regular readers.

The distinctive symbiosis between an author and their fan club, all of them privy to a common "secret," can be seen by taking a look at the blogs of the writer Denis Dragunskii (*clear_text*), the historian Nikolai Shaburov (*furlus*), the writer and philosopher Mikhail Bezrodnyi (*m-bezrodnyj*) and several thousand other LiveJournal blogs launched as "authors' projects." The people who set up these blogs propose separating their projects into short-term (the launch of a book as a LiveJournal "annual compendium") and medium-term cycles (devirtualization during book launches at fairs, by working with students).

## Conclusion

In tracking the development of the Russian blogosphere from the late 1990s to the early 2010s, we can highlight a number of principal and contrasting signs.

First, there is the combination of the civic counter-cultural practices of the internet era with the older practices of dissidence (alternative thinking) in the late Soviet period, leading to the emergence of two coexisting models: the citizen platform and the personal blog. In the post-Soviet Russian environment, the blogosphere has fitted itself into the traditional late Soviet subculture of dissidence. In this way, it is perceived as a new-fangled culture and counter-cultural practice, and at the same time as a reinforcement of old cultural stereotypes. This leads to the contradictory attitude to blogging adopted by those taking part in and observing the process—as a useful activity which expands the boundaries of the traditional media (Navalny), and as a pointless and harmful pastime (Dugin).

Second, oppositional bloggers have found it increasingly difficult to promote politically significant information offline, due to growing administrative harassment. As seen in the state-led campaigns waged against well-known bloggers (Navalny, Adagamov et al.), there is a clear desire among Russian officialdom to marginalize the blogosphere. On the other hand, among the blogosphere's active users and creators alike, the points of contact between virtual content and offline social reality are constantly changing. The impulse triggered by the blogosphere is not always picked up by the social environment, but is becoming an ever more important feature of the media landscape.

Finally, the blogosphere is still perceived by most users as an environment for recreation and micro-group cultural consumption. Only a small portion of people using the blogosphere view this environment as a space for "real" (offline) social creativity. The rich traditions of elite cultural leisure find form in the blogosphere as personal artistic projects. The volume of texts produced and processed in this space–time continuum makes the blogosphere a parallel reality. This reality either pushes active users away from taking practical social, artistic, and political action, or offers itself up as a genuine lifestyle alternative. Just as this chapter goes to press, Aleksei Navalny has demonstrably taken the latter tack, publicly declaring his ambition to become the next president of the Russian Federation (Lenta 2013). The declaration would hardly be useful in his attempts to avoid reprisals by the Prosecutor General of Russia, but it stands as a clear challenge to Russian political bloggers less inclined to take the fight from the virtual to the real. Are they ready for a new positioning of the blogosphere or not? Will the very core of Navalny's activities, some of which have led to the sacking of corrupt politicians, become a new trend in Russia? Or, maybe Navalny will suffer the fate of quite a few stubborn businessmen and politicians right now in jail? Negotiating these two main strategies remains a key issue for the self-perception of bloggers and the Russian blogosphere at large.

## Acknowledgments

I express my gratitude for criticism and help provided by Michael Gorham, Ingunn Lunde and Martin Paulsen in order to make this chapter clearer. However, the responsibility is entirely mine.

## Notes

* Translated from the original Russian by Kyrill Dissanayake.
1 Based on data from Rambler's list of the top 100 online media (http://top100.rambler.ru/navi/?theme=440).
2 The harassment of Mikhail Verbitskii is described in detail on the Wikireality website: http://www.wikireality.ru/wiki/Миша_Вербицкий.
3 This is also the view of Ilya Kukulin, who even suggests that among the most radical members of the language environment, a favorable attitude towards the state's radical anti-democratic position is refracted as a paradoxical distortion of the language of culture and the intelligentsia. From the standpoint of the most active counter-culture groups, the standard language is a hypocritical discourse among dissidents and liberals, which threatens Russia with collapse and destabilization (Kukulin 2012).
4 http://www.russia.ru/video/dugin_lj/ (accessed January 2013).
5 Slon (slon.ru), Forbes (forbes.ru), Grani.ru (grani.ru), Snob (snob.ru).
6 For photographs of the devastation at the Saiano-Shushenskaia hydroelectric power station, see *socro* (2009). Compare with an analysis of blogging in the USA in connection with Hurricane Katrina: Kay Trammell's (2005) conclusion—"blogging will not change the world in crisis, but it will make it more human"—fully applies to the function of the blogosphere in Russia as an environment that offers an alternative to or supports the media.
7 See the LiveJournal blog Vybir 2004 (2004-vybory-ua.livejournal.com/).

8 For more on the intelligentsia as a source of critical ideas on development, see Beyrau (1993).
9 See, for example, the German history of the "thick journal" in Philpotts (2009).
10 Zhurnal'nyi zal (magazines.russ.ru).

## References


988. 2012. "Ot chego umerlo protestnoe dvizhenie." *"988!"—khroniki novogo obshchestva*, 7 December. Available at: http://988.livejournal.com/340949.html (accessed 18 April 2013).

Belokurova, Elena. 2012. "Staroe i novoe v diskurse grazhdanskogo obshchestva i kharaktere obshshestvennykh dvizhenii" *Neprikosnovennyi zapaz* 4 (84). Available at: http://magazines.russ.ru/nz/2012/4/b6.html (accessed 18 April 2013).

Beyrau, Dietrich. 1993. *Intelligenz und Dissens: Die russischen Bildungsschichten in der Sowjetunion 1917–1985*. Göttingen: Vandenhoeck & Ruprecht.

Dragunskaia, Irina. 2012. "Art-partizany." *The New Times* 29(256), 17 September. Available at: http://newtimes.ru/articles/detail/57343/ (accessed 18 April 2013).

Grin, Sam. 2012. "Konets virtual'nosti." *Tsentr izucheniia Interneta i obshchestva*, 19 January. Available at: http://www.newmediacenter.ru/ru/2012/01/19/the-end-of-virtuality-2/ (accessed 18 April 2013).

Guseinov, Gasan. 2000. "Zametki k antropologii russkogo interneta: osobennosti iazyka i literatury setevykh liudei. *Novoe literaturnoe obozrenie* 43. Available at: http://magazines.russ.ru/nlo/2000/43/main8.html (accessed 18 April 2013).

Kukulin, Ilya. 2012. "Ressource Ressentiment: Internet-Subkultur und Politmarketing." *Osteuropa* 6–8: 191–208.

Lenta. N.d. "Blogosfera." *Lenta Slovar'*. Available at: http://x.lenta.ru/abc/0251.htm (accessed 18 April 2013).

—— 2013. "Naval'nyi zaiavil o namerenii stat' prezidentom Rossii." *Lenta*, 5 April. Available at: http://lenta.ru/news/2013/04/05/navalny/ (accessed 18 April 2013).

Mal'gin, Andrei. 2011. "Podslushanoe." *Zapiski mizantropa*, 18 September. Available at: http://avmalgin.livejournal.com/2631615.html (accessed 18 April 2013).

Manovich, Lev. 2001. *The Language of New Media*. Cambridge, MA: The MIT Press.

Martinsen, Deborah A., ed. 1997. *Literary Journals in Imperial Russia*. Cambridge: Cambridge University Press.

Mil'man, Zolik. 2009. "Saiano-Shushevskii urok." *Rossiiskaia gazeta*, 28 August. Available at: http://www.rg.ru/2009/08/20/shoigu.html (accessed 8 April 2013).

Naval'nyi, Aleksei. 2013. "Korruptsionnaia latinitsa i kak ee pobedit'." *Aleksei Naval'nyi: final'naia bitva mezhdu dobrom i neitralitetom*, 23 January. Available at: http://navalny.livejournal.com/768312.html (accessed 18 April 2013).

Philpotts, Matthew. 2009. "Polyphonic Traditions: Schiller, 'Sinn und Form' and the 'Thick' Literary Journal." In *Contested Legacies: Constructions of Cultural Heritage in the GDR*, edited by Matthew Philpotts and Sabine Rolle, 184–97. Rochester, NY: Camden House.

Rettberg, Jill Walker. 2008. *Blogging*. Cambridge: Polity Press.

Rokina, Anna. 2007. "Za negativ otvetish'!" *Bortovoi zhurnal*, 28 January. Available at: http://www.netmind.ru/blog/general/za-negativ-otvetish (accessed 18 April 2013).

Rukhakasia. 2009. "Osnovanii dlia paniki net: no telefonnaia sviaz' uzhe ne rabotaet." *Dnevnik provintsial'nogo zhurnalista*, 17 August. Available at: http://rukhakasia.livejournal.com/2009/08/17/ (accessed 18 April 2013).

Sherman. 2011. "Zhizn' onlain." *lokutrap*, 12 May. http://sherman.livejournal.com/195771.html (accessed 18 April 2013).

Simanowski, Roberto. 2008. *Digitale Medien in der Erlebnisgesellschaft: Kultur—Kunst—Utopien*. Reinbek bei Hamburg: Rowohlt.

Schulze, Gerhard. 1992 *Erlebnisgesellschaft: Kultursoziologie der Gegenwart*. Frankfurt: Campus Verlag.

Socro. 2009. "Foto s mesta avarii S-SH GES." *socro*, 17 August. Available at: http://socro.livejournal.com/2009/08/17/ (accessed 18 April 2013).

Tolstaia, Tatiana. 2011. "Prokhorov." *tanyant*, 17 September. Available at: http://tanyant.livejournal.com/85823.html (accessed 18 April 2013).

—— 2012a. "Kremlevskie stsenarii." *tanyant*, 12 May. Available at: http://tanyant.livejournal.com/94852.html (accessed 18 April 2013).

—— 2012b. "Knizhka vtoraia." *tanyant*, 22 March. Available at: http://tanyant.livejournal.com/94129.html (accessed 18 April 2013).

Timchenko, Galina. 2012. "Zhurnalistika eto tiazheloe remeslo i ser'eznaia professiia: o transformatsii otnoshenii chitatelei i SMI." YOungJOurnalists, 19 March. Available at: http://yojo.ru/?p=8621.

Tönnies, Ferdinand ([1887] 1957) *Community and Society: Gemeinschaft und Gesellschaft*, translated and edited by Charles P. Loomis, Ann Arbor, MI: The Michigan State University Press.

Trammell, Kay D. 2005. "Slogging, and Blogging, through Katrina." *Washington Post*, 3 September. Available at: http://www.washingtonpost.com/wp-dyn/content/article/2005/09/02/AR2005090202120.html (accessed 18 April 2013).

# 4 Social network sites on the Runet

## Exploring social communication

*Tine Roesen and Vera Zvereva*

In the second half of the 2000s, both the global web and the Runet witnessed a boom in social network sites (SNS).[1] In Russia, the growth of SNS coincided with a dramatic rise in the number of Internet users (their number increased by approximately 25 percent between 2008 and 2012, by which point they accounted for 57 percent of the whole population; Fomin 2012). The aim of this chapter is to discuss some noticeable shifts in the communicative culture on the Runet related to the spread of SNS.

In 2007, boyd and Ellison presented a definition and a history of SNS that have helped to delineate a distinct, interdisciplinary field within internet studies and studies of computer-mediated communication (CMC): SNS are regarded as a particular kind of online culture and a specific type of social media, as distinct from blogs, for example, or content-sharing sites, virtual game worlds, forums and wikis. According to their widely accepted w, SNS are

> web-based services that allow individuals to (1) construct a public or semi-public profile within a bounded system, (2) articulate a list of other users with whom they share a connection, and (3) view and traverse their list of connections and those made by others within the system.
>
> (boyd and Ellison 2007: 2)

To this list of distinguishing features, Tuor (2009: 14) has added: (4) the possibility of posting news and comments. Social network sites can be studied as cultural and social tools as well as new media technologies, and the main issues to have been analyzed so far have been identity management, friendship, networking, privacy and security. Accordingly, attempts have been made to categorize types of SNS further. Mike Thelwall has suggested distinguishing between three sub-categories, based on the different purposes for which SNS-friendship connections are made and on the extent to which the SNS functionality is core to the users: (1) General purpose, socializing SNS (e.g. Myspace, Facebook); (2) Networking SNS, designed for non-social interpersonal communication (e.g. LinkedIn); (3) (Social) Navigation SNS, aimed at finding information or resources via interpersonal connections (e.g. LiveJournal, deviantART) (Thelwall 2009: 24–5; Thelwall and Stuart 2010: 265–6). Some SNS are powerful enough to be used for all these purposes (Thelwall and Stuart 2010: 266). In similar vein, Zhang and Wang (2010) have suggested distinguishing between interest-oriented and relation-oriented SNS, presenting Douban.com as an example of the former, and Ziaonei.com as an example of the latter. The mention of SNS such as the Chinese Douban and Ziaonei, which are relatively unknown outside of their national web, is rare in the scholarly literature; the same goes for Russian SNS and Russian uses of global SNS.[2]

Focusing our attention on the question of social communication, and presuming SNS to be an important object of study capable of shedding light on a society's broader communicative developments, we begin this chapter with a survey of the specific features of those network sites that are popular among Runet users. It is a difficult task to ascertain the linguistic and communicative specifics of SNS as distinct from other forms of CMC.[3] As shown elsewhere in this book, in Russia significant shifts in the linguistic culture appeared before the rise of online social networks. However, with the advent of SNS and as most Runet users set up accounts, major changes in the digital *communicative* culture became clearly visible. By "communicative culture" we understand the forms of communication and practices of interaction fostered by the use of certain new media technologies in a networking environment. Our focus on the social aspects of SNS communication reveals that networking communicative practices reflect existing ideological tensions and social divisions among Runet users. At the same time, forms of communication on SNS do not merely duplicate offline forms of social interaction, and new patterns of social unification can be seen emerging in web practices.

## Social networking on the Runet

By 2012, 82 percent of Russian internet users had one or more SNS accounts ("Reiting" 2012).[4] Representing such a significant share of the population, these users necessarily come from different social backgrounds, and, as we will show below, this is an important factor that shapes the communicative culture.

Web statistics reveal that among the ten websites currently most visited in Russia, four are social network sites and another four (Mail.ru, Liveinternet and two Google sites)[5] have sub-site SNS functionalities. The remaining two sites in the top 10 are the search engine Yandex (linking to its own SNS, Moi krug) and Wikipedia.[6] Moreover, the globally used Facebook and LiveJournal (ranking 11) are presently the third and fourth most visited SNS in Russia, but even more popular are the indigenous Russian SNS VKontakte and Odnoklassniki.[7] In the following overview of social network sites on the Runet, we will concentrate on these four popular SNS, before proceeding to examples of their communicative culture. For contextualization, Table 4.1 shows the most popular Russian SNS, as well as SNS widely used in Russia and globally well-known SNS.

As Table 4.1 shows, 2006 was a big SNS year globally, but even bigger in Russia, given the launch of not one but two indigenous Russian network sites, as well as the new global arrivals. The influence of an online network is related not only to the originality or convenience of its services, but also to the particular ways it is used in a society, which has, in turn, been formed by historical and cultural contexts.[8] This

*Table 4.1* The most popular SNS in Russia and globally

| *Runet SNS* | *URL* | *Year launched* | *Rank in Russia 2012* | *Global rank 2012* |
|---|---|---|---|---|
| Google+ | google.com<br>google.ru | 2011 | — | — |
| Snob | snob.ru | 2008 | 827 | 15,105 |
| Tumblr | tumblr.com | 2007 | 135 | 34 |
| Moi mir | my.mail.ru | | — | — |
| Facebook* | facebook.com | 2006 | 8 | 2 |
| Twitter | twitter.com | | 15 | 9 |
| VKontakte | vk.com/vkontakte.ru | | 2 | 28 |
| Odnoklassniki | odnoklassniki.ru | | 7 | 63 |
| Mir tesen | mirtesen.ru | | 161 | 2755 |
| Ning | ning.com | 2005 | 78 | 398 |
| Moi Krug | moikrug.ru | | 256 | 4,139 |
| Flickr | flickr.com | 2004 | 224 | 60 |
| Tagged | tagged.com | | — | 285 |
| LinkedIn | linkedin.com | 2003 | 54 | 13 |
| Myspace | myspace.com | | 545 | 204 |
| Last FM | lastfm.com | | 2,292 | 934 |
| Hi5 | hi5.com | | 5,020 | 680 |
| Live Internet | liveinternet.ru | | — | — |
| Friendster | friendster.com | 2002 | 72,481 | 17,972 |
| Skyrock (2007; orig. Skyblog) | skyrock.com (skyblog.com) | | 5,344 | 848 |
| deviantART | deviantart.com | 2000 | 315 | 137 |
| LiveJournal | livejournal.com<br>livejournal.ru | 1999 | 11<br>723 | 122<br>11,058 |

Sources: Boyd and Ellison (2007), Alexa.com, web sites' own information, Prokhorov (2006), and, in a few instances, Ru.wikipedia.org. Ranking numbers are according to website traffic in Russia and the world, respectively, as given on Alexa.com 15 December 2012.

Note:
*We list only the version of Facebook that was open to everyone in 2006.

helps explain why online networks with similar functionalities serve different communicative functions. In Russian culture of the 2000s, global as well as Russian SNS have been adapted to particular social, political and cultural tasks and goals.

## LiveJournal

Launched in 1999, LiveJournal combined the online diary (one of the first blogging platforms) with an early version of online networking, including friends' lists and comment trees.[9] In the first half of the 2000s, LiveJournal began to function as a global SNS. It soon came to be dominated by Russian users (Gorny 2006: 73–90), and whereas the website's global traffic ranking is currently 122, its Russian ranking is 11.[10]

Since LiveJournal preceded all other SNS on the Runet, for a period it united almost *all* Russian SNS users, who then later dispersed among various online networks. Consequently, for a while, this was a platform for every possible kind of online communicative behavior, and quite a few linguistic innovations were tried or even invented here. In the early 2000s, this platform was regarded not least as a sphere of cultural innovation, of literary and linguistic experiments. Unlike future Facebook and VKontakte practices, a LiveJournal account could be linked to an invented virtual persona rather than to a real person. The members of the Russian LiveJournal community were often unknown to each other beyond their usernames and "avatar" identities. In the early days of LiveJournal, users would add to their friends list not only existing offline friends, but also users they regarded as interesting authors/bloggers. Thus, LiveJournal witnessed a rapid growth of new social links, which exceeded the limits of existing "real-life" contacts. Communication within the newly created LiveJournal communities was characterized by a considerable social and cultural flexibility, allowing borders of age, subculture, gender, etc. to be crossed. Only in the mid-2000s did the fashion for anonymity fade under the influence of other popular SNS.

In contrast to more recent SNS, the Runet LiveJournal-segment had a hierarchy of users, achieved by means of users' ratings and a constantly updated top ten (now top 25) of popular entries. The rating service is built into LiveJournal and statistics published on the LiveJournal front page, thus facilitating personal promotion as well as drawing public attention to specific topics. It could be argued that the ratings served as a proclaimed LiveJournal "agenda," a common list of discussion topics, providing all bloggers with a common ground for debates. Another crucial feature of LiveJournal was the opportunity to publish long texts and comments. LiveJournal offered a new outlet for the urge to write and read texts, an urge sometimes self-ironically referred to as graphomania. This feature fitted well into the Russian nineteenth-century tradition of "literaturecentrism," which prevailed throughout the twentieth century and was still strong among the intellectual elites in the 1990s and early 2000s. It also gave Runet users the possibility of engaging in serious public discussions. In the early 2000s, LiveJournal was the first, and for a long time the most important, web space to display features of a public sphere, i.e. a place where problems in Russian society could be freely discussed with a view to influencing political action (Gorny 2006: 76; MacLeod 2009). For Russian Internet users, the possibility of launching open discussions in blogs on this platform, which lay outside Russian jurisdiction,[11] became all the more important given the still weakly developed civic society and increasingly centralized control of the media, and LiveJournal soon gained a reputation as the best place for voices to be heard and answered. For many users, setting up a profile on LiveJournal was thus equivalent to joining Russia's virtual civic society. This culture has produced a number of figures who have developed from high-ranking bloggers into famous political activists (such as Aleksei Navalny) and new media journalists (such as Rustem Adagamov and Il'ia Varlamov).

In the mid-2000s, the creative elite were joined on LiveJournal by less experimental and less political users and their more banal blogging topics. Measured both by user activity and the frequency of significant discussions, LiveJournal remains popular in Russia, although other SNS with more functionalities have also established themselves solidly among Russians.[12] Apart from a sense of loyalty, habit, and the fact that LiveJournal is still the best SNS for sharing long texts and personal diaries, its popularity might also be explained by the fact that users can asymmetrically befriend other users,[13] including well-known journalists and writers, such as Linor Goralik, Boris Akunin, and other celebrities.

## Odnoklassniki

First appearing in March 2006, the indigenous Russian and Cyrillic SNS, Odnoklassniki ("Classmates"), like the American SNS on which it was modeled, was launched as a means of facilitating contact between schoolmates in Russian-speaking regions, allowing them to search for friends by school name (or rather: school number, as is the custom in the former Soviet Union), and serving socializing and relation-oriented purposes. Odnoklassniki is widely accessed across the whole of the former USSR, and it is currently the most popular SNS in Moldova and Uzbekistan, and second to Facebook in Kyrgyzstan, Georgia, Armenia and Azerbaijan. Odnoklassniki presented a different approach to networking than LiveJournal. It identified users not with their invented, virtual persona and online expressions, but with real people, including their biographies and personal histories. Odnoklassniki encouraged users to turn previous offline contacts into a virtual form, but it envisaged virtual communication as a temporary stage between real meetings. For the Runet, this approach was innovative, and Odnoklassniki was welcomed as a sort of time machine, which would connect a person to his or her past. During a short "romantic" period, thousands of Runet users rushed to join this network, in order to search for their old classmates and forgotten memories.

As a result, not only experienced users but people who for various reasons had never participated in LiveJournal blogging became involved in digital communication. Despite its wider reach, this communication has in many respects been much simpler than its LiveJournal-based counterpart. Users reduced their communicative and discursive varieties to the limited set of speech acts and online actions prescribed by the situation of talking to "strangers" they used to know long ago. For a while, Odnoklassniki expanded extensively, but soon, when everyone in the network had established all possible contacts, the initial interest faded, and its profile changed slightly. More sophisticated users left to communicate on other platforms. The conventional rather than creative forms of communication on Odnoklassniki have also weakened the status of this SNS in comparison with competing network sites. Moreover, its low social prestige has led many users to close their accounts.

## VKontakte

Launched in October 2006 as a clone of the American Facebook, the Russian and Cyrillic VKontakte ("In Contact") is now the Runet's most popular social network, with a daily audience that exceeds 38 million users (September 2012). It is currently widespread in the former Soviet republics, not least in Belarus, Ukraine and

Kazakhstan. Open and flexible, VKontakte provides its users with various tools; it is primarily employed as an instrument to create and maintain contacts with like-minded people, friends and colleagues in the post-Soviet cultural space, and also as a dating service and a sphere for political discussions. At the same time, commercial companies have set up a multitude of public pages, and users interact in diverse interest-oriented communities.

This network site takes a trait inherent in most SNS—interaction between various social groups—to the extreme. People of different social and cultural origins and backgrounds communicate with the help of the same tools (short texts and comments, uploaded media files, profile pages, "statuses," etc.), and observe or break similar rules of online behavior.

VKontakte functions as a free store of (pirated) films, videos and music and as a platform for online multi-user games. In the light of improved implementation of copyright restrictions in most other significant parts of the global internet, VKontakte is a uniquely free and very large online space. Many users do not download anything, but keep their favorite media products online and access them via their network profiles. The access to games attracts a younger audience and gives the network the image of being a great deal "less serious" than Facebook. Finally, easy access to pornography must also be assumed to account at least in part for its popularity.

The opinion has been voiced that the "Russianness" of this network site is a problem: "VKontakte is a horribly local service, and that is unacceptable for a social network in our global age. This locality carries with it not only the risks of censorship and burdensome regulation; it also limits personal and professional communications" (Merkurov 2012). However, this feature actually seems to be cherished by the bulk of the audience. VKontakte is widely regarded as "our own" SNS, specially designed to fulfil the needs of Runet users and to facilitate local, Russian-based communication. According to this view, Cyrillic letters protect VKontakte users from foreign gaze and invasion.

## Facebook

Opening up to all internet users in September 2006, Facebook seems to have become widespread among Russian users in the first half of 2009,[14] undoubtedly in part as a result of the introduction of Cyrillic services in 2008. Since its services were initially exclusively in English, it was only accessible to Russian users with at least some English-language skills, and this impacted on the social structure of the Russian Facebook segment. Sociologically speaking, the Russian Facebook was the opposite of Odnoklassniki, and seems in this respect to have differed demographically and communicatively from Facebook in the USA, and probably also elsewhere. Early Russian users of Facebook appreciated its international character, including the access it afforded to globally famous celebrities. As some of these users told us in personal communication, social interaction on Facebook allowed them to "come out of the Runet ghetto" and "feel themselves part of the global Internet."

Similarly to Odnoklassniki, Facebook enhances existing offline contacts, not least by suggesting that users import email contacts into their Facebook account. Facebook is therefore generally regarded as a platform not only for informal but also for professional communication. The implied social gaze of Facebook friends, who are also meaningful in one's offline life, sets certain communicative rules. Although in practice many users communicate there with their close friends, Facebook is regarded as a more demanding space, where users tend to avoid "wild" forms of online behavior (such as abusive language, obscene photos or pornography), reserving these for LiveJournal, VKontakte, Odnoklassniki and Twitter.

The Facebook tool of "likes"—in Russian slang *laik*—proved to be a significant success. Since nearly all online media sites have by now added a Facebook "like" button to their pages, this SNS has, in Russia as well, become a mediator between users and other digital media resources.

Runet users criticize Facebook for its restriction on long texts (texts exceeding a few lines being automatically truncated), which simplifies communication, and causes postings to be not so much read as browsed. They voice their critique directly in discussions of the constraints, but also indirectly by posting links to more complicated texts elsewhere on the internet. On the other hand, Facebook communication is valued for its closeness to real time: it links a person to a current moment as well as to topical news, and is widely used as an efficient service for organizing prompt action and discussing burning issues online. While the number of Russian users on Facebook is growing fast, it is still less popular in Russia than in Europe and its Runet audience is much smaller than VKontakte's ("Facebook" 2011; Malakhov 2011).

## Russian SNS and communicative culture

From a user's perspective, the popular services of LiveJournal, Odnoklassniki, VKontakte and Facebook vary according to their more specific functions; they are often seen as mutually reinforcing as well as stimulating different kinds of self-expression and communication, and users may simultaneously be active on several of them. Through the ways in which they are used, these essentially similar technological systems inevitably acquire different statuses, e.g. fashionable and unfashionable platforms, "teenage" and "adult" blogs. The way they are used assumes a symbolic significance, which brings about a division of communication tasks: certain genres and types of interaction dominate particular networks. For example, extended texts including detailed argumentation and discussion, debates on current politics, exercises in literature and various forms of art are mostly posted on LiveJournal. Searching for old and new friends, including dating, joking and small talk, takes place in Odnoklassniki and VKontakte. Online cultural consumption and the sharing of diverse media products are distinctive features of VKontakte. Professional communication and the exchange of links to news and topical media publications are characteristic of Facebook. All of these SNS, except for Odnoklassniki, with its focus on private issues, are to some extent used for political and public communication. For Russian society, the development of an SNS infrastructure means that, in addition to official and unofficial offline networks, people have voluntarily committed themselves to many additional social links, which partly overlap with and partly supplement existing ones. Not all relationships in these new digital communities are thought to be meaningful, but they all imply important collective practices, such as discovering and recognizing "others."

If plurality and exposure are essential to internet communication in general, they are particularly so for the interactions and "masspersonal" communications on SNS.[15] By creating accounts and exposing their writing in online diaries, on "walls" and in group interactions, millions of Runet users display themselves to each other. Regarded as a common space for visibility and public self-representation, the digital communities may be likened to a social theater, currently being played out in and perhaps playing its role in a fragmented Russian society (Gudkov 2004; Dubin 2011).

## Establishing (social) differences

As mentioned above, new SNS friends are often recruited from existing groups of online and offline acquaintances. In many cases, however, people continue to make new contacts not only according to interests, but also according to SNS attractiveness (i.e. real and/or virtual standing, online reputation and popularity). In doing so, users tend to identify with particular languages and discourses, which carry a load of cultural and social markers that are decisive in virtual communication (Jacobson 1999). In SNS-based communication, dissimilarities between the languages used by various groups become more noticeable and important, because these groups represent themselves on the same media platforms. Therefore, apart from grouping according to views, ideologies and discourses, a social stratification also takes place on different levels in Runet networks. Important factors in this process are taste (as a tool of social control; Bourdieu 1984) and linguistic competence. For example, members of the group "Culinary nightmare" on VKontakte mock the participants of another popular community, "Magic cooking," not because of their recipes but because of their pretentious self-representations:

> I am deeply touched and delighted by some pious ladies. Good photo of tuna salad. But the text that follows is just an anecdote. "It's Lent at the moment, can I eat this salad? Tuna's seen as a fish, right?" I wanted to answer that "Nah, we don't think so. Let's call it sausage."

The discussion of this episode on "Culinary nightmare" then switches to criticizing other women for adding markers of their Orthodoxy to texts about meals.[16]

As mentioned earlier, a stratification of the various popular SNS has already taken place. Odnoklassniki is generally considered a network for the lower social segments, a common offensive name for it being *Bydloklassniki* ("Redneck-mates"): "How do you hack a webpage on Odnoklassniki?—Do you really need to It's called Bydloklassniki because 95 percent of the users there are redneck glamorpusses and he-cats. Let them hang out."[17] Not infrequently, VKontakte is associated with the same social characteristics: "Your goof-contacts and redneck-mates (*lokhtakty i bydloklassniki*) branched out and got noticed three years ago at the most."[18] Commercials addressed at users of these networks sensitively capture their interests and tone. For example, one advertising slogan read: "The most beautiful girls are on Odnoklassniki. Prove it right now."[19] Similar advertising is hardly imaginable in the Runet segments of LiveJournal or Facebook, where it would run the risk of being accused of primitiveness.

The critical attitude of socially more privileged SNS users towards Odnoklassniki and VKontakte has even led to the emergence of special communities for the purpose of posting and ridiculing "tasteless" photos from public accounts on the lower-status SNS.[20] In popular LiveJournal groups such as "In Carpet we trust," "Freak School" and "Pussy-mates," users mock the desire to shape one's own image by posing in the manner of glossy magazine models, in squalid apartments and with a wall carpet (a symbol of cheap Soviet chic) in the background, e.g.

> Here we collect photos of "terribly glamorous young men and women" from the vast expanse of social network sites [. . .] In order to guarantee the attention of the "Pussymates" [members], you should have gel-swollen lips and use bronzer in very large quantities. Blonde-colored hair, "duckface" and pink accessories are also very welcome.[21]

The ability to write correctly is also considered a sign of higher social status, the demarcation line, according to SNS users of higher standing, dividing those who distort the Russian language intentionally or by negligence (which is fine) from those who simply do not know how to write correctly (which invites contempt), e.g. a girl from VKontakte who sends illiterate and aggressive demands for her photos to be deleted from "Pussymates" provokes even more bitter irony on LiveJournal:

> A girl from the social network. Ksenia says: Application already submitted to the court! If 35 photos are not removed from your livejournal site in the next week, you personally will have major problems with the law! You still have time to come to your senses! (ЗАЯВЛЕНИЕ В СУД УЖЕ ПОДАНО! если на протяжении недели 35 фото небудет удалено у твоего сайта livejournal и лично у тибя будут огромные трудности с законом! у тибя есть время взятся за мозги!)
>
> [comment]: judging by the many mistakes, this girl is, as they say, "not disfigured by intelligence." I feel like saying: author, write more (аффтар пишы истчо).[22]

## Facing others

On the internet in general and in SNS in particular, any user's self-identification (subcultural, political, religious, gender, ethnic, professional, etc.) is, in principle, exposed for anyone to see. Anyone can produce a text and can see the texts of "others" (except in those cases where communities, sites or profiles choose to be invisible[23]). This sort of exposure leads to certain shifts in the communicative culture, which go beyond the characteristics of digital communication in general.

In the 2000s, researchers studying Russian society talked about its growing atomization and the crisis of social trust, a consequence of state cultural policy (Gudkov 2004; Dubin 2011). As the most influential medium, the main Russian TV channels, which were forced to focus on the "unification" of all Russian citizens around the "power vertical," artificially reduced the cultural diversity of Russian society (Hutchings and Rulyova 2009). As a result of internet communication, however, this picture has started to change. By the end of the 2000s, SNS were providing a developed infrastructure which allowed Russians to represent this plurality and diversity of values, attitudes, lifestyles and subcultures. When "everybody" began to discover "everybody else" and to speak to each other on these Runet networks, Russian society embarked on a process of learning about itself. Centers and regions, major cities and smaller towns, as well as state officials and representatives, marginalized groups, minorities, subcultures, professional associations and representatives of various ideologies have now become involved in SNS communication. As popular as it has been, the discovery of the actual diversity of Russian society has not, however, been an easy challenge, as it requires that people acknowledge their cultural differences. For example, currently the most popular community on LiveJournal is "One day of my life";[24] it is followed by nearly 40,000 users and is registered on Facebook.[25] Its members publish photo reports about their lives. People of different occupations and ages share their routines, successes and problems, allowing other members to comment on and discuss their "days." Detailed accounts allow users to abandon stereotypical images such as "businessmen," "students," and "housewives," and learn about the experiences of "a father wishing to adopt a child," "an amateur actor," "a Russian biologist in Japan," "the mother of a boy with Down's syndrome," "a night watchman," etc.

SNS communication has made it clear that the real "others" live side by side with "us," and that it is necessary to interact with them as fellow members of society. "They" use the same SNS functionalities to express their thoughts online. But if these groups cultivate and spread opposing views and unacceptable ideologies, how should we then interact with them on the internet? Establishing such relations have turned out to be a difficult test for Runet users. In this process, it is clearly important for users to reach a definition of "us" and "them" by ideology and attitudes. It is obviously difficult to build relationships of solidarity with users of different opinions or orientations. This is why many SNS interlocutors prefer talking inside groups of associates, and when they cannot ignore the "others," they initiate quarrels and trolling.

The impossibility of ignoring opponents, or the unwillingness to do so, often leads to the cultivation of hate speech, and this practice also has its own cultural implications. An extremely high level of hostility and hatred, unwarranted aggression, mockery and cynicism in virtual communications in VKontakte and LiveJournal indicates the persistency of a collective Soviet trauma.[26] Of course, foul language and hostility are also found elsewhere on the global internet, but on the Runet these practices seem to be a "trademark," connected to the post-Soviet identity complex, including weak social bonds and public and political powerlessness (Gudkov 2004; Dubin 2011). It reveals itself in the constant challenging of someone else's authority, competence and value, and in the popularity of formulas that invert power relations and lower the status of the interlocutor. All subtypes of aggressive talk and all variants of obscene lexicon are present there. For example, in the VKontakte group, "White ribbon movement," whose members declare that "elections must be fair, mass media independent, and everyone equal before the law!," non-members regularly enter this territory to condemn the followers: "Revolution . . . what bullshit, America has run out of bucks, there's fucking nothing to do here, and you bastards are too thin on the ground to instigate a riot."[27] Judging by the listed interests of the group coordinator (#Hospital no. 31, Let's keep the protest going in the regions, The Right movement of St. Petersburg, The Lunacharskii Theater in Sevastopol, The press-club Green Lamp, The AdVita charity foundation For Life) and of the opponent cited (World of Tanks the official group, Being funny 18, Modern tanks, Hunting & fishing, Street Fights only, The motorists' club Your Car, Kirishii furniture), they would hardly meet on common VKontakte ground. The opponent pays deliberate and repeated visit purely to stigmatize the group's members.

## The active role of the user

The increased user activity in new media is of great consequence for cultural communications. The role of a user differs from the role of a consumer of media products. It presupposes constant interaction, involvement in the production, consumption and exchange of messages, and the use of research strategies, creativity and play in working with information.

In the Russian culture of the early 2000s, civic and political passivity was a kind of extension of the passive role of an audience of centralized and controlled media. By the late 2000s, however, this situation had changed, and these changes are largely associated with the spread of online networking communities, the growing significance of social media and the transfer of online activity onto the streets. SNS communities facilitated a shift from litany and lamentation (widespread post-Soviet rhetorical strategies) towards a discussion of practical solutions to problems and further to concrete action (Zvereva 2012). Now, quite a few groups on LiveJournal, VKontakte and Facebook are focused on finding solutions to diverse problems, from private psychological challenges to public social and political ones.[28]

Members of these groups support each other in various difficult situations, practice therapeutic conversations, or exchange advice on "what to do if . . ." Many of their virtual communities try to perform small but practical acts and to bring together users for specific projects, such as protecting rights (of drivers on the roads, people who suffer at the hands of officialdom, etc.), organizing social assistance (raising money for the sick and homeless, care for the elderly), and coordinating joint civic actions (support for environmental initiatives). To be an "active citizen" and to communicate in this manner is becoming a popular mode of online behavior among Runet users. Activist SNS groups produce and present a networking/networked identity which is associated with "positive" thinking and acting, not focused on the past, but based on "connective" (Hoskins 2011) experiences in the present.

The shift towards civic networking has resulted in an increasing number of volunteer movements. This new social trend became visible in July–August 2010, when thousands of SNS users united to fight the fires in European Russia and to help the victims of these fires. The trend peaked in July 2012, when without waiting for any decision or prompting from central or local government, volunteers joined forces to help victims of a disastrous flash flood in Krymsk in Krasnodarskii Krai. Another side of this activity reveals itself in Runet users' increased interest in the "networking city" problem and in the collective designing of urbanscapes by citizens.[29] Against the backdrop of these digital communities, which seek to solve offline problems, the Russian political movements of 2012–13 may be regarded as a practice anticipated for years by effective social networking communication.

## Conclusion

In the late 2000s, a distinctive shift occurred in Runet communicative culture: whereas the first years of the new millennium were dominated by LiveJournal blogging and proto-networking among a relatively small group of internet pioneers—a LiveJournal elite, forming a distinct post-Soviet public sphere with its own playful and sophisticated language culture and text-centered communicative style—the second half of the decade saw explosive growth in the number of internet users, as well as in SNS platforms. These platforms brought about new kinds of communicative behavior.

Interactions in what we have described as the social theater of SNS are to some extent a continuation of existing, offline social structures, but we also see an intensification of social contacts and communication, and, in addition to existing networks, new kinds of networks are being formed. These may be interest- or information-oriented, focusing on discussions and expertise, or they may be relation-oriented, with users navigating according to similar backgrounds, curiosity or desired digital status. The most visible patterns in these interactions seem to confirm social differences. Users tend to group according to social backgrounds, culture and innate taste. Everybody is visible to and befriendable by everybody, but self-identifications and preferences, as well as the need for recognition and distinction, lead to the formation of alliances and the declaration of oppositions. This social stratification of different SNS and of groups within them may also lead to mutual attacks, including accusations of low culture and bad taste, such as when LiveJournal users unite to attack groups on VKontakte and Odnoklassniki. Despite the fundamentally "democratic" network structure of each SNS, we have also seen hierarchies being introduced, such as the "top bloggers" list on LiveJournal. With the rise in both SNS platforms and the number of users, such hierarchies are likely to multiply, but they will only be known to smaller segments of users, and their authority will be limited to specific sub-themes, such as children's education, ecology, the Romanovs, or which smart phone is the best. In this sense, social communication on SNS has come to resemble the complex structure of Russian society as such.

Nonetheless, alongside this stratification and compartmentalization, we have also identified patterns of consolidation across social classes and across different SNS, when new communicative habits not only are used as socio-cultural markers keeping others out, but also serve to unite users across platforms. Thus, we venture to conclude that the wide range of SNS available to Russian internet users offers potent tools for civic discussion and action. Where the tendency to unite rather than differ combines with the active role of new media users, civic action may move from online discussions onto the streets.

## Notes

1 Social network sites are also called social networking sites, social network services or online social networks.

2 By scholarly literature we are referring here to Anglo-American, Russian, German, French and Scandinavian literature. In the wake of the ground-breaking study by Schmidt, Teubener and Konradova (2006), the online journal *Digital Icons* has, since 2008, formed the exception concerning the study of Russian SNS, especially with its second issue (Strukov et al. 2009). See also Etling et al. (2010), Alexanyan (2009) and Panchenko (2011).

3 Tuor (2009: 133) insists that communication in SNS is not of a particular kind: "Eine Kommunikationsform *soziale Netzwerke* gibt es nicht. Vielmehr bieten diese mehrere Möglichkeiten des Austauschs, welche alle der Kommunikationsform E-Mail (im weiten Sinn) zuzuordnen sind." Thelwall (2009: 59) sums up the linguistic features of CMC in general (acronyms, abbreviations, repeated letters, swearwords, slang, pictograms, multiple languages, etc.), underlining the rise in spelling and other language variations as an important characteristic in its own right, and concludes that all the various styles of electronic communication are probably to be found to some extent in a typical SNS.

4 The article refers to statistics from VTsIOM, a Russian polling organization. For 2009 statistics, see Alexanyan (2009: 6–11). Setting up your own SNS is a widespread business venture in present-day Russia, and not all of these sites prosper or reach the rating lists. Examples of unsuccessful SNS are Atlaskit.com (atlaskit.com), Webby (webby.ru) and 7 ruk (7ruk.ru), which were all launched in 2005–6 but do not play any role today. See Prokhorov (2006).

5 Google (here represented by both google.ru and google.com), Mail.ru (mail.ru) and Liveinternet (liveinternet.ru). Liveinternet combined the earlier rux.ru and li.ru. Its core has exactly the same structure as LiveJournal, and it hosts 2,788,062 individual blogs, with the additional functionalities of adding friends and setting up communities.

6 Yandex (yandex.ru), Wikipedia (wikipedia.org). Moi krug ("My crowd", moikrug.ru) was launched in 2005 as the first genuine Runet SNS. In 2007, it was bought by Yandex and turned into a Yandex service, though it retained its own URL. Moi krug functions as an SNS for professionals, much like LinkedIn. See Prokhorov (2006).

7 VKontakte (vkontakte.ru), Odnoklassniki (odnoklassniki.ru). The precise traffic rank of sub-site SNS on Google, Mail.ru and Liveinternet, etc. cannot be measured by the available statistics, and therefore Table 4.1 does not supply rankings for sub-site SNS.

According to "Reiting" 2012, Moi mir (my.mail.ru) was used by 31 percent of internet users in 2012, making it the third most popular SNS, behind VKontakte and Odnoklassniki.

8 Cf. Schmidt, Teubener and Konradova (2006: 8): "The global communication technologies function on a worldwide scale but encounter very specific, local contexts, leading, in consequence, to a growing diversity of media usages."

9 The word for online friend/contact, *frend* (*frendy* in the Russianized plural), with the by now common derived forms *frendit'* (to become online friends with), *otfrendit'* (to unfriend), were born on the Russian LiveJournal (Gorny 2006: 76). Friendship on LiveJournal is not limited to the mutually acknowledged kind but can be asymmetric: essentially, to befriend on LiveJournal is the same as following.

10 That Russians have truly embraced LiveJournal is also evident from the fact that it has a Russian nickname, *zhivoi zhurnal*, fondly abbreviated as *zhzh* (in Cyrillic жж, pronounced "zhezhe").

11 On the protests by Russian LiveJournal users in 2006 when the Russian segment of LiveJournal (including service and management rights) was being bought by the Russian media holding SUP, see Schmidt, Teubener and Zurawski (2007).

12 See also Alexanyan (2009: 11):

> With the notable exception of LiveJournal . . ., "pure" social networking sites are more popular than blogging sites. Based on this data, I suggest that the locus of online social activity in Russia may be shifting from blogs and blog/social network hybrids to pure social networking sites, a stylistic shift from keeping an "online diary" for an interactive network of "readers" to simply (re)connecting with friends.

13 See note 9.

14 Golynko-Volfson (2009: 102).

15 "Masspersonal" meaning neither interpersonal nor impersonal, but personal messages to a(n indefinite) number of people, cf. Walther et al. (2009: 34).

16 http://vk.com/topic-19189245_26070260?post=3842 (accessed 2 February 2013); http://vk.com/topic-19189245_26070260?post=3844 (accessed 2 February 2013).

17 http://otvet.mail.ru/question/65471095 (accessed 2 February 2013).

18 http://lubopitniy-1978.livejournal.com/5497.html (accessed 2 February 2013).

19 Unfortunately, we cannot provide a reference here, since I-net banners do not have permanent links and addresses.

20 http://carpet_rise.livejournal.com/?style=mine (accessed 2 February 2013); http://shkola_urodov.livejournal.com/?style=mine (accessed 2 February 2013).

21 http://kisoklassniki.livejournal.com/ (accessed 25 February 2013).

22 http://nafanko.livejournal.com/896018.html?thread=28915218#t28915218 (accessed 25 February 2013).

23 The Russian SNS Snob (snob.ru, 2008) being a case in point, see Roesen (2011). Snob and similar elite SNS, such as A Small World (asmallworld.net, 2004) or Elixio (elixio.net, 2007), may thus be regarded as internet versions of Manuel Castells' residential and leisure-oriented "gated communities" (Castells 2000: 446–7).

24 http://odin-moy-den.livejournal.com (accessed 2 February 2013).

25 http://www.facebook.com/Onemyday (accessed 25 February 2013).

26 On Facebook, Runet users tend to avoid extreme forms of self-expression. In Odnoklassniki, users do quarrel and attack each other, but the format of this network does not stimulate verbal battles.

27 http://vk.com/wall-31708188_21161?reply=21192 (accessed 25 February 2013).

28 See, for example, http://girls-only-off.livejournal.com/ (accessed 2 February 2013), http://www.facebook.com/moscow.comes.back (accessed 2 February 2013), http://ru-vederko.livejournal.com/ (accessed 2 February 2013), http://musora.bolshe.net/ (accessed 2 February 2013).

29 See topics and discussions in popular blogs: http://zyalt.livejournal.com/ (accessed 2 February 2013), http://maxkatz.livejournal.com/profile (accessed 2 February 2013).

## References

Alexanyan, Karina. 2009. "Social Networking on Runet: The View from a Moving Train." *Digital Icons* 2: 1–12.

Bourdieu, Pierre. 1984. *Distinction: A Social Critique of the Judgement of Taste.* Cambridge, MA: Harvard University Press.

boyd, danah m. and Nicole B. Ellison. 2007. "Social Network Sites: Definition, History, and Scholarship." *Journal of Computer-Mediated Communication* 13(1): 210–30.

Castells, Manuel. 2000. *The Rise of the Network Society* (2nd edn.). Oxford: Blackwell Publishers.

Dubin, Boris. 2011. *Rossiia nulevykh: politicheskaia kul'tura—istoricheskaia pamiat'—povsednevnaia zhizn'.* Moscow: Rossiiskaia politicheskaia entsiklopediia.

Etling, Bruce B., et al., 2010, "Public Discourse in the Russian Blogosphere: Mapping RuNet Politics and Mobilization." Available at: http://cyber.law.harvard.edu/publications/2010/Public_Discourse_Russian_Blogosphere (accessed 22 February 2013).

"Facebook" 2011. "Facebook ne populiaren v Rossii," online at HR-Expert.net: vse ob upravlenii personalom. Available at: http://hr-expert.net/2011/03/05/facebook-ne-populyaren-v-rossii/ (accessed 15 September 2012).

Fomin, Sergei. 2012. "Kolichestvo pol'zovatelei Interneta v Rossii." *Internet v mire i v Rossii*, 25 November. Available at: http://www.bizhit.ru/index/users_count/0-151 (accessed 22 February 2013).

Golynko-Volfson, Dmitrii. 2009. "Sotsial'nye seti v nesetovom sotsiume," *Digital Icons* 2: 101–13.

Gorny, Eugene. 2006. "Russian LiveJournal: The Impact of Cultural Identity on the Development of a Virtual community." In *Control + Shift: Public and Private Uses of the Russian Internet.* Edited by Henrike Schmidt, Katy Teubener, and Natalja Konradova, 73–90 Norderstedt: Books on Demand GmbH. Available at: http://www.katy-teubener.de/joomla/images/stories/texts/publikationen/control_shift_01.pdf (accessed 23 January 2013).

Gudkov, Lev. 2004. *Negativnaia identichnost': stat'i 1997–2002.* Moscow: Novoe Literaturnoe Obozrenie.

Hoskins, Andrew. 2011. "Media, Memory, Metaphor: Remembering and the Connective Turn." *Parallax* 17(4): 19–31.

Hutchings, Stephen, and Natalia Rulyova. 2009. *Television and Culture in Putin's Russia: Remote Control.* London: Routledge.

Jacobson, Dave. 1999. "Impression Formation in Cyberspace: Online Expectations and Offline Experiences in Text-Based Virtual Communities." *Journal of Computer-Mediated Communication* 5(1). Available at: http://jcmc.indiana.edu/vol5/issue1/jacobson.html (accessed 22 February 2013).

MacLeod, Heather. 2009. "Examining Political Group Membership on LiveJournal." *Digital Icons* 2: 13–26.

Malakhov, Aleksandr. 2011."Ъ-Gazeta—Facebook ne gruzitsia." 25 February. Available at: http://www.kommersant.ru/doc/1591130 (accessed 15 September 2012).

Merkurov, Anton. 2012. "Pochemu 'Vkontakte' luchshe, chem Facebook—Slon.ru." 9 November. Available at: http://slon.ru/future/pochemu_vkontakte_luchshe_chem_facebook-850183.xhtml (accessed 1 February 2013).

Panchenko, Egor. 2011. "Integratsiia Internet-SMI i sotsial'nykh setei v Runete: novaia publichnaia sfera ili prostranstvo kontrolia?" *Digital Icons* 5: 87–118.

Prokhorov, Aleksandr. 2006. "Sotsial'nye seti i internet." *Komp'iuter Press* 10 (special issue: Sekrety Internet. Available at: http://compress.ru/article.aspx?id=16723&iid=776 (accessed 18 January 2013).

"Reiting." 2012. "Reiting populiarnosti sotsial'nykh setei v Rossii," *DV-Reclama.ru*, 14 February. Available at: http://www.dv-reclama.ru/russia/analytics/internet/detail.php?ELEMENT_ID=24570 (accessed 11 December 2012).

Roesen, Tine. 2011. "www.snob.ru: A Social Network Site for the Elite." *Digital Icons* 6: 81–92.

Schmidt, Henrike, Katy Teubener, and Natalja Konradova, eds. 2006. *Control + Shift: Public and Private Uses of the Russian Internet*. Norderstedt: Books on Demand GmbH. Available at: http://www.katy-teubener.de/joomla/images/stories/texts/publikationen/control_shift_01.pdf (accessed 23 January 2013).

—— 2007. "Update Diaspora—September 2007." In *Control + Shift: Public and Private Uses of the Russian Internet*, edited by Henrike Schmidt, Katy Teubener, and Natalja Konradova, 1–5 [inserted between pages 146 and 147]. Norderstedt: Books on Demand GmbH. Available at: http://www.katy-teubener.de/joomla/images/stories/texts/publikationen/control_shift_01.pdf (accessed 23 January 2013).

Strukov, Vlad, et al., eds. 2009. *From Comrades to Classmates: Social Networks on the Russian Internet* (= *Digital Icons* 2). Available at: http://www.digitalicons.org/issue02 (accessed 1 November 2012).

Thelwall, Mike. 2009. "Social Network Sites: Users and Uses." In *Advances in Computers* 76 [Social Networking and The Web], edited by Marvin Zelkowitz, 20–73. Boston: Academic Press.

Thelwall, Mike and David Stuart. 2010. "Social Network Sites: An Exploration of Features and Diversity." In *Social Computing and Virtual Communities*, edited by Panayiotis Zaphiris and Chee Siang Ang, 263–82. Boca Raton, FL: CRC Press.

Tuor, Nadine. 2009. *Online-Netzwerke: Eine kommunikationstheoretische, sozial-psychologische und soziolinguistische Analyse* (Networx 55). Available at: http://www.mediensprache.net/networx/networx-55 (accessed 29 January 2013)

Walther, Joseph B., et al. 2009. "Interaction of Interpersonal, Peer, and Media Influence Sources Online: A Research Agenda for Technology Convergence." In *A Networked Self: Identity, Community, and Culture on Social Network Sites*, edited by Zizi Papacharissi, 17–38. London: Routledge.

Zhang, Weiyu, and Rong Wang. 2010. "Interest-Oriented versus Relationship-Oriented Social Network Sites in China." *First Monday* 15(8). Available at: http://firstmonday.org/htbin/cgiwrap/bin/ojs/index.php/fm/article/viewArticle/2836/2582 (accessed 29 January 2013).

Zvereva, Vera. 2012. *Setevye razgovory: kul'turnye kommunikatsii v Runete* (Slavica Bergensia 10). Bergen: Department of Foreign Languages, University of Bergen.

# 5 Testing and contesting Russian Twitter

*Martin Paulsen and Vera Zvereva*

## Introduction

In December 2011, Russians took to the streets to protest against their government. The demonstrations in a number of Russian cities, which marked the beginning of "the movement for just elections," were provoked by massive fraud during the 2011 parliamentary elections. For the 2000s, this gathering was unprecedented. To many it resembled the protests which had preceded the fall of the Soviet Union in 1991.

The protests continued into 2012 and united leftists, liberals and nationalists in a hitherto unseen fashion. Tens of thousands joined protests that were consistently non-violent and original: Russians made their voices heard through creative posters ridiculing Vladimir Putin and the Kremlin. As might be expected, the protests met with highly unfavorable coverage on Russia's main television channels, but times had changed since the early 1990s and the predominantly middle-class protesters made use of social media to get their message through.

Over the course of the 2000s, new digital media have gained a prominent place in Russian society. The massive spread of smartphones has intensified interpersonal connections between their users. Mobile devices have radically reshaped the landscape of media communication, as they enable immediate access to blogs, micro-blogs and social networks from virtually any location.

As a consequence of their technological characteristics, such media influence language and the way people communicate on a day-to-day level. Just as importantly, since the social and political worlds are shaped on a discursive level, linguistic and discursive changes mediated through such technological gadgets have a direct effect on social forms and political practices. During the 2000s, these changes were of particular importance to civic and political communication globally. In political movements in the Arab world and Eastern Europe, new mobile personal media have contributed to the challenging of established political systems, with Twitter as one of the key instruments.

In this chapter, we investigate the role of Twitter and specifically the use of hashtags in communicative practices related to the Russian protest movement. Our chapter adds to existing research by introducing a qualitative approach, focusing on Twitter's role in relation to a specific street event, the "Test Walk," which took place in Moscow on 13 May 2012, just under a week after Putin's inauguration as president.

## Twitter as a tool of communication

Twitter is a micro-blogging-cum-social-networking service that allows users (Tweeters) to publish messages—tweets—of up to 140 characters. These tweets can be read either from Twitter's website, through specially designed programs on computers or on other digital devices such as mobile phones and tablet computers. Indeed, the rapid spread of Twitter can be partly explained by the simultaneous spread of smartphones ideally suited to using the medium (Hutchins 2011).

Another reason for Twitter's global popularity is its role as a social service where you can *follow*, or subscribe to, the updates of others and react to these by *replying* to them or forwarding—*retweeting*—them. While a tweet can be seen as the opening of a conversation, replies and retweets can be seen as ways of entering into this conversation. In general, a reply is the most direct way of engaging in a conversation on Twitter, while a retweet signals a desire to include more people in the conversation. A tweet usually consists of a short statement conveying what the Tweeter is doing or a reaction to something experienced, quite often including a link to material on webpages or to photos (boyd, Golder and Lotan 2010).

Twitter stands out as a markedly public medium: even though the messages can be protected as private, most Tweeters allow them to be openly accessible to everyone, including people who do not have Twitter accounts themselves. Each tweet is assigned a unique URL, a permanent address in the internet infrastructure. This means that it is easy to integrate Twitter into other web services, e.g. a constantly updated Twitter feed relating to a particular topic on a news site. The social aspect of following others, combined with open access to the published material, places Twitter in a position in between blogs and social network services such as Facebook and VKontakte.

Another important feature of Twitter today is the *hashtag*. While a basic way of using Twitter is to read updates from the people you follow, hashtags allow users to follow tweets relating to a specific topic, regardless of whom you follow. In this way you can tune in to discussions on a specific political event or, say, your favorite TV show. A hashtag serves as a headline or keyword for the content of the tweet. Hashtags have been of great interest to Twitter researchers. Some researchers focus on how they are used in political debates to create "ad-hoc publics" (Bruns and Burgess 2011a), both in relation to prolonged debates and unfolding news stories (Bruns and Burgess 2011b). Zappavigna (2011, 2012) describes how, through hashtags, Twitter produces "searchable talk," i.e. a discourse where the use of key words and the service's inbuilt search function creates affiliation among people.

The political significance of Twitter communication has attracted a great deal of attention following social unrest in different parts of the world. Summing up recent research into social media and dissent, Christian Christensen (2011) discusses the relationship between *techno-utopianism* and *techno-dystopianism* that has dominated the public debate on these political events, particularly in the USA. Adherents of the first point of view see social media as an important contributor in the erosion of oppressive state power, while those who subscribe to the latter school of thought warn of the dangers of exaggerating the role of social media in these events. At the heart of the matter, says Christensen, is the relationship between the "affordances of social media technologies, and the materialities of the offline world" (ibid.: 156). A study of the use of Twitter during social protests in Tunisia and Egypt found that Twitter is being used by bloggers and activists to participate in the construction of news alongside journalists (Lotan et al. 2011).

In a research project on the internet's impact on Russian politics, media and society, a group from the Berkman Center at Harvard University identified

> the emergence of a vibrant and diverse networked public sphere that constitutes an independent alternative to the more tightly controlled offline media and political space, as well as the growing use of digital platforms in social mobilization and civic action.
>
> (Alexanyan et al. 2012: 2)

In another publication, the same group of researchers found that, by enabling rapid information-sharing, Twitter is becoming increasingly important for political communication in Russia (Kelly et al. 2012; see also: Grin 2012).

## Twitter in Russian politics

Following its launch in 2006 and ascent in 2007, Twitter has become highly popular worldwide, including in Russia (Glaser 2007). It is difficult to determine the exact number of Tweeters in Russia, but statistics indicate that the numbers run into the millions. As of January 2013, the Russian search engine Yandex identifies 6.6m Russian Twitter accounts publishing some 7m tweets daily. The year before, the international analytics firm Semiocast released a report indicating that, in July 2012, there were around 8m accounts in Russia. Interestingly, a third of these had been created since the beginning of the year. According to Alexa.com, the internationally recognized website statistics service, in January 2013 Twitter was the 14th most popular website in Russia.

In Russia's new media landscape, Twitter has become important for journalists, leading bloggers, celebrities, businesses and advertising agencies because of the way in which it provides them with additional channels of communication with followers, fans and consumers. It has also proved to be a significant tool for politicians. In 2010, there was clear evidence of the increasing use of Twitter by volunteer groups, by civil and political activists and by the country's ruling party, United Russia. That year, Dmitry Medvedev, the incumbent president, started tweeting on political and personal issues, followed soon after by a number of high-ranking officials (see Chapter 13 by Gorham, in this volume).

By the end of 2011, Twitter was being used to plan, organize and publicize protests, marches and rallies, and acquired mobilizing and coordinating functions.

It facilitated the instant exchange of messages between large numbers of protesters, while its special features, such as hashtags and retweets, proved to be useful in organizing the flow of relevant information.

In order to explore some general aspects of Twitter's linguistic and social functioning, we opt for a detailed analysis of communication on Twitter, and take as our point of departure Michael Warner's (2002) understanding of a "public" as a self-organized body of strangers actively taking part in a social discourse. He stresses that the creation of a public is the direct effect of media communication. A public is text-based, and is created when its participants pay attention to a certain discourse that is presented in a mediated flow of information. The features of this community are defined discursively by means of a recognizable language. Proceeding from its keywords, circulating meanings and stylistic markers, potential members of the community are eager either to identify themselves with this language or to oppose it. In this sense, a public is a temporary, voluntarily self-organizing entity. We will argue that the new sociocultural and political forms of protest movements that have become possible thanks to the mobile digital media are constituted in the language and discourse of Twitter.

We will investigate the extent to which Twitter served as a communication platform/channel, and how the protests were construed and maintained discursively. Moreover, how is political communication shaped by using Twitter, and how do hashtags function in organizing Tweeters' communication? And, finally, how are new civic and political phenomena generated through language and communication on digital gadgets and platforms?

## #Kontrolnaiaprogulka: creating an arena for public discourse on Twitter

On 7 May, the Russian authorities sent large numbers of police and soldiers to Moscow, to clear the city center of people and prepare the way for Putin's inauguration as president. These measures, together with widespread police violence the previous day, had provoked Muscovites into a series of actions designed to reassert people's right to assembly on the city's streets.

The next day, on his LiveJournal blog, the writer Boris Akunin published an invitation to join a march, organized by himself and other writers, designed to clarify—or *test*—the limits of their rights as inhabitants of the Russian capital. The walk was to be named the Test Walk (*Kontrol'naia progulka* in Russian). The invitation was first discussed in the blogosphere and then cited on Twitter. The Cyrillic hashtag #kontrolnaiaprogulka was first used on 9 May, and, on 13 May, the day of the protest, it was one of the trending hashtags not only on the Runet, but also globally. Despite general concerns about possible provocations and police intervention, the Test Walk, from Pushkin Square to Chistye Prudy and the protest camp there, was held as a peaceful event, and attracted between 10,000 and 20,000 people, including prominent writers, musicians and activists.

Our study is based on the Russian search engine Yandex's service for searches in Russian-language Twitter. We focus on the Twitter representation of a localized offline event, both in terms of time and place—it lasted no more than a few hours, and was geographically confined to two boulevards in central Moscow.

With the help of the search engine, we have been able to establish a chronology of tweets relating to the Test Walk through the hashtag #kontrolnaiaprogulka. Some 34,525 tweets with this hashtag were posted on 13 May. This represents the core of our data. Among these we have delimited the dataset to tweets in the time span from 11 a.m. to 1 p.m., from one hour before the street march started until one hour into the event.

Our decision to restrict ourselves to this specific hashtag does not mean that coverage of the event relied exclusively on tweets containing #kontrolnaia-progulka. Indeed, many tweets relating to the street event will have appeared without any hashtag, or will have used other hashtags. Our aim was to study how a hashtag is used to establish a Twitter event, parallel to the street march.

## Hashtags as a rhetorical device for organizing Twitter discourse

The hashtag #kontrolnaiaprogulka first appeared on 9 May in a tweet posted by the Tweeter *@kominanton.*

> 13 May #kontrolnaiaprogulka from #Pushkin to #Chistyeprudy. I believe ordinary citizens may join. **LINK**.[1]

Before this, the event had already been mentioned by several users who regularly read Akunin's blog on LiveJournal. While the initial discussion of the event on Twitter had included references to Akunin's blog post, *@kominanton* refers to a news story on Svobodanews.ru. This indicates that Akunin's proposal had become something bigger than the blog post. If we look more closely at the relationship between Akunin's blog post and the hashtag #kontrolnaiaprogulka, we see that, while 360 tweets refer to the blog post, only two of them use the hashtag. Even though the event was widely discussed on both Twitter and LiveJournal in the days following Akunin's post, the hashtag appeared only sporadically. Only on 12 May, the eve of the march, did it start to be used more frequently.

Specific comments on the hashtag among Tweeters demonstrate an awareness of its importance to the organization of the event. On 12 May, the Tweeter *@kurashev* asks whether #kontrolnaiaprogulka is the proper hashtag, and proclaims that a unified, popular hashtag is needed.[2] *@kurashev* is not a very popular Tweeter, with less than 100 followers, but he includes the Tweeters *@WakeUpR* and *@doblag* into his message. They represent two important civic initiatives in Moscow in the Spring of 2012—the organization *Za chestnye vybory* (For fair elections) and the newspaper of the Chistye prudy protest camp respectively. By doing so, *@kurashev* seeks to draw broader attention to his proposal. His proposal is successful and, the following day, @*WakeUpR*'s call to use #kontrolnaiaprogulka to coordinate activities is retweeted 19 times.[3] In this way, existing resources within Twitter are used to coordinate the event, and the initiative comes not from the event's instigator, Akunin, but from other participants.

The Tweeters' choice to send a hashtagged message implied a certain knowledge of how to organize effective Twitter communication. The Twitter event was "administrated" by means of retweets, links to media sources, spam, etc., aimed at increasing its "weight" in the media. A hashtag presupposes that a message becomes visible and accessible to many Tweeters who are interested in the same offline event and its online coverage. From the point of view of Twitter discourse, the use of several hashtags strengthens the utterance, since it makes the tweet more easily accessible to other Tweeters, those who follow other hashtags. This combination of hashtags is a way of creating a public.

The Tweeter @*shokmary* eloquently includes two other hashtags relating to Moscow protests:

> From #marshmillionov to #kontrolnaiaprogulka through #chistyeprudy)))[4]

The same tactic is pursued throughout the event. The hashtag #kontrolnaiaprogulka is used, along with #okkupaiabai.[5] In fact, if we disregard the flooded messages (see below), on the day of the march, half of the tweets in our data use the two hashtags together. Similarly, the hashtag helped to spread the Moscow protest virtually to other Russian cities:

> #kontrolnaiaprogulka Thanks to the transmission, we are with you. Vologda[6]

Such tweets also serve to "objectify" the hashtag and support its interpretation as a "real" event, as something collective and tangible. The same can be said of the use of retweets and links to other digital platforms relating to the event.

## Participants

Those who tweeted using the hashtag #kontrolnaiaprogulka can be arranged into several groups. "Regular Tweeters" constituted the majority. Whether followed by many or few, these people pooled their resources with the help of a hashtag. In so doing, they constructed the social space of an online broadcast, presenting themselves as participants in this political event, and created a virtual audience of readers of their tweets. The commonest role was that of eyewitness, transmitting first-hand information, sharing impressions and posting photos. Such witnesses are particularly important in Russia, where general trust in the ability of journalists to report freely is shown to be low as compared to other countries around the world (BBC poll 2006).

> A lot of people – Pushkin square is full. Everybody wants to go to #kontrolnaiaprogulka. It seems [we] have started moving towards the "Rossiia" cinema.[7]

But the purpose of such hashtagged tweets extends beyond coverage of events alone. Through this sort of representation, a street event becomes a live, "true" happening. It unfolds in real time, its results are as yet unknown and the tension is maintained. Its participants are people "like us."

As they used #kontrolnaiaprogulka, new media grassroots journalists, popular bloggers and Tweeters (or those seeking popularity) occupied a prominent position. They set the tone for the assessment of the Test Walk on the Runet. The civic journalist Kirill Mikhailov uses Twitter on a regular basis to report from street events:

> I left for #kontrolnaiaprogulka and am reproaching myself. I'M BEGGING for someone to replace me at #okkupaisud [Occupy court]. Pass the message on![8]

The voices of professional journalists were also clearly heard. Sometimes they kept a distance. In other instances they wrote as "ordinary participants," but in this case their reputation lent their words more authority.

> Symbolic! RT @KSHN The Avengers. **PIC** #okkupaiabai #kontrolnaiaprogulka[9]

In this tweet, the well-known journalist Oleg Kashin posted a picture of protesters on Pushkin Square with a poster for the movie *The Avengers* in the background. Kashin himself did not include the hashtag, which was added in a retweet by the regular Tweeter @*VladiannaS* and thereafter retweeted 37 times.

Within the hashtagged stream, the accounts of journalists were present in the form of retweets and links to online newspapers, radio stations and news agencies. In this way journalists connected Twitter broadcasting with external media and provided #kontrolnaiaprogulka with publicity.[10] Despite the silence of the main Russian TV channels, which did not report the event, the Test Walk was covered in the media and was constructed on multiple platforms—on Twitter, LiveJournal,

Facebook, the webpages of some newspapers such as *Novaia gazeta*, on radio (Svoboda, Ekho Moskvy) and on internet TV (Dozhd')—as a media event with a networking structure.

Since the Test Walk was organized as a "civic" action and its political dimension was implied but not explicitly stated, most opposition politicians and activists abstained from participating. The strategically important actors in the Test Walk were celebrities—writers (e.g. Boris Akunin, Dmitrii Bykov, Liudmila Ulitskaia) and musicians (e.g. Andrei Makarevich). They were not actively involved in #kontrolnaiaprogulka—the Twitter event—but were indirectly present in reports and photos posted by other Tweeters. Thus their popularity was a resource that directed the attention of Twitter readers to the hashtagged event.

> Dmitrii Bykov has arrived at #kontrolnaiaprogulka, and created much ado. Giving out autographs. **PIC.**[11]

In other words, the groups of people taking part in the Test Walk and #kontrolnaiaprogulka overlapped, but were not identical: some of the march's participants also took part in #kontrolnaiaprogulka, but not all of them. Similarly, while some participants in #kontrolnaiaprogulka were out on the streets, others were at home, in front of their computers.

## Performativity 1: coordinating action

Handheld digital devices make Twitter useful in several ways. Due to the brevity of its messages and its dynamic nature, as well as its multimedia functionality and the ease with which links can be posted, Twitter is a convenient tool for organizing communication between people simultaneously involved in street events. This meant that the same participants could join the walk along Moscow's boulevards and instantly discuss their actions online. For this reason, it would be incorrect to treat #kontrolnaiaprogulka as a purely virtual event, or to limit its function to representation.

Communication during the Test Walk had a strong performative effect: the event was shaped by means of talking about what went on. All activities (the gathering at Pushkin Square, moving along the streets, meeting celebrities, granting interviews, etc.) were immediately reported, evaluated and discussed on #kontrolnaiaprogulka. The walk's participants interacted on Twitter not only with remote audiences, but also with each other. Thus, the transmission of emotions in tweets was also addressed to other protesters – for mutual reassurance, caution and the adjustment of personal feelings to presumably common experiences. Sometimes such coordinative actions were intended to remind the Test Walk's participants of their common goals and to explain how the march should be interpreted.

> All of us share the same conviction: that we can walk around in our own city, where we like and when we like. #kontrolnaiaprogulka #okkupaiabai **LINK**[12]

On #kontrolnaiaprogulka one can find messages from those who tried to coordinate the movement of the column, or tweets to the people at the rear of the procession about what was happening at the very front. This strategy was used in order to address practical issues. It was assumed that people who were walking along the boulevards could not have full information on the event. For example, after hearing people chanting political slogans, one of the participants quickly issued a reminder that such declamations were strictly prohibited:[13]

> Someone in the crowd at #kontrolnaiaprogulka has started to shout slogans. Guys, don't do it!!![14]

Thus, posting tweets was not only a supportive action but part of the unfolding event itself. This communications strategy proved its usefulness during the parallel "occupy" events in Moscow. Followed by the police, people who took part in those events had to move from place to place around the city. To make this happen, they were arranging their meetings on Twitter and via SNS, proclaiming new streets and squares temporarily occupied zones.

Twitter also allowed protesters to lend new meanings to various urban locations. On #kontrolnaiaprogulka participants bestowed the monuments they were seeing and the boulevard along which they were moving with new meanings in connection with their views and values. For instance, a Tweeter "re-appropriates" the Vladimir Vysotsky monument on Strastnoi Boulevard:

> #kontrolnaiaprogulka we are passing Volodia Vysotsky [the statue]. Govorukhin! Vysotsky is with us! #okkupaiabai[15]

Thus, Twitter serves as another tool for influencing public discourse, in addition to traditional media. It is also innovative when viewed alongside blogs, since it can be taken out on the streets and is both more immediate and more geographically mobile.

## Performativity 2: constructing the event

At the beginning of the event, emphasis was given to tweets that—at first glance—merely described what was happening. They served a greater purpose, however:

the discursive constitution of the Test Walk as a successful event. The use of Twitter thus illustrates an important principle of media culture: the mere physical existence of a certain phenomenon does not make it real, it must be represented in discourse. The need for storytelling implies that the success or failure of a political event, as well as its chances of achieving its goals, depend to a great extent on its verbal description and visual presentation. What is important is whose representation wins, how the event is retold by its participants, which narrative prevails in the press, on the internet and on TV. Since Twitter is a real-time medium, Tweeters compete to be the first to describe an event in "proper" terms.

The first tweets from Pushkin Square pursued this goal. The tweets constituting this event sought to convince people at the location that they had not come in vain. At the same time they addressed those who were waiting in front of their PCs at home—inviting them to join in this fascinating street event. Elements of visual communication were important, i.e., images designed to prove the success of the Test Walk. Many of the first tweets contained pictures of the street event, followed by a short phrase highlighting desirable meanings. These photos were actively retweeted:

> Look how many people there are at #kontrolnaiaprogulka **PIC PIC**[16]
>
> Behind me there are even more than on the photo #kontrolnaiaprogulka **PIC**[17]

These are works of representation: i.e. a certain image of the march is created by means of symbols—words and pictures—that are never neutral. Most often, people used words and metaphors intended to raise the spirits of participants and provoke their ideological opponents. The reference to numbers (one thousand, two, five, ten thousand participants on Moscow's boulevards) also fulfilled this task.

> I believe this is what they call a sea of "people". People are everywhere right up to the horizon and [more] are coming #kontrolnaiaprogulka **PIC**[18]
>
> Several thousand [participants] started #kontrolnaiaprogulka in the streets! There are a lot of people![19]

A "good" representation means describing the offline subject in the most cheerful tones. Since there is competition for attention, the most successful tweets are the ones that are most frequently retweeted. Tweeters therefore look for "intensive" words, striking metaphors and epithets.

> All in all #kontrolnaiaprogulka towards the #okkupaiabai is a mega creative and interesting form of communication and protest. Come.[20]
>
> #Kontrolnaiaprogulka in this river of peaceful people [creates] an unbelievable feeling of freedom and solidarity #okkupaiabai[21]

Most of these tweets are either emotional, or mention people's feelings, emotions and affects. Subjective evaluations, metaphors, constant repetitions and quotations occupy a significant place in public communication (Warner 2002: 63, 82–3). The sharing of emotions and affects in tweets is designed to build and maintain networking communities on the basis of understandable feelings and experiences (Zappavigna 2012). In this case, communication relating to a political event was not about "informing" the audience, but about telling stories of personal experiences, as well as sharing opinions on what a person should feel about the event, followed by emoticons and exclamation marks. Thus, we are reminded that this political communication is taking place using personal means of communication—mobile phones, tablets and PCs. In this discourse, an account of what is happening is inseparably connected to the Tweeters' personal experiences.

> This is amazing! People are walking in the streets without police or any sorts of organizers! The elderly, children and . . . writers! #kontrolnaiaprogulka[22]

Though initially Twitter is oriented towards one's circle of friends, it often becomes a channel through which to address the public. These circumstances led to the remarkable blending of semi-private messages with the hashtagged flow of information aimed at a non-specific audience. In #kontrolnaiaprogulka, some Tweeters addressed semi-private statements to their followers. Marked with the same hashtag, these messages contained personal information. This informality and personalization also served to increase the Twitter event's popularity.

> Aa! I'm only now heading off to #kontrolnaiaprogulka, wait for me! I'll have flowing hair and be wearing a black jacket, [I'm] short and cute.[23]
>
> Alright, I'll have some tea and head off to #kontrolnaiaprogulka fast as a bullet.[24]

Thus, the hashtagged broadcasting gave Tweeters the opportunity to engage in an identity performance, where individual meanings intertwined with civic ones.

Consequently, a political event—mediated via Twitter—takes on certain features: it is personalized due to the individual participation of a narrator; it happens in real time; it is constructed by means of a language of emotional solidarity among its participants. Online coordination of such events presupposes solidarity among a number of people who share certain values.

The fact that, in 2012, the people who took part in the Russian protest movement were largely unsuccessful in altering the outcome of the elections (neither the results of the parliamentary elections nor those of the presidential elections were reconsidered) is of only partial importance. The protesters fought not only for "material" but also for symbolic results, i.e. to establish the civil right to protest and to call the authorities to account. This is why the emotional component and affective evaluation of such events in the media were of vital importance. An array of "positive" tweets united by the hashtag created a field of communication that was supposed to be attractive to other social media users. From the point of view of new media political communication, the tweets in #kontrolnaiaprogulka were inviting people to join the event; thus they functioned as advertising for a street protest that was to be perceived as an interesting, outstanding event supported by the most creative users and popular celebrities. Though the Tweeters and their audience were not homogeneous or unanimous, the Twitter broadcasting constructed a politically oriented public: this comes as the result of individual spontaneous tweets. In the construction of a virtual public, there is an important role for the signs that can activate the "hidden network," i.e. a network based not on existing (overt) links between friends and followers but on potential connections between users interested in the same searchable words. A hashtag makes it possible to join a hidden network. In turn, this becomes a place for a contest among Tweeters, who are looking for like-minded users, and fighting those whose values they reject. Semantic connections in this network are maintained by means of retweets and mutual users' references, which generate a sense of commonality in the conversational context. Users address their messages both to their friends and to "familiar strangers" who speak the same language.

## Contestation: flood

The story of #kontrolnaiaprogulka would not be complete without one significant element, i.e. the voices of opponents of the Test Walk. In earlier studies of Twitter in Russia, researchers at the Berkman Center (Alexanyan et al. 2012) and Sam Greene (Grin 2012) found significant variations between groups of different political affiliations in the way that they used the service, and the variations were particularly significant between pro- and anti-government groups. Though the opponents used the same hashtag, they pursued different communications goals. One aim was to present an alternative point of view and to undermine the confidence of followers of #kontrolnaiaprogulka. But more often they intended to mock, offend or provoke the march's participants, or even to destroy its Twitter representation:

#kontrolnaiaprogulka through Moscow by provocateurs and non-Russians calling themselves "writers"[25]

#kontrolnaiaprogulka the country's destructive forces call upon people to walk through the streets.[26]

One of the most striking features of our material is the amount of spam, or more precisely the flood of hostile tweets.[27] In our context, these are tweets that are deliberately written to disrupt the ongoing communication within the hashtag, referred to as "trend hijacking" by Grier et al. (2010). On 13 May, there were 33,369 tweets with the same text "Because Putin loves you (X number of times)," where the X would represent a new number with every tweet:

#okkupaiabai #kontrolnaiaprogulka Because Putin loves you!:) 5068 times![28]

The preceding day, 12 May, saw a similar level of activity, with 23,196 tweets using this formula, while there was a significant drop on 14 May, with only 521 tweets. The important point for us here is that this message was used with the #kontrolnaiaprogulka hashtag. On 13 May, there were 26,336 tweets which combined this text and our hashtag. This implies that three out of four messages sent on 13 May using the hashtag #kontrolnaiaprogulka were flooded messages.

The typical profiles of Tweeters posting these messages are very similar: they have posted several thousand tweets, but do not follow any other Tweeters, nor do they have followers themselves. This picture is confirmed by existing research on Twitter spam, which claims that the metadata of Tweeters can indicate whether they are spammers or not—spammers tend to deviate from regular Tweeters in the number of followers and accounts they follow (Lee, Eoff, and Caverlee 2011; Kelly et al. 2012).

In their analysis of Russian Twitter, Kelly et al. (2012) noted the presence of such flooding, but pointed out the lack of successful flood attacks in relation to the March 2012 presidential elections. Unfortunately, the authors did not discuss the criteria for the success of a flood attack. The implications of the flooding should be seen in relation to the uses and purposes of the hashtag. If the purpose was to create a public related to the street event, the flood of irrelevant messages will certainly have been a major obstacle. People on the streets will have been accessing Twitter via handheld devices (i.e. smartphones) and the limitations of the handheld devices—their size—make them more vulnerable to flooding. In the case of #kontrolnaiaprogulka the flood attack was initiated at 12:23 p.m., 20 minutes after the Test Walk itself had started, and for the remainder of the period observed it completely dominated the hashtag.

If, however, the purpose of the hashtag was to draw attention to the Test Walk, on 13 May, the flooding helped the hashtag reach the top of that day's list of

Russian hashtags, even the top list of hashtags world-wide, making the event much more visible to a larger audience than those initially interested in it.[29]

## Conclusion

On 13 May 2012, Twitter became a battleground for opposing forces in Russian politics. Our analysis has shown how a purposeful, coordinated and massive attack was launched on #kontrolnaiaprogulka from several spam accounts specially created for this purpose. While the Test Walk was allowed to proceed undisturbed, the flood attack clearly sought to undermine the relevance and functioning of #kontrolnaiaprogulka. The fact that the hashtag made it to the top of Twitter's global trends was taken as a signal that the Test Walk had achieved a certain level of success. Part of the reason for this popularity, however, was the flood attack, which rendered meaningful communication using the hashtag all but impossible.

#kontrolnaiaprogulka is a case that shows the relevance of the Runet to Russian public discourse and politics. A specific feature of *Russian* Twitter communication is that this medium is not "owned" by a certain political force: it is used actively (though in different ways) by both the opposition and by supporters of the authorities. We are not only dealing with a simple opposition between old and new media, where old media are controlled by the government and new media are used by opposition forces. The struggle for power is also unfolding in computer-mediated discourse; the battle for the digital space has become a significant factor in Russian political and civic life. While generally allowing the Runet and social networking platforms such as Twitter to thrive, the Russian authorities are apparently concerned by their allegedly subversive potential during periods of political tension, such as those witnessed during the Winter of 2011 and Spring of 2012. Subtle though a flood attack may be when compared to a complete shutdown of Twitter in Russia, it still signals the authorities' determination to control the playing field and their ability to interfere when they deem it necessary. The authorities try to recruit their online supporters from the same Runet milieu. The common cultural background of the Runet enables one side to seek opportunities for digitalized political communication, and another side to destroy these efforts. Thus, the ability to find creative solutions becomes crucial.

This case could lead to speculation about the further possibility of using Twitter and hashtags as tools for political communication. We have seen their role in linking two different events, the street march and the online action, as well as in the rooting of these events in political and civic discourses in the Runet. After Akunin invited people to the walk on his blog, his LiveJournal entry became a news story in Russian online media and acquired a life on its own on Twitter. This medium was used to mobilize people for the demonstration, and during the march a hashtagged account of the march constituted and shaped the Test Walk. A public was created linking the street protests with online discourse, which, in turn, gave the street event relevance and a digital afterlife.

Thus, our study has demonstrated that political communication on Twitter is performative. This fact helps to explain the importance of a discursive representation of an event. For the Test Walk's participants, a successful protest march implies its advantageous representation in social media. At the same time #kontrolnaiaprogulka has shown the limits of Twitter communication. Knowledge of the potential and constraints of the medium gives Tweeters the power to use them both to create and destroy channels of political and civic interactions. In our case, the decisive features of a hashtagged communication are shaped by Twitter's dependence on a real-time collectivity of users' actions, as well as the mobility and limited traffic capacity of personal digital devices. Political communication via hashtagged tweets implies collective production and the simultaneous performance of identity. The product of such real-time performance is intensive, exposed and short-term; hence, this communication faces the challenge that its channel could immediately be captured and reappropriated, its content substituted.

Despite its obvious vulnerability, Twitter has potential as a medium for political communication among civic initiatives. It is voluntary, grassroots, network-based and requires minimal organization. In contemporary Russia this communication is confronted by a seemingly similar, but in fact rather more organized and structured force, relying not so much on human resources as on programmed "bots." Still, at the moment, acts of political communication on Russian Twitter are only followed, rather than being preceded or anticipated, by repressive counter-action.

The example of the Test Walk demonstrates that the new media participant in political and civil events is a "connected" person, who finds himself on the streets with others and, at the same time in a flow of virtual communication. While moving and acting, he writes and posts links and pictures. In Twitter communication a public is united by weak bonds. Its collective identity is presented as political, intense, short-term and renewable upon request.

Twitter is used reflectively as a medium that links a physical urban space with social virtual spaces. Protesters affirm the right of the people and grassroots communities to reassign spaces in their everyday life by erasing authoritative meanings and conferring their own. The short-term nature of Twitter, coupled with the exposure of communication to flooding, prevents the long-lasting discursive appropriation of urban places. At the same time, Twitter demonstrates the capacities of tactical media, creating temporary zones of alternative meanings. Tweeting, walking through a city's streets and sitting in boulevards are becoming forms of political protest. A flâneur, a listener to an open-street lecture, as well as a person who performs an unexpected act in a public place, turns into a representative of political protest. An integral part of this strategy is posting photos and comments on these actions in real time, as well as making this information searchable with the help of keywords, tags and hashtags. Despite the seemingly innocent nature of most of these materials and actions, they are qualified as political acts, both by protesters and state authorities. Thus, we are dealing with a form of political communication organized by means of mobile digital media on social networking platforms.

## Notes

1 http://twitter.com/KominAnton/statuses/200260017532833793, 9 May at 6:24 p.m. Note that in this example and those that follow, the codes LINK and PIC in bold are given as abbreviated references to links and pictures in the original tweets.
2 http://twitter.com/kurashev/statuses/201379519335108608 and http://twitter.com/kurashev/statuses/201383238978125825.
3 http://twitter.com/WakeUpR/statuses/201582733355524096.
4 http://twitter.com/Shokmary/statuses/200263917379919872, 9 May at 6:40 p.m.
5 The hashtag (Occupy Abai) refers to the street occupation in Moscow of the monument to the Kazakh poet Abai Qunanbaiuli.
6 http://twitter.com/luana_dio/statuses/201595422450515968, 13 May at 12:49 p.m.
7 http://twitter.com/istechkin/statuses/201584712328818688, 13 May at 12:08 p.m.
8 http://twitter.com/ReggaeMortis1/statuses/201573699323834368, 13 May at 11:24 a.m.
9 http://twitter.com/VladiannaS/status/201586303773581312, 13 May at 12:14 p.m.
10 This tendency is also reflected in Sam Greene's research on use of Twitter in Russia during and immediately after the presidential elections in March 2012 (Grin 2012).
11 http://twitter.com/sashakots/statuses/201582019325591552, 13 May at 11:57 a.m.
12 http://twitter.com/Estraniero/statuses/201580983869378560, 13 May at 11:53 a.m.
13 The organizers of the march presented it as a non-political spontaneous "walk." Any organized declamation could give the police legal reasons to start arresting people.
14 http://twitter.com/hmoll/statuses/201593714286669825, 13 May at 12:44 p.m.
15 http://twitter.com/OlegPshenichny/statuses/201589814678654976, 13 May at 12:28 p.m. This tweet requires explanation. Its author says that the march was approaching a monument to Vladimir Vysotsky. Vysotsky's most popular role in cinema was in Stanislav Govorukhin's cult film *The Meeting Place Cannot Be Changed* (1979). For many Russians, Vysotsky still remains a symbol of personal freedom. At the same time Govorukhin ran Putin's campaign headquarters in the run-up to the presidential election in 2012. The author of this tweet encodes the monument in his own way—he reminds his readers of freedom, linking Vysotsky's memory with the Test Walk while reproaching Govorukhin for his "betrayal."
16 http://twitter.com/antonb_ru/status/201599343667589121, 13 May at 11:06 a.m.
17 http://twitter.com/mrButt/statuses/201587930811219968, 13 May at 12:21 p.m.
18 http://twitter.com/nikel1309/statuses/201593985100296192, 13 May at 12:45 p.m.
19 http://twitter.com/AndreyShabaev/statuses/201587606415351808, 13 May at 12:20 p.m.
20 http://twitter.com/blinov001/status/201584402122280960, 13 May at 12:25 p.m.
21 http://twitter.com/OlegPshenichny/statuses/201588432785510400, 13 May at 12:23 p.m.
22 http://twitter.com/AndreyShabaev/statuses/201588414049562624, 13 May at 12:23 p.m.
23 http://twitter.com/aliaazamat/statuses/201578934582788097, 13 May at 11:45 a.m.
24 http://twitter.com/John_Glabb/statuses/201576779218038784, 13 May, at 11:37 a.m.
25 http://twitter.com/swarog09/statuses/201576606630805504, 13 May at 11:36 a.m.
26 http://twitter.com/ssecondhandd/statuses/201584985390587904, 13 May at 12:09 p.m.
27 The difference between spam and flood in computer-mediated communication is that spam is the result of a commercial enterprise, where someone sends out advertisements in large numbers with the hope that at least one person will pay. Thus spammers have a direct economic interest in distributing the spam. A flood is a political phenomenon, with someone sending out large numbers of messages to obstruct the communication of their political opponents.
28 http://twitter.com/nangdua/statuses/201588407766482944, 13 May at 12:22 p.m.
29 http://twitpic.com/9kqdn7 and http://twitter.com/VitasTweet/status/201609557351477248/photo/1.

## References


Alexanyan, Karina, Vladimir Barash, Bruce Etling, Bruce Faris, Urs Gasser, John Kelly, John Palfrey, and Hal Roberts. 2012. "Exploring Russian Cyberspace: Digitally-Mediated Collective Action and the Networked Public Sphere." Berkman Center Research Publication. Berkman Center. Available at: http://papers.ssrn.com/sol3/papers.cfm?abstract_id=2014998&http://cyber.law.harvard.edu/publications/2012/exploring_russian_cyberspace (accessed 15 April 2013).

BBC poll 2006, "Trust in the Media." Available at: http://news.bbc.co.uk/2/shared/bsp/hi/pdfs/02_05_06mediatrust.pdf (accessed 15 April 2013).

boyd, danah, Scott Golder, and Gilad Lotan. 2010. "Tweet, Tweet, Retweet: Conversational Aspects of Retweeting on Twitter." In *Proceedings of HICSS-42, Persistent Conversation Track*. Kauai, Hawaii: IEEE Computer Society. Available at: http://www.danah.org/papers/TweetTweetRetweet.pdf (accessed 15 April 2013).

Bruns, Axel, and Jean Burgess. 2011a. "The Use of Twitter Hashtags in the Formation of Ad Hoc Publics." Paper presented at the European Consortium for Political Research conference, Reykjavik. Available at: http://www.ecprnet.eu/MyECPR/proposals/reykjavik/uploads/papers/2090.pdf (accessed 15 April 2013).

—— 2011b. "New Methodologies for Researching News Discussions on Twitter." Paper presented at The Future of Journalism, Cardiff, September 8–9.

Christensen, Christian. 2011. "Twitter Revolutions? Addressing Social Media and Dissent." *The Communication Review* 14: 155–7.

Glaser, Mark. 2007. "Twitter Founders Thrive on Micro-Blogging Constraints." *MediaShift*, May 17. Available at: http://www.pbs.org/mediashift/2007/05/twitter-founders-thrive-on-micro-blogging-constraints137.html (accessed 15 April 2013).

Grier, Chris, Kurt Thomas, Vern Paxson, and Michael Zhang. 2010. "@spam: The Underground on 140 Characters or Less." *ACM Conference on Computer and Communications Security*. CCS.

Grin, Samuel'. 2012. "Tvitter i rossiiskii protest: memy, seti i mobilizatsiia." *Rabochie materialy TSIIO*, Moscow. Available at: http://www.scribd.com/doc/94393467/Твиттер-и-российский-протест-РМ-ЦИИО-2012-1 (accessed 15 April 2013).

Hutchins, Brett. 2011. "The Acceleration of Media Sport Culture: Twitter, Telepresence and Online Messaging." *Information, Communication & Society* 14: 237–57.

Kelly, John, Vladimir Barash, Karina Alexanyan, Bruce Etling, Bruce Faris, Urs Gasser, and John Palfrey. 2012. "Mapping Russian Twitter." *The Berkman Center for Internet & Society Research Publication Series*. Boston: Berkman Center for Internet & Society Research.

Lee, Kyumin, Brian David Eoff, and James Caverlee. 2011. "Seven Months with the Devils: A Long-Term Study of Content Polluters on Twitter." *Fifth International AAAI Conference on Weblogs and Social Media*. Barcelona. Available at: http://www.aaai.org/ocs/index.php/ICWSM/ICWSM11/paper/view/2780/3296 (accessed 15 April 2013).

Lotan, Gilad, Erhardt Graeff, Mike Ananny, Devin Gaffney, Ian Pearce, and danah boyd. 2011. "The Revolutions Were Tweeted: Information Flows During the 2011 Tunisian and Egyptian Revolutions." *International Journal of Communication* 5: 1375–1405.

Warner, Michael. 2002. "Publics and Counterpublics." *Public Culture* 14: 49–90.

Zappavigna, Michele. 2011. "Ambient Affiliation: A Linguistic Perspective on Twitter." *New Media & Society* 13: 788–806.

—— 2012. *Discourse of Twitter and Social Media*. London: Continuum.

# Part III

# Language and diversity

# 6 The written turn

## How CMC actuates linguistic change in Russian

*Aleksandrs Berdicevskis*

## Introduction: the actuation problem

One of the main tasks of sociolinguistics is the identification of general patterns of language change. How do languages change, why do they do it that way, and what causes particular changes? The latter question is also known as the *actuation problem*, formulated by Weinreich, Labov and Herzog (1968: 102) in the following way: "Why do changes in a structural feature take place in a particular language at a given time, but not in other languages with the same feature, or in the same language at other times?" They referred to it as "perhaps the most basic" question facing students of language change.

Most sociolinguists acknowledge that the quest to solve the actuation problem does not have to be limited to language-internal factors. As Weinreich, Labov and Herzog (1968: 186) themselves note, stimuli and constraints that affect the process of language change can be found in both society and the structure of language. Well-recognized external causes of language change include, for instance, changes in social structure or language contact (see Cheshire, Agder and Fox 2012). This chapter discusses the potential role of computer-mediated communication (CMC) in the actuation of language change in Russian. I focus on one aspect of CMC influence, the fact that it enhances the so-called "written turn" (Baron 2005), i.e. increases the role of written speech and visual communication in general.

## CMC and language change

CMC has long been recognized as a factor in language change. Baron (1984) made one of the very first declarations of interest, Herring (2012) and Androutsopoulos (2011a) offer brief reviews of what has been done since then. The interest in CMC has reinvigorated the long-standing interest in the more general question of the role of the communication channel (medium) in language change (Herring 2003). To the best of my knowledge, however, there has been little explicit discussion of whether studies of language change in CMC allow us to arrive at a partial solution of the actuation problem.

One reason might be that the actuation problem lies within the field of "classic" sociolinguistics, and this field's questions and methods are not exactly the same as those in CMC studies. Androutsopoulos (2011b), for instance, discusses several of the limitations of a variationist sociolinguistics approach to CMC. First, the narrow understanding of a linguistic variable (on various understandings of linguistic variables, see Wolfram 1991; Tagliamonte 2006: 70–98) excludes certain features, which can nonetheless be of importance. Second, quantitative-based sociolinguistics excludes features that are scarce in frequency, even though they are not necessarily marginal. Third, sociolinguistic analysis often relies on non-linguistic parameters (age, gender, region) that are to a large extent predefined by scholarly conventions. These categories, however, are not necessarily those that are most relevant to variation in the linguistic behavior observed in CMC.

These divergences between the two fields can be seen quite clearly in this chapter. The innovations that will be discussed are not linguistic variables *stricto sensu*. For most of them, it is difficult to estimate the frequency reliably, for some, that frequency is likely to be low. Further, I do not show any link with traditional social parameters such as age and gender (instead, I claim that a parameter that facilitates their emergence is the communication channel). Finally, it is possible that these innovations will be short-lived, and some of the new patterns are very unlikely to replace the existing ones, and may at best co-exist with them.

Nevertheless, all examples in this chapter attest to the fact that a new pattern has emerged in the speakers' linguistic behavior. In each case, I explain which pattern is new, what is new about it and why the innovation is worth attention. Milroy and Milroy (1985: 345) claim that "[i]f we are to address the actuation problem . . . we must break with tradition and maintain that it is not languages that innovate; it is speakers who innovate." In my examples, speakers do innovate in some way, and the important question is: why do they do it?

## A two-stage model of innovation and its importance for CMC

It is important to distinguish between the two processes involved in language change (Croft 2000: 4–5): the initial *innovation* and the subsequent *diffusion* (or propagation). I refer to the former as *speaker innovation* (after Milroy and Milroy 1985), to the latter as *diffusion*, and to the result of diffusion as *community innovation*. The word *innovation* is used to denote any new pattern in the language, either one that is represented by a single speaker innovation or one that has already diffused into the community. There is, of course, no strict boundary between the two types of innovation, rather a continuum.

One of the key claims of this chapter is that most of the influence that CMC exerts on language change occurs at the stage of diffusion, cf. a hypothesis put forward by Maslova (2008: 15): "selection-level processes may play a more prominent role in determining universal tendencies of language change than commonly assumed." In other words, if something new has appeared in language because of the existence of CMC, it is most likely that that has happened because the stage of diffusion has been affected, not the stage of speaker innovation. For many novel patterns, the emergence of which is typically associated with

CMC, very similar speaker innovations can be found in "traditional" channels, long before the advent of CMC.

A textbook example of a CMC-born innovation are emoticons, created, according to the most widely held belief, in 1982 (Fahlman ?2002). Zimmer (2007), however, provides examples of features which are virtually identical to emoticons, both in form and function, and which date back to 1967, 1969 and 1887 [*sic*!]. All these were independent one-speaker innovations that were not adopted by other members of the community and did not diffuse further. Thus, emoticons did not diffuse into community innovation prior to 1982 not because they had not been invented previously (they had), but because there was no medium where they could easily spread. Text-based CMC, with its lack of non-verbal cues, limited set of characters, high informality and playfulness and other properties, provided such a medium. It also provided a multiplex social network where the innovation was able to spread and establish itself extremely quickly. In other words, if we focus on speaker innovations, post-1982 emoticons are not really new. As community innovations, however, they are.

It might be that CMC also creates new opportunities for speaker innovations, and that some fundamentally novel speaker innovations occur. For instance, in CMC, language change can be actuated by a typo. Consider leet speak (an Internet slang, notable primarily for its non-standard orthography), which produced neologisms such as *pwn* ("own") and *teh* ("the"), both the result of a typo (Ross 2006), or Russian *psto* ("blogpost"), most likely of the same origin. Even in this case, however, the main effect of CMC occurs at the stage of diffusion: typos could have occurred (and most likely did) in traditional channels, but only in CMC did speakers pick them up and start using them intentionally.

Taking all of this into account, I investigate the forces that are at work at the diffusion stage: not the structure of the social network and its role in the spread of innovation, as many sociolinguistic studies do (see Paolillo 2001, regarding the application of the social network approach to CMC), but rather the selective forces that either promote the speaker innovation or prevent it from diffusing into the community.

To analyze these selective forces, we must abandon the uniformitarian principle (Labov 1972), the assumption that linguistic forces operating today are the same as those that operated in the past, or at least in the not-too-distant past (Labov 1994). On the contrary, these forces can change when social structure changes (Trudgill 2011: 167–9), or when important cultural and technological changes take place. This view allows us to address the actuation problem.

To return to our earlier example: emoticons were actuated several times prior to the advent of CMC, but the selective forces against them were strong, and they did not diffuse. The spread of CMC changed the selective forces, and the actuation in 1982 was successful.

The advent of CMC, a communication channel with a peculiar set of properties, launched several trends that influence which selective forces are at work and in which direction they operate. The trend on which I focus in this chapter, "the written turn," can briefly be described as follows: due to the increased use of written speech, speaker innovations which can easily diffuse in written speech, but not in oral speech, enjoy much higher chances of success.

## The written turn

The fact that CMC changes the traditional relationship between written and oral speech, and cannot easily be classified as either, has been mentioned on innumerable occasions. Jones and Schieffelin (2009), Tagliamonte and Denis (2008), Dresner (2005), Zitzen and Stein (2004), Ko (1996), Yates (1996), Collot and Belmore (1996) and Ferrara, Brunner and Whittemore (1991) discuss either some of the aspects of this complex relationship, or the manifestation of oral and written features in CMC, or the status of CMC: hybrid register or the medium in its own right, or many other aspects of "written" and "spoken" constituents of CMC. Androutsopoulos (2011b) emphasizes the need to rethink the methods of "classic" sociolinguistics (that were designed with oral speech in mind) in order to study language change in the visual environment. Baron (2005) offers a brief overview of the "written turn" in modern language culture and the role of CMC in it.

Of importance to this chapter are the novel patterns of linguistic behavior that provide evidence about this written turn, the changing role of written speech, its increased autonomy and salience. Werry (1996: 58), examining data from IRC, identifies "an almost manic impulse to produce auditory and visual effects in writing, a straining to make written words simulate speech." In the next section, I analyze several patterns in Russian CMC that can be classified as the results of the opposite "impulses." First, I focus on a written-speech pattern that is in *direct contradiction* with oral speech. Second, I use several examples to demonstrate how *the effects from writing are reproduced in auditory and visual communication.* Finally, I review a case of language change where the written turn actuates the change and directs it, with both the trends identified in previous sections in operation.

It can be argued that some of the observed patterns are somewhat peripheral.[1] It is, however, important that the innovations *exist* (cf. Labov's (2010: 90) claim that "[t]he actuation problem demands that we search for universals in particulars"). The mere fact of their existence reveals certain cognitive and social features of the current language situation. In fact, each pattern requires separate and thorough study, so what is presented here is instead an overview, intended to outline a trend and show the possible directions for future, more detailed research.

## Facets of the written turn: autonomy of the written speech

Writing has often been considered to be just "a way of recording language" (Bloomfield 1933: 21). According to this view, orthography is a mere representation of phonology, and the features of written texts, for the most part, mirror those of oral speech. Consider in this light the following metalinguistic comment by a Russian Internet user:

(1) Радуют блондинки, которые пишут "пожалууууйста", явно не имея представления об ударениях. *FACEPALM*

*Raduiut blondinki, kotorye pishut "pozháluuuuuista", iavno ne imeia predstavleniia ob udareniiakh. *FACEPALM**[2] (bash.org.ru, 2010)

It's fun to observe blondes who write "pozháluuuuuista" ["please"], while clearly having no idea about stress

Here, the speaker ridicules those users who write "pozháluuuuuista" (classifying them as dumb "blondes"). What is wrong with this spelling? The elongation of a vowel or a consonant is often used in spoken Russian to express emphasis of some kind. The same device is often used in writing, mirroring the emphatic pronunciation. There are, however, certain restrictions on what can be elongated, and since the use of this device in writing is supposed to be a mere recording of language, the restrictions in both registers are defined by the properties of oral speech.

As regards vowels, the general rule is that only the stressed vowel can be elongated. The reasons are purely phonetic: if a non-stressed vowel is elongated, while the stressed one is not, the word is likely to sound as if the stress shifts to the elongated vowel, i.e. to the wrong place. Thus, *pozháaaluista*, for instance, is a "licensed" elongation, acceptable in standard written Russian.[3] The general rule has certain exceptions. The first vowel can be elongated, even if it is not stressed (*taaakói* "such," *bo-ol'shói* "large"). A pronunciation where the last vowel is elongated (even if it is not stressed), or all vowels are elongated, can also be imagined. They might sound somewhat artificial, but they are not blatantly incorrect.[4] The form *pozháluuuuuista*, however, cannot sound like correct Russian when pronounced. The elongation of *u* is unacceptable in this word, both in writing and in speech.

In the unregimented realms of CMC, in blogs, fora, chatrooms and any channels where one can write without being edited by a professional editor, it can occur. Moreover, other instances of the pattern "elongate whatever vowel you want" can be found: consider examples (2–5) (keywords are italicized in the translations).

(2) убиииивать таких уродов

*ubiiiiivát' takikh urodov* (vk.com, 2012)

morons like these have to *be killed*

(3) ой смехооота какая

*oi smekhoootá kakaia* (pesikot.org, 2007)

oh, how *funny*

(4) ласкоооовый такой
*láskooovyi takoi* (zverushki.tomsk.ru, 2009)
[it is] so *tender*

(5) матч заеееeебись
*match zaeeeeebís'* (chat at cspl.ru, 2012)
the game was *fucking cool*

As regards consonants, the restrictions existing in standard language are less clear. Viktorova (2008) provides some limited evidence that the first consonant is elongated more often than other consonants and that sonorants are elongated more often than other types, but the patterns are not as clear-cut as is the case with vowels. Still, CMC obviously shows more variation in the elongation of consonants than traditional channels do, consider:

(6) и как побббежала
*i kak pobbbezhála* (bash.org.ru, 2012)
and then she *really broke into a run*

(7) оттгстань
*otttstán'* (beon.ru, 2011)
*leave me alone*

The elongation of a stop consonant such as [b] or [t] is a difficult venture, especially in a [tst] cluster, as in example (7). The phonetic results will resemble stuttering rather than emphasis (though the context in both cases clearly indicates emphasis).

Finally, the Russian alphabet includes two letters that are neither vowels nor consonants, but so-called "signs," a soft sign *Ь* (') and a hard sign *Ъ* ("). These do not denote any sound and, obviously, cannot be elongated in standard language. In CMC, however, counter-examples can be found, consider:

(8) брысььь отсюда
*brys''''* *otsiuda* (twitter.com, 2012)
*get out* of here

(9) ноут вообще вещьь
*nout voobshche veshch''* (bash.org.ru, 2012)
a laptop is a cool *thing*

(10) так въъъебать охото ему
*tak v”””ebat’ okhoto emu* (clipiki.ru, 2011)
I want to *smack* him so much

In example (8), the soft sign denotes only the softness of the preceding consonant [s], while in example (9) it has no phonetic value at all and is retained for historical reasons. The hard sign in example (10) does not denote any sound either, indicating instead how the preceding consonant and the following vowel should be pronounced (fulfilling the so-called separating function). Still, speakers find it perfectly possible to express emphasis by elongating these mute letters.

To sum up, the novelty of the observed pattern can be described as follows. Traditionally, in standard written Russian it is possible to express emphasis by mimicking an emphatic device of oral speech, namely, by elongating one or more letters in a word. The letters have to denote sounds that would have been elongated in emphatic pronunciation. In informal CMC, however, it is possible to express emphasis by elongating *any* letters, even if they denote sounds which cannot be elongated in oral speech or do not denote any sound at all.

How could CMC have fostered the emergence of this innovation? First, through the visual nature of the channel: mostly text, no sound (voice, video and multimodal communication via computers is, of course, possible and is becoming increasingly frequent, but the large share of CMC has been, and still is, text-based, sometimes text-only). This means that traditional prosodic and non-verbal cues are unavailable, and the need to compensate for their absence is strong. In particular, people are eager to convey emphasis by one means or another.

Second, Saussure (2011: 31–2), describing the “tyranny of writing,” noted that “[b]y imposing itself upon the masses, spelling influences and modifies language” (ibid.: 31), and that this happens “only in highly literate languages where written texts play an important role.” CMC enhances this effect. It has become extremely popular and plays an important role in the daily life of many speakers, in some cases *replacing* auditory communication such as a phone conversation or a face-to-face meeting. Speakers become more accustomed to writing and less dependent on oral speech.

Third, CMC is highly tolerant of deviations from the standard norm, and allows considerable freedom. To provide an example related to the elongation device: in “traditional” written channels (books, press), a letter is seldom repeated more than three times, while in CMC occurrences like *pozhaluuuuuuuu-uuuuuuuuuuuuuuuuuuuuuuuista* are quite possible. There is no editor to suppress this rich variation, and it is this variation which paves the way for innovative patterns to emerge.

Fourth, it is easy to produce an additional letter: just hold a key down for several moments longer (or press it several times). This is easier than writing a letter by hand, although not necessarily easier than elongating a sound in oral speech (it depends on which sound is being elongated).

Why is this innovation important? It shows that people can write without thinking of how they speak, that the visual channel can become decoupled from the auditory channel. This fact challenges the Bloomfieldian view of writing as a mere "recording" of language (the repercussions of which are still strong among linguists) and supports the view, as expressed by Aaron and Joshi (2006), that writing is as natural as spoken language.

Returning to the actuation perspective, writing as a linguistic domain is becoming more autonomous, and changes that are independent of oral speech are more likely to occur. Contrary to Werry's observation (cited above), in this case there is no "straining to make written words simulate speech;" users do not care whether writing simulates speech or not.

## The salience of written speech

In this section, I will discuss a trend which runs counter to the "impulse to produce auditory and visual effects in writing" observed by Werry. While users are certainly keen to do that, it is also the case that *effects from written speech are reproduced audibly or visually*. Consider example (11):

(11) Теперь, после достаточного знакомства с интернетом, моя младшая сестра, когда видит или слышит что-то "смешное", то с абсолютно спокойным лицом произносит "хд" и все.

*Teper', posle dostatochnogo znakomstva s internetom, moia mladshaia sestra, kogda vidit ili slyshit chto-to "smeshnoe", to s absoliutno spokoinym litsom proiznosit "khd" i vse.* (bash.org.ru, 2010)

Now that she is pretty familiar with the internet, my younger sister, when she hears something "funny," just keeps an absolutely calm face and says "khd," and that's it.

The etymology of *khd* (*хд* in Cyrillic) is as follows. Both in English and in Russian CMC, the emoticon *xD* (sometimes *XD*) is often used to convey laughter. It is an iconic representation of a laughing face, *D* representing a wide open mouth. In Russian CMC, however, the Cyrillic counterpart *хД* is often used (sometimes lowercase *хд*). It is the result of two different types of transliteration: in Androutsopoulos's (2009) terms, *Д* or *д* is a phonetic transliteration of *D*, while *x* is a orthographic transliteration (visual subtype) of *x*. Russian *x* denotes sound [h], not [ks], and thus is used due to its visual similarity to English *x*. Importantly, *хД* bears very little resemblance to a laughing face, *хд* even less so. Still, speakers use it, since *xD* requires the additional action of switching the keyboard layout from Russian to English, while *хД* does not. In example (12), the speaker claims that their sister uses *хд* in oral speech. It can be pronounced as [hd], or [hede], or, less likely, [hade] (the standard name for the letter *x* is [ha], but it is seldom used in vernacular speech).

It is, of course, possible that the example was invented by the speaker and is not actually true. It was, however, posted on a website (bash.org.ru) where all posts are rated by site visitors, who vote either for (if they find them funny, interesting and, importantly, plausible, unrealistic posts tend to get low score) or against them. This one has a rating of more than 25, which means that at least 25 other users did not find the situation described completely unrealistic. Moreover, other similar statements about the use of [hd] in oral speech can be found on the Internet. Finally, further evidence for the process of "voicing" emoticons can be provided. Consider the following fragment of a rhyme from the same website, bash.org.ru:

(12) Кот, хуясе, 0_о, одмин,
Я надеюсь не один!
*Kot, khuiáse, 0_o, odmín,*
*Ia nadéius' ne odín*[5]
Cat, whatthefuck, 0_o, sysadmin,
I hope I am not alone

The first line is a list of well-known "old" memes from the website: 0_o is an emoticon conveying surprise (representing the eyes of a surprised person). They are often used together in the form of a similar list at the end of a post (without any connection to the post content). In the preceding lines, the author laments the fact that site visitors are beginning to forget these memes, and then claims he has not, before expressing hope that he is not alone.

Here, it is the metrical foot of the rhyme which is of importance. Most of the previous lines (not cited here) are written in a trochee: DUM-da-DUM-da-DUM-da-DUM. The same clearly applies to the second line of the cited extract: ***Ia*** *nad**é**ius' **ne** od**í**n*. The first line, however, does not fit well: *K**o**t, khu**iá**se, 0_o, odm**í**n*, or DUM-da-DUM-da-da-DUM. Both the number of syllables and the structure of the line are wrong. The rhyme can be read correctly only if we assume that the emoticon 0_o functions as a single stressed syllable. In this case the line can be read as *K**o**t, khu**iá**se,* ***0_o****, odm**í**n*, or DUM-da-DUM-da-*DUM*-da-DUM.

Most likely, the author reads 0_o as [o], thus ignoring the fact that the first symbol is not *o*, but zero, and that *o* is used here not to denote a sound, but to represent an eye. Alternatively, he may have gauged the suitability of the foot only by looking at the written lines, almost without trying to read them aloud. If he perceives 0_o as a monosyllabic word, it could act as the required DUM.

Of which novel pattern are these two examples evidence? A linguistic feature which emerged in written speech and is typically associated with writing is borrowed into oral speech. This is not new *per se*. In Russian, for instance, the set phrase *v kavychkakh* has been used for ages (literally "in quotes," actual meaning "metaphorically, ironically"). Nowadays, CMC fosters the emergence of new features (in these examples, emoticons *хД* and 0_o, but similar contexts can be provided for features of other types), which, despite their visual nature, are also borrowed into oral speech.

Why is this important? It shows that the speakers do not perceive emoticons as features confined to the written space, but are ready to invent a way to pronounce them, thus enriching oral speech with devices borrowed from written speech. In example (12), the speaker is aware that something unusual has happened, while in example (13), the speaker uses 0_o in a rhyme without any explicit comment, being sure that his readers will have no trouble reading it.

## Written speech as the actuator of change

In this section, I will briefly describe a morphosyntactic innovation in Russian which has recently diffused through CMC.[6] In the early 2000s, an anti-standard idiom called *Olbanian language* became immensely popular in Russian CMC (see Chapter 7 by Berdicevskis and Zvereva, in this volume). One of its basic principles is to "break all rules of orthography," and one manifestation of this principle is the spelling of *o* instead of the unstressed *a* (it violates orthographic but not phonological norms: in unstressed positions both vowels are reduced and sound the same). Thus, nouns with unstressed ending—*dévushka, knízhka, naúka, muzhchína* ("girl," "book," "science," "man")—sometimes assume the form *dévushko, knízhko, naúko, muzhchíno.*

Nouns ending in *-o* in Russian are strongly linked to the neuter gender. As a consequence of this link, words like *dévushko* (originally feminine) or *muzhchíno* (originally masculine) can be reclassified as neuter, with their declension and agreement following suit. We are witnessing a rare phenomenon: orthography influencing morphology. The "orthographic neuter" has become frequent and productive (almost losing its connection with Olbanian, the popularity of which is fading). Nouns belonging to other formal classes, not only those ending in unstressed *-a*, are also migrating to the new gender.

The innovation is, of course, used playfully and does not replace any of the three traditional genders (masculine, feminine and neuter), but instead adds a new one. While the original substitution of the letter *o* instead of the unstressed *a* was a purely visual phenomenon, its grammatical consequences affect oral speech as well, cf. standard *tupoi blondinke* (dumb-DAT.SG.F blonde-DAT.SG) vs. orthographic-neuter *tupomu blondinku* (dumb-DAT.SG.N blonde-DAT.SG) or standard *nemytyi admin* (dirty-NOM.SG.M admin-NOM.SG) vs. orthographic-neuter *nemytoe admino* (dirty-NOM.SG.N admin-NOM.SG).

Moreover, there is anecdotal evidence that speakers sometimes do pronounce non-fully-reduced [o] instead of a reduced [a], imitating the orthographical neuter: *kóshk[o], kís[o], Polínk[o]* instead of standard *kóshk[a]* "cat," *kís[a]* "pussycat," *Polínk[a].*

As a speaker innovation, the orthographic neuter is not new. It was used in fiction, poetry and the press throughout the twentieth century (and the earliest known example dates back to 1888). Two things, however, are important. First, it did not become a community innovation until the early 2000s. Second, prior to that, it was used as a salient artistic device, usually adding certain (often pejorative) connotations to the meaning of a noun (for instance, it could imply the asexuality of a denoted person). Now, on the contrary, having diffused widely enough in CMC, the innovation has lost most of its original semantic connotations, and has become a means of adding some general ironic flavor to one's utterance.

The features of CMC which were instrumental in transforming a rare wordplay into a productive model are as follows. First, CMC provided a written channel of communication: in standard oral speech, *dévushka* and *dévushko* are indistinguishable. Second, unlike traditional written channels, CMC is both public and unregimented: anybody can write, anybody can read, and nobody edits, i.e. enforces the standard norm. This, as I mentioned above, makes the channel tolerant of norm deviations. The public nature of the channel, the fact that it is a multiplex network with a high speed of information exchange, makes the rapid spread of innovations possible.

When the orthographic neuter is finally diffused, both trends identified in the previous sections are in operation. The readiness of speakers to use in writing features that *contradict* oral speech enables the spelling of *o* instead of *a*. The readiness of speakers to *borrow* features from writing into oral speech makes the innovation visible in spoken Russian (since people can pronounce *tupomu blondinku* instead of *tupoi blondinke* or even *kís[o]* instead of *kís[a]*). While the phenomena analyzed above (the non-standard vowel elongation, the "voicing" of emoticons) can be said to be peripheral, the orthographic neuter is frequent, productive, salient and stable.

It is informative to compare the orthographic neuter with a trend observed by Polinsky (2006: 223–4) in what she terms "American Russian," the incompletely learned language of those Russians who moved to the USA and became English-dominant in childhood. In American Russian, a shift in the opposite direction happens: neuter nouns are often treated as feminine: *bol'sháia iábloko* (big-NOM.SG.F apple-NOM.SG) instead of standard *bol'shóe iábloko* (big-NOM.SG.N apple-NOM.SG). This shift, however, affects neuter nouns with stem stress (like *iábloko*) less frequently than nouns with end stress (*litsó* "face"). The noun *iábloko* sounds *iáblok[a]* and is thus more easily associated with feminine (for which the ending *-a* is typical) than *lits[ó]*.

Thus, the situation with morphological gender in Russian resembles what Labov (2010) terms "a fork in the road."[7] Depending on which forces are operating, the linguistic system can follow one route or the other. In this case, the *incomplete acquisition* in American Russian causes nouns to migrate from neuter, the most unstable gender, to feminine, partially destroying the gender system and simplifying it. The *influence of CMC* in mainland Russian causes nouns to migrate from both masculine and feminine to neuter, thus enriching the system with a new "ironic" gender, which complicates the system, and reinforcing the position of the neuter (Zubova 2010).[8]

## Conclusion

Discussing language change, Labov distinguishes between *triggering events*, which are "particular accidents of history" (2010: 184), *governing principles*, which constrain the direction of a change, and *driving forces*, which motivate the continuous process of change.

Andersen (1989: 8) notes that while linguistic change in some sense is a product of the speaker's free will, its development also depends on "the universal principles which govern language use and grammar formation."

In this chapter, I foreground a concept of *selective forces*, related to Labov's notions of governing principles and driving forces and Andersen's of universal principles. A selective force is a factor that either promotes or inhibits the diffusion of a speaker innovation. The main theoretical claim of this chapter is that, in order to explain the actuation of language change in CMC, it is necessary to focus on how CMC changes the selective forces.

This does not presuppose that speaker innovations are of no interest. They are, though in actual fact they seldom become the focus of sociolinguists' attention. Croft (2000: 55) notes that discussions of variation almost never explain how variants arise, and instead most research focuses on their early diffusion. Since in CMC the data are archived and searchable, there are new opportunities to study speaker innovations. The innovations become potentially more searchable, and direct observation of the actuation process, which Milroy and Milroy (1985: 370) claimed to be "difficult, if not impossible," turns out to be possible in some cases.

Still, finding a speaker innovation does not always solve the actuation problem. When emoticons were invented by Fahlman in 1982, they diffused and change happened, but why did it not happen when they were invented in 1967 by Nabokov or in 1887 by Bierce? Why did orthographic neuter in Russian not diffuse in 1888? The list can be continued: variation in language is immense, and one can find a great number of speaker innovations at any point in history. For virtually any feature that is presumably new, some older equivalent can be found. Crudely put, at the level of speaker innovations almost everything is possible, but few novel patterns develop into community innovations. Which speaker innovations are successful depends on the combination of actual selective forces.

Moreover, in some cases there may be no single speaker innovation to actuate the change. This is most likely the case with the orthographic neuter: the playful device of converting nouns into neuter has been in use for ages—in the 1960s, 1990s and 2000s. After the spread of Olbanian, however, speakers started using this device with increasing frequency, and, given that selective forces acting against the innovation were now less strong, it diffused rapidly. There was no "zero patient," no single "author" of the innovation. The idea was obvious enough, and many speakers started using it independently.

The identification and description of selective forces enable us to explain the observed changes, and, potentially, to predict which changes are likely to occur and which are not. Obviously, in order to pursue the ambitious goal of predicting changes, sociolinguists also have to achieve a better understanding of the mechanism of speaker innovations (to what extent are they random? can they be predicted?). Likewise, much remains unknown about the mechanism of innovation diffusion through social networks, although this is probably the most widely researched aspect of language change. The mechanism of selection, however, is of most importance, at least if one is interested in the role of CMC, the new communication channel, in linguistic change.

As is obvious from the discussion above, selective forces can be very heterogeneous and include cognitive factors, technological affordances, the structure of social networks and many other things. In this chapter, I offer neither a strict definition of selective force, nor a formalized way of describing it, confining myself to informal descriptions of the written turn in Russian.

The partial solution to the actuation problem, promised above, can be formulated as follows. *A particular change X can take place in a particular language at a given time because selective forces, which operate in a given language, in a given society and at a given time, and which play an important role in determining which speaker innovations will diffuse and which will not, promote particular speaker innovations, namely, those that can trigger the change X.*

One factor which affects how selective forces operate is the communication channel. As this chapter shows, some of the recent innovations in Russian were successfully actuated because of the availability of CMC. While the comparative analysis was not among the aims of this chapter, it is reasonable to expect that written turn is visible in other languages as well, and might be actuating similar changes.

## Acknowledgments

I am grateful to all the participants of the Future of Russian "F4" workshop (Bergen 2012) who participated in the discussion of this chapter, in particular to Sali Tagliamonte. This work also benefited from comments by Alexander Piperski and Arkadii Avdokhin.

## Notes

1 One argument in favor of their unimportance might be that they all come from written speech, and it is exactly this view that this chapter argues against. The focus of sociolinguistics on oral speech is understandable, but a sociolinguistics of writing is also required (cf. Sebba 2009; Lillis 2013).
2 Examples are quoted without any changes. Stress marks are added in the transliterated Russian where relevant. Deviations from the standard norm are not translated or commented on unless directly relevant to the discussion.
3 The claims relating to the acceptability of a particular spelling in standard written Russian are based not only on my intuition, but also on verification in the Russian National Corpus (ruscorpora.ru, which includes predominantly fiction and non-fiction books), the Integrum database of contemporary Russian press (integrumworld.com) and Google books (books.google.com). Details are not provided here for the sake of brevity.
4 Further exceptions can possibly be found in songs, but, even there, elongation of one and only one non-stressed vowel, if it is neither the first nor the last one, is unlikely.

5 It is important to keep in mind that *ia* and *iu* stand for letters *я* and *ю*, i.e. are pronounced as [ja] and [ju] and represent thus *one* syllable, not two.
6 For a detailed analysis of the innovation and the evidence for the causal link between its spread and CMC, see Berdichevskii (2012).
7 The difference is that Labov defines "a fork in the road" as an unstable situation when two routes are nearly equiprobable, and the choice depends on some "small forces."
8 It has to be noted that orthographic neuter is considerably less salient on a scale of mainland Russian than neuter-to-feminine conversion on a scale of American Russian.

## References


Aaron, P., and R. Malatesha Joshi. 2006. "Written Language Is as Natural as Spoken Language: A Biolinguistic Perspective." *Reading Psychology* 27: 263–311.

Andersen, Henning. 1989. "Understanding Linguistic Innovations." In *Language Change: Contributions to the Study of Its Causes*, edited by Leiv Egil Breivik and Ernst Håkon Jahr, 5–28. Berlin: Mouton de Gruyter.

Androutsopoulos, Jannis. 2009. " 'Greeklish': Transliteration Practice and Discourse in a Setting of Computer-Mediated Digraphia." In *Standard Languages and Language Standards: Greek, Past and Present*, edited by Alexandra Georgakopoulou and Michael Silk, 221–249. Farnham: Ashgate.

—— 2011a. "Language Change and Digital Media: A Review of Conceptions and Evidence." In *Standard Languages and Language Standards in a Changing Europe*, edited by Nikolas Coupland and Tore Kristiansen, 145–61. Oslo: Novus.

—— 2011b. "From Variation to Heteroglossia in the Study of Computer-Mediated Discourse." In *Digital Discourse: Language in the New Media*, edited by Crispin Thurlow, and Kristine Mroczek, 277–98. Oxford: Oxford University Press.

Baron, Naomi. 1984. "Computer Mediated Communication as a Force in Language Change." *Visible Language* 18(2): 118–41.

—— 2005. "The Written Turn." Review of *The English Writing System*, by Vivian Cook. *English Language and Linguistics* 9: 359–76.

Berdichevskii, Aleksandr. 2012. " 'Orfograficheskii' srednii rod: grammaticheskaia innovatsiia v iazyke russkogo Interneta." In *Variativnost' v iazyke i kommunikatsii*, edited by Liudmila Fedorova, 51–72. Moscow: RGGU.

Bloomfield, Leonard. 1933. *Language* (revised from 1914 edition). New York: Holt.

Cheshire, Jenny, David Agder, and Sue Fox. 2012. "Relative *Who* and the Actuation Problem." *Lingua*. doi 10.1016/j.lingua.2012.11.014 (accessed 9 January 2013).

Collot, Milena, and Nancy Belmore. 1996. "Electronic Language: A New Variety of English." In *Computer-Mediated Communication: Linguistic, Social and Cross-Cultural Perspectives*, edited by Susan Herring, 13–28. Amsterdam: Benjamins.

Croft, William. 2000. *Explaining Language Change: An Evolutionary Approach*. Harlow: Longman.

Dresner, Eli. 2005. "The Topology of Auditory and Visual Perception, Linguistic Communication, and Interactive Written Discourse." *Language@Internet* 2, article 2. Available at: http://www.languageatinternet.org/articles/2005/161 (accessed 23 January 2013).

Fahlman, Scott. ?2002. "Smiley Lore." http://www.cs.cmu.edu/smiley/history.html (accessed 20 January 2013).

Ferrara, Kathleen, Hans Brunner, and Greg Whittemore. 1991. "Interactive Written Discourse as an Emergent Register." *Written Communication* 8(1): 8–34.

Herring, Susan. 2003. "Media and Language Change: Introduction." *Journal of Historical Pragmatics* 4(1): 1–17.

—— 2012. "Grammar and Electronic Communication." In *The Encyclopedia of Applied Linguistics*, edited by Carol Chapelle. Hoboken, NJ: Wiley-Blackwell. Available at: http://onlinelibrary.wiley.com/book/10.1002/9781405198431 (accessed 20 January 2013).

Jones, Graham, and Bambi Schieffelin. 2009. "Enquoting Voices, Accomplishing Talk: Uses of be + like in Instant Messaging." *Language & Communication* 29: 77–113.

Ko, Kwang-Kyu. 1996. "Structural Characteristics of Computer-Mediated Language: A Comparative Analysis of InterChange Discourse." *Electronic Journal of Communication* 6(3). Available at: http://www.cios.org/www/ejc/v6n396.htm (accessed 8 April 2013).

Labov, William. 1972. *Sociolinguistic Patterns.* Philadelphia, PA: University of Pennsylvania Press.

—— 1994. *Principles of Linguistic Change, Internal Factors.* Hoboken, NJ: John Wiley & Sons, Ltd.

—— 2010. *Principles of Linguistic Change, Cognitive and Cultural Factors.* Hoboken, NJ: John Wiley & Sons, Ltd.

Lillis, Theresa. 2013. *The Sociolinguistics of Writing.* Edinburgh: Edinburgh University Press.

Maslova, Elena. 2008. "Unidirectionality of Grammaticalization in an Evolutionary Perspective." In *Studies on Grammaticalization*, edited by Elisabeth Verhoeven, Stavros Skopeteas, Yong-Min Shin, Yoko Nishina, Johannes Helmbrecht, 15–24. Berlin: Mouton de Gruyter.

Milroy, James, and Lesley Milroy. 1985. "Linguistic Change, Social Network and Speaker Innovation." *Journal of Linguistics* 21(2): 339–84.

Paolillo, John. 2001. "Language Variation on Internet Relay Chat: A Social Network Approach." *Journal of Sociolinguistics* 5(2): 180–213.

Polinsky, Maria. 2006. "Incomplete Acquisition: American Russian." *Journal of Slavic Linguistics* 14(2): 191–262.

Ross, Nigel. 2006. "Writing in the Information Age." *English Today* 22(3): 39–45.

Saussure, Ferdinand de. 2011. *Course in General Linguistics.* Translated by Wade Baskin, edited by Perry Meisel and Haun Saussy. New York: Columbia University Press.

Sebba, Mark. 2009. "Sociolinguistic Approaches to Writing Systems Research." *Writing Systems Research* 1(1): 35–49.

Tagliamonte, Sali. 2006. *Analysing Sociolinguistic Variation.* Cambridge: Cambridge University Press.

Tagliamonte, Sali, and Derek Denis. 2008. "Linguistic Ruin? LOL! Instant Messaging and Teen Language." *American Speech* 83(1): 3–34.

Trudgill, Peter. 2011. *Sociolinguistic Typology: Social Determinants of Linguistic Complexity.* Oxford: Oxford University Press.

Viktorova, M. 2008. "Emotivnyi aspekt prodleniia soglasnykh zvukov (na materiale pesen V. Vysotskogo i Zh. Brelia)." *Izvestiia Rossiiskogo gosudarstvennogo pedagogicheskogo universiteta imeni A. I. Gertsena* 60: 68–73.

Weinreich, Uriel, William Labov, and Marvin Herzog. 1968. *Empirical Foundations for a Theory of Language Change.* Austin: University of Texas Press.

Werry, Christopher. 1996. "Linguistic and Interactional Features of Internet Relay Chat." In *Computer-Mediated Communication: Linguistic, Social and Cross-Cultural Perspectives*, edited by Susan Herring, 47–61. Amsterdam: Benjamins.

Wolfram, Walt. 1991. "The Linguistic Variable: Fact and Fantasy." *American Speech* 66(1): 22–32.

Yates, Simeon. 1996. "Oral and Written Linguistic Aspects of Computer Conferencing: A Corpus Based Study." In *Computer-Mediated Communication: Linguistic, Social and Cross-Cultural Perspectives*, edited by Susan Herring, 29–46. Amsterdam: Benjamins.

Zimmer, Ben. 2007. "The Prehistory of Emoticons." *The Language Log*, September 21. Available at: http://itre.cis.upenn.edu/~myl/languagelog/archives/004935.html (accessed 13 January 2013).

Zitzen, Michaela, and Dieter Stein. 2004. "Chat and Conversation: A Case of Transmedial Stability?" *Linguistics* 42(5): 983–1021.

Zubova, Liudmila. 2010. "Ironicheskaia grammatika: srednii rod v igrovoi neologii." *Voprosy iazykoznaniia* 6: 16–25.

# 7 Slangs go online, or the rise and fall of the Olbanian language

*Aleksandrs Berdicevskis and Vera Zvereva*

## A. Olbanian in context[1]

The Russian Internet speaks with multiple voices: it is multilingual not only from the point of view of national languages, but also in the broader cultural sense. Offline subcultures, clubs and professional communities continue their lives in a digital space, while new groups with diverse interests emerge online. Quite a few of them have their own ideas on how best to observe grammatical rules and use the Russian language. The Internet absorbs different slangs, each of them with their own principles in terms of orthography, grammar and lexicon.

Thus, when they move online, groups that already exist bring their own words and expressions with them. At the same time, new digital communities on the Runet adjust the Russian language to their needs and produce slangs, introducing their linguistic innovations into daily practices.

This chapter looks at how users' attitudes towards linguistic norms relate to the emergence of new slangs in Runet communities. In two separate sections, we discuss the instructive case of the "Olbanian language."[2] This slang, originating in the narrow circle of early Runet users, gained mass popularity, and for a while claimed the role of the Russian language of new media. It also delivered a powerful blow to the idea of "sacred" literacy. This case allows us to study the phenomenon of linguistic fashion on the Internet, since the relatively rapid disappearance of *padonki* slang is no less noticeable than its rise. And yet its effect on Russian digital linguistic culture has been a lasting one.

### *Social and cultural background*

The linguistic environment of the Runet is not the same as it was ten years ago. Unlike the current situation, where there is a rich diversity of slang belonging to different communities, some years ago there reigned one dominant slang—"*padonki* language," which to very different groups of Russian-speaking web users seemed provocative and attractive. During the period 2004–2006, the *padonki* style of writing and communication attracted growing public attention. Both in new and old Russian media, it was considered a symbol of the Runet. Its main features included deliberately erroneous writing, in which a word's written form imitated its pronunciation, a large proportion of clichés, the use of low style and foul words, and the declarative denial of repressive literacy. This slang introduced a set of new words, expressions and memes into popular communication. Various groups of users endowed *padonki* language with different meanings. It was used for creative writing and everyday communication, online play and speech aggression, counter-cultural and mainstream speak, and as a tool of self-identification that made it possible to unite and subdivide different kinds of "us" and "them." It can be assumed that this semantic and functional flexibility is characteristic of a slang that is not "owned" by a particular social or sub-cultural group.

The Olbanian language emerged in the second half of the 1990s, when the Russian cyberspace was in the process of evolving into a new cultural territory, with its own regulations. The slang was shaped by several processes: removing the taboo on foul language in literature and media, working out a conventional vocabulary for computer-mediated communication and a pragmatic orthography suitable for instant textual exchange, and building online hierarchies that differentiated between various virtual groups.

In the 1990s, the so-called elite of the Russian Internet was formed (Kuznetsov 2004; Gornyi 1999). This circle included IT specialists, professional and amateur authors, and journalists. Even before the advent of blogs, writing became a fashionable online practice. It developed vigorously on the Runet's "people's resources" (*narodnye resursy*)—websites like Fuck.ru, Fuckru.net, and Udaff.com.[3] These sites allowed users to publish creative texts—short stories, poems and reviews of music and films (*kreativy*) and commentaries to these texts (*kamenty*).[4] The way in which Russian was altered on these websites was labeled *padonki* style, that is, the slang of uneducated "scumbags," who were trying to sound provocative and offensive to adherents of "pure Russian" and advocates of classical Russian literature.

What was in dispute was the language. Did users have to adhere to the established rules of the standard language? Both linguistic norms and "good manners" were declaratively canceled; in order to contrast their writings and speech with "normal" (i.e. boring and sanctimonious) Internet communication, *padonki* chose obscene topics and privileged erroneous orthography. "Padonki decided . . . to disfigure the 'regular Russian language' beyond recognition. In their version it turned into a *pravel'nyi Ruskei ezyk*. And they started calling each other nothing other than *pesatel'* and *chetatel'*" (Sokolovskii 2008: 13).

The emerging practice of writing and commenting was networked: it presupposed the rapid spread of approved models of successful texts, while users collectively acquired the attractive rules of *padonki* style. The slang was used not only for creative writing and communication, but also for self-positioning in terms of linguistic norms and cultural standards.

The authors of a text which was popular among Runet users, and proclaimed a *padonki* "reform" of the Russian language, stated:

> Order No.116 of the 26th of October 2005 (On the reform of the Russian language). In connection with the planned reduction in education funding, as well as the natural evolution of the Russian language, I encourage:
>
> 1 [sending] all norms of Russian orthography and grammar to Bobrujsk;

2 [throwing] all Russian language and literature textbooks into the oven;
3 all school and higher school teachers of Russian language and literature to take poison;
4 to entrust the further development of the Russian language to Fuck-it-institute.

(jack_patterson 2006)[5]

The online spread of *padonki* slang resembles the patterns by which fashionable samples spread (Blumer 1969). Extremely popular within a community of *k&k* resources in the late 1990s, the *padonki* style was regarded as the plaything of the Runet's "old users," and added to this group's symbolic prestige. The appropriation of this fashionable sample by regular Internet users outside the realm of *k&k* sites made its trendy creators less interested. For newcomers, however, the real excitement around this slang was still just beginning.

The popular blogging platform LiveJournal played a crucial role in the mass spread of the Olbanian language. In 2003, when LiveJournal canceled special invitations and became open to everyone, thousands of Russian users rushed into this new space. There they found "elite" or "old users," already tired of linguistic games. The newcomers, however, started playing with the *padonki* slang, which was often interpreted as a set of ready-made clichés. There began a mass reproduction of posts and comments.

The years 2004–06 saw a peak of interest in Olbanian, both on the Runet and in offline culture. On the Runet there were heated debates between supporters and opponents of erroneous orthography. A series of articles in magazines and newspapers drew further attention to this issue (Vernidub 2005; Subbotin 2006; Vil'ianov 2006). By this time—as we will demonstrate in the second part of this chapter—the "true" *padonki*, who had promoted this slang in the late 1990s, had almost ceased using it. But for the mass audience, the wave was at its peak. For many users this slang was known as "Olbanian language." This name was coined in 2004 (though the Internet meme "learn Albanian," which meant "before speaking to us, learn essential things," existed in the 1990s). The term cropped up in the midst of comments on a Russian LiveJournal post, when an English-speaking user expressed his indignation about the "unknown" language and attracted a series of mocking responses from Russian bloggers urging him to "learn Albanian."[6] In 2006, the apotheosis of the *padonki* style coincided with the explosion of the "Medved" meme ("Medved" 2013). The Russian translation of John Lurie's picture "Bear Surprise" on the collective blog Dirty.ru employed the formulation "Preved!," which was followed by "Medved," "Krosavcheg," "Kagdila?," etc. This image, together with associated *padonki*-stylized formulations, provoked a multitude of jokes, reinterpretations, pictures and texts, in which users exercised their Olbanian skills.

In 2006 and 2008, when presidents Putin and Medvedev held internet conferences, Runet users employed Olbanian to pose some of the top questions. Thus, the *padonki* slang gained new meaning in the context of Russian political culture (Internet-konferentsiia 2007).

Between 2008 and 2010, public interest in the Olbanian language waned, the slang went out of fashion and discussions about it subsided. Only a few recent literary texts written in Olbanian can be found on the Runet. *Padonki* slang is no longer an attribute of a group that can oppose itself to "the others" by means of its use. However, its elements—erroneous orthography and some of its formulations—have been widely integrated into the daily linguistic practices of Runet users.

## *Uses of the Olbanian language*

### *A convenient language*

*Padonki* slang was regarded by many users as an adaptation of the Russian language to the possibilities and demands of new media communication. Those who used to spend a great deal of time online were attracted by the convenient spelling of Olbanian, which made it possible for virtual interlocutors to avoid the constraints of formal rules. *Padonki* slang was praised for the sense of intimacy and immediacy it lent to communication.

### *Opposition to the norm*

In their discussions of Olbanian, people often said they were tired of linguistic norms supported by "repressive" institutions. Users dreamed of the Internet as a free space, where they could do anything, at least in terms of everyday communicative practices. The easiest way to create an unofficial atmosphere in blogs and fora was a demonstrative violation of the normative orthography, perhaps as a compensation for their conformity in "real life."

> I write rather serious texts on politics and economics: it's my job. I am SICK of the correct spelling; I want to have a rest and to act like a hooligan. *"Paetamu ia idu na forum i peshu kak bog na dushu palozhyt."* [That's why I go to a forum and write any old way.]
>
> (N.n. 2006)

On the one hand, *padonki*, the creators of the slang, claimed that the opportunity to reject the norms of the standard language was a special counter-cultural virtue. On the other hand, common users practiced Olbanian without identifying with the *padonki* group, but simply demonstrating their desire to be liberated from the restrictions of the predominant linguistic culture.

### *Writing creatively*

For some users, deliberate errors in the words stressed their own human nature. Blind adherence to the standard language was considered to be robotic. Meanwhile, the ability to invent new words and to modify norms was seen as an art.

> Manifesto Against Literacy. We are fundamentally opposed to so-called "literacy" on the Internet . . . With the improvement in computer spell-checkers, the Russian language will lose even more of its spontaneity and charm. Therefore, all the artists of the Russian word must defy the murder of our living language by soulless machines! The main principle of our great movement, POST-CYBER, says: "The real art of the new millennium is what a computer cannot do, and only a human can do it!"
>
> (Meri Shelli 1999)[7]

The Olbanian language was thus understood as the invention of the "giants" of the new literature. The supporters of this position valued witty transformations of the orthography, as well as creative ways of avoiding spelling one and the same word in one and the same manner. In this way, choosing to use Olbanian was an attempt to compete for the readers' recognition. Creative vs imitative uses of *padonki* style allowed the establishment of a hierarchy of Runet writers.

### *The true Russian vs the anti-Russian language*

The Olbanian language was used by supporters of different ideological positions. Some of the proponents of nationalist movements spoke of the "anti-patriotic" nature of this slang. According to them, the Russian language, preserved by means of grammatical rules, was a profound expression of the national spirit; any mocking attitude towards the norms of the Russian language was therefore seen as "anti-Russian." In this context, *padonki* slang was read as a manifestation of the general decline of the great cultural traditions:

> In my opinion, this is a case where simplicity is worse than stealing . . . "Olbanian" produces a change in thinking. [This is] of the same nature as the visible changes in the language. That is—nihilistic and destructive in terms of culture.
>
> (Kazerskii 2008)

At the same time, other proponents of anti-Western views advanced an alternative interpretation. They viewed *padonki* slang as a natural protection of the Russian Internet from foreigners, to whom it was "not given" to understand the subtleties of the Russian language and grasp the irony contained in the denial of linguistic norms.[8]

### *Supporters of common sense*

Despite the fact that a certain protective attitude toward the Russian language was widely represented on the Runet, the majority of users believed that the new slang was not a genuine threat to Russian culture. First, it was seen as a temporary passion; even in the periods of greatest indulgence in *padonki* games, there were many voices predicting the end of this fashion cycle:

> I agree that language always develops and "medveds-preveds," and all Olbanian literature illustrates it. However, all these "Olbanisms" will pass, and rather quickly; people will get bored and start inventing something new.
>
> (Vzhdanov 2006)

To others, modifications of the Russian language seemed to be part of a common process of linguistic development:

> Community "write right": "Here it is—a community for anyone who is not indifferent to the fate of the Russian Language. Remember that the Russian language is not a frozen monolith, although it has absolute rules; it is a living, breathing, moving and changing organism."[9]
>
> (Peshu_pravellno 2004)

Here, linguistic changes were seen as natural and dependent on the cultural context; the boundaries of the norm were transparent; and it was important to update lexicon and spelling regardless of the concrete sources of and reasons for this transformation.

*Intellectual slang vs illiterate language*

The most popular debates about the Olbanian language focused on the cultural competence or otherwise of the slang's proponents. Were they intellectuals who had perfect grammar and had appropriated the right to break the norms? Or were they, on the contrary, "illiterate idiots?" The self-representation combined these extremes. The founders of *padonki* slang stressed its democratic potential: everyone had the right to be an author and to ignore the rules. At the same time, they emphasized the differences between the "real scumbags" and the imitators, who were masking their own ignorance.

Users who doubted their own competence in literacy exploited the rhetoric that praised the *padonki* for their love of freedom. Not knowing how to write correctly, they exaggerated the erroneousness of the spelling:

> It happens that sometimes I communicate with teenagers . . . As they, for some reason, cannot write competently, they commit errors DELIBERATELY, in order to use the "fashionable" language as a cover for their ignorance. For example, I found a word in an ICQ message: "vyzdOravlEvaii". As we can see, two letters have been selected. "O" is the correct letter, but the person is not sure . . .; however, "E" is obviously wrong.
>
> (Stass 2006)

Others were indignant that the symbolic capital of "anti-literacy" was shared unequally: their view was that, despite the exercises of the intellectuals, the winners were those who could hide their ignorance among intentional mistakes. In articulating this claim, these users presented themselves as truly competent people who were insulted by "unpunished" erroneous writing.

*Counter-culture vs mainstream*

As the Olbanian language began to spread among Runet users, some participants of the early communities on Udaff.com and connected websites tried to claim primacy and spoke of the counter-cultural nature of this slang. There were also disputes about the "*Padonki* Manifesto" written by a collective of authors on Udaff.com in 2001. This lengthy text contained a set of regulations which related to multiple social situations. "Scumbags" were presented as a group with a certain system of views and attitudes toward society. In this representation, they were protesting against the System, and their slang expressed these protest meanings:

> Padonok, as a fighter for a civilized society without the population being duped, first of all carries the cumulative charge of destruction, targeted at the System. The main purpose of a padonok is to be free . . . Padonok is a life-style, an inner state of mind. Cynicism and mockery of the reality—those are the distinctive qualities of a padonok.
>
> (Idiolag nakh, Pachti Doktar 2001)

Initially, however, this slang did not revolve around the idea of counter-cultural resistance; this idea was introduced later. Most of Olbanian's adherents were opposed neither to the authorities nor to the lifestyle of the middle class. Their shared protest was directed mainly against the routine of everyday life. In the second half of the 2000s, users talked bitterly of the transformation of Olbanian into the mainstream language of mass culture, the inclusion of the language's top authors in the commercial industry of popular literature, and the appropriation of formulations by advertising, consumer culture and political propaganda.

## *After Olbanian*

The trend for *padonki* slang came in two waves: the first reached its peak in 2001, in the very community where it had been developed and promoted since the 1990s. The second wave, which rose in 2006 with the "Medved" meme, attracted mass users. It was this second wave that triggered the rapid spread of Olbanian, which, in turn, caused the fracturing of different sub-communities, each seeking to protect its own version of the slang.

By the early 2010s, *padonki* slang had come to be viewed as being outdated. While some elements still enjoyed common usage, their origins had come to be largely forgotten:

*@norguhtar:* AAAAAAAATLIChNAAA
*@kaliy:* this is not the first time I have come across such an entry. where does it come from?

*@norguhtar:* I can't remember, but, as far as I can tell, from the *padonki* language.

(Kaliy 2013)

Though violations of the linguistic norm still outrage many Runet users, many have taken delivery of the message: erratic spelling is a sign of convenient and informal digital communication. "The most important thing is not to write correctly, but to write so that people can understand the meaning of what is written!"[10] Olbanian has legitimized irregularities that users insert randomly into their everyday Internet discourse.[11]

## B. Diachrony of Olbanian

### *Linguistic background*

One of the many possible ways of spelling the name of the slang in question is *йазык падонкафф/iazýk padónkaff*, while the only standard spelling would be *язык подонков/iazýk podónkov*. Let us briefly review the deviations from the standard norm in the former variant, in order to obtain some insight into the essence of this phenomenon.

The letter *я* (*ia*) denotes a combination of two phonemes, /ja/, which means that the erratic, two-letter combination *йа* (*i+a*) is actually pronounced in the same way. Three out of four deviations in the second word are of a similar type. The pronunciation of the word *подонков/podónkov* can be transcribed as [padónkaf].[12] Phonemes /o/ and /a/ are distinct only in stressed position, while in an unstressed syllable both are realized as a reduced vowel, which in the given phonetic contexts is close to [a]. Phoneme /v/, as with all paired voiced consonants, is devoiced at the end of the word and pronounced as [f].

These deviations follow the phonetic principle "write as you hear." The standard orthography, however, often ignores that principle in favor of a principle which can be labeled as *phonemic*—"write an underlying phoneme," or *morphemic*—"write in a way that retains the most consistent spelling of morphs across different word forms" (on the principles of Russian orthography, see Kniazev and Pozharitskaia 2012: 376–86).

The remaining erratic spelling, *фф/ff* instead of *ф/f*, is somewhat different. Just like the others, it does not change the pronunciation of the word: double consonants in this position sound as a single one in normal speech. It cannot, however, be said to follow the "write what you hear" principle, rather the opposite one: "write *not* what you hear, but what would sound the same." One hears [f], not [ff] in *падонкафф/padónkaff*, so the spelling does not approach pronunciation, but in fact moves away from it.

This introduction provides some insight into the spirit of the Olbanian language: the violation of linguistic norms, predominantly the norms of orthography, most often by following the principle "write as you hear." Some deviations also concern phonology and morphology, but they are marginal compared to those that relate to orthography (see Sebba 2003, for an overview of the cases where violation of orthographic norms manifests a rebellion spirit). Another distinctive feature of Olbanian is the active use of clichés. Some of these clichés contain words that have not existed previously or have acquired new meaning (see Guseinov 2005, for a brief wordlist with explanations), but for the most part they also depend heavily on anti-orthography to make them visible and distinguishable.

This triggers the question of whether Olbanian is indeed a *slang*. Eble (1996: 11) defines slang as "an ever changing set of colloquial words and phrases that speakers use to establish or reinforce social identity or cohesiveness within a group or with a trend or fashion in society at large." Lighter (1994: xi) offers the following working definition (which, in his own view, is not fully adequate, since it fails to take the social dimension into account): "an informal, nonstandard, nontechnical vocabulary composed chiefly of novel-sounding symbols for standard words and phrases." The latter is rather close to Halliday's (1976) notion of *anti-language*. Note that Halliday (1976: 571) also considers relexicalization ("new words for old") to be a basic means of creating an anti-language, although he acknowledges that foregrounding of certain nonstandard elements also occurs at other levels, such as the phonological, lexicogrammatical and semantic.

In our case, the level which conveys most of the *anti* spirit is orthography. Relexicalizing a word usually means rewriting it using Olbanian orthographical (anti-) conventions. The increased importance of orthography is unsurprising, given the general trend in modern language culture towards both greater autonomy and greater salience for written language (see Chapter 6 by Berdicevskis, in this volume). Another widely-known idiom that manifests its slang-like nature primarily through the distortion of writing system is leet speak (see, e.g., Blashki and Nichol 2005). Just like Olbanian, it has some distinctive features on other levels, including lexical clichés, and it has also emerged online. In some other respects, however, it is noticeably different.

The role of Olbanian within the Russian-speaking community is quite close to that of slang, and so *orthographical slang* (or anti-language) seems to be an appropriate label for it.

Olbanian has received a fair amount of linguistic attention (Guseinov 2005; Krongauz 2008; Shapovalova 2007; Zvereva 2009, not to mention numerous articles in the mass media and a self-description [Sokolovskii 2008]). The late Daniela Hristova (2011) offered the most detailed linguistic description to date. When it comes to diachronic descriptions, however, what is available is mostly speculation.

Studies of slang diachrony have never been frequent, and this is understandable, given that slangs usually do not "fossilize," or leave a written record, at least not one that is easily accessible. In CMC, the situation with data availability is much better, but still, as Androutsopoulos (2011: 150) notes, "[T]here is a striking lack of systematic micro-diachronic studies within CMC. While the implicit assumption seems to be that digital language innovations are here to stay, 'rise and fall' patterns are just as possible." Some diachronic studies of language in CMC, however, can be mentioned, cf. Herring (1998), and Rowe (2011).

Returning to the phrase *йазык падонкафф / iazýk padónkaff*, we can see that here the anti-normative spirit manifests itself five times in the space of two short words. Producing and perceiving texts with so many deviations can be quite difficult, and Krongauz (2008) assumes that, while the original core principle was to violate the norm as many times as possible, this standard, in fact, turned out to be unreachable and eroded with time, and it became enough to make at least some errors. This assumption seems plausible. Regardless of whether it is actually true, there is a common view that Olbanian has already passed its peak and in recent years has been dying out, probably as a result of a simple fading of the fashion. This, however, is an intuitive impression that has never been empirically verified, and the exact dates of alleged peaks and troughs are unknown, although it is usually assumed that public interest towards the slang peaked in 2004–2006 (see above).

In this section, we aim to verify the existing intuitive assumptions about the diachrony of the Olbanian language, both within the community of its active users (experiment 1) and outside it (experiment 2), thus extending our understanding of how an online slang can develop. We will focus on the behavior of one parameter that provides crucial information about the status of the slang and is easily measurable—the frequency of the actual usage of the slang's distinctive linguistic features. In the case of Olbanian, this means the frequency of norm violations, predominantly of erratic spellings.

## *Experiment 1*

All the data were taken from the website Udaff.com (as mentioned above, it is the center of *padonki* culture and one of the cradles of the Olbanian language), from the section *kreativy* ("creative stories"), where users upload their own short stories. This is one of the oldest and most important sections on the website, and its name is a symbol of *padonki* culture. It was chosen as the largest and most diachronically representative collection of texts (a) with a large number of erratic spellings; and (b) written by people who identify themselves as *padonki*, i.e. "native speakers" of Olbanian. It should be kept in mind, however, that these data do not necessarily reflect patterns of use of the Olbanian language elsewhere.

Texts were selected from 975 webpages covering the time period from January 2001 to December 2011. One text was selected randomly from each page (each page contained 50 texts), and a random fragment of 100 words was extracted for analysis. If a text was for some reason not suitable for analysis (e.g. it was shorter than 100 words), another random text was selected.

This resulted in 975 100-word fragments produced by 729 authors (156 authors produced more than one text, the largest number of texts per author was 9, the mean was 1.34). No adjustment was made for the fact that some authors had more than one fragment included in the sample: while this gives their idiolect additional chances to contribute to the observed variation, that must mirror the actual situation. For every word, it was noted how many deviations from the norm it contained.[13] All kinds of deviations were counted, and not all of them are strictly Olbanian. However, the analysis of distribution of deviations across different types (Berdicevskis 2013) shows that the number of indisputably non-Olbanian deviations is relatively small and constant and does not distort the general picture.

Results are shown in Figure 7.1. It can be seen that there is a sharp decrease in frequency from 2001 to 2002 and then a gradual decrease from 2002 to 2011. In 2001, the general trend is to sprinkle one's text with deviations. On average, there are not so many (the median lies rather low down), but some texts contain a fair

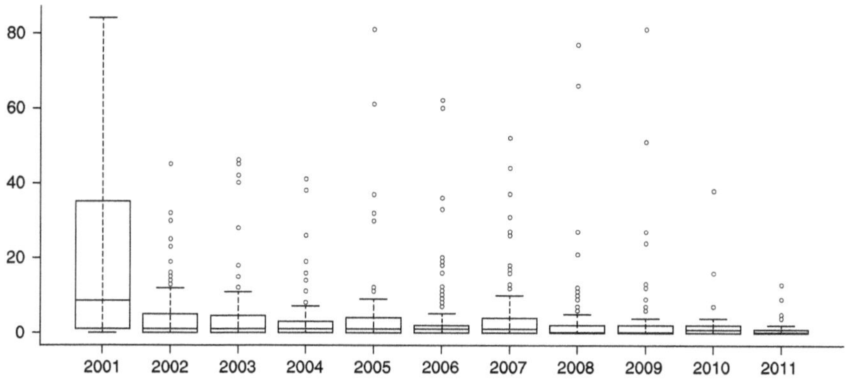


*Figure 7.1* Frequency of use of the Olbanian language on the Udaff.com website (*kreativy* section): number of deviations from the norm per 100 words.*

Note:

* This a boxplot, or a box-and-whiskers plot. Since some readers may be unfamiliar with it, I am providing a brief explanation of what it is and how it should be interpreted. For each year, several dozens of text fragments (from 34 in 2001 to 142 in 2007) were analyzed, which provides us with 11 *distributions* of data points. Each point is a number of deviations in a text fragment. The boxplot uses *five-number* summary to represent a numerical distribution visually. The black horizontal line is the *median* (half of the observations lie above this point and half lie below, this is the middle of the dataset). The box in the middle indicates the "core" of the distribution (technically speaking, the horizontal edges of the box are hinges, which are almost equivalent to upper and lower quartiles). The length of the box makes it possible to estimate how *dispersed* the distribution is (the longer the box, the higher the dispersion), the position of the median within it indicates whether the distribution is *skewed* (in Figure 7.1, for instance, the median lies close to the lower edge, which means that there are more texts with a small number of deviations than with a high number). Whiskers indicate the range within which all the observations are expected to fall (technically, they show the largest or smallest value within a distance that is 1.5 times the box size from the nearest hinge). Dots that lie beyond the whiskers are data points considered *outliers*, observations that strongly deviate from other members of the sample. Informally speaking, these are the points which can be considered "unusual."

number (the upper edge of the box is high, and the upper whisker is sky-high). There are, however, no outliers: even the texts saturated with deviations can still be said to fall within the general trend. Starting from 2002, the median lies much lower down, the box size and the whisker range are smaller and continue to decrease over a period of years. Some authors still produce texts rich in deviations, but these texts are rare now, they are outliers, and even their number falls noticeably towards the end of the period.

## *Experiment 2*

The data from *kreativy*, used in experiment 1, tell us nothing about the use of the Olbanian language outside the Udaff.com community (moreover, even in the other sections of the website, the diachronic patterns may be different), and it is interesting to know what happens on a broader scale. For that purpose, a "Pulse of the blogosphere" service offered by Yandex, a major Russian search engine, was used.[14] "Pulse" indexes a significant part of the Russian blogosphere and returns a share of all the blog posts that were written within a given month (starting from June 2001) and contain a given search query (that is, a word or a phrase).

To select a number of appropriate queries, the following was done. During experiment 1, a list of all the word forms containing deviations from the norm was compiled. The list contained 3,109 word forms. To constitute a good query, a word had to meet the following criteria: (a) an average monthly frequency of occurrence within the blogosphere of at least 100 blog posts (otherwise "Pulse" did not provide reliable results); and (b) to be the result of using specifically Olbanian slang and not committing a random error or allowing deliberate norm violations for other reasons. To narrow the list down, only forms which had been classified as containing exactly three deviations from the norm were selected (those which contained more were likely to violate condition (a), those which contained less were likely to violate condition (b). The remaining forms were manually checked to satisfy conditions (a) and (b).

This procedure resulted in ten words: *исчо/ischó* "more, yet" (from *ещё/eshché*), *ниибет/niibét* "I am not concerned" (from *не ебёт/ne ebét*,[15] literally "this does not fuck [me]"), *канешна/kanéshna* "of course" (from *конечно/konéchno*), *штоле/shtóle* "or what?" (from *что ли/chtó li*), *йопт/iopt*, profane interjection (derived in a somewhat unclear way from the verb *ебать/ebat'* "to fuck"), *нимагу/nimagú* "I cannot" (from *не могу/ne mogú*), *апстену/apsténu* "against the wall" (from *об стену/ob sténu*), *ниибаца/niibátsa*, *ниибацца/niibátstsa* "very" (from *не ебаться/ne ebát'sia*, literally "not to fuck"), *беспезды/bespezdý* "certainly, honestly" (from *без пизды/bez pizdý*, literally "without a cunt"). Some of these words are parts of frequent clichés (e.g. *убиться апстену/ubít'sia apsténu* "kill oneself against the wall"), but this fact was not taken into account. It is assumed that the frequency of use of these ten words can serve as a proxy for estimating the general popularity of the Olbanian slang. Results are shown in Figure 7.2. The pattern is noticeably different from that observed in Figure 7.1: here, the frequency peaks in 2006 with a gradual increase in preceding years and gradual decrease (nearly to extinction) in subsequent years.

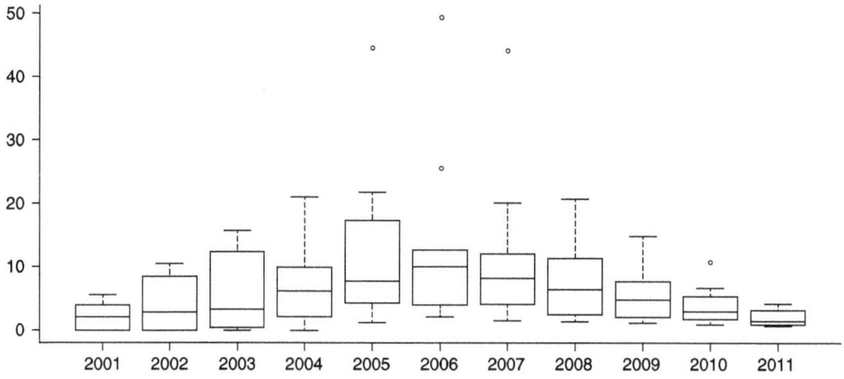


*Figure 7.2* Frequency of use of the Olbanian language in the Russian blogosphere: ratio of the number of blog posts where a query word occurs to the total number of blog posts in the given year; per mille. For each year, the frequency was calculated as the arithmetic mean of frequencies for all 12 months (apart from 2001, for which the data are available only starting from June). The query words were the ten words from the selected set.

To test whether the observed differences are indeed due to the different data source (Udaff.com vs. blogosphere) and not the measuring method (number of deviations in text fragments vs. frequency of a few erratically spelled words), the same method was applied to all the *kreativy* available on Udaff.com (i.e. the population from which the data for experiment 1 were sampled). Results are shown in Figure 7.3. The pattern is very similar to that observed in Figure 7.1, although the decrease after 2001 is more gradual. Thus, the results of experiment 1 are confirmed.[16]

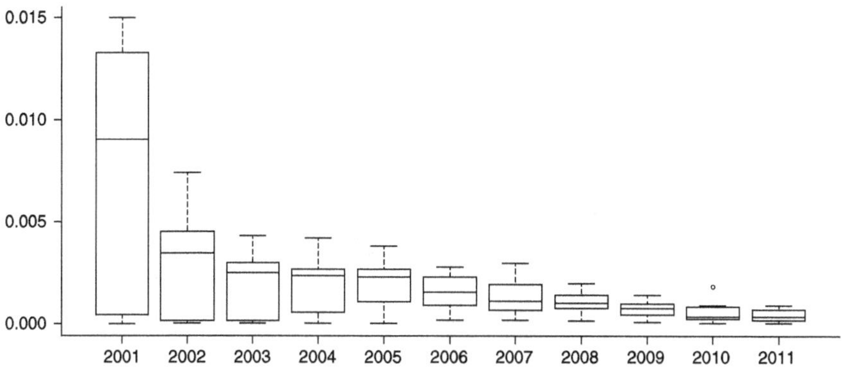


*Figure 7.3* Frequency of use of the Olbanian language on the Udaff.com website (*kreativy* section): weighted frequency of the ten selected words, calculated as the mean number of their occurrences divided by the size of the text file containing all the *kreativy* for the given year.

### *Discussion*

The common view that the Olbanian language has fallen out of fashion is confirmed by both experiments: in 2011, the frequency of deliberate norm violations falls to almost zero. It is, however, unlikely that the decrease in frequency after 2001, observed in Figures 7.1 and 7.3, is a result of the same extinction process. In 2002, Olbanian is still a fashionable new practice. The more plausible explanation for this decline is offered by Krongauz's (2008) insight that, after toying extensively with new anti-orthographical devices, speakers start using them more economically and in a more symbolic way. It is somewhat surprising that this happens so early, just a year after the Udaff.com website was created and the slang began gaining prominence.

The observation that public interest in Olbanian peaked in 2004–2006 fits in with the results of experiment 2, although Figure 7.2 suggests that the heightened interest lasted for a longer period, 2004–2008, with a peak in 2006. In any case, it is noteworthy that speakers *inside* and *outside* the Olbanian community use anti-normative devices most actively in different periods. Interestingly, the absolute number of texts in the *kreativy* section of the Udaff.com website also undergoes a rather gradual increase and decrease, with a peak in 2007 (see Figure 7.4). It is difficult, however, to tell whether this is the consequence of the increased public interest or the cause. In any case, at Udaff.com, there is no upsurge in the frequency of deviations from the norm.

The early-year decrease is less steep in Figure 7.3 than in Figure 7.1. This can probably be attributed to the method of measurement: as I mentioned earlier, some of the ten words selected are part of oft-used cliché, and thus their frequency can fall in a more gradual way and exhibit less variation. Interestingly, at the end, it also approaches zero. Thus, the data do not support the common view that Olbanian, while nearly extinct, has been survived by a number of clichés.

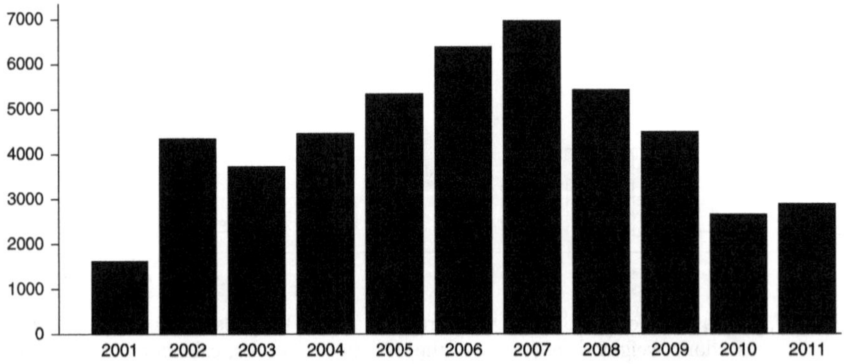


*Figure 7.4* Number of texts per year in the *kreativy* section of the Udaff.com website.

## Conclusion

The conclusions about how typical or atypical the development of Olbanian was are necessarily limited, since, as was mentioned above, there is very little systematic research on slang diachrony. We are aware of no data that would make it possible to carry out a comparison of Olbanian with another online slang, or, more interestingly, with an offline one. In the absence of such data (but with the hope that someday they will be collated, at least for relatively accessible online slangs), only some preliminary observations can be made. First, we witness the increased role of writing and orthography. It was the denial of orthography and its norms that gave birth to the Olbanian language and has been the main source of relexicalization. Second, the online processes happen with remarkable speed. Again, in the absence of reliable data it is impossible to claim that they are slower in offline slangs, but it is still impressive that a very salient idiom can go through a rise-and-fall cycle in less than two decades.

As regards the popularity of Olbanian outside the *padonki* community, it might have been the rise that precipitated the fall. The end of the fashion was probably connected not only with the boredom induced by the endless copying of *padonki* formulations, but also with the fact that the slang, having become too widespread, ceased to operate as a tool of separation of certain groups from the others.

The mass spread of *padonki* elements and the increase in public attention in the mid-2000s provoked discussions about the possible long-lasting influences of this slang on the Russian language as a whole. Nevertheless, the life-cycle of Olbanian ended without leaving any notable linguistic traces in the offline language. The Olbanian language did have some long-lasting effect on the linguistic practices of speakers of Russian, but in a less direct way. In spite of the fading of interest in *padonki* slang, the mass participation of users in this linguistic game has established a general consensus as to the right of any user to break the rules of orthography. Olbanian has changed attitudes to linguistic norms. As a result, the principle of conscious distortion or simple neglect of linguistic norms, without making references to *padonki* sub-culture, became massively popular.

## Notes

1 Vera Zvereva is the author of part A, "Olbanian in Context," and Aleksandrs Berdicevskis is the author of part B, "Diachrony of Olbanian." Conclusion was written jointly.
2 In this chapter, we use the terms *Olbanian* and *padonki language* (*iazyk padonkov*) entirely interchangeably, although some researchers (e.g. Hristova 2011) endow these terms with different meanings.
3 Fuck.ru (fuck.ru), Fuckru (fuckru.net), Udaff.com (udaff.com).
4 Subsequently, sites that enabled users to post *kreativy* and *kamenty* were called *k&k* resources.
5 This text (like several texts quoted below) is written in Olbanian slang.

> Прекас № 116 от 28 актибря 2005 (О риформи рускава йазыка): Фсвязи с плановым сакрощением фенонсиравонийа аброзаваннийа и истественной ывалйуцыей рускава йазыка призывайу: 1. Фсе правела рускай арфаграфии и громатеки – в Бобруйск. 2. Фсе учепники рускава йазыка и лейтеротуры— фтопку. 3. Фсем учетилям рускава йазыка и лейтеротуры школ и вузов—

выпеть йаду. 4. Дольнейжее розвитее рускава йазыка паручить энстетутам НИИ БАЦА и НИИ БЕТ.

(*Prekas № 116 ot 28 aktibria 2005 (O riformi ruskava iazyka): Fsviazi s planovym sakroshcheniem fenonsiravoniia abrozavanniia i istestvennoi yvaliutsyei ruskava iazyka prizyvaiu: 1. Fse pravela ruskai arfagrafii i gromateki—v Bobruisk. 2. Fse uchepniki ruskava iazyka i leiterotury—ftopku. 3. Fsem uchetiliam ruskava iazyka i leiterotury shkol i vuzov—vypet' iadu. 4. Dol'neizhee rozvitee ruskava iazyka paruchit' enstetutam NII BATsA i NII BET.*)

6 By 2012 this thread has been saved as a "historical" one: see http://onepamop.livejournal.com/240305.html?thread=2070193#t2070193 (accessed 13 April 2013).

7

МАНИФЕЗД АНТИГРАМАТНАСТИ.Мы прынцыпиально протиф так называимай "граматнасти" в Сити . . . Па мери савиршенства кампютырных спилчекирав руский изык ишо болще патеряит сваих нипасредствиннасти и абаяния. Паэтому все художники рускава слова далжны бросить вызав убиванию нашива живова изыка биздушными автаматами! Галавный Принцып нашева великава движения ПОСТ-КИБЕР гаварит: "настаящие исскувство новава тысичулетия—это то что ни можыт делать кампютыр, а можыт делать тока чилавек!!!"

(*MANIFEZD ANTIGRAMATNASTI My pryntsypial'no protif tak nazyvaimai "gramatnasti" v Siti . . . Pa meri savirshenstva kampiutyrnykh spilchekirav ruskii izyk isho bolshche pateriait svaikh nipasredstvinnasti i abaianiia. Paetomu vse khudozhniki ruskava slova dalzhny brosit' vyzav ubivaniiu nashiva zhivova izyka bizdushnymi avtamatami! Galavnyi Printsyp nasheva velikava dvizheniia POST-KIBER gavarit: "nastaiashchie isskuvstvo novava tysichuletiia—eto to chto ni mozhyt delat' kampiutyr, a mozhyt delat' toka chilavek!!!"*)

8 Supporters of this point of view stated their case in the flash mobs "Learn Olbanian" and "Madonna, learn Olbanian!" ("Zhargon padonkov" 2013; N.n. 2005).

9

И, вот, ано—Со-обсщество для всех каму неравно душна сутьба Рускага Езыка. Помните што, Руский Езык это—незастывшый, маналитъ хатя он и имеит обсалютные правелла но, он жывой дышащийся шевелящий и, из-мяняющщий аргонизм.

(*I, vot, ano—So-obsshchestvo dlia vsekh kamu neravno dushna sut'ba Ruskaga Ezyka. Pomnite shto, Ruskii Ezyk eto—nezastyvshyi, manalit" khatia on i imeit obsaliutnye pravella no, on zhyvoi dyshashchiisia sheveliashchii i, iz-mianiaiushchshchii argonizm.*)

10 Самае главное ни правильно песать,а писать так,читобы понять смысл написаного! (*Samae glavnoe ni pravil'no pesat',a pisat' tak,chitoby poniat' smysl napisanogo!*) (Mansur 2012).

11 E.g.: тебе природа подсовывает всяко разно,а ты берешь только то,что нравицца именно тебе; (*tebe priroda podsovyvaet vsiak**o** razn**o**,a ty beresh' tol'ko to,chto nravi**tstsa** imenno tebe*); ("the nature palms off various things, but you take what you like"). (Julia 2013). нихачу пока в Мск . . . а то сегодня полдня мечтала вслух, что надо бы собраться на недельку и повидаться . . . (***nikhachu** poka v Msk . . . a to segodnia poldnia mechtala vslukh, chto nado by sobrat'sia na nedel'ku i povidat'sia . . .*; ("I do not want to Moscow yet . . . though I've been dreaming out loud a half of the day that it would be good to go for a week as well as to see everybody . . ."), (lesqualita 2013).

12 A simplified transcription is used, IPA would be [pɐdónkəf].

13 The coding was carried out by two research assistants (linguists and native speakers of Russian) and AB. We are grateful to Alexander Piperski and Liudmila Zaydelman for doing the majority of the coding-and-counting work.

14 http://blogs.yandex.ru/pulse/. Standard Internet search engines are notoriously imprecise with year-specific search queries, but since "Pulse" was created especially for diachronic studies, the hope is that it can be more reliable.

15 The spelling of *e* instead of *ë* is allowed by the norm.
16 Note that Figures 7.1, 7 2, and 7.3 all measure different things, so one cannot make any meaningful direct comparison of absolute numbers provided in them. It only makes sense to compare diachronic trends.

## References


Androutsopoulos, Jannis. 2011. "Language Change and Digital Media: A Review of Conceptions and Evidence." In *Standard Languages and Language Standards in a Changing Europe*, edited by Kristiansen Tore and Nikolas Coupland, 145–61. Oslo: Novus.

Berdicevskis, Aleksandrs. 2013. Language Change Online: Linguistic Innovations in Russian Induced by Computer-Mediated Communication. PhD diss., University of Bergen.

Blashki, Katherine, and Sophie Nichol. 2005. "Game Geek's Goss: Linguistic Creativity in Young Males within an Online University Forum (94/\/\3 933k'5 9055oneone)." *Australian Journal of Emerging Technologies and Society* 3(2): 77–86.

Blumer, Herbert. 1969. "Fashion: From Class Differentiation to Collective Selection." *Sociological Quarterly* 10(3): 275–91.

Eble, Connie. 1996. *Slang and Sociability: In-group Language among College Students*. Chapel Hill: The University of North Carolina Press.

Gornyi, Evgenii. 1999. *Letopis' russkogo Interneta: 1990–1999*. Available at: http://www.netslova.ru/gorny/rulet/ (accessed 1 October 2008).

Guseinov, Gasan. 2005. "Berloga vebloga: vvedenie v erraticheskuiu semantiku." *Govorim po-russki*. Available at: http://www.speakrus.ru/gg/microprosa_erratica-1.htm (accessed 12 April 2013).

Halliday, M.A.K. 1976. "Anti-Languages." *American Anthropologist* 78(3): 570–84.

Herring, Susan. 1998. "Le style du courrier électronique: variabilité et changement." *Terminogramme* 84–85: 9–16. English version at http://ella.slis.indiana.edu/~herring/term.html (accessed 23 January 2013).

Hristova, Daniela S. 2011. "Velikii i moguchii olbanskii iazyk: The Russian Internet and the Russian Language." *Russian Language Journal* 61: 143–62.

Idiolag nakh, Pachti Doktar. 2001. "Manifezd Padonkaff." Available at: http://podonki.irk.ru/html/manifezd.html (accessed 7 August 2008).

"Internet-konferentsiia s Dmitriem Medvedevym." 2007. 5 March. Available at: http://www.d-a-medvedev.ru/dialog.html (accessed 10 March 2011).

jack_patterson. 2006. "Samaia pravil'naia istoriia padonkaff" *padonki_history*, 15 March. Available at: http://padonki-history.livejournal.com/1836.html (accessed 24 April 2013).

Julia. 2013. "Vot interesno . . ." *Moi mir*, 30 March. Available at: http://my.mail.ru/community/man/8FCC8EEB1CEC622.html?thread=6469D9181B45C6D3 (accessed 31 March 2013).

Kaliy. 2013. "Ne pervyi raz . . ." *Juick*, 30 March. Available at: http://juick.com/kaliy/2288212#1 (accessed 31 March 2013).

Kazerskii, Valentin K. 2008. "Budem uchit' 'Olbanskii'?" *Pravoslavnyi forum apostola Andreia Pervozvannogo*, 28 September. Available at: http://www.cirota.ru/forum/view.php?subj=81064&fullview=1&order=asc (accessed 13 April 2013).

Kniazev, Sergei, and Sof'ia Pozharitskaia. 2012. *Sovremennyi russkii literaturnyi iazyk: fonetika, orfoepiia, grafika i orfografiia*. Moscow: Akademicheskii proekt.

Krongauz, Maksim. 2008. "Utomlennye gramotoi." *Novyi mir* 5: 153–9. Available at: http://magazines.russ.ru/novyi_mi/2008/5/kr11.html (accessed 12 April 2013).

Kuznetsov, Sergei. 2004. *Oshchupyvaia slona: zametki po istorii russkogo Interneta.* Moscow: Novoe Literaturnoe Obozrenie.

Lesqualita. 2013. "Positivchiku." *disposable thoughts*, 30 March. Available at: hhornton.livejournal.com/1264120.html?thread=13458936& (accessed 31 March 2013).

Lighter, Jonathan. 1994. Preface to *Historical Dictionary of American Slang*, xi–xxxix. Oxford: Oxford University Press.

Mansur. 2012. "Samoe glavnoe . . ." Moi mir, 20 December. Available at: http://blogs.mail.ru/bk/mansur_83/49C05C94A357177D.html (accessed 31 March 2013).

"Medved." *Wikipedia.* Available at: http://ru.wikipedia.org/wiki/Медвед (accessed 10 March 2013).

Meri Shelli. 1999. "Manifezd Antigramatnasti." *Fuck.ru*, 18 February. Available at: http://www.guelman.ru/slava/manifest/istochniki/shelli.htm (accessed 13 April 2013).

N.n. 2005. "Madonna, uchi albanskii!" *Polit.ru* 15 December. Available at: http://www.polit.ru/news/2005/12/15/madonna/ (accessed 13 April 2013).

N.n. 2006. "Arfagrafiia ili Afftar, peshi ishcho!" *Nauka i obrazovanie*, 3 September. Available at: http://krd.best-city.ru/articles/?id=26, (accessed 1 February 2013).

Peshu_pravellno. 2004. "Profile." *Peshu_pravellno*, 23 September. Available at: http://community.livejournal.com/peshu_pravellno/profile (accessed 7 August 2008).

Rowe, Charley. 2011. "*Whatchanade?* Rapid Language Change in a Private Email Sibling Code." *Language@Internet* 8, article 6. Available at: http://www.languageatinternet.org/articles/2011/Rowe (accessed 23 January 2013).

Sebba, Mark. 2003. "Spelling Rebellion." In *Discourse Constructions of Youth Identities*, edited by Jannis Androutsopoulos and Alexandra Georgakopoulou, 151–72. Amsterdam: Benjamins.

Shapovalova, Nadezhda. 2007. "Karnaval'noe obshchenie v Internete (na materiale saita www.udaff.com)." *Vestnik Cheliabinskogo gosudarstvennogo universiteta* 16(20): 164–7.

Sokolovskii, Dmitrii. 2008. *Bibliia padonkov, ili Uchebneg albanskogo iazyka.* Moscow: Folio SP.

Stass. 2006. "Preved pobedit." *Akuna matata*, 26 April. Available at: http://blog.kp.ru/users/895883/post14634579/#comment52797158 (accessed 13 April 2013).

Subbotin, Igor'. 2006. "Novoiaz Interneta." *Sovershenno konkretno* 20(332). 20 April. Available at: http://www.soverkon.ru/2006/20/4.php (accessed 10 March 2011).

Vernidub, Artem. 2005. "U iazyka est' aftar." *Russkii Newsweek* 17(47). 16 May.

Vil'ianov, Sergei. 2006. "Polnyi preved." In *Komp'iuterra* 11(631). 22 March. Available at: http://offline.computerra.ru/2006/631/259101/ (accessed 1 February 2013).

Vzhdanov. 2006. "Nash otvet prevedu." *putevye zametki*, 25 May, Available at: http://vzhdanov.livejournal.com/68108.html (accessed 1 February 2013).

"Zhargon padonkov." *Wikipedia.* Available at: http://ru.wikipedia.org/wiki/Жаргон_падонков (accessed 13 April 2013).

Zvereva, Vera. 2009. "'Iazyk padonkaf': Diskussii pol'zovatelei Runeta." In *From Poets to Padonki: Linguistic Authority and Norm Negotiation in Modern Russian Culture* (Slavica Bergensia 9), edited by Ingunn Lunde and Martin Paulsen, 49–79. Bergen: Department of Foreign Languages, University of Bergen.

# 8 Language on display

## On the performative character of computer-mediated metalanguage

*Ingunn Lunde*

### Introduction

The internet, and especially the various interactive online environments of recent years, have opened up "a range of discursive spaces to individuals and groups who may not have traditionally had access to public media fora" (Johnson and Milani 2009: 6). While the "digital divide" may somewhat modify this postulation, there is no question that the sheer mass of online conversation taking place in digital forums has greatly increased scholarly access to informal, often spontaneous writing. This gigantic "corpus" provides us not only with a rich variety of linguistic usage, but also with "naturally occurring reception evidence" (Cameron 2007: 239), that is, people's more or less spontaneous reactions to all sorts of things, including language.

Language issues have long been a popular topic of debate in Russia, a debate that rises to particularly passionate heights in times of linguistic turbulence, both in response to linguistic innovations or radical changes in language culture, and in response to attempts to meet such changes with regulations, language policies and speech cultivation programs. The venues for language debates have been manifold: conferences and round tables organized by institutions such as the Academy of Sciences, universities or other academic establishments, radio broadcasts devoted to the language question, and the state-sponsored internet portal Gramota.ru, which features dictionaries, library resources, language games and information services. A presidential decree by Vladimir Putin declared 2007 as the "Year of the Russian Language," with numerous events in Russia and abroad promoting the study of Russian as well as its status as an international means of communication. The written mass media also provide much space for linguistic discussion, featuring columns or series of articles devoted to language, with contributions from linguists, teachers, journalists, critics and writers. Meanwhile, the internet provides a number of more informal venues: Facebook and VKontakte groups, blog communities, discussion forums, comment sections on news sites and similar.

Is online "talk about talk," or metalanguage, different from its offline variants? As Jannis Androutsopoulos (2011: 153) points out, "what is new in 'new media language' is not just a number of innovative constructions or structures, but new resources and strategies for written language production and meaning making, from graphology to discourse structure." Just as language usage itself has become more diversified with the new forms of public spheres provided by the internet, talk *about* language can also be expected to take on new forms. If we look at representations of "new media language" in particular, recent research suggests that metalinguistic talk about the characteristics, status and potentials of online linguistic practices differ in new media environments when compared to traditional outlets (Thurlow 2007; Jones and Schieffelin 2009). In addition, studies of online discussions not confined to *new media* language, but looking at more general linguistic issues, point to some core characteristics in online metadiscursive language. These characteristics, which we will see examples of below, may be summed up in terms of a broad, folk-linguistic nature (cf. Preston 2004), ideological pluralism and principally democratic stance (for studies of Russian online metalanguage, see Gorham 2009; Zvereva 2012; Lunde 2013; for a general perspective, see Androutsopoulos 2011).

Such studies demonstrate that the *attitude* to language (new media or general) in computer-mediated environments tends to differ from what we see in traditional media (e.g. newspapers and magazines). Most notably, it is more pluralistic, articulating a great variety of different view-points and opinions, and it is less oriented towards standard language ideology. The latter point applies both to the ideological stance adopted in online discussions about language and the concrete linguistic practices witnessed online, which fancy deviations from the norms of the standard language.

Continuing along the lines of this research, in this chapter I shift the focus from attitudes and representation to the *form, style* and *rhetoric* of computer-mediated metalanguage. In exploring reactions to language-related matters in a selection of YouTube videos, I look at the ways in which understandings, views and opinions on linguistic issues are articulated and negotiated online. I contend that linguistic metadiscourse is not only quantitatively influenced by its new media framework, but may also, in a digital environment, be shown to take on certain new forms or emphases. The chapter has two goals. First, it aims to characterize the style of Russian online metalanguage in a particular setting, that of a user-generated site such as YouTube. Second, it wishes to contribute to the study of verbal interaction on sites such as YouTube in general.

My material includes three videos with commentaries. The videos address language issues in one form or other. Two are humoristic sketches: one about the invention of the Cyrillic alphabet, one featuring the teaching of Russian in Kazakh schools, and one is a lecture on the Russian internet slang known as *iazyk padonkov* or *Olbanian* (see Chapter 7 by Berdicevskis and Zvereva, in this volume). In the comments (502 in total), users voice their reactions to the video, or comment on other users' comments. These particular videos have been chosen because they discuss and represent language and, in so doing, urge users to comment on language-related issues as well. In this way they constitute an ample and representative, yet manageable source of online Russian metalanguage.

YouTube belongs to the "participatory culture" (Jenkins 2006) of modern web environments, including social networking sites such as Facebook or Twitter, content-sharing sites such as Flickr and YouTube, blogs and forums. Androutsopoulos (2013) suggests a new term to designate YouTube and similar user-generated content-sharing sites as "participatory spectacles," a term that captures well the complexity of modes and media that we see in YouTube content (e.g. audio-visual content, dialogic interaction), in that it emphasizes its "collaborative production and visual character." Androutsopoulos (ibid.: 50) sums up the main characteristics of "participatory spectacles" in the following way: "Viewed as an organic whole, participatory spectacles are multiauthored, multimodal, multimedia, inherently dialogic, dynamically expanding, and open-ended."

I would argue that the term "spectacle" also points to a particular characteristic of discourse (including metalinguistic discourse) on sites such as YouTube: the quality of *display* and *performance*. In Bauman's and Brigg's words (1990: 73), performance "puts the act of speaking on display—objectifies it, lifts it to a degree from its interactional setting and opens it to scrutiny by an audience." In participatory online cultures, users put their texts, pictures, movies and voices on display, for other users to see, like, comment on or share. Accordingly, in online metalinguistic discussions, users put their views on language on display. Participating in a collaborative production of text and culture, people are eager to show off, play, be original and creative. This characteristic of online metalinguistic discourse is the point of departure for the present chapter. I argue that the feature of display and performance, so characteristic of online participatory spectacles, also influences the form and style of online metalanguage. This kind of discourse belongs to a broader field of *performative metalanguage*, a term I will outline in the following section.

## Metalanguage and performativity

Language's reflexive capacity has received considerable attention within various branches of linguistics, semiotics, anthropology and psychology over the past few decades (e.g. Gumperz 1982; Lucy 1993; Schieffelin, Woolard, and Kroskrity 1998; Silverstein 1998). *Metalanguage* is what happens "on the contextual margins of speaking" (Coupland and Jaworski 2004: 15). Within sociolinguistics, where studies of metalanguage have proliferated in recent decades, *metalanguage* is a broadly applied concept (Jaworski, Coupland and Galasiński [2004] call it a "family of concepts"), and the literature displays a wealth of different methodological, theoretical and analytical approaches.

Even so, recent reviews of metalanguage as a concept have taken the field to a new level, in particular as regards its social and ideological framing (Jaworski, Coupland, and Galasiński 2004). Moreover, an important step forward is the broad acceptance of the fact that reflexivity—the *meta* component—is inherent in language use as such (e.g. Lucy 1993: 11; Davis and Taylor 2002; Cameron 2004). For analytical and methodological purposes we may speak of *metalanguage, a metalinguistic function* or *reflexive linguistic elements*, but, in a broader sense, metalinguistic activity is inseparable from language use in general, allowing us to speak of a *metalinguistic dimension* of language.

However, while sociolinguists are aware of language's strong reflexive component in general, and appreciate the close connection between reflexive and poetic language (Lucy 1993; Coupland and Jaworski 2004: 22; Ensslin 2007; Jones and Schieffelin 2009) in particular, what I call *performative metalanguage* (Lunde 2009) has received far less attention. *Performative metalanguage* amounts to statements about language communicated implicitly, through a concrete linguistic practice. It involves all kinds of linguistic usage where a reflective attitude towards language is in play, such as quotation, imitation, stylization, word play, irony, a sudden insertion of a dialect word, an unexpected turn of phrase, a distorted idiom.

Questions concerning language, linguistic norms and values are often among the burning issues in a society. The resulting language debates are usually studied in the form of explicit utterances and statements about language, linguistic policy and language cultivation, for example, in round-table discussions, newspaper articles or language promotion programs. In this chapter my material will consist of explicit language discussions, but I will focus on arguments, elements and qualities within these commentaries on language that are not stated straightforwardly, but conveyed through language-in-use, through verbal performance, for instance, in language play, quotation or stylization.

## Case study: three YouTube videos

Once registered as a user, one can respond to YouTube videos by posting a comment, a reply to another comment, or even add additional video material (video replies). In this study, I shall focus on the textual comments, which, in terms of genre, may be very generally defined as "public asynchronous computer-mediated communication." Even if we exclude the visual element of the YouTube site for this study, we should keep in mind that the comments form part of a "participatory spectacle," that is, it is multiauthored, multimodal, dialogic, dynamically expanding and open-ended (Androutsopoulos 2013: 50). Users include a wide range of people from many countries who write in different, and occasionally more than one, language.

*Kirill i Mefodii pridumyvaiut russkii iazyk* (KM)
(Cyril and Methodius invent the Russian language)
Added: 17 December 2007
Views: 414,986 (24 January 2011)
Comments: 96 (24 January 2011)
Comments in: Russian (Cyrillic and Latin letters), Bulgarian (Cyrillic), Church Slavonic (quote from the video)

Summary: A sketch by the comedy group Ural'skie pel'meni ("Ural dumplings"). The main characters are the brothers Cyril and Methodius, "apostles of the Slavs," credited with devising, in the ninth century, the first script to render the Church Slavonic language. In the video the brothers are given the task of inventing the Cyrillic alphabet by the Byzantine emperor, and use this as an opportunity to create all kinds of problems for Russian schoolchildren—based on peculiarities in spelling, e.g. *legko* (with *g* pronounced as an unvoiced glottal fricative), *solntse* (with an unpronounced *l*), and to invent seemingly unnecessary punctuation marks.[1]

*KVN kak Kirill i Mefodii pridumyvali russkii iazyk* (KM2)
(KVN [Comedy Club] on how Cyril and Methodius invented the Russian language)
Added: 30 July 2009
Views: 55,796
Comments: 21 (17 August 2012)
Comments in: Russian (Cyrillic and Latin letters)[2]

*Anatolii Vassermann—"albanskii" iazyk* (AV1)
(Anatolii Vasserman—"Albanian [Olbanian] language")
Added: 11 March 2009
Views: 63,871 (9 August 2012)
Comments: 158 (9 August 2012)
Comments in: Russian (Cyrillic letters), English (4), Albanian (i.e. real Albanian) (1)

Summary: Anatolii Vasserman (AV), journalist and political consultant; intellectual figure, famous for his achievements in various quiz shows, and also famous for his provocative views, for instance, on the status of the Ukrainian language (which he considers to be a dialect of Russian). He is also a folkloric internet hero who goes by the name of "Onotole." In this lecture, he offers his positive view of "internet subculture," including *Olbanian.* This subculture, Vasserman says, is not of harm to "general culture," but contributes to and supports this culture.[3]

*Anatolii Vassermann—"albanskii" iazyk* (AV2)
(Anatolii Vasserman—"Albanian" language)
Added: 16 March 2009
Views: 3789 (9 August 2012)
Comments: 16 (9 August 2012)
Comments in: Russian (Cyrillic letters)[4]

*Urok russkogo iazyka* (UR)
(Russian Language Lesson)
Added: 21 November 2010
Views: 827,127 (9 August 2012)
Comments: 232 (9 August 2012)
Comments in: Russian (Cyrillic and Latin letters), English (4), Kazakh (1)

Summary: A humorous sketch featuring a Russian language lesson for Kazakh schoolchildren, explaining why Kazakh people know Russian so well. The sketch focuses on the rich possibilities of Russian syntax for the construction of complex sentences, spelling out every punctuation mark in actual speech ("Good morning comma children exclamation mark"; "Knock dash knock comma knock dash knock three dots").[5]

## Core features: diversity of content and style, proximity to folk linguistics

Before turning to the central question of *how* metalanguage is expressed in these three cases, a quick look at the contents, attitudes and the users' motivations for writing will give us a sense of its core features. Why do users comment and what are their opinions? In this material, the comments can roughly be divided into three groups: positive comments, negative comments and explanatory comments (both "positive" and "negative"). The "explanatory comments" may be of a provocative nature, they may question the content or style of the video, they may support or refute its statement by adding more or less relevant information. Without applying any sort of evaluative attitude, we can notice that the criterion of relevance ranges from "clearly relevant" to cases where certain themes, notions or concepts seem to function as trigger words for launching particular views or topics, not necessarily thematized directly in the source video. This phenomenon has been observed in Russian online commentaries generally, in particular on websites devoted to news (Zvereva 2012), and is probably not restricted to the Russian-language internet. The recourse to commonplace topics is one of several characteristics that reveal the folk linguistic status of this material (Niedzielski and Preston 2003). So is the tendency to come over (or give the impression of doing so) as spontaneous and often emotional:

(1) mansik93: Онотоле все знает! (AV1)
Onotole knows everything!

(2) kirgiz1981: казахи лучшие! (UR)
the Kazakhs are the best!

(3) artemba3: Блин как я люблю эту команду)))особенно старичков Турсунбек вообще мужик) (UR)

Oh sugar how I love that team)))in particular the old fellows Tursunbek's really a great fella

Furthermore, when expressing their views, users often rely on intuition, association and comparison, rather than on strict logic and sustainability of argument, as shown in the following examples:

(4) Pujardoff1: Это не албанский язык, а беларуская мова! Её главный принцип: как слышишь, так и пиши, главное чтобы не так похоже было на русский (AV1)

This is not Albanian, but Belarusian! Its main principle is: write what you hear, the main thing is that it shouldn't be too similar to Russian

(5) Megafrostmage: Анатолий молодец, но йазыг падонкафф одобрять нехорошо. Русский язык тем и хорош, что всё пишется не так как читается. (AV1)

Anatolii is a fine fellow, but it's not good to approve of *iazyg padonkaff*. That's what makes Russian a nice language—that everything's written not as it's read.

Negative comments are often rather harsh and use coarse language. The problem of hate speech is a general one in many digital environments, political themes are likely to pop up, and nationalist discourse is quite frequent:

(6) KhanKazakhe: @камилл кеппель Дебил! Ты хоть понимаешь что означает слово Европеоид?? Европеоид это раса! К нему относятся узбеки(памиро-ферганский подтип с монголоидной смесью), турки, азери, туркмены(закапийский подтип с монголоидной смесью), персы, таджики, арабы, кавказцы!!! Европеец это тот который живет в Европе дебил сука! Я не сказал что казахи европейцы! Я сказал что казахи смешанной монголоидной и европеоидной расы, южносибирской! Иди учи что такое раса! (UR)

Moron! Do you even understand what the word Caucasian [*Evropeoid*] means? Caucasian is a race! It includes the Uzbeks (the Pamir-Fergana subtype mixed with the Mongoloid one), Turks, Azeris, Turkmens

(Transcaspian subtype mixed with the Mongoloid one), Persians, Tajiks, Arabs, Caucasians [*kavkaztsy*]! A European is someone who lives in Europe moron bitch! I didn't say that Kazakhs are Europeans! I said that Kazakhs are of mixed Mongoloid and Caucasian race, a South Siberian one! Go and learn what a race is!

Positive comments tend to assume some stylistic element of the source text, supporting its content and style by *performing* in the same manner, as I will show in more detail below. Consider this example from the video about the teaching of Russian in Kazakh schools, where the user adopts the video's funny habit of spelling out punctuation marks in actual speech and combines this with a positive evaluation of the video:

(7) SashaDise: Вхахахаха круто восклицательный знак, особенно про барана без всяких знаков))) (UR)

Hahahaha cool exclamation mark, especially about the mutton-head without any marks)))

The 502 comments in the material used for this study display a great variety of different styles and attitudes. Consider these two different replies to a user comment by "Zenon3x":

(8) Dmitryi Moroz: @Zenon3x Уважаемый, я не имел в виду этимологию, о которой вы пытаетесь сказать,а только культуру и владение русской речью,которой Вассерман владеет блистательно.Кстати слово лестница пишется с буквой "т", а не так как у вас написано. (AV1)

Distinguished user, I did not have in mind the etymology that you are trying to talk about, but only speech culture and mastery of the Russian language, in which Vasserman is superbly skilled. By the way, the word *lestnitsa* is written with a "t," and not in the way you wrote it.

(9) MrAssertor: @Zenon3x че ты херню всё время несёшь, мудило безграмотное?!!! (AV1)

@Zenon3x Why do you talk rubbish all the time, you illiterate scumbag?!!!

While one commentator politely makes his or her point clear, using highly literate and conservative forms and constructions and even allowing him/herself to correct a small spelling mistake in the original poster's comment, the other is rather aggressive, scolding the original poster, using slang terminology ("scumbag," "rubbish") and vernacular forms (*che* for *chego*). This is just one example of the very different styles of two replies to one and the same comment. Stylistic diversity and pluralism of opinion are key factors in this material, as in many digital environments (cf. Androutsopoulos 2011).

## Performative metalanguage

Let us return to what I termed performative metalanguage, metalinguistic comments that take on the form of verbal performance. I will look at three subtypes: stylization, quotation and creative variation. Needless to say, these forms may overlap.

First, *stylization*: a comment mirrors the style of the video in that some sentence, catchphrase or word is brought in from the source text, revoiced and often accompanied by a comment. Alternatively, the comment itself performs in the style of the source text/video.

Consider this series of comments on the Vasserman video on internet subculture, all approving of the video, its message and style, in a performative manner:

(10) shvonts: праффильно роскозал, панашыму, па-олбански! (AV2)

Well said, in our idiom, in Olbanian [The commentator approves of what Vasserman says, using *Olbanian*, which is also the topic of Vasserman's lecture. In other words, he or she approves of the style both explicitly and implicitly, through the very use of it.]

(11) neodoc1976: ОНОТОЛЕ!!!
ОНОТОЛЕ!!!
ОНОТОЛЕ!!! (AV1)
[a threefold exclamation/apostrophe of Vasserman/Onotole]

(12) aqsw79: автор!
не вздумай пить яд!
жжошь!!! (AV1)

Author [a common apostrophe in *olbanian* of the user who's written the blog post one is commenting on]! Don't dare to drink poison! You're cool! [The commentator uses elements of *Olbanian*, including the negation of a typical "negative" comment: "Drink poison!"]

(13) BlackTurismoMR: Да, действительно, в условиях конкуренции прогресс движется быстрее. Она стимулирует его развитие.
Уважаю Анатолия. (AV1)

Indeed, in a competitive environment progress is faster. It stimulates its development. I respect Anatoly.

(14) IVePoison116: воистину мы внемлем твой глас онотоле
Verily we hear thy voice onotole

Of these examples, the first three perform in the very style that Vasserman comments on, but certainly does not use, in the video, the well-known internet slang *iazyk padonkov*, many elements of which have become common style in blogs, forums and social networks. The next is an adaptation of Vasserman's own highly cultivated standard language style, repeating and approving one of his main explicit points. The last comment takes this style, characterized (or rather, downplayed) by another commentator as "slightly archaic," one step further and gives an approving response in Church Slavonic.

What we can see in all these examples is a combination of explicit and implicit, or performative, metalanguage, as users apply a particular style in order to re-inforce their argument. The style may match the topic of Vasserman's lecture (*iazyk padonkov*), his own style (high-style Russian standard language), or exaggerate this style (Church Slavonic). As the examples show, the effect can be humoristic, compelling and elegant.

Second, *quotation*: is in itself a reflexive mode, creating a certain distance from the words, observing them, as it were, from an outside perspective. Below are three comments from the Cyril and Methodius video (KM): the first user simply quotes a funny phrase, the second adds a lot of smileys to the quote in order to show his or her appreciation, and the third adds a similarly approving commentary and smileys to the quotation:

(15) SetaSoieSeda: Осторожно, кавычки открываются "Осторожно, кавычки закрываются!" (KM)
Attention, quotation marks opening "Attention, quotation marks closing!"

(16) ma3xim: Великий Могучий Русский Рот )))))))))) (KM)
Great, Mighty Russian Mouth ))))))))))

(17) Nordddd: Я взял лесТницу, пошёл на соЛнцЕ смотреть леГко)) ржу нимагу))) (KM)
I took the ladDer, and went easIlY to look at the sUn))
Can't bear it)))

The first comment plays with the common metro announcement about closing doors, applying them, just as in the video, to opening and closing quotation marks. The next is a variation of the phrase "Great, mighty Russian language" from a short prose piece by the nineteenth-century writer Ivan Turgenev, a very common dictum in Russian standard language ideology. The last comment, again a quotation from the video, combines three words with peculiar spelling rules in Russian, which, according to the video, Cyril and Methodius made up purely to make Russian schoolchildren suffer.

It is rather seldom that quotations are formally marked as quotations (i.e. by quotations marks), but it happens, as in this Church Slavonic phrase:

(18) Caledoniadream: "Ликую я аки отрок младой"))))))) (KM)
"I rejoice like a young child")))))))

Third, *creative variation.* In an even more creative manner, users perform in the style of the video, adding some new element as they offer their comments on, or positive evaluation of, the style it features—occasionally also interacting with, or responding to, other user comments:

(19) prototip2002: глаз не отрвать это так смешно ну что сказать смешно смешно не подетски (UR)
can't withdraw my eyes it's so funny what to say funny funny very much

(20) uralfilm @prototip2002: А теперь запетая со знаками препинания запятая пожаулста восклицательный знак точка с запятой скобка закрывается (UR)
And now comma with punctuation marks comma please exclamation mark semicolon closing bracket

This user reacts to "prototip2002's" comment pointing out the lack of punctuation marks. He or she does so in the manner of the video, spelling out the punctuation marks of his or her own "correction," but takes the humoristic effect to a new level by adding an emoticon in the same style "semicolon closing bracket," that is, ";)." This is a device not used in the video. Since emoticons are visual elements created by punctuation marks, the device of spelling out its constituents becomes even more pronounced than the spelling out of ordinary punctuation marks and gives the comment an additional twist.

(21) sogryanin1: Ребята просто хороши, безо всяких кавычек. (UR)
The guys are just good, without any quotation marks

This user performs in the manner of the video, with a variation of the phrase "without any punctuation marks" (a quote from the video). By changing the quotation into "without any quotation marks," he or she is able to add, in a humoristic way, a serious touch to the statement, emphasizing his or her sincerity in praising the authors of the sketch.

(22) sergeyemelin: Онотоле! Без комментариев (AV1)
Onotole! Without comments

This user, finally, plays cleverly with the genre of commentary altogether, as he/she performs what is clearly a positive evaluation. It has a similar effect to the previous example, adding a hint of sincerity in a playful manner.

In a number of instances, the forms of metalanguage in play come close to poetic language. These are uses of language that draw attention to themselves. They create a certain distance from the language, observe it from the outside and thus apply the *meta*-perspective. But they do so not, or not only, by taking the explicit meta-perspective, but by performing linguistically in ways that place emphasis on the reflexive dimension of their utterance. As the examples show, users apply performative language to approve of, celebrate, or play with catchwords and styles. Occasionally users comment or elaborate on other users' commentaries. Frequently an explicit, metadiscursive comment and a linguistic practice, or use of a particular linguistic element, combine to give force to the user's argument. The great majority of "performative" comments in this study are positive. This indicates that users who wish to express critique or disapproval are less likely to use performative metalanguage, but this may be different in other contexts.

## Performative metalanguage: a cross-linguistic perspective

Why is it that metalanguage in this material has this strong *performative* character? In many instances, we saw that the verbal performance was directly inspired by the source text or video performance. Similarly, in a study of YouTube comments on AT&T commercials, Jones and Schieffelin (2009) found that many users, in their playful responses to the language of the commercials, are inspired by the style of this language (playing on text messaging), showing an impressive attentiveness to language and displaying this linguistic reflexivity in their verbal practice:

> The original AT&T commercials are brilliantly crafted artifacts of speech play that assemble elements of everyday language in highly artificial but eminently entertaining verbal performances. These performances, in turn, provide not only resources for further verbal play, but also an impetus for metalinguistic commentary and assessment. In short, we argue that there is a direct, if not causal, connection between the ads' poetic deployment of texting language and the critical discussions about texting language they have occasioned.
>
> (Jones and Schieffelin 2009: 1074–5)

It is true, as Jones and Schieffelin note, that the style of the video influences the style of the comments, but the performativity is also triggered by the particular characteristics of the venue itself as a "participatory spectacle."

The practice of putting one's language, and one's views on language, on display has a visual component to it. As Fairclough argued back in 1995, "written texts in contemporary society are increasingly becoming more visual . . ., not only in the sense that newspapers, for instance, combine words with photographs . . ., but also because considerations of layout and visual impact are increasingly salient in the design of a written page" (quoted from Johnson and Milani 2009: 11). In the context of discussion forums, blogs, social networking sites and not least all kinds of "participatory spectacles," one can observe a growing visualization not only in the multimodal combination of textual and visual material, but also on a micro-level, in the structure of the word, phrase, sentence, comment or punctuation, and all these features may be used and interpreted and represented in metalinguistic terms, as we saw, for instance, in the "performative" representation of an emoticon above.

The performativity, furthermore, has to do with the style of much computer-mediated communication itself. Language use in many digital contexts has acquired a high degree of playfulness, a self-reflexive and often ironic attitude. We can see this as a general trend in commentary fields, social networks, blog posts and discussion forums: a shift from the *informative* to the *performative.*

Just as people are eager to respond to questions about language in online "participatory spectacles" (see Gorham 2009), people are also eager to play, display, perform, be different, original, and, not least, challenge or subvert the traditional status of the standard language, at least in societies with a hegemonic standard language culture, such as Russian or English. If the style of meta-language may perhaps also reflect a particular conception of language, of linguistic hierarchies and ruling or alternative language ideologies, to what extent are the features of computer-mediated metalanguage in a context such as the YouTube site language-specific? To what extent can they be linked to the individual language's linguistic culture and traditions of discussing language? These are questions that cannot be solved within the framework of the present chapter. An analysis of a larger data collection in different languages from diverse online venues may be able to determine variables that are related to the digital context and to the specificity of the concrete venue (such as the "participatory spectacle," as opposed to news sites or a moderated forum) and variables that may be linked to, and partly explained by, factors that depend on a particular language's historical development, traditions of linguistic debate and policy, history of standardization, inventory of linguistic varieties and similar. Together with other case studies of online metalanguage (Jones and Schieffelin 2009 for English; Lunde, in preparation for Norwegian and Danish), this chapter shows that, at least as far as a core set of devices (quotation, stylization, language play) is concerned, performative metalanguage seems to share general features across cultures and languages.

## Notes

1 http://www.youtube.com/watch?v=soO10_qVDbc (accessed 24 January 2011, no longer available; the video can be viewed at http://www.youtube.com/watch?v=riHjf9f5Rso as of 9 August 2012).
2 http://www.youtube.com/watch?v=riHjf9f5Rso (accessed 17 August 2012). This is the same video as the above, but with other comments.
3 http://www.youtube.com/watch?v=JMxvNGSGZCA (accessed 17 August 2012).
4 http://www.youtube.com/watch?v=S8taIp85rQs (accessed 17 August 2012). This is the same video as the above, but with other comments.
5 http://www.youtube.com/watch?v=PzusVXZ7h-I (accessed 17 August 2012).

## References

Androutsopoulos, Jannis. 2011. "Language Change and Digital Media: A Review of Conceptions and Evidence." In *Standard Languages and Language Standards in a Changing Europe*, edited by Nikolas Coupland and Tore Kristiansen, 145–60. Oslo: Novus.

—— 2013. "Participatory Culture and Metalinguistic Discourse: Performing and Negotiating German Dialects on YouTube." In *Discourse 2.0: Language and New Media*, edited by Deborah Tannen and Anna-Marie Trester, 47–72. Washington, DC: Georgetown University Press.

Bauman, Richard, and Charles L. Briggs. 1990. "Poetics and Performance as Critical Perspectives on Language and Social Life." *Annual Review of Anthropology* 19: 59–88.

Cameron, Deborah. 2004. "Out of the Bottle: The Social Life of Metalanguage." In *Metalanguage: Social and Ideological Perspectives*, edited by Adam Jaworski, Nikolas Coupland, and Dariusz Galasiński, 311–21. Berlin: Mouton de Gruyter.

—— 2007. "Dreaming of Genie: Language, Gender Difference and Identity on the Web." In *Language in the Media: Representations, Identities, Ideologies* (Advances in Sociolinguistics), edited by Sally Johnson and Astrid Ensslin, 234–49. London: Continuum.

Coupland, Nikolas, and Adam Jaworski. 2004. "Sociolinguistic Perspectives on Metalanguage: Reflexivity, Evaluation and Ideology." In *Metalanguage: Social and Ideological Perspectives*, edited by Nikolas Coupland, Adam Jaworski, and Dariusz Galasiński, 15–51. Berlin: Mouton de Gruyter.

Davis, Hayley, and Talbot J. Taylor. 2002. *Rethinking Linguistics* (Routledge Advances in Communication and Linguistic Theory). London: Routledge.

Ensslin, Astrid. 2007. "Of Chords, Macines and Buble-bees: The Metalinguistics of Hyperpoetry." In *Language in the Media: Representations, Identities, Ideologies* (Advances in Sociolinguistics), edited by Sally Johnson and Astrid Ensslin, 250–70. London: Continuum.

Gorham, Michael. 2009. " 'We Speak Russian!' New Models of Norm Negotiation in the Electronic Media," In *From Poets to Padonki: Linguistic Authority and Norm Negotiation in Modern*

*Russian Culture* (Slavica Bergensia 9), edited by Ingunn Lunde and Martin Paulsen, 315–35. Bergen: Department of Foreign Languages, University of Bergen.

Gumperz, John J. 1982. *Discourse Strategies*. Cambridge: Cambridge University Press.

Jaworski, Adam, Nikolas Coupland, and Dariusz Galasiński, eds. 2004. *Metalanguage: Social and Ideological Perspectives*. Berlin and New York: Mouton de Gruyter.

Jenkins, Henry. 2006. *Convergence Culture: Where Old and New Media Collide*. New York: New York University Press.

Johnson, Sally, and Tommaso M. Milani, eds. 2009. *Language Ideologies and Media Discourse: Texts, Practices, Politics* (Advances in Sociolinguistics). London: Continuum.

Jones, Graham M., and Bambi B. Schieffelin. 2009. "Talking Text and Talking Back: 'My BFF Jill' from Boob Tube to YouTube." *Journal of Computer-Mediated Communication* 14: 1050–79.

Lucy, John A. ed. 1993, *Reflexive Language: Reported Speech and Metapragmatics*. Cambridge: Cambridge University Press.

Lunde, Ingunn. 2009. "Performative Metalanguage: Negotiating Norms Through Verbal Action." In *From Poets to Padonki: Linguistic Authority and Norm Negotiation in Modern Russian Culture* (Slavica Bergensia 9), edited by Ingunn Lunde and Martin Paulsen, 110–28. Bergen: Department of Foreign Languages, University of Bergen.

—— 2013. " 'A Stroll through the Keywords of My Memory': Digitally Mediated Commemorations of the Soviet Linguistic Heritage." In *Memory, Conflict and New Media: Web Wars in Post-Socialist States*, edited by Ellen Rutten, Julie Fedor, and Vera Zvereva, 101–11. London: Routledge.

—— (in preparation). "Displayed and Discussed: Performative Metalanguage on YouTube (Danish, Norwegian, English)."

Niedzielski, Nancy A., and Dennis R. Preston. 2003. *Folk Linguistics*. Berlin: Mouton de Gruyter.

Preston, Dennis R. 2004. "Folk Metalanguage," In *Metalanguage: Social and Ideological Perspectives*, edited by Adam Jaworski, Nikolas Coupland, and Dariusz Galasiński, 75–101. Berlin: Mouton de Gruyter.

Schieffelin, Bambi B., Kathryn A. Woolard, and Paul V. Kroskrity, eds. 1998. *Language Ideologies: Practice and Theory* (Oxford Studies in Anthropological Linguistics 16). New York: Oxford University Press.

Silverstein, Michael. 1998. "The Uses and Utility of Ideology." In *Language Ideologies: Practice and Theory*, edited by Bambi B. Schieffelin, Kathryn A. Woolard and Paul V. Kroskrity, 123–45. New York: Oxford University Press.

Thurlow, Crispin. 2007. "Fabricating Youth: New-Media Discourse and the Technologization of Young People." In *Language in the Media: Representations, Identities, Ideologies* (Advances in Sociolinguistics), edited by Sally Johnson and Astrid Ensslin, 213–33. London: Continuum.

Zvereva, Vera. 2012. *Setevye razgovory: kul'turnye kommunikatsii v Runete* (Slavica Bergensia 10). Bergen: Department of Foreign Languages, University of Bergen.

# 9 Translit

## Computer-mediated digraphia on the Runet

*Martin Paulsen*

@janajordane xorowo znajew anglijskij?!

"Do you know English well?" This question, recently posed by one Russian girl to another on Twitter, epitomizes a key challenge for the Russian language community in the post-Cold War era. The demise of the Soviet Union led to a sharp increase in the influence of English-language and Western-language technologies on the Russian language community. While the influence of the English language has been a recurrent topic, both in the language community itself and in the scholarly literature, the technological influence has received comparatively little attention, especially among scholars.

One of the most visible outcomes of this technological shift has been the notable increase in the use of the Latin alphabet to write Russian in digital settings, as seen above. Simultaneously, digital technology has become an indispensable part of everyday life for Russians. As a result, we now have a situation where both Cyrillic and Latin are used by Russian speakers in day-to-day communication. In sociolinguistics, this phenomenon is referred to as *computer-mediated digraphia* (Androutsopoulos 2009).[1] Despite technological innovations that have made the use of Cyrillic much easier, the digraphic situation persists. In order to understand the full scope of the issue, there is a need to investigate the technological preconditions further.

In Russian public discourse the use of Latin to write Russian in digital settings is known as *translit*, derived from "transliteration." However, while transliterations have traditionally been based on well-established systems and used for limited and quite specific purposes, *translit* is characterized by a great degree of variation, and is used for full-fledged communication. The issue has also been ideologically charged, due to the fact that the Russian language and Cyrillic alphabet are important to the national identity of Russians, and consequently the spread of *translit* has led to strong reactions in the Russian language community. The following discussion will address three aspects of Russian computer-mediated digraphia key to understanding the phenomenon: (1) the *technological* background for its appearance and further existence; (2) the *linguistic* features of translit; and, finally, (3) the *metalinguistic* reactions to the phenomenon.

## The technology behind computer-mediated digraphia

The introduction of digital technology and computer-mediated communication (CMC) seems to have re-actualized digraphia as a research object. To my mind, computer-mediated digraphia should be seen not only as a digraphic situation *in* CMC, but also as something that appears *as a result of* the technological specificities of CMC, i.e. we should pay attention to the constraints of CMC that make many people turn to the Latin alphabet to write Russian. This does not mean, of course, that there was no digraphia before digital media, but that it has gained new relevance with the introduction of new technology. This section will show that the technical reasons for computer-mediated digraphia are related to both the hardware (keyboards) and the software (script encodings) of CMC.

Indeed, we could talk of a digital script, the basic and most robust way of writing in CMC. This script is based on the ASCII (American Standard Code for Information Interchange) encoding system, which was the first to be widely adopted by the early developers of the internet as a basis for online communication. It includes the 26 letters of the English alphabet, numerals and some punctuation marks. Despite the later development of more advanced encodings, ASCII has become the "lowest common denominator" of online communication, the only code that can guarantee the successful delivery of a message in any CMC setting. This has led researchers to talk of an "ASCII-ized Arabic" or an "Internet Slavic" (Magner 2001; Palfreyman and al Khalil 2007).

Even though Soviet industry had a long history of developing computers,[2] the breakthrough in personal computers in the former Soviet Union came with the import of relatively cheaper and more technologically advanced computers from abroad (Prokhorov 1999: 12–13; Khairullin 2010), and with the cloning of foreign computers (Markelov 2004). This development became visible at the end of the 1980s (Rohozinski 2000: 336). In 1988, new customs regulations made it possible for individuals to import computer equipment, and from the early 1990s computers sold on the Russian market were based on foreign parts (Ganley 1996: 29; Prokhorov 1999: 12).

This eventually led to the problem of incompatible keyboards. How could the 33 letters of the Russian alphabet be fitted onto keyboards that had originally been designed for the 26 letters of English? Even if there had been Russian typewriters with a standardized layout before the advent of PCs, as Artemii Lebedev notes in his history of keyboards in Russia, the introduction of digital technology in Russia did not take this into account:

> At the end of the 1980s we got PCs of foreign origin. No one in the world made or has any intention of making keyboards that took the length of the Russian alphabet into account. As a result, someone simply Russified what already existed.
>
> (Lebedev 2004)

This incompatibility was not nearly as complex for Russian as it was for non-alphabetical languages like Japanese and Chinese (Gottlieb 2000; Sproat 2010), but it was complex enough to affect the availability of punctuation marks and some Cyrillic letters. There are several different versions of Cyrillic computer keyboards in use today, but, according to Lebedev, they all struggle with a shortage of keys. While on a Latin keyboard you can render the comma and the full stop with a single key stroke, typing them on a Cyrillic keyboard requires the shift key as well. This solution slows down the typing of Cyrillic texts (Lebedev 2004).

Even if the early 1990s seem far away now, similar hardware problems are found today, in the development of handheld digital devices. With the introduction of products like the iPhone, iPad and Kindle, mobile phones or PDAs are playing an increasing role in CMC. Frehner (2008: 28) points out that computer keyboards are much more comfortable than mobile phone keypads, and that this difference influences typing. Similarly, in a review of new mobile phones, Iar Sobolev compares the solutions offered by different mobile phone producers available on the Russian market, and concludes that some letters in the Russian alphabet are not available on the standard keyboard of most PDAs:

> Once again, the abundance of keys was not enough to enable complete Russification of the machine: the letters "ё," "ъ" and, what is particularly sad, most of the punctuation marks, were only available either through additional key-combinations, or in the English version. This illness, I should note, has turned out to be chronic, and has not been cured even to this very day.
>
> (Sobolev 2009)[3]

This same issue lay behind a petition from the Russian NGO Zaria[4] in Ul'ianovsk to the president of the Finnish company Nokia, asking him to make sure that the Cyrillic letter "ё" was restored to the mobile phones Nokia makes for the Russian market. In a news story in *Rossiiskaia Gazeta* on 25 March 2010 reporting this petition, the journalist draws attention to the fact that the letter is also difficult to access on computer keyboards.

The problem for individual users is also a practical one, relating to the availability of Cyrillic keyboards in different situations. It is, for instance, possible to set up a keyboard designed with Latin letters to write Cyrillic letters, but many will find it difficult to type Russian without seeing the Cyrillic letters on the keyboard. Cyrillic letters are often missing on mobile phones that have been imported from outside Eastern Europe. Until recently such illegally imported mobile phones dominated the local market (Anon 2007).

Still, the software issue regarding the encoding of digital communication is even more complex. For even if there is often a correspondence between the letter on the key we strike on our keyboard and the letter that appears on the screen, digital typing is a highly complex matter of binary codes turned into letters on the screen, and this is where the similarity between typewriters and computers ends. On a typewriter, what you see is what you get, while a computer keyboard can be programmed to do just about anything (Sproat 2010: 170–83). In other words, the software is what makes the mechanical technology of typewriters different from the digital technology of computers and keyboards.

The most common way of rendering text in the early development of digital technology was through the ASCII standard, tailored to the English language. Later, as it became obvious that you needed to be able to write in other alphabets as well, the ISO standard was introduced, using parallel standards, so you would have one standard for Western European languages (ISO–8859–1), and one for Cyrillic (ISO–8859–5). The problem with this was that, if you received a text written in a standard other than the one you used yourself, the text would become illegible. In the early 2000s the Russian IT expert and journalist Iurii Revich pointed out:

> It got to the point where it was easier to send an e-mail using translit than to deal with the encoding. The situation improved slightly when almost everyone went over to Outlook. But even today you occasionally stumble upon e-mails which contain something like "Sb'f'el{e cnqond'! Ndmnbpelemmn on Mnbn-phfqjnls m'op'bkemh~" or simply "???? ?????! ?????? ???? ??"
>
> (Revich 2002)[5]

The problem of several parallel standards was, in principle, solved by the introduction and gradual implementation of the UNICODE standard—a code that allows for more than a million distinct characters, which should be sufficient to meet the needs of contemporary languages (Danet and Herring 2007: 11, see also Paulsen 2011: 129–30).

Meanwhile, encoding continues to play an important role in mobile phone communication, where the length of an SMS message is dependent on the alphabet. Messages written in Latin letters can contain 160 characters, while messages written in other alphabets, such as Cyrillic, can contain only 70 characters (Hillebrand et al. 2010: 93). The topical interest of this issue is supported by the Russian linguists Marina Avdonina and Sergei Nikitin (2006b: 88), who claim that in SMS communication Latin is perceived as "fashionable, shorter and cheaper" than Cyrillic.

Today, the problem is particularly relevant outside Russia. A look at the backgrounds of users who write in *translit* on Russia's most popular social networking service, VKontakte, indicates that the vast majority of those who named their home country live outside Russia.[6] Figures from VKontakte also show that it is still widely used today (the number of messages in *translit* runs into the hundreds of thousands).

## The linguistics of *translit*

The technological constraints described above have implications for the linguistic characteristics of *translit.* Parallel phenomena have been studied for many languages in similar situations, such as Japanese (Gottlieb 2000, 2005, 2009), Greek (Androutsopoulos 2006 and 2009; Koutsogiannis and Mitsikopoulou 2007, Tseliga 2007), Arabic (Abdulla 2007; Palfreyman and al Khalil 2007; Warschauer, el Said and Zohry 2007) and Bulgarian (Spassov 2012). There has also been some research into the phenomenon in the Russian language community, but so far it has been more limited in scope (Birtser 2004; Avdonina and Nikitin 2006a and 2006b). And whereas earlier research on *translit* has drawn examples from email and SMS communication, the present study relies on linguistic material drawn from small-scale samples of CMC in the openly accessible services Twitter and VKontakte—an approach which allows for an in-depth analysis of the linguistic characteristics of *translit* at the level of individual letters.[7]

While, as I showed in the previous section, the ASCII code has been followed by the introduction of more elaborate codes, with a greater variety of symbols, my data show that the 26 letters of ASCII still define the terms for *translit*. With three exceptions, all 100 tweets in my material are written entirely with symbols available in the ASCII code. Two of the exceptions combine text written by the user with text produced by others, copied and pasted, or automatically generated by an online service. Example 1 is most likely written in Cyrillic and Latin by the same person.

(1) не стала делать цветуху.menya ub'yut
/не стала делать цветуху.меня убьют/
I decided not to do my homework in chromatics. They will kill me.[8]

The point in this chapter is not that it is not possible to switch between Cyrillic and Latin, or that people do not do it, but rather to focus on what makes it difficult or inconvenient for some people to write Cyrillic (previous section), and what they choose to do when they write Russian in CMC without Cyrillic (this section).

The remaining 97 messages in my material consist only of symbols from the ASCII encoding. *Translit* is therefore different from several existing transliteration systems for Russian into other languages that are based on diacritic symbols unavailable in ASCII (Birtser 2004: 83–6). This implies that, since there are 33 letters in the Russian alphabet, and only 26 in the ASCII code, it is impossible to create a system based on one-to-one correlations between the two. At least four distinctive linguistic features result from these constraints: (1) the loss of graphemes; (2) the use of a combination of Latin letters to render one Cyrillic; (3) the use of numerals for letters; and (4) the conflation of several Cyrillic letters into one Latin.

A basic approach to the study of *translit*, which informs all of the features enumerated above, is to establish categories based on the different techniques used to transliterate (Androutsopoulos 2009). This approach distinguishes fundamentally between phonetic transliteration and orthographic transliteration, the former based on correspondences between Russian phonemes and Latin graphemes (related to the phonetic aspect), while the latter is based on a preservation of the Russian orthography (related to the visual aspect).

(2) Otnoshus' kak k drugu, no vse je est nechto bolshoe o chem ya i sam ne mogu ponyat'! Tvoi golos dlya menya bolshaya podderjka) Serikbayev

/Отношусь как к другу, но все же есть нечто большое о чем я и сам не могу понять! Твой голос для меня большая поддержка) Серикбаев/

I relate to you as a friend, but there is something big which even I cannot really understand! Your voice is a great support to me) Serikbayev[9]

(3) @janajordane xorowo znajew anglijskij?!

/@janajordane хорошо знаешь английский?!/

@janajordane do you know English well?![10]

Example 2 demonstrates the phonetic principle, with the *translit* based on the phonetic correlations between Russian and Latin letters and the Russian *ш* rendered as "sh." Example 3 illustrates the orthographic principle: both "x" and "w" are used because they resemble the Cyrillic characters *х* and *ш* visually.

Even if the basic concept of a computer-mediated digraphia is common to languages that use non-Latin scripts, what actually goes on might be conceptually different from language to language. Androutsopoulos (2009) refers to *Greeklish* as a form of transliteration, while Palfreyman and al Khalil point out that what is happening in ASCII-Arabic is "in many respects a transcription of what writers would say, rather than a transliteration of Arabic script" (2007: 53).

The term *translit* suggests a connection with transliteration, and one of the strategies applied in my material is to base *translit* on one or more of the existing systems of transliteration from Russian to other languages, such as English, German or French. Earlier research has shown that the English system is the most influential for *translit* (Birtser 2004: 71) and for Latinized variants of other Slavic languages (Magner 2001: 24; Chemerkin 2009: 37).

(4) Samoe luchshee mesto na zemle-eto tvoi nejnye ob'yatiya.

/Самое лучшее место на земле – это твои нежные объятия./

Your tender embrace is the best place on earth.[11]

Example 4 is one of the best examples of influence from the most popular English transliteration in my material. The letters are rendered according to their sound values in English, such as "ch" for the Cyrillic *ч* and "ya" for Cyrillic *я*. The "j" in "nejnye" and the apostrophe are the only deviations. The "j" is taken from the French system, and the apostrophe should have been double according to the most widely used English system.

This combination of the English and French systems suggests that it would be better to treat *translit* as an alternative orthography for Russian that cannot be reduced to any one system of transliteration, but is the result of linguistic creativity that goes beyond the framework of established schemes of transliteration. It is important to bear in mind that while existing transliteration systems are made to fit the phonetics of the language into which a text is transliterated, *translit* takes place within the framework of a single language. This explains why the user in Example 4 can include "j" in his *translit*. The use of "j" makes sense in the French system, since the phonetic qualities of the Cyrillic letter *ж* resemble those of the French "j." This is different in English phonetics, which is why the English transliterate the same letter as "zh." This Russian user is not constrained by English or French phonetics, instead he opts for the most economical, one-letter solution from the French system. In my material there are 30 messages with renderings of the Cyrillic *ж*, 16 of them write "j" (e.g. examples 2, 4, 6, 15), nine write "zh," four write "z," and one writes "gh" (e.g. example 9).

The partial overlap between the Cyrillic and Latin alphabets means that some letters are less prone to variation within *translit* than others. In my material, there is a total overlap between 15 letters: *а* (a), *б* (b), *г* (g), *д* (d), *з* (z), *к* (k), *л* (l), *м* (m), *н* (n), *п* (p), *р* (r), *с* (s), *т* (t), *ф* (f), and *э* (e). That is, every instance of the Cyrillic letter renders the respective Latin letter. The letters "v" and "i" also overlap with one or two exceptions, as seen in the following examples.

(5) @FeruzaFattohova xorowo cto retvitnula asalim i eto retweetni
/@FeruzaFattohova хорошо что ретвитнула асалим и это ретвитни/
@FeruzaFattohova Good that you retweeted Asalim, retweet this as well.[12]

(6) 2 rasskaza Za den' eto silno [SMILEY] Azerbaijan jdu menya
/2 рассказа за день это сильно [SMILEY] Азербайджан жди меня/
2 short stories in one day, that's impressive [SMILEY] Azerbaijan, wait for me[13]

Example 5 concerns the Cyrillic letter *в*. We see that the stem "tvit," as in the Russian word for Twitter (i.e. *Tvitter*), is rendered differently, first as "retvitnula" (retweeted) and then as "retweetni" (retweet) influenced by English spelling. In my material there is one similar example with "tvit" and one with the word "wow." Example 6 is the only instance in my material where the Cyrillic *и* is rendered not as Latin "i," but as Latin "u." While the first is an example of the phonetic approach, the latter is an example of the orthographic approach, with the graphic form of the Latin "u" resembling to the Cyrillic *и*.

The remaining 16 letters of the Cyrillic alphabet are represented by different Latin letters or symbols. A good example is the letter *ш*, which comes out as "w" (example 3), "6" (example 7), or "sh" (example 8).

(7) Odno radyet iz vsei et sityei6en). 4to po skaipy govorila s odnim 4elovekom*. Gde-to okolo 6 hourse)).

/Одно радует из всеи эт ситуэйшен). Что по скайпу говорила с одним человеком*. Где-то около 6 hourse [*sic*!]./

One thing makes me happy in this situation). That I spoke with one guy on Skype. For some 6 hours)).[14]

(8) @sandraa666 @datKiwii 1.ja ne slushaju russkij rap 2.eto ne bilo skazano v obidu tebe i vsem ostaljnim gitaristam. prosto mojo mnenie

/@sandraa666 @datKiwii 1.я не слушаю русский рап 2. это не было сказано в обиду тебе и всем остальным гитаристам. просто моё мнение/

@sandraa666 @datKiwii 1. I don't listen to Russian rap 2. this was not said to offend you or other guitar players. It is just my opinion.[15]

The correlation of letters varies depending on the perspective, i.e. whether we take a standardized Cyrillic Russian text as our point of departure, or look at the Latin text at hand. For several of the letters in the above list of overlaps, the Latin representation is shared between several Cyrillic letters. Latin "g" is one such example: in my material it represents the Cyrillic *г*, *ж*, and *х*.

(9) @fyfars a ya,moi dryg,k soghaleniu ne v Yakutii (: no na schet loghek . . . Y menya est',vozmoghno mogy popolnit' tvou kollekciyou

/@fyfars а я, мой друг, к сожалению не в Якутии (: но на счет ложек . . . У меня есть, возможно могу пополнить твою коллекцию/

@fyfars But I, my friend, am not in Yakutia (: But when it comes to spoons . . . I have, I might be able to add to your collection[16]

(10) @ButskoS 9 dumau 4to u takoi devuwki kak ti ne gvatit smelosti poiti na takoe))))

/@ButskoS Я думаю что у такой девушки как ты не хватит смелости пойти на такое))))/

@ButskoS I think that a girl like you doesn't have enough courage for something like that))))[17]

In Example 9, Latin "g" is used both for Cyrillic *г* and, together with the Latin "h," for Cyrillic *ж*. In Example 10, Latin "g" is used for Cyrillic *х*.

Variation can also be seen at the level of words. In my material, the pronoun *что* is represented 17 times in 75 messages.[18] Table 9.1 shows that the forms

*Table 9.1* Variants of the pronoun "Что" in Twitter and VKontakte

| *Variant* | *Instances Twitter* | *Instances VKontakte** | *Characterization* |
|---|---|---|---|
| chto | 8 | 680,000 | Phonetic approach, English transliteration |
| 4to | 5 | 345,000 | Orthographic approach |
| wto | 2 | 45,000 | Orthographic approach (transcription) |
| cto | 2 | 34,000 | Quasi-academic |

Note: *The search on VKontakte was done 22–23 January 2013.

"chto" and "4to" are the most popular: the former is an example of the phonetic approach, which is also identical to common English transliteration, the latter is an example of an orthographic approach. "Wto" is another example of an orthographic approach, where the pronoun is transcribed as pronounced in Russian—*што*—and then rendered in Latin letters. The final example, "cto," resembles academic transliteration (čto), but without the diacritics. The latter example illustrates the limitations of the ASCII code, where diacritic symbols are not available. A similar pattern to that seen in Twitter occurs if we search for these variants on the Russian social networking service VKontakte. The search function in VKontakte renders a multiplex material of personal messages and links, but a quick look at the extracted hits indicates that they are relevant for my purpose.

The numbers in Table 9.1, with several hundred thousand messages written in *translit*, also indicate that it is widely used among the Russian-speaking community online.

As we have seen from these examples, the different number of letters in the Cyrillic and Latin alphabets means more than one Latin letter must be used to represent one Cyrillic letter in some instances. This is particularly common for some consonants *ш* (e.g. example 8), *щ*, *ж* (e.g. example 9), *ц*, *х*, and for the so-called soft vowels *е*, *ю*, and *я*. The latter are often represented by one standard letter "j" (e.g. examples 3, 8 and 14) or "y" (e.g. examples 1, 2, 4, 9, 12, 13 and 16) that indicates softness, and a letter to represent the vowel sound in question (e.g. "e," "u," and "a").

As seen in one of the examples above, there is also a tendency, where possible, to avoid using more than one Latin letter to represent one Cyrillic. One of the ways to achieve this goal is by using numerals for some Cyrillic letters. Example 11 demonstrates this, where "4" is used for Cyrillic *ч* and "9" is used for Cyrillic *я*.

(11) @Skatesoul2 tu witaew 4to y teb9 babskij harakter? o.O
/@Skatesoul2 ты считаешь что у тебя бабский характер? o.O/
@Skatesoul2 Do you think that you have a sissy character? o.O[19]

The use of the numerals to represent letters can be understood in two ways. One interpretation is what Androutsopoulos calls "graphemisation," where the visual resemblance is taken into account, as in an orthographic transliteration, e.g. "4to" for Cyrillic *что*. Alternatively, the numeral "4" can be seen as representing the first letter in the Russian word "four"—*четыре*. This latter interpretation is different from the homophones well known from English, where the phonetic resemblance allows the numeral "4" to represent "for" as a word or suffix, as in "4ever", a phenomenon that is also described for Greek by Androutsopoulos (2009). It is similar, however, to the situation in Arabic, where the numeral "5" is used to represent the sound "x," since "the Arabic word for 'five,' 'xamsa,' begins with this sound" (Palfreyman and al Khalil 2007: 54). Avdonina and Nikitin (2006b) have suggested calling this phenomenon a phonogram, since the numerals are to be read as letters independently of their visual characteristics, as was the case with some Egyptian hieroglyphs.

While "4" can be understood both as a graphemization and as a phonogram, "9" can only be read as a graphemization, since there is no relationship between the name of the numeral, *девять*, and the letter it is taken to represent, *я*. The relationship is a visual one. However, the concept of phonogram is crucial to understanding the use of "6" in Example 7 above, as it represents the Cyrillic letter *ш*, which is also the first letter in the Russian word for "six"—*шесть*. Note that the use of "6" as a phonogram does not prevent it being used as a proper numeral in the same tweet.

We also observe a tendency towards conflation and loss of graphemes. This is seen among both vowels and consonants. In the following two examples we see a conflation of the Cyrillic vowels *и* (govorit, priwla, velikaya, im, opravdaniya) and *ы* (ti, sliwy, papi, vivodu, nepriyazn', tolstim) into one Latin "i."

(12) 'a on mne govorit:ti poslednee vremya takaya profyra, a ya emy: a 4to eto?' dadada. Ya sliwy eto slovo ne tol'ko v sarapyle ot papi

/"а он мне говорит: ты последнее время такая профура, а я ему: а что это" дадада. Я слышу это слово не только в Сарапуле от папы/

"And he tells me: lately you have been such a Fury, and I tell him: what's that?" yesyesyes. Sarapul isn't the only place I've heard this word from dad.[20]

(13) priwla k vivodu, 4to u menya velikaya nepriyazn' k tolstim lyudyam!!! Im net opravdaniya!!!

/пришла к выводу, что у меня великая неприязнь к толстым людям!!! Им нет оправдания/

I came to the conclusion that I have a great dislike for fat people!!! There is no excuse for them[21]

This practice leads to a reduction of the Russian alphabet by one letter. We also find conflation in consonants. In my material, *ш*, (example 15) *щ*, (example 14) *ч* (example 15) and the combination of letters *сч* (example 11, above) are all represented by Latin "w."

(14) @AnnaTurchak hahahaa eto ewe tot prikol na samom dele bojus predstavit 4to u malenkoj tur4ak tam tvorilos haahahahah :D

/@AnnaTurchak хахаха это еще тот прикол на самом деле боюсь представить что у маленькой Турчак там творилось хахахаха :D/

@AnnaTurchak hahaha that's the same joke I really don't dare to imagine what the young Turchak was up to there hahahah :D[22]

(15) @Aziza_Mzadeh jaaaan spasibo bolwoooe:)sdala i daje ne ojidala wto tak xorowo vse budet :)

/@Aziza_Mzadeh jaaan спасибо большое:) сдала и даже не ожидала что так хорошо все будет :)/

@Aziza_Mzadeh jaaan Thank you so much:) I passed and didn't even expect that it would all turn out so well :)[23]

While the use of "w" for *ш* can be explained by a graphic similarity, the rest of the solutions are better explained with reference to Russian phonetics. There is a tendency in Russian pronunciation towards a conflation of the sounds represented by the graphemes *ш* and *щ*. Similarly, according to Russian orthography, the combination *сч* is pronounced as the letter *щ*, and the pronoun *что* is pronounced as if it were written *што*.

Palfreyman and al Khalil ask whether transliteration or transcription inform practices of ASCII-ized languages. The examples mentioned above with "w" indicate that transcription is indeed used for some of the consonants in my material, but in general the transliteration approach dominates. This is particularly visible in the rendering of Russian vowels. Instead of *transcribing* the vowel phonemes according to the vowel reduction that is so characteristic of spoken Russian, users prefer to *transliterate* the vowel graphemes from written Russian. This can be seen in Example 16, where the letters in bold are pronounced more like "a" than the written "o." Note also the rendering of the pronoun in genitive "togo," which is pronounced "tavo." Thus we are clearly dealing with transliteration, rather than transcription.

(16) ahahahahah kaaak et**o** mil**ooo**)) d**o**vesti parnya d**o** t**o**go 4to on ydalilsya ahahahahahaahah

/ахахахах каак это милооо))) довести парня до того что он удалился ахахахах/

ahahahaha Ho-ow nice it is)) to irritate a guy so much that he takes off[24]

In doing so, users are choosing to ignore the trend towards phonetic script, *olbanskii iazyk*, that was so popular on the Runet in the first decade of this century (see Hristova 2011; Zvereva 2012: 51–82; and Chapter 7 by Berdicevskis and Zvereva, in this volume).

## The politics of computer-mediated digraphia

As a new phenomenon that has gained prominence in the Russian language community over the last two decades, and one that violates the expectations we harbor towards modern standardized orthographies, it is natural to see some debate about the use of *translit*. Following the liberal linguistic policies of the 1990s, which led participants in the public discourse to talk about a lack of restraint in public language behavior and a fall in language culture (Paulsen 2009), the 2000s have seen moves by Russians politicians to restore the greatness of the national language, particularly through state-sponsored programs of language support (Ryazanova-Clarke 2002; Gorham 2009). There have been several key events over the last decade. In 2002, the Duma amended "the Law on the Languages of the People of the Russian Federation" to make it mandatory for all languages in the country to use the Cyrillic alphabet. A couple of years later "the Law on the State Language of the Russian Federation" was passed (Ryazanova-Clarke 2006). And the same year, Vladimir Putin decreed 2007 the "Year of the Russian Language," thus ensuring that matters of language would receive much funding and attention, both within Russia and abroad.

One of the key issues for Russian politicians recently has been the conditions for Cyrillic in digital settings. The opportunity to use Cyrillic in internet address domains became a test case, and in June 2008 then president Dmitry Medvedev made it clear that the Russian government "must do all [it could] to make Cyrillic domain names possible" (Anon. 2008). The Russian Ministry of Communications applied to the Internet Cooperation for Assigned Names and Numbers (ICANN), and in May 2010 the Cyrillic top-level domain *.рф* was established. Interestingly, the fact that the new domain took its name from the official name of the Russian Federation—RF—indicated that the state was now heavily involved in the development of the Russian segment of the internet. This was further emphasized when the two first sites within the new Cyrillic domain were opened, representing the Presidential Administration and the Government: prezident.rf and pravitelstvo.rf.

According to official information from the Ministry of Communications website, the introduction of the Cyrillic domain is seen as an important step towards boosting the creation of a national identity and broadening the Russian-language segment of the internet. The website points out that a Cyrillic domain is seen as necessary because not all Russians are equally comfortable with the English language, i.e. the Latin alphabet.

*Translit* is also discussed widely among Russians online. In an investigation of the language policies of more than 80 Runet forums, Sidorova (2006: 182–4) found that one of the most widely used rules is to restrict the use of *translit*. For the purposes of this chapter I have collected materials from the youth discussion site, lovehate.ru.

Lovehate.ru is a discussion site where users write their reasons for "loving" or "hating" various phenomena. The site keeps a complete track file of all contributions and is thus a convenient site for establishing the development in attitude towards a phenomenon. A reasonably popular discussion about *translit* was set up in February 1999 and contains 103 messages, 20 in support of *translit* and 83 opposed.[25]

The supporters of *translit* point to technological, technical, economical and cultural explanations for their preference: (1) Not everyone has access to Cyrillic letters in CMC; (2). Some have become used to writing in Latin letters and find it more convenient; (3) Due to different encodings, SMS messages are cheaper with Latin letters (160 symbols per message) than with Cyrillic (70 symbols per message); (4) One or two point out that Russians should replace Cyrillic with the Latin alphabet to join the more developed Western civilization. The fact that technological constraints were mentioned in the period 1999–2002 and limited, in later posts, to people traveling or living outside Russia, or to the language of SMS messages, indicates that, in general, when using PCs, people in Russia no longer experience technological constraints in writing Cyrillic. However, the spread of digital technology, along with the increased use of handheld digital devices such as mobile phones, indicates that the Latin alphabet is still used for writing Russian today. The latest comment in support of Latin for SMS messages was written in August 2012.

The comments written by those opposed to *translit* are generally very aggressive. "I hate it when someone writes in Russian with Latin letters!" was how user Inga opened a discussion in February 1999, "and I hate those who write like that," she went on. The arguments against *translit* are mainly linguistic, technological and cultural: (1) It is much harder to read a text in *translit* than in Cyrillic; (2). It is very easy to set up your computer to support Cyrillic; (3) People who use *translit* are lazy, stupid, too influenced by Western values, or just want to show off; (4) There is no common standard for writing *translit*. Several users relate *translit* to English through the alphabet and claim that they would rather read proper English than Russian in Latin letters. Others are more accommodating, noting that *translit* can be excused when writing SMS messages. In general, however, the decade-long discussion about *translit* on lovehate.ru suggests that *translit* is an unpopular phenomenon among members of the Russian language community online.

## Conclusion

The technical reasons for the rise of *translit* and the appearance of a digraphical situation are based on the fact that the digital technology we use today has been developed in an English-language setting. Language communities using other scripts have had to play a game of catch up: even if solutions have been found for some of the fundamental challenges, new technological developments have created new challenges. Today *translit* is particularly relevant for SMS messages (where it remains cheaper) and for people writing Russian outside the borders of Russia. The latter often find themselves in multilingual surroundings where digital devices have not been adapted for the use of Cyrillic letters. This is key to understanding the computer-mediated digraphia: as Artemii Lebedev pointed out, since digital devices are made outside of Russia, they are by default not created to be used with the Cyrillic alphabet and have to be adapted to the Russian alphabet. This does not make it impossible to use Cyrillic, but the adaptation involves an extra cost of effort or money (in the case of SMS messages). As a result many still find it more convenient to use *translit*.

The linguistic character of *translit* is that of variety. The common English transliteration system appears to influence many of the solutions chosen by users in the data examined here, but the total picture of the linguistic output investigated differs significantly and *systematically* from any established system of transliteration. For Russians, the established transliteration systems have become linguistic smorgasbords from which they pick and choose the options that fit their needs. Different approaches are used for different letters even within the same, very short, messages. Some letters are rendered according to principles of transliteration, others follow principles of transcription. Still others go beyond the borders of traditional transliteration and transcription, using numerals. The data also indicate a tendency towards conflation and loss of graphemes.

This suggests that we are dealing with a new orthography, or rather a multitude of individual new orthographies that share some more or less common features. Based on the linguistic resources at hand (the available letters, existing systems of transliteration and transcription), different individuals use their linguistic creativity to establish their own systems of rendering Russian in Latin letters. Future research should continue to map out the existence of *translit* in various digital settings, as well as its typological features. Will we see a koineization towards a more stable orthography, or will the variation continue?

The magnitude of the phenomenon means that the study of *translit* and the Russian computer-mediated digraphia is important for our understanding of contemporary Russian. This is especially true for our understanding of Russian outside Russia's borders. In addition, my findings, together with Birzer's (Birtser 2004), have shown that the study of *translit* can tell us something about common tendencies towards convergence in Russian phonetics.

While figures of actual usage from VKontakte and metalinguistic discussions on lovehate.ru suggest that *translit* is still a common phenomenon, especially in SMS messages and among Russian-speakers outside the country, the attitude towards the phenomenon is generally negative. This is reflected in official Russian policies: Russian laws oblige the country's citizens to use Cyrillic, and the government uses its prestige also to make the use of Cyrillic possible in areas where this has so far been impossible. The big question in determining the future of *translit* is whether the general attitudes among users of CMC and the efforts of the government are enough to counter the technological bias towards Latin script.

## Notes

1 See Dale (1980), DeFrancis (1984), Grivelet (2001) for introductions to digraphia.

2 The proud history of Russian and Soviet computer development is portrayed at the internet museum *Virtual'nyi komp'iuternyi muzei*: http://www.computer-museum.ru/index.php.

3 It should be noted that the letter "ë" has for a long time had only semi-official status in the Russian language. See Es'kova (2000, 2008).

4 *ZA Russkii IAzyk*—"For the Russian language."

5 Doshlo do togo, chto proshe bylo posilat pisma na translite, chem vozit'sya s perekodirovkami. Polozhenie neskol'ko vypravilos', kogda pochti vse pogolovno pereshli na Outlook. No i seichas prihoditsya stalkivat'sya s pis'mami, v kotoryh soderzhitsya chto-nibud' vrode "Sb'f'el{e cnqond'! Ndmnbpelemmn on Mnbnphfqjnls m'op'bkemh~" ili voobshe "???? ?????! ?????? ???? ??" . . . [Original in Latin letters, MP].

6 Based on searches for "chto," "4to," "wto" and "cto" in VKontakte, see Table 9.1. Out of 100 messages, seven were written by people who indicated Russia as their home country, 58 indicated that they lived outside Russia, whereas 30 did not indicate any geographical belonging.

7 My data was collected in January 2013 from Twitter using Yandex's Twitter search, based on 25 tweets for each of the search words "4to," "xorowo," "eto," and "menya." The selection of search words reflects popular norms of *translit*, and allow for comparison across the material.

8 Polina Malibu, @polina_malibu (15 January 2013), http://twitter.com/polina_malibu/statuses/291258672481464320 (accessed 15 April 2013).

9 Ainura A, @ainura_at (15 January 2013), http://twitter.com/ainura_at/statuses/291266614731624448 (accessed 15 April 2013).

10 Yelena Trifonova, @trifonovayelena (14 January 2013), http://twitter.com/TrifonovaYelena/statuses/290920237677805568 (accessed 15 April 2013).

11 A****, @ajara_k (15 January 2013), http://twitter.com/Ajara_K/statuses/291268264754020352 (accessed 15 April 2013).

12 Kamola Oripova BMK, @bonowim28 (11 January 2013), http://twitter.com/bonowim28/statuses/289669732058152960 (accessed 15 April 2013).

13 UkenovA, @aruwka (15 January 2013), http://twitter.com/ARUWKA/statuses/291248744358354944 (accessed 15 April 2013).

14 Anna Modei, @modei15 (15 January 2013), http://twitter.com/MODEi15/statuses/291026500138971136 (accessed 15 April 2013).

15 milanie, @a_milanie (15 January 2013), http://twitter.com/miljkastar/statuses/291259809561444353 (accessed 15 April 2013).

16 Ischenko Viktoria, @vikulush (15 January 2013), http://twitter.com/VikuLish/statuses/291263892481519617 (accessed 15 April 2013).

17 Fedor Mironov, @fedor_mironov (14 January 2013), http://twitter.com/Fedor_Mironov/statuses/290948881410310144 (accessed 15 April 2013).

18 The material collected through the search word "4to" was excluded from this comparison.

19 Zzayots, @zzayots (15 January 2013), http://twitter.com/Zzayots/statuses/290975261451763712 (accessed 15 April 2013).

20 Valentina Semenova, @valundij (15 January 2013), http://twitter.com/Valundij/statuses/291075765087383552 (accessed 15 April 2013).

21 Nata, @natalienataalie (15 January 2013), http://twitter.com/NatalieNataalie/statuses/291229661332127744 (accessed 15 April 2013).

22 Kaitly Harris, @chakkat (15 January 2013), http://twitter.com/ChakKat/statuses/290987632752750592 (accessed 15 April 2013).

23 Aytaj Kerimli, @aitaj_k (14 January 2013), http://twitter.com/aitaj_k/status/290729039654711296 (accessed 15 April 2013).

24 Lika, @lika_likushaa (15 January 2013), http://twitter.com/lika_likushaa/status/291170709286313985 (accessed 15 April 2013).
25 See: lovehate.ru/opinions/975/.

## References


Abdulla, Rasha. 2007. *The Internet in the Arab World: Egypt and Beyond*. New York: Peter Lang.

Androutsopoulos, Jannis. 2006. "Introduction: Sociolinguistics and Computer-Mediated Communication." *Journal of Sociolinguistics* 10: 419–38.

—— 2009. " 'Greeklish': Transliteration Practice and Discourse in the Context of Computer-Mediated Digraphia." In *Standard Languages and Language Standards: Greek, Past and Present*, edited by Alexandra Georgakopoulou and Michael Silk, 221–49. Aldershot: Ashgate.

Anon. 2007. "Mobile Handset Market Shrinks." *IT & Telecom Russia*. February 22. Available at: http://www.ictrussia.com/46845/Mobile_handset_market_shrinks.shtml (accessed 31 March 2013).

Anon. 2008. "Medvedev nastaivaet na kirillicheskikh domennykh imenakh." *Klerk.ru*. June 11. Available at: http://www.klerk.ru/soft/news/110807/ (accessed 31 March 2013).

Avdonina, Marina, and Sergei Nikitin. 2006a. "Sovremennoe neformal'noe pis'mennoe obshchenie na russkom iazyke (leksikograficheskoe i orfograficheskie problemy v SMS-soobshcheniiakh i Internet)." In *Russkii iazyk v Evrope: metodika, opyt prepodavaniia, perspektiv*, edited by Sergio Pescatori, Stefano Aloe and Iuliia Nikolaeva, 112–16. Verona: The Coffee House art & adv.

—— 2006b. "SMS—novyi etiket, pravila i konventsii neformal'nogo pis'mennogo obshcheniia na russkom iazyke." In *Rechevaia kommunikatsiia na sovremennom etape: sotsial'nye, nauchno-teoreticheskie i didakticheskie problemy*, edited by Liudmila Minaeva, 87–90. Moscow: Institut Russkogo iazyka im. A.S. Pushkina, MGUS.

Birtser [Birzer], Sandra. 2004. *Transliteratsiia russkikh grafem v latinitsu v elektronnoi perepiske na russkom iazyke*. St Petersburg: Izdatel'stvo SPbGU.

Chemerkin, Serhii. 2009. *Ukraiinska mova v Interneti: pozamovni ta vnutrishn'ostrukturni protsesy*. Kyiv: Natsional'na akademiia nauk Ukraiiny, Instytut ukraiinskoii movy.

Dale, Ian. 1980. "Digraphia." *International Journal of the Sociology of Language* 26: 5–14.

Danet, Brenda, and Susan Herring. 2007. "Introduction: Welcome to the Multilingual Internet." In *The Multilingual Internet: Language, Culture, and Communication Online*, edited by Brenda Danet and Susan Herring, 3–39. Oxford: Oxford University Press.

DeFrancis, John. 1984. "Digraphia." *Word* 35: 59–66.

Es'kova, Natal'ia. 2000. "Pro bukvu ë." *Nauka i zhizn'* 4. Available at: http://www.nkj.ru/archive/articles/6983/ (accessed 31 March 2013).

—— 2008. "I eshche raz o bukve ë." *Nauka i zhizn'* 7. Available at: http://www.nkj.ru/archive/articles/14333/ (accessed 31 March 2013).

Frehner, Carmen. 2008. *Email—SMS—MMS: The Linguistic Creativity of Asynchronous Discourse in the New Media Age*. Bern: Peter Lang.

Ganley, Gladys. 1996. *Unglued Empire: The Soviet Experience with Communication Technologies*. Norwood, NJ: Ablex Publishing Corporation.

Gorham, Michael S. 2009. "Linguistic Ideologies, Economies and Technologies in the Language Culture of Contemporary Russia (1987–2008)." *Journal of Slavic Linguistics* 17: 163–93.

Gottlieb, Nanette. 2000. *Word-Processing Technology in Japan: Kanji and the Keyboard*. Richmond: Curzon.

—— 2005. *Language and Society in Japan*. Cambridge: Cambridge University Press.

—— 2009. "Language on the Internet in Japan." In *Internationalizing Internet Studies: Beyond Anglophone Paradigms*, edited by Gerard Goggin and Mark McLelland, 65–78. London: Routledge.

Grivelet, Stéphane. 2001. "Introduction." *International Journal of the Sociology of Language* 150: 1–10.

Hillebrand, Friedhelm, Finn Trosby, Kevin Holley, and Ian Harris. 2010. *Short Message Service (SMS): The Creation of Personal Global Text Messaging*. Chichester: Wiley.

Hristova, Daniela S. 2011. "Velikii i moguchii olbanskii iazyk: The Russian Internet and the Russian Language." *Russian Language Journal* 61: 143–62.

Khairullin, Lenar. 2010. "Istoriia poiavleniia komp'iuterov v Rossii." *Mega Obzor*, January 25. Available at: http://megaobzor.com/newsnew-11646.html (accessed 31 March 2013).

Koutsogiannis, Dimitris, and Bessie Mitsikopoulou. 2007. "Greeklish and Greekness: Trends and Discourses of 'Glocalness'." In *The Multilingual Internet: Language, Culture, and Communication Online*, edited by Brenda Danet and Susan Herring, 142–60. Oxford: Oxford University Press.

Lebedev, Artemii. 2004. "Tragediia zapiatoi." *Kodovstvo*. Available at: http://www.artlebedev.ru/kovodstvo/sections/105/ (accessed 31 March 2013).

Magner, Thomas F. 2001. "Digraphia in the Territories of the Croats and Serbs." *International Journal of the Sociology of Language* 150: 11–26.

Markelov, Andrei. 2004. "Domashnie PK v SSSR i ikh emuliatsiia." *Upgrade* 167. Available at: http://stfw.ru/page.php?id=9911 (accessed 31 March 2013).

Palfreyman, David, and Muhamed al Khalil. 2007. " 'A Funky Language for Teenzz to Use': Representing Gulf Arabic in Instant Messaging." In *The Multilingual Internet: Language, Culture, and Communication Online*, edited by Brenda Danet and Susan Herring, 43–63. Oxford: Oxford University Press.

Paulsen, Martin. 2009. "Hegemonic Language and Literature: Russian Metadiscourse on Language in the 1990s." PhD dissertation, University of Bergen, Bergen.

—— 2011. "Digital Determinism: The Cyrillic Alphabet in the Age of New Technology." *Russian Language Journal* 61: 119–40.

Prokhorov, Sergei. 1999. "Computers in Russia: Science, Education, and Industry." *IEEE Annals of the History of Computing* 21: 4–15.

Revich, Iurii. 2002. "Polnyi CHARSET (okonchanie)." *Russkii zhurnal*. December 29. Available at: http://old.russ.ru:8085/netcult/20021229_revich-pr.html (accessed 31 March 2013).

Rohozinski, Rafal. 2000. "How the Internet Did Not Transform Russia." *Current History* 99: 334–8.

Ryazanova-Clarke, Lara. 2002. "Developments in the Russian Language in the Post-Soviet Period." *Journal of Communist Studies and Transition Politics* 18: 97–116.

—— 2006 "?The State Turning to Language?: Power and Identity in Russian Language Policy Today." *Russian Language Journal* 56: 37–55.

Sidorova, Marina. 2006. *Internet-lingvistika: Russkii iazyk. Mezhlichnostnoe obshchenie*. Moscow: 1989.ru.

Sobolev, Iar. 2009. "Zhertvy dizainerov: zametki o mobil'nykh klaviaturakh." *Mobi.ru*. January 28. Available at: http://www.mobimag.ru/Articles/3955/Zhertvy_dizainerov_zametki_o_mobilnyh_klaviaturah.htm (accessed 31 March 2013).

Spassov, Orlin. 2012. "Contesting Bulgaria's Past Through New Media: Latin, Cyrillic and Politics." *Europe-Asia Studies* 64(8): 1486–504.

Sproat, Richard. 2010. *Language, Technology, and Society*. Oxford: Oxford University Press.

Tseliga, Theodora. 2007. " 'It's All Greeklish to Me!': Linguistic and Sociocultural Perspectives on Roman-Alphabeted Greek in Asynchronous Computer-Mediated Communication." In *The Multilingual Internet: Language, Culture, and Communication Online*, edited by Brenda Danet and Susan Herring, 116–41. Oxford: Oxford University Press.

Warschauer, Mark, Ghada el Said, and Ayman Zohry. 2007. "Language Choice Online: Globalization and Identity in Egypt." In *The Multilingual Internet: Language, Culture, and Communication Online*, edited by Brenda Danet and Susan Herring, 303–18. Oxford: Oxford University Press.

Zvereva, Vera. 2012. *Setevye razgovory: kul'turnye kommunikatsii v Runete* (Slavica Bergensia 10). Bergen: Department of Foreign Languages, University of Bergen.

# Part IV

# Literature and new technology

# 10 Russian literature on the internet

## From hypertext to fairy tale

*Henrike Schmidt*

### Literary dot-ru addiction: introduction

Есть точка в космосе с названьем кратким «ru»,
В которой я завис давно и прочно.
Боюсь, что в этой точке и помру . . .

There is a dot in space with the brief name .ru,
Where I've already long been caught,
I'm afraid, at this dotty point I will snuff it, too . . .

Igor' Irt'enev's (2007) ironic verse on getting addicted to the Russian internet, designated by the typical abbreviation dot.ru, summarizes the symbolic meaning and the practical significance of networked communication environments for Russian writers. The poetic dedication characterizes the attachment of the Russian creative class to the Runet as an efficient publication technology, a captivating communication network and a new public sphere. In its intensity, this attachment is interpreted ambivalently, in positive as well as in negative terms. Such a paradoxical identification with the literary—and political—culture of the web is rather common among the *runetchiki*, a popular neologism for the internet professionals and digital bohemia. An especially insightful case is the poet, writer and journalist Dmitrii Bykov, who polemicizes against "the Runet" by describing it as a place where "programmers, grads, moms, and dads" are given the power to judge aesthetic works according to their individual likings (Bykov 2005: 66). For that reason, the "professional" writer Bykov spontaneously regrets having been born in the "most reading country of the world." He also compares life on the *Rulinet*—the "Russian Literary internet"—with popular novels by Fyodor Dostoevsky (ibid.: 64–5): "In fact, it would be no great exaggeration to say that it was Fedor Mikhailovich who invented the Rulinet . . . 150 years before it actually appeared." While Bykov fundamentally admires the work of Russia's famous novelist, the analogy here is in no way positive. It is Dostoevsky's bored, cynical, malicious "underground man" who, according to Bykov is today reincarnated in the ordinary Russian user, with his cultural inferiority complex and literary ambitiousness.

At the same time Bykov, a multimedia jack-of-all-trades participating in talk shows on radio and TV, uses the internet intensively. For example, to propagate his extremely popular literary "newsical" *Citizen poet* (*Grazhdanin poet*), where, at the height of the political protests which accompanied the elections in the winter of 2011–12, he rewrote classical Russian poems as Putin parodies (performed by the well-known artist Mikhail Efremov). When asked to explain this contradiction, Bykov lists a variety of arguments: he likes, once again in the tradition of Dostoevsky, to keep a writer's diary (*Dnevnik pisatelia*); many of his ideas, which were first expressed on the Runet, constitute important material for his novels, and some forum discussions have even passed into his books in their entirety. Despite such pragmatic reasons, Bykov finally admits experiencing a kind of cyberpassion which runs counter to his own will: he reads distinct texts or sites as well as the majority of forum discussions with "an aesthetic, possibly even erotic, pleasure" (ibid.: 74).

Such quasi-erotic attractiveness is grounded, at least during the early development of the Runet, in its marginality, what made its literary pioneers feel as if they were virtually colonizing a new cultural field. Even Sergei Kostyrko, literary critic for the "thick journal" *Novyi mir* and opponent of any media euphoria, recalls the "virginal purity of the Russian internet" (Kostyrko 2000–2008, here from 2006), populated in the following years by opposing interest groups.

## "Lyricists and physicists": early history

The "pure" space of the literary Runet was first settled by representatives of the technical "intelligentsia," which in Russia has traditionally been strong. Mathematics, physicists, engineers and programmers were among the first to have access to computer technology and to the internet. Besides their professional activities, they used the new communication technologies for their own literary amusement. Thus, it comes as no surprise that the first wave of Russian-language resources focusing on literary content was created to a large extent by the so-called "technicians" (*tekhnari*), reflecting their specific literary tastes.

In November 1994, the programmer Maksim Moshkov launched his electronic library, which even today remains one of the Runet's most prominent "institutions" (see Chapter 12 by Mjør, in this volume). Only a year later, in 1995, the mathematician Dmitrii Manin founded the first collective literary game *Burime* (from the French: "Bout-rimé"), including a guestbook and a complaints book, which provided the opportunity for interactive exchange among authors and readers. That April saw the launch of *DeLitZyne*, the first electronic literary magazine to be published in the Russian language, which was initiated by the geophysicist Leonid Delitsyn, who at the time was studying in the United States. His insider magazine for technology freaks with literary interests developed rapidly and within a few years turned into the biggest online literary award on the Runet, the *Teneta* (*Snares*). Last but not least, late 1995 witnessed the emergence of yet another cult resource on the Runet, *Anekdot.ru* (Anekdoty iz Rossii/Jokes from Russia), initiated once again by one of the "technicians" living abroad, namely the astrophysicist Dmitrii Verner. This project—as was the case with the Moshkov library—was started as a private hobby for the sake of personal entertainment and turned into a huge resource with ten thousands of users, still popular today. The Anekdoty.ru collection of jokes, funny stories and other humoresque genres was one of the early examples of the emerging net folklore which would achieve such popularity on the Runet (Gorny 2009: 289): "[it] represent[s] the present-day Russian folklore and, through it, give[s] an unbiased picture of the Zeitgeist."

The digital literary field of the time was small, as was the number of protagonists, with a high *tusovka*-factor (Russian jargon for "get-together," "partying"), as they virtually and physically "clubbed around," for example at the famous "headquarters" of the early Runet elite, based in the Moscow apartment of the literary scholar, publisher and cultural activist Dmitrii Itskovich (Gorny 2009: 162). Accordingly, among the early *runetchiki* the feeling of a digital subculture emerged, at the same time elitist and oriented towards the grass roots. Its self-consciousness was determined by the ideal of unrestricted cultural autonomy, totally free of political and commercial interests; through their projects they promoted aesthetics, texts and authors which had been forbidden or marginalized throughout Soviet times, ranging from science fiction to esoterism, from vanguard poetry to bard song culture. While many of them were programmers and thus "code experts," the early Runet protagonists were not particularly engaged with critical net art or conceptual codeworks, as was the case, for example, in the English- or German-speaking segments of the web. They were interested in "content" that had been inaccessible throughout the decades of Soviet political and aesthetic domination.

From the external perspective of the established literary institutions, the anarchic Runet mix of Soviet bard and song culture (Vladimir Vysotsky), science fiction (the Strugatskii brothers) and post-modern aesthetics (Viktor Pelevin) constituted a "distorted" picture of Russian literature and a provocation to recognized canons and institutions (Kostyrko 2006).

## Cyber-graphomania and web samizdat

The representatives of the established literary institutions and professions, when they entered the Runet in the mid-1990s, clearly articulated their aim of correcting the "distortions" and preparing the virtual ground for the arrival of the "professional writers." They encountered resolute resistance from the "technicians," on the one hand, and from the rather sub- or counter-culturally-oriented protagonists, on the other, who did not want the old structures and hierarchies, some of them still partly Soviet, to be reproduced in what continued to be a non-hierarchic internet.

The ideal of a literary space free from hierarchical structures was viewed as a negative utopian vision by others, such as the poet and literary critic Dmitrii Kuzmin, who acquired the notoriety of an ardent defender of "professional literature" on the Runet (Kuzmin 2000; Levin n.d.). The uncontrolled growth of the Russian literary internet, which had been created in the years 1994–97 principally by "people not adhering to literature," in keeping with this position, was to be civilized.

The provocative terms of dilettante, amateur or graphomaniac turned into the starting point for heated debates which erupted throughout almost every cycle in the development of the Runet, from its marginal beginnings in the mid-1990s through to the massive use of Web 2.0 in the 2000s. Such discussions are not confined to the Runet, but take place right around the world, focusing on online creativity and its mass nature (Keene 2007). In Russia, such disputes are partly "nationalized" when placed within the terminological and historical framework of samizdat (Klimontovich 2003). The term samizdat, literally "self-publication" (*sam* "self"; *izdat'* "to publish"), denotes the publication of texts which in Soviet times were excluded from print for political reasons. Samizdat as a reference frame is thus used when issues of censorship in contemporary Russia are discussed and the Runet appears as an alternative publication channel for otherwise suppressed or inaccessible materials.

But samizdat is not only positively used for current self-publishing initiatives on the web. Thus, Dmitrii Kuzmin differentiates between a political samizdat, which does not reject basic editorial and selection procedures, and a *sam-sebia-izdat* as a "do-it-yourself" publishing policy, which avoids the application of external quality standards. While Kuzmin himself efficiently uses the Runet in order to propagate his own literary projects, he demonizes the phenomenon of amateur web samizdat as a threat to "Great Russian literature." In practice, the graphomaniacs defend themselves by maintaining enormous self-publication platforms such as stihi.ru or proza.ru, which contain millions of literary texts, and by positioning themselves provocatively as the only writers free of pressure in a contemporary Russian culture dominated by commercialization and commodification.

The graphomanian furore of the Runet provoked reactions that were mostly negative or suffused with amused irony, interpreting Russian net samizdat as a symbol for cultural degradation induced by a democratization of publishing technology. The philosopher and media theoretician Oleg Aronzon was among the first observers to try to make sense of the graphomanian samizdat by stressing a significant shift from cultural semantics to affective economy (Aronzon 2006).

## Cultural essentialism

As the Runet evolved from a marginal communication technology for techno geeks and underground writers into an easy-to-use mass medium, so more and more "professional" authors entered the internet. Personal homepages were used not only as an innovative communication channel, but as virtual extensions of carefully styled authorial *personae* (Boris Akunin, Viktor Erofeev, Aleksandra Marinina, Viktor Pelevin, Vladimir Sorokin). Writers entered into direct interaction with their readership via (micro-)blogs. While doing so they discussed—among themselves or with their readers—the extent to which the direct exposition of their writer's ego to the Runet community might change their style of writing, their aesthetics and their poetics, for better or for worse (see Chapter 4 by Roesen and Zvereva, in this volume). Last but not least, almost any text by a Russian contemporary writer sooner or later became available in one of the legal or illegal

Russian-language online libraries, sometimes with the approval and sometimes against the wishes of the respective authors (see Gornyi 1999). Such pragmatic publication policies caused not only verbal controversies but also led to trials and court proceedings (see Chapter 12 by Mjør, in this volume). Despite these conflicts, currently the Runet still abounds with literary texts and activities, even when compared with other segments of the global internet.

As an explanation for the astonishing vitality of the literary Runet, one nevertheless does not have to adhere to the myth of Russia as a literature-centered country, but can rely instead on historical, geographical and demographic aspects. With a readership living not only in the metropolises but also in regions geographically far away from the centers, with a Russian-speaking diaspora dispersed throughout the whole world and a book market which, especially in the 1990s, suffered from dysfunctionalities (Lovell and Menzel 2005), the internet offered and continues to offer an efficient marketing instrument for Russian authors and an important place for them to meet one another and their respective audiences.

While the quantitative growth of literary production on the Russian internet was thus acknowledged as an undeniable fact, provoking controversial discussions, the qualitative nature of the changes induced by digital and networked media for literary aesthetics has been questioned by a considerable number of Russian writers, critics and scholars. "What did the internet bring to literature that was new?" asks, for example, the poet Aleksandr Levin, in a discussion concerning the existence of a specific "net-literature" (in Russian called *seteratura* from the Russian word *set'* "web," "net," see Diskussiia o seterature 2000). And he provides a negative answer himself, by repudiating not only the idea of a specific net-literature, but also the idea of the significance of writing technology for the literary text in general (Levin n.d.): "The way of writing remained the same: with a pen scratch scratch, with a keyboard tak tak, with your head—think think." Such essentialist positions are popular not only among "paper writers," but also among Russian authors labeled as "net writers" (Gorchev 2000). Thus, Bykov, whom I cited above, concurs with the views expressed by Levin (Bykov 2000): "A specific form of *seteratura* does not exist in principle, just as there does not exist a manuscript-literature, a typewriter-literature, a tape-recorder-literature or anything of the kind."

Bykov's brief history of writing technologies aims to prove the resistance of literature to media change, to underline its ahistorical essence and identity, encompassing different epochs and cultures. Such "ahistorism," to use a term by Bourdieu, stands in distinct opposition to established positions in global media studies, starting with Marshall McLuhan's famous dictum about the "media being the message."

Of course, some Russian writers also represent the opposite opinion, articulating the point of view that the materializations of literature play an important role in literary aesthetics (Kuritsyn 2001). However, a significant part of the literary establishment *and* the literary Runet remains firmly opposed to positions that are commonplace in global media studies and were articulated by German literary scholars Peter Gendolla and Jörgen Schäfer (2007: 27): "[Literature] changes with and through the respective media through which it is processed and experienced . . . We therefore might say that the medium always inscribes itself into the content."

The blogger and writer Dmitrii Gorchev (2002) even suggested that analyzing the specific aesthetics of a subsumed net-literature is a favorite obsession of foreigners rather than of Russian scholars. Gorchev's rather sarcastic commentary contains some truth: "Russian" and "Western" literary studies are, at least partly, characterized by different research perspectives. Ulrich Schmid, in his book on *Russian Media Theory*, points out that there persists a distinct essentialist world-view within some parts of Russian humanities, where "'culture' is understood as an autonomous factor which exists apriori to its manifestations" (Schmid 2005: 83).

How then does one explain the ontological trait in (parts of) Russian literature and literary science? My hypothesis would be that, within Russian society as a whole, including academia, there remains a tendency towards cultural essentialism (see Franklin and Widdis 2004), which was only partly overcome during perestroika. The idea that literature has an eternal, timeless substance can be understood as a backlash against its marginalization during the (post-)perestroika period. Paradoxically, the essentialist view on literature did not hinder, but, on the contrary, fostered the development of a lively literary segment on the Runet. Without restricting themselves to avant-garde experiments in the field of electronic and digital aesthetics, Russian writers were free to explore and "fill" the internet with such—seemingly—anachronistic activities as the collective creation of sonnets and limericks or digital soap operas.

## Hyperfiction

Despite the cultural essentialism and the skepticism concerning the existence of a specific net-literature, literary works experimenting with the distinct technological features of new media do, of course, exist on the Runet. These experiments were framed by the respective theoretical discourses, embedding digital poetics in the contexts of vanguard poetics, on the one hand, and post-modern philosophy, on the other.

As in other segments of the global web, hypertext technology fascinated the minds of writers and artists and was discussed as a liberation technology, in the political as well as in the literary sense. Due to its interactivity and non-hierarchical nature, hypertextuality would free political discourses from power play and the reader from the narrative dictatorship of the author (Landow 2006). Criticism of such a utopian vision soon followed, focusing either on pragmatic facts, such as the question of internet access and the digital divide, or on philosophical issues such as the cognitive impossibility of a completely non-linear reading (Aarseth 1997; Porombka 2001; Simanowski 2002). Russian discourses concerning the promises and delusions of hypertext technology in the 1990s did not differ much in their arguments for and against, but, once again—as was the case with amateur literature and graphomania—became partly "nationalized" with regard to the specific historic situation of the time, when regime change and media "revolution" coincided (Afanasev 2001; Kuritsyn 2001; Kuznetsov 1999; Vizel' 1999).

While theoretical reflections on the potential of hypertextuality for literary writing—and its criticism—abounded, the number of literary works relying in their aesthetics and narratives on hyperlinking and digressive narratives remained fairly small. For North American hyperfiction, for example, among the canonical texts are Michael Joyce's *Afternoon* (1987), as well as Stuart Moulthrop's *Hegirascope* (1995/1997). The German literary scholar Nicole Mahne, in her book on trans-medial storytelling, asserts (2007: 110), that hyperfiction "enjoys the reputation of an experimental, vanguard phenomenon of rather marginal significance and has indeed not been able to establish itself since its beginnings on the literary market."

The situation on the Runet is not much different from the one in other languages or national segments of the web. The literary online award *Teneta*, mentioned earlier, elaborated a sophisticated categorization for its jury, distinguishing the following subgenres: "hypertextual literature" (*gipertekstovaia literatura*), "multimedia literature" (*mul'timedial'naia literatura*) and "dynamic literature" (*dinamicheskaia literatura*). The terminological differentiation suggests variety, where literary works were actually lacking. Thus, out of approximately 1,500 works nominated for the *Teneta* in 2002, only 94 were nominated in the relevant categories of net-literature. The rest constituted traditional poetry and prose.

Thus, for the Runet, the number of acknowledged hypertextual literary works is similarly narrow. Undoubtedly, the hypertextual interactive project *Novel* (*Roman* 1995) by Roman Leibov is recognized as the origin and at the same time the masterpiece of Russian hypertextual literature. The multimedia hypertext *When My Boyfriend Came Back from the War* (1996) by net artist Olia Lialina is often also cited, and has acquired international attention due to the fact that the text is written in English. Also popular is the "philosophic novel" *The Infinite Deadlock (Beskonechnyi tupik)* by Dmitrii Galkovskii, which in effect represents a pre-electronic form of hypertextual writing, realized, with the advent of computer technology, in electronic form. With the self-confident exaggeration which is typical of the author, Galkovskii states that, to date, his *The Infinite Deadlock* "represents the only serious hypertextual work" if not within world literature, then certainly on the Runet.

## Case study 1: hypertext: "ingeniously unreadable": *Novel* (Roman Leibov et al.)

Aleksandr Maliukov (1999) wittily calls the hypertextual novel *Novel* by Roman Leibov an "ingeniously unreadable work." Indeed, from its beginnings, *Novel* was conceived as a text to be written and not to be read. Leibov positioned his hyper-textual project as a collective interactive game, an experiment in co-authorship. The threefold meaning of the title, which in Russian designates at the same time the work's genre (novel), topic (a love affair) and author (Roman Leibov), testifies to the high level of self-reflectivity. It might be added that, as a representative text of early Runet literature, the *Novel* has also been written in the Roman alphabet.

The beginning of the novel is decidedly banal. The hero deposits a love letter in the postbox of his beloved, but instantly regrets his affective deed, since, at the moment he leaves the letter, he discovers his girlfriend with another lover. The classic intrigue of the story to be written by the co-authors revolves around the question of how the love triangle will play out.

As the initiator of the collective hypertext, Roman Leibov provided the starting point of the narrative, a text of roughly half a page, including 16 hyperlinks. Within one-and-a-half years the text had grown to 252 pages; the number of added hyperlinks is not documented. As a result, a narrative hypertext emerged, which in the multiplicity of its digressions is indeed fundamentally unreadable. "The tree of chapters is more threatening than the scheme of a tube TV," remarks Maliukov (1999) once again with sharp humor. As postulated by Jorges Luis Borges, who is worshipped (not only) by Russian authors as the father of pre-electronic hypertextual literature, in Leibov's *Roman*, different futures evolve simultaneously, proliferate and sprawl. After a year of "free" existence on the internet, the *Novel* grew so fast that it ran the risk of death, so Leibov decided to close the text to any further amendments.

From the beginning, Leibov's hypertextual project was planned as an experiment that was doomed to fail (Leibov n.d.). It was to demonstrate in practice that it is impossible to co-author a non-sequentially structured text which would at the same time allow the reader to be captured by the story. The fatal success of Roman Leibov's *Novel* marks at the same time the beginning, the apogee and the end of Russian hypertextual literature understood as narrative hyperfiction. When interpreted as literary play, though, as a form of ergodic literature in the sense of Espen Aarseth, *Novel* inscribes itself into the large and fruitful tradition of literary games so popular on the Runet, where thousands of users interactively co-author mostly lyric genres, such as sonnets, haiku, limericks or Bout-rimés (see Chapter 11 by Leibov, in this volume).

## Weblogs: serial self and serialized satire

"My diary: my life with typos," notes the writer and literary scholar Aleksandr Markin in one of his blog posts, thus conveying the idea of an authentic, unstyled autobiographical self-portrait. Such excessive exposure of the narrating subject is mirrored by a voyeuristic impulse (2006: 332): "I am magnetized by spying and eavesdropping. I hope this is not an illness, but purely down to the conditions of contemporary culture." Markin's blog posts comprise central aspects of blogging philosophy and aesthetics: the nature of the blog as an ego-document in its historic relationship to the diary; the imperfect, seemingly authentic appearance of the blogging self; the voyeuristic impulses dominating the emotionalized networked publics. Excerpts from his blog appeared in 2006 under the succinct title *Diary [2002–2006]*, and comprised diverse literary genres and styles such as notes from Moscow's (sub-)urban life and the narrator's love affairs, sentimental descriptions of nature and landscapes, philosophical aphorisms and philological analysis.

It is precisely against the background of this idea of a blog representing an authentic person that the appearance of fake identities acquires its specific ethical and aesthetic thrill (Rettberg 2008: 121–6). As the case of *lonely_girl 15* has shown in the English-speaking segment, the adoption of a fictitious identity may deeply disturb the readership. Under the nickname *lonely_girl 15*, a professional actress had performed typical scenes from a teenager's life in the form of a video blog on YouTube. For the Russian context, Eugene Gorny (2009) has documented the existence of such fake identities in the early period of blogging. Regarding the decade of Russian blogging from 2001/2002 until 2011/2012 one might, nevertheless, state the following dynamics: fake identities, mask play and the creation of fictitious identities declined in popularity and were replaced by an authenticity claim, typically embodied in the Markin diary. This tendency reflects a general trend in global digital culture away from mystification and towards authenticity (Kitzmann 2004).

Russian theoretical discourses and blogging practices thus do not differ much from their global counterparts. Partly, they have been embedded into a national cultural framework in order to explain the successes and failures of Russian blogging. Thus, Eugene Gorny (2009: 259–61) argued that the specific collectivity of—early—Russian blogging, concentrated on the blogging platform LiveJournal (in Russian translation *Zhivoi zhurnal* or abbreviated *ZheZhe*), might be explained through a different understanding of "friendship," grounded in the experience of Russian/Soviet commonality. In order to sustain his hypothesis, Gorny refers to the especially high number of "friends" the average Russian blogger collected in his "friend-list" (*frend-lenta*), as well as to specific "unification tools," which forced the individual user to participate in the larger community of Russian-language bloggers. The argument is sustained by the writer and editor Dmitrii Volchek, who published the Markin diary, but judged in negative terms: Volchek sees the deeply individual experience of blogging being discredited by his fellow Russian writers, who turned the private textual experiment into a "peep show" for the collective, following patterns of deeply rooted Soviet mentality (cf. Maizel 2003: 4).

If we move from aesthetics to poetics, the "generic instability" (Morrison 2007: 378) of blogging as a software-based communication format is typically highlighted. Irina Kaspe and Varvara Smurova are among the first Russian scholars to propose an analytical approach towards (literary) blogging on the Runet. They highlight the eclectic mixture of literary genres and textual formats sampled through blogging (Kaspe and Smurova 2002): "*ZhZh* [LiveJournal] includes diaries, forums, memoirs, essays, poems, lyrical prose, short chapters from novels, funny stories, real-life stories, letters, annotations, notes, . . ."

It is thus not by chance that the first blogging experience in (literary) Runet history was related to the idea of genre variety. And nor is it an accident that this experiment was initiated by Roman Leibov, the renowned pioneer of Russian hyperfiction. On 1 February 2001, Leibov wrote the first entries in his LiveJournal. His historic blog post was tellingly titled "trying out a new pen" (*proba pera*). The term has a double meaning: it alludes to first steps taken in a new literary epoch and literally refers to the pen in the sense of a quill. With this historic reference to the pre-print era, Leibov marks the (dis)continuities in writing technology and exposes the anachronisms inherent in media change in a subtle and witty manner, while at the same time exploring himself the aesthetic challenges of the new communication format. On the same day Leibov authored 18 posts, comprising—as in the case of the Markin diary—such different genres as aphorism, citation, commentary, observation and anecdote (see Gorny 2009: 264). By doing so, in only a few hours he sketched the whole panoply of literary blog usages, which in the years that followed would come to define literary blogging on the Runet.

Kaspe and Smurova stress that the communication format of the blog encourages the production of potentially endless "text cycles" and narratives. Such serial narratives can constitute (auto-)biographical life texts in diary style as well as fictional serial novels. According to Rettberg, both sub-genres are characterized by a "narrative desire for continuity" (Rettberg 2008: 115), and both are popular on the Runet.[1]

Whereas blogging discourses do not differ much on a global and a national level, what is different is the extent to which Russian authors engage in blogging activities (Rutten 2009a). An impressive number of established Russian writers maintain personal diaries, ranging from prominent novelists such as Boris Akunin, Evgenii Grishkovets, Sergei Lukianenko or Tatiana Tolstaya to vanguardist poets such as Georgi Lukomnikov or Dmitrii Vodennikov and ending up with popular glamour writers such as Sergei Minaev.[2]

## Case study 2: weblog: "a year of life in LiveJournal": Evgenii Grishkovets

For several years, from 2007 until 2011, the Russian performer, playwright and novelist Evgenii Grishkovets maintained his own personal diary-style blog, based on the blogging service LiveJournal. Grishkovets had almost 40,000 friends and up to 100,000 readers a day. He was thus among the most popular bloggers on the Runet. He did not use nicknames or pseudonyms, and the internet address of his blog clearly indicated its owner. Regardless of the characteristic heterogeneity of the postings, some recurrent topics can be identified:

- stories and anecdotes from family life;
- memories of childhood and early adulthood, especially from military service in the navy;
- reports from the everyday life—and sufferings—of a creative writer;
- notes from his travels, especially in the Russian regions and ex-Soviet republics (Ukraine, Georgia);
- meta-reflexive accounts of the significance of blogging and the phenomenon of the blogosphere in general.

The heterogeneity of the episodic posts and disparate topics is integrated through the personality of the author and his personal perspective, as well as through the shared time of the narration (Rettberg 2008: 118). Despite all the doubts concerning the significance of blogging, Grishkovets explains his diaristic activities on the web by referring to his desire to express "real passion," the "desire and the opportunity to be authentic" and the challenge to be "honest" (Grishkovets 2008: 5). The Grishkovets blog as a whole is an example of carefully styled simplicity as an equivalent to authentic self-exposure. It thus illustrates what Andreas Kitzmann characterizes as "staged authenticity," and relates to the return of the aura of the author, on the one hand, and the real as a "belief system," on the other (Kitzmann 2004: 115).[3]

In 2011, Grishkovets finally abandoned his LiveJournal blog. His explanation was that, over time, the Russian blogosphere had turned from a platform for personal communication into a popular mass medium. And thus, one might continue his argument, it is losing its appeal as a platform for authentic communication (as such, his argument resonates with the positions pro and contra the Russian blogosphere as expressed by Gorny and Volchek). Grishkovets, nevertheless, is still maintaining his diary on his personal website at odnovremenno.com, which seems to be a virtual space that offers more privacy and intimacy than the open communication environment of Russian LiveJournal.

In 2008, Grishkovets published excerpts from his blog in book form. The blog-book turned out to be a success, and two further volumes followed in 2010 and 2011. As a sequel, the publication clearly illustrates the "narrative desire for continuity," identified by Walker Rettberg as a distinct characteristic of blogging. Publication as a book does not, however, automatically mean being turned into literature. Grishkovets clearly distinguishes the diary type of blogging from literature in the proper sense (cf. Zaslavskii 2009): "The *ZhZh* is a diary, a note for the moment. But when I am writing, I take a certain distance. In other words: I am unable to write a literary work in a state of lived experience."

The question of whether blogging is a—primarily—literary activity has been the subject of heated debate. Kaspe and Smurova (2002) introduced the term of "half-literariness" (*okolo-literaturnost'*) in order to characterize its hybrid status. Ellen Rutten takes the argument further when asserting that many blogs by Russian literary writers function as a "safety zone," where the authors can engage in writing and communicating without adhering to the established norms of literary language (Rutten 2009a, 2009b). Rutten embeds this diagnosis in the broader, and even global, framework of a return to authenticity in times of overall digital artificiality. Concerning the Russian contexts specifically, the authenticity topos is discussed against the background of a return to "new sincerity" (*novaia iskrennost'*), as a tendency which runs counter to postmodern playfulness. I myself propose to approach the problem by relying not on fixed genre definitions but on the dynamic approach of Russian formalism, notably Iurii Tynianov's concept of the "facts of everyday life" being turned for a specific time period into "literary facts" (Schmidt 2011: 629).

## The Medved meme: neo- and post-folklore literary genres on the Runet

Folklore genres are among the most popular literary forms practiced on the Runet (Burkhart and Schmidt 2009; GRCF 2007). World-wide, a new kind of net-lore emerged, consisting of jokes, anecdotes, urban legends or fairy tales, mixing old forms and new content (Krawczyk-Wasilewska 2006). Folklore genres and traditions criss-cross with what in today's media theory is called an internet meme: that is, phrases, topics or narratives which are spread by the channels of digital culture in a virus-like manner. The Runet fascinates with the large quantity and variety of such neo- or post-folklore-genres.[4]

Among the most notable folkloristic memes in Runet culture is the narrative of the "bear Medved." The evolution of the meme and its hero started in early 2006, and, as is often the case with nascent internet memes, the trigger was rather banal. A Russian blogger, the user *Lobzz* (Roman Iatsenko), (re-)posted a watercolor picture by the American artist, musician and actor John Lurie, showing a couple making love in the woods and being disturbed by a bear. The anthropomorphized bear thrusts his arms into the air in a friendly gesture and shouts "Surprise!"

The scenery is adopted by Lobbz simply by changing "surprise" into a more informal "hi" (*privet* in Russian), which is linguistically distorted to *preved*, according to the "rules" of Russian internet slang (see Chapter 7 by Berdicevskis and Zvereva, in this volume). As a result, the funny linguistic play not only rhymed with the Russian word for "bear" (*medved'*), but also alluded to Dmitry Medvedev, Russia's president from 2008 to 2012.

In the months and years that followed, the *medved* meme was collectively spread and modified through such diverse online communication channels as blogging communities, forums and social networks. Its narrative ingredients, including pictures, videos, literary texts and songs, were collected and catalogued in wikis and net encyclopedias. I therefore suggest that these post-folklore genres and practices should be related to the narratological concept of "transfictionality," as coined by Marie-Laure Ryan and describing "the migration of fictional entities across different texts" and media (Ryan 2013). Especially during the period of its greatest popularity, between 2006 and 2008, the *preved-medved* meme turned into a transmedial phenomenon, which was even exploited for offline political propaganda and commercial PR.

## Case study 3: "the male fairy tales of the padonki subculture"

As products of a genuine internet-lore, neo-mythological creations such as the bear *medved* are introduced into traditional folklore genres, such as the anecdote or the fairy tale. Russian online fairy tales are often characterized by subcultural aesthetics, including non-normative and obscene language and the propagation of politically incorrect content. Thus, it is less astonishing that on their web platform at Udaff,[5] the subcultural community of the *padonki*, the net scumbags, engages in contemporary fairy tale production. As a popular phenomenon of Russian internet culture, the *padonki* slang combines linguistic inventiveness with a programmatic transgression of the communicational, social and political norms. Udaff is an example of what media theoretician Olga Goriunova calls an art platform, an online environment encouraging "a process of globally open non-individual but truly communal creation in large volume" (2007: 171). The virtual scumbags themselves label their production as *kreatiff*, a distorting derivation of the English "creative." Since 2001, the *padonki* have maintained a specific section for their male fairy tales on the udaff.com-platform. Typically, those transgress established linguistic and social norms in a carnivalesque manner.

The Russian internet's bear *medved* is introduced directly into a number of *kreatiff*-fairy tales, for example, in the animal tale with the telling title *Masha and Medved*, written by the author *Krokokot* (Krokokot n.d.). The story, as well as the plot, corresponds to the original: the little girl Masha gets lost in the woods and finds shelter in the hut of a bear; the bear, in turn, forces the girl to stay with him; Masha succeeds in outwitting the bear and returns to her grandparents' home. But the mythological bear is replaced by the Runet bear *medved*, and the basic narrative is sexualized, with Masha and *medved* as the erotic heroes.

The magical *kreatiff* of the *padonki* thus stands at the crossroads of canonic and non-normative textual practices, following the tradition of the famous *Secret tales* (*Zavetnye skazki*) collected by the Russian scholar and philologist Aleksandr Afanasev in the nineteenth century and banned from publication until perestroika. Russian net folklore continues to be strongly political today, not only by its sometimes openly erotic or even obscene nature which undermines accepted norms of standard language (see Lunde and Paulsen 2009), but because of its subversive potential, making fun of political leaders. Other than in Soviet times, the extraordinarily popular satirical folklore on the web is not censored. Sometimes it is even used actively by recoding the folkloristic memes as a kind of pro-government PR. The latter approach can be illustrated by Dmitry Medvedev's playful self-identification with the funny and friendly internet bear *medved*. In addition, Russian novelists such as Viktor Pelevin (*The Helmet of Horror* 2005) or Sergei Minaev (*Media sapiens* 2007) explore the new collective forces and forms of linguistic and literary creation and use them as a raw material for their own work.

## Conclusion

The media theoretician Geert Lovink characterizes the change from Web 1.0 to Web 2.0 communication formats as a development from code to content. The user-friendly platforms of the Web 2.0 era allow for "practical media analphabetism," a formulation coined by the artist and literary scholar Florian Cramer (in Lovink 2007: 133). In other words, not even a basic knowledge of computer programming is needed any more in order to use the internet for creative work. As a consequence of this increasing inability to look behind the screen surfaces, the aesthetic reflection of the coded nature of digital and networked culture gradually fades, which can result in a shortage of self-reflexivity. At the same time, the liberation of content creation from code knowledge has led to a democratization of screen culture and paved the way for mass creative productivity.

But how does one explain the abundance of literary practices and texts specifically on the Runet? I suggest the following explanation: Russian literary culture on the internet, with its (partly) essentialist views, was from the very beginning dominated by content and not by code. The geographic and diasporic dispersal of authors and readers gave rise to communicative needs, which could only be satisfied via the internet. A "soft" interpretation of copyright regulations further fostered the development, sometimes grounded in pragmatic needs, sometimes justified with reference to historically distinct concepts of individual property. As a result, from its earliest times, the Runet was characterized by a richness of literary production not comparable to other—Western—segments of the internet. In turn, Russian authors who fundamentally rejected the idea of *seteratura* moved to the internet, attracted by the vitality of the online literary field. The result was a process of self-generated growth—with quantity turning into quality.

Paradoxically, cultural essentialism, combined with pragmatic communication needs, turned out to be one of the reasons for the amazing growth and popularity of Runet literary practices. While not restricting itself to vanguard or postmodern literary aesthetics, Russian literature on the internet was free to engage in seemingly anachronistic literary practices, such as literary games, collective mystifications, poetic miniatures, serial narratives or even folklore genres. In consequence, the genre structure of Runet literature differs largely from what is traditionally subsumed by the term *seteratura* or *net-literature* (see Glazier 2002; Siemens and Schreibmann 2007; Simanowski 2002), and may be roughly sketched by the following tendencies (without, of course, pretending to map the whole bandwidth of literary practices on the Runet): transfictionality and serial narrative instead of digressive hypertextuality; linguistic innovation of poetic language instead of technologically animated poetry; pre-modern instead of post-modern literary genres (fairy tale instead of hypertext).

A consequence of the specific genre structure of the Runet is a remarkable tendency towards remediation, in the sense of Bolter and Grusin, who understand it as "the representation of one medium in another" (2000: 45). Blog-books are published (Grishkovets, Markin), internet novels printed (Kononenko), volumes edited which collect Runet poems or *padonki-kreatiff* (Minaev and Bagirov 2007). Despite being moved onto paper, they retain aesthetic traces of their digital origins.

## Notes

1 For the latter type see, for example, the blog-style novels by Aleks Eksler (*The Diary of Vasia Pupkin* 2004) or Maksim Kononenko's political satire *Vladimir Vladimirovich*™ (2005).

2 Boris Akunin (Grigorii Chkhartishvili), (borisakunin.livejournal.com), Evgenii Grishkovets, (e-grishkovets.livejournal.com), Sergei Lukianenko, (dr-piliulkin.livejournal.com),

Georgii Lukomnikov, (lukomnikov-1.livejournal.com), Sergei Minaev, (amigo095.livejournal.com), Tatiana Tolstaya, (tanyant.livejournal.com), Dmitrii Vodennikov, (vodennikov.livejournal.com).

3 For a discussion of authorship in the new media, see Chernoritskaia (2005), Chesher (2005), Hartling (2009).

4 For a distinction between neo- and post-folklore, see Nekhliudov (n.d.).

5 Udaff (udaff.com).

## References


Aarseth, Espen J. 1997. *Cybertext: Perspectives on Ergodic Literature.* Baltimore, MD: Johns Hopkins University Press.

Afanasev, Pavel. 2001. "Rulinet: nabroski nekrologa." *Setevaia slovesnost'*, 16 November. Available at: http://www.netslova.ru/afanasiev/rulinet.html (accessed 31 October 2012).

Aronzon, Oleg. 2006. "Narodnyi siurrealizm (Zametki o poezii v internete)." *Polit.ru*, 4 August. Available at: http://www.polit.ru/research/2006/08/04/aronson.html (accessed 31 October 2012).

Bolter, Jay D., and Richard Grusin. 2000. *Remediation: Understanding New Media.* Cambridge, MA: MIT Press.

Burkhart, Dagmar, and Henrike Schmidt. 2009. " 'Geht ein Bär durch den Wald': Zu Status und Varietät der russischen Internet-Lore." *Zeitschrift für Slavistik* 54(1): 20–43.

Bykov, Dmitrii. 2000. "Detiratura: nikakoi 'seteratury' ne sushchestvuet." *Literaturnaia gazeta* 28–29 (5797). Available at: http://www.lgz.ru/archives/html_arch/lg28-292000/Literature/art9.htm (accessed 31 October 2012.)

—— 2005. "Dostoevsky and the Psychology of the Russian Literary Internet." *Russian Studies in Literature* 41(2): 64–74.

Chernoritskaia, Olga. 2005. "Fenomenologiia setevogo avtora." *Topos*, 21 March. Available at: http://www.topos.ru/article/3393/ (accessed 31 October 2012).

Chesher, Chris. 2005. "Blogs and the Crisis of Authorship." *Blogtalk Downunder*. Available at: http://incsub.org/blogtalk/?page_id=40 (accessed 31 October 2012).

"Diskussiia o seterature 1997–98gg v kratkom izlozhenii." 2000. *Setevaia slovesnost'*. Available at: http://www.netslova.ru/teoriya/discus.html (accessed 31 October 2012).

Franklin, Simon, and Emma Widdis, eds. 2004. *National Identity in Russian Culture: An Introduction.* Cambridge: Cambridge University Press.

Galkovskii, Dmitrii. 2008. *Beskonechnyi tupik.* Moskva: Izdatel'stvo Dmitriia Galkovskogo. Available at: http://www.samisdat.com/3/31-bt.htm (accessed 31 October 2012).

Gendolla, Peter, and Jörgen Schäfer, eds. 2007. *The Aesthetics of Net Literature: Writing, Reading and Playing in Programmable Media.* Bielefeld: Transcript.

Glazier, Loss Pequeño. 2002. *Digital Poetics: The Making of E-Poetries.* Tuscaloosa: University of Alabama Press.

Gorchev, Dmitrii. 2000. "Seteratura." *Terabait* 2. Available at: http://www.netslova.ru/gorchev/seteratura.html (accessed 31 October 2012).

—— 2002. "Inter(akti)viu 50." *Russkii zhurnal*, 14 March. Available at: http://old.russ.ru/netcult/interactiview/20020314.html (accessed 31 October 2012).

Goriunova, Olga. 2007. *Art Platforms: The Constitution of Cultural and Artistic Currents on the Internet.* Helsinki: University of Art and Design.

Gorny, Eugene. 2009. *A Creative History of the Russian Internet: Studies in Internet Creativity.* Saarbrücken: VDM. Cited from the online version available at http://citeseerx.ist.psu.edu/viewdoc/summary?doi=10.1.1.132.1099.

Gornyi, Evgenii. 1999. "Problema kopiraita v russkoi seti: bitva za 'Goluboe salo'." *Zhurnal. ru* September. Available at: http://www.zhurnal.ru/staff/gorny/texts/salo.html (accessed 31 October 2012).

GRCF [Gosudarstvennyi respublikanskii centr russkogo folklora]. 2007. *Folk-art-net: novye gorizonty tvorchestva: ot tradicii—k virtual'nosti*. Moscow: GRCF.

Grishkovets, Evgenii. 2008. *God zhzhizni*. Moscow: Ast.

Hartling, Florian. 2009. *Der digitale Autor: Autorschaft im Zeitalter des Internets*. Bielefeld: Transcript.

Irt'enev, Igor'. 2007. "S nazvanem kratkim 'ru': stikhi." *Oktiabr* 4. Available at: http://magazines.russ.ru/october/2007/4/ii4-pr.html (accessed 31 October 2012).

Kaspe, Irina, and Varvara Smurova. 2002. "Livejournal.com, russkaia versia: poplach' o nem, poka on zhivoi." *Neprikosnovennyi zapas* 24 (4). Available at: http://magazines.russ.ru/nz/2002/4/ kaspe-pr.html (accessed 31 October 2012).

Keene, Andrew. 2007. *The Cult of the Amateur: How Today's Internet Is Killing Our Culture*. New York: Doubleday.

Kitzmann, Andreas. 2004. *Saved from Oblivion: Documenting the Daily from Diaries to Web Cams*. New York: Lang.

Klimontovich, Nikolai. 2003. "Nostalgiia po samizdatu." *Nezavisimaia gazeta*, 4 February. Available at: http://www.ng.ru/style/2003-02-04/12_nostalgia.html (accessed 31 October 2012).

Kostyrko, Sergei. 2000–2008. "WWW-obozrenie Sergeia Kostyrko." *Novyi mir* 1, 3, 11 (2000), 6, 8, 11 (2001), 2 (2004), 4 (2005), 3 (2006), 6 (2008). Available at: http://magazines.russ.ru/novyi_mi/ (accessed 31 October 2012).

Krawczyk-Wasilewska, Violetta. 2006. "E-Folklore in the Age of Globalization." *Fabula: Zeitschrift für Erzählforschung* 47: 248–54.

Krokokot. N.d. "Masha i medved." *udaff.com*. Available at: http://udaff.com/read/skazki/60391.html (accessed 31 October 2012).

Kuritsyn, Viacheslav. 2001. "Son o seti: literatura kak predchustvie interneta." *Kuritsyn-weekly*. May 11. Available at: http://www.netslova.ru/teoriya/son.html (accessed 31 October 2012).

Kuzmin, Dmitrii. 2000. "Tonus nerazlicheniia." *Literaturnaia gazeta* 31. Available at: http://www.netslova.ru/kuzmin/tonus.html (accessed 31 October 2012).

Kuznetsov, Sergei. 1999. "Rozhdenie Igry, smert Avtora i virtualnoe pismo." *Inostrannaia literatura* 10. Available online in *Setevaia slovesnost'*. Available at: http://www.netslova/teoriya/kuznet.html (accessed 31 October 2012).

Landow, George. 2006. *Hypertext 3.0: Critical Theory and New Media in an Era of Globalization*. Baltimore, MD: Johns Hopkins University Press.

Leibov, Roman. 1996. *ROMAN*. Available at: http://www.cs.ut.ee/~roman_l/hyperfiction/ (accessed 31 October 2012).

—— N.d. "Kniga dlia vsekh i ni dlia kogo." *Klassika russkoi pautiny*. Available at: http://kulichki.com/classic/Leibov.htm (accessed 12 December 2012).

Levin, Aleksandr. N.d. "I vse-taki o professionalizme." *Setevaia slovesnost'*. Available at: http://www.netslova.ru/teoriya/profi_levin.html (accessed 31 October 2012).

Lialina, Olia. 1996. *When My Boyfriend Came Back from the War*. Available at: http://myboyfriendcamebackfromth.ewar.ru/ (accessed 31 October 2012).

Lovell, Stephen, and Birgit Menzel, eds. 2005. *Reading for Entertainment in Contemporary Russia: Post-Soviet Popular Literature in Historical Perspective*. Munich: Kubon & Sagner.

Lovink, Geert. 2007. *Zero comments: Elemente einer kritischen Internetkultur*. Bielefeld: Transcript.

Lunde, Ingunn, and Martin Paulsen, eds. 2009. *From Poets to Padonki: Linguistic Authority and Norm Negotiation in Modern Russian Culture* (Slavica Bergensia 9). Bergen: Department of Foreign Languages, University of Bergen.

Mahne, Nicole. 2007. *Transmediale Erzähltheorie: Eine Einführung*. Göttingen: Vandenhoeck & Ruprecht.

Maizel, Evgenii. 2003. "Subject: Zhivoi zhurnal slovami pisatelei." *Russkii zhurnal* 2–4, 6, 15, 16, 19, 23. Available at: http://old.russ.ru/krug/20030606_em.html (accessed 31 October 2012).

Maliukov, Aleksandr. 1999. "Velikii russkii pisatel' Roman Leibov." *Sovremennaia literatura s Viacheslavom Kuritsinym*. Available at: http://www.guelman.ru/slava/black_sot/mal.htm (accessed 31 October 2012).

Markin, Aleksandr. 2006. *Dnevnik [2002–2006]*. Moscow: Kolonna Press.

Minaev, Sergei, and Eduard Bagirov. 2007. *Litprom.ru: antologiia*. Moscow: Ast.

Morrison, Aimée. 2007. "Blogs and Blogging. Text and Practice." In *A Companion to Digital Literary Studies*, edited by Ray Simens and Susan Schreibmann, 369–87, Malden, MA: Blackwell.

Nekhliudov, Sergei Iu. N.d. "Neskol'ko slov o 'postfolklore'." *Fol'klor i postfol'klor: struktura, tipologiia, semiotika*. Available at: http://www.ruthenia.ru/folklore/postfolk.htm (accessed 31 October 2012).

Porombka, Stephan. 2001. *Hypertext: Zur Kritik eines digitalen Mythos*. Munich: Wilhelm Fink Verlag.

Rettberg, Jill Walker. 2008. *Blogging*. Cambridge: Polity Press.

Rutten, Ellen. 2009a. "Literary Weblogs? What Happens in Russian Writers' Blogs?" *kultura. Russland-Kulturanalysen* 1: 15–19. Available at: http://www.kultura-rus.de/kultura_dokumente/artikel/englisch/k1_2009_EN_Rutten.pdf (accessed 31 October 2012).

—— 2009b. "Wrong Is the New Right. Or Is It? Linguistic Identity in Russian Writers' Weblogs." In *From Poets to Padonki: Linguistic Authority and Norm Negotiation in Modern Russian Culture* (Slavica Bergensia 9), edited by Ingunn Lunde and Martin Paulsen, 97–109. Bergen: Department of Foreign Languages, University of Bergen.

Ryan, Marie-Laure. 2013. "Transmedial Storytelling and Transfictionality." In *Medien–Erzählen–Gesellschaft*, edited by Karl Renner, Dagmar von Hoff, and Matthias Kringel, 88–117. Berlin: Walter de Gruyter. Available online on Ryan's personal homepage. http://users.frii.com/mlryan/transmedia.html (accessed 30 January 2013).

Schmid, Ulrich, ed. 2005. *Russische Medientheorien*. Bern: Hauptverlag.

Schmidt, Henrike. 2011. *Russische Literatur im Internet: Zwischen digitaler Folklore und politischer Propaganda*. Bielefeld: Transcript.

Siemens, Ray and Susan Schreibmann, eds. 2007. *A Companion to Digital Literary Studies*. Malden, MA: Blackwell.

Simanowski, Roberto. 2002. *Interfictions: Vom Schreiben im Netz*. Frankfurt a.Main: Suhrkamp.

Vizel', Mikhail. 1999. "Giperteksty po tu i etu storonu ekrana." *Inostrannaia literatura* 10. Available at: http://www.netslova.ru/viesel/visel-ht.html (accessed 31 October 2012).

Zaslavskii, Grigorii. 2009. " 'Nelineinaia zhizn'." *Antrakt*, 16 January. Available at: http://antrakt.ng.ru/people/2009-01-16/9_grishkovets.html (accessed 31 October 2012). Archived copy available in archive.org: http://web.archive.org/web/20090320221323/http://antrakt.ng.ru/people/2009-01-16/9_grishkovets.html.

# 11 Occasional political poetry and the culture of the Russian internet*

*Roman Leibov*

In loving memory of P.S. Reifman.

Russians traditionally see in the New Year with their televisions switched on. At the start of 2011, as usual, the president delivered his traditional speech, and pop stars performed their traditional song and dance. But this time there was also something else. For its New Year programming, Dozhd', a new independent TV channel catering for people who would subsequently come to be known around Moscow as the "creative class," recruited three presenters: Andrei Vasiliev, Dmitrii Bykov and Mikhail Efremov. That night, the three of them—a producer, a poet and an actor—came up with a new project, which they called "Citizen Poet." It ran for a year, in a range of formats (broadcasts on Dozhd' and the Ekho Moskvy radio station, video clips at the F5.ru website, concerts, digital copies, books), and, according to Forbes.ru, over that period brought in around 3 million dollars (Zhokhova 2012). The point, however, is not that this was an unprecedented financial success. What the project's popularity really signaled was a new stage in the development of an old poetic genre.

## An overview of the history of the genre

We will focus on "occasional political poetry" in present-day Russian culture, as presented primarily on the internet, with a special emphasis on lyric-epic verses that are:

- created as a spontaneous response to socially significant events (the notion of the significance of an event being historically fluid and currently equal to information about it in the media);
- characterized more by their topicality than any historical perspective;
- frequently characterized by a predominance of wittiness rather than emotion; and
- widespread as a separate literary genre owing to professional writers in daily and weekly periodicals but also existing outside of them.

Given the practically total lack of research on this thematic and genre field in Russian poetry, a brief historical overview of the subject matter is in order.[1]

Russia has a long history of occasional political lyric poetry. In fact, the first text in verse of modern Russian literature was a response to events of state importance: the capture by Russian troops of the Turkish Khotyn Fortress. Thanks to its wide genre range, occasional poetry is able to go beyond the limits of pure lyricism and acquire properties of plot-driven narratives.

The era of the democratic mass media that arrived in the latter half of the nineteenth century and flourished in the early twentieth century not only ushered in social-satire poetry but also enabled it to reach a wide readership. At the same time (indeed, as early as the beginning of the Epoch of the Great Reforms) there occurred a radical transformation of the perception of what a media fact was. Widespread newspaper coverage of criminal and court cases, administrative abuse, extraordinary incidents, and, later, details of the campaigns and private lives of prominent political figures enabled these narratives to switch genres—they crossed over from the oral to the print domain. The public began to view media-presented facts as part of history.[2] In other words, the early twentieth century saw a dramatic expansion of the range of "immediate occasions" that triggered occasional poetry. Following the usurping of state power by the Bolsheviks, the official culture—or the variety of culture that was laying claim to being official—encouraged both low and high literary genres. In the 1930s, Soviet occasional poetry entered its Stalinist socialist realist phase, continuing to sing praises of the regime in the pages of *Pravda* and to lambaste the birthmarks of capitalism and the intrigues of internal and external enemies in the satirical magazine *Krokodil* and variety show satirical songs. This mass-produced poetry was oriented toward the tastes and habits of the new readership and consisted of endless variations on the same themes, intonations, and plots. Throughout the Stalin era, the political sphere was totally controlled by the state, leaving no space for alternative occasional poetry. The repressive apparatus made sure of that.

The few poetic reactions to the events of the 1930s through the early 1950s that survived censorship and made it to our time (from Mandel'shtam's anti-Stalin poem to Nikolai Glazkov's epigrammatic response to the beginning of the Great Patriotic War) became widely known in a different political and cultural epoch. The new situation that arose during the "Khrushchev Thaw," becoming entrenched in the Brezhnev period, brought us back to the beginning of the nineteenth century: official literature that responded with another hackneyed ode to another unremarkable Communist Party Congress or with an epigram castigating some predictable crimes by the forces of imperialism was opposed by post-folkloric/samizdat texts. As for occasional poetry, it was practiced, with varying degrees of intensity, by some of the greatest Russian "tape-recording" authors of censorship-defying songs, such as Iulii Kim, Vladimir Vysotsky, Aleksandr Galich, and even Bulat Okudzhava. The genre limits had undoubtedly shifted into the domain of satire, but some of the texts in this genre were far from comic.

The satirical "post-folklore," popular among the intellectuals of this era (the humorous ditties/songs that paralleled political jokes and were indirectly related to traditional folklore), included the still remembered poetic responses to the exchange of Luis Corvalán for Vladimir Bukovsky,[3] the expulsion of Solzhenitsyn,[4] and another increase in the price of vodka.[5]

Injecting irony into Russian occasional political-lyric poetry played a substantial role in its development: irony became this poetry's defining element and basic emotional coloring. Irony spilled over into ever new genre fields (from ode to satire), defamiliarizing and objectifying the focus of lyric poetry—its lyric subject. The twentieth-century experimenting with creating an ironical and detached subject of speech that took over various genre fields in Russian literature could not but affect occasional poetry.

The period of transition that began with Gorbachev's perestroika and ended in 1991 removed any censorship restrictions and returned the situation to the status of 1905. The new independent press was quick to revive the genre of social satire in verse. At the turn of the new millennium this genre (and the whole of occasional political poetry) began to be shaped by the precipitate growth of a fundamentally new medium—the internet.

Given the way things are developing, I submit that we have to rethink the traditional dichotomy "online" culture vs "offline" culture in general and our perception of the mode of existence of poetry in particular. But, even as we are witnessing this global process of verbal culture moving into a new medium, the traditional forms of verbal culture ("paper" journals and magazines, literary prizes, book publishing, and book trade) continue to fulfill important social functions. These functions are first and foremost connected with the hierarchy of cultural processes and with the mechanisms of social recognition. There is little doubt, however, that literary texts (and, to a large extent, their evaluation) are increasingly relocating into the sphere of social networks on the internet. It seems that the development of the genre of "occasional poetry" provides us with a highly eloquent model for this sort of transformation in the hierarchy of mechanisms of cultural evaluation. In order to construct such a model, we need to draw on an analysis of the work of individual authors and an examination of specific texts. In this respect it would be appropriate to rely on auto-meta-description, and open the floor up to the authors themselves (an unacceptable action from a historico-literary standpoint, but entirely justified in the context of a discussion on modern culture). These interviews form the second part of our work, while the third provides an analysis of several texts.

## Russian occasional lyric poetry on the internet today: four interviews

The history of the Russian political-poetic internet grew out of the text-exchanging internet communities of the 1990s (for example, USENET and the early literary projects using hypertext).[6] Instrumental in the relocation of occasional poetry to the internet were the following factors:

1 the radical change in the demography and the technological platform of the Russian internet;
2 the increase in the number and prestige of internet-based and mixed-based (having alternative internet versions) mass media;
3 the development of Web 2.0 that enabled the creation of cross-genre "new media" legitimately hosting both spontaneous responses to political news and lyrical emotions;
4 the sense (fostered by the above-listed factors) that the ever increasing flood of information and replicated texts and commentaries was becoming too depersonalized and needed a counterbalance in the form of some unique lyrical intonation; and
5 the hijacking and privatization at the beginning of the twenty-first century of Russian public politics and power by a small group of people that put itself in control of social mobility and began an active promotion in the mass media of *étatist* paternalism and personal unaccountability.

Toward the latter half of the 2000s, the Russian virtual space became a thickly populated instantaneous-response medium, enabling its users to react to the pressing issues of the day and to replicate information very quickly and independently of any controls. Poetic responses to socially significant events occupy a special place among the texts disseminated online. Of course, one should not overestimate their role in this alphabet soup, but one thing is clear—immediately posted occasional verses do not go unnoticed against the general background of the fan-like spreading of newspaper allusions and quotations. In fact, a simple list of poetic responses to the events of the beginning of the new millennium would provide a reliable chronicle of these events and would make it possible to rank them in order of importance. Besides, a comparative statistical analysis of responses in other speech genres would help understand the mechanisms of thematic selection.

It should be noted that the new medium greatly facilitates transforming texts into folklore. The minimal and very widespread form of present-day occasional poetry is the "joke"—a subphrasal or short supraphrasal text based on assonance and/or semantic shifts. Jokes are often minimalist in form, being one-line verses or couplets. Such mini-texts, whose ideal medium of dissemination is micro-blogs, are the easiest to transform into folklore. In contrast to traditional folklore or twentieth-century post-folklore, folklorization today involves not so much transforming texts as stripping them of authorship. The blogosphere becomes the main medium through which such poetry is disseminated, and it is also the medium that stimulates the rise of such poetry. It is, therefore, interesting to identify, using texts by specific authors, the shifts in the established genre, stylistic and pragmatic coordinates of occasional poetry in this new medium.

The choice of the poets that I consider has been determined, first, by the popularity of their texts (the frequency of their being quoted and evaluated by critics and readers) and, second, by the desire to illustrate the different ways different authors have of dealing with the burning issues of the day. It should be noted that these authors belong to different generations, and their range of creative work is not confined to occasional poetry alone.[7] In the interviews, while posing questions that varied on a case-by-case basis, I pursued the following goals: (1) to search for meta-poetic reflections on the specificity and history of the genre; and (2) to make a list of texts and authors working in this genre-thematic field and considered "relevant" at the time of this writing (beginning of the 2012).[8]

## *Igor' Irten'ev*

A veteran of the genre of occasional poetry in the new medium is Igor' Moiseevich Irten'ev (b. 1947). He made his debut in 1979, becoming famous for his ironic texts already in the 1980s (his first collection of poetry was brought out in Paris). In recent years he has been publishing his social satires in verse in different venues—the online Gazeta and Grani,[9] as well as the print editions of *Gazeta*. Apart from Irten'ev's verses being published as separate collections (18 items in his bibliography), he became widely known as a participant in Viktor Shendrovich's show Itogo[10] on the NTV television channel. His trademark act included assuming the comic role of someone expressing "fervent approval" of something and belaboring to the point of absurdity some controversial issue, with the central lyrical figure of many of his texts being the ironically ridiculed *homo (post)sovieticus*. Irten'ev's genre range is not limited to poetic occasional responses to topical issues, but they form a significant part of his literary output. (Irten'ev's new texts posted on Gazeta regularly appear in his blog on LiveJournal.)

*Roman Leibov (RL): What is the history of your relationship with this genre as a reader and as an author?*

Igor' Irten'ev (II): As a reader, I'm mostly familiar with this genre through the works by A.K. Tolstoi, who even today remains an unsurpassed master of the genre. In Soviet times this genre was quite widespread, but all of that claptrap (produced by Sergei Mikhalkov, Nikolai Entelis, and some other vampires) was totally impossible to read.

*RL: How do you explain the prominence of versified social satire in Russian culture in recent years?*

II: I think society has grown somewhat tired of the unscrupulousness of the authorities and feels a natural need for some articulate and witty response.

*RL: Whose occasional responses in verse to current events do you read on a regular basis?*

II: Regularly—only Dmitrii Bykov's.

*RL: Can you name three recent most vivid texts in this genre?*

II: I'm afraid I don't have an answer to that.

*RL: Can you identify some occasional poetry that resonates with you? You could just give a few names.*

II: If you actually mean direct responses to specific political events, then, besides Tolstoi and Bykov, nobody else comes to mind. Taking a broader view and talking about poets that respond to various social and political trends in society as whole, I would name Vsevolod Emelin, Vadim Zhuk, Sergei Plotov, Vladimir Vishnevskii, and Andrei Orlov (Orlusha).

## *Dmitrii Bykov*

Another author who debuted in the Gorbachev era and is undoubtedly the most prolific and popular among the occasional poetry authors today is the poet (11 collections of poetry), social commentator, television and radio host, novelist, essayist, and author of biographical monographs, Dmitrii L'vovich Bykov (b. 1967). Bykov's poetic output is prodigious, his popularity is so pervasive that he is openly imitated (by Leonid Kaganov, for example, who, clearly under the influence of Bykov's style, writes his social satires in verse in the form of regular prose text), and his genre and intonational range is truly vast. Bykov's versified texts are marked by their epic scope and pastiche-like density of quotations. And this is true not only of the parodic cycle "The Citizen Poet," posted online as a video show, in which Bykov's verses, recited by the famous actor Mikhail Efremov, are direct variations on canonical texts. In comparison with Irten'ev, Bykov resorts more often to open non-ironic lyricism, and this makes his texts similar to Russian lofty civic-minded poetry.

*RL: What is the history of your relationship with this genre as a reader and as an author?*

Dmitrii Bykov (DB): As a reader, I have none. As an author, I once (in 1996) got tired of painting a political portrait of Chubais in prose and did it in verse. I discovered that a lack of new facts could be adequately made up for by the novelty of intonation. From that time onward, this kind of writing first became a rubric in the weekly newspaper *Sobesednik*, then in *Ogonek* magazine, and then in *Novaia gazeta*.

*RL: You didn't mention the "Citizen Poet" project. How did it come into being?*

DB: After *Koshechka*,[11] Misha wanted to do impersonations of people far removed from and dissimilar to his character in that film. We decided to impersonate different poets, picking topics from contemporary life, but not necessarily political ones.

*RL: Is this acted poetry that relies on recitation an entirely different genre or a continuation of your poetic cycle in a different medium?*

DB: Stylization has, of course, an entirely different focus. In *Novaia gazeta* I have more leeway, but, then, it is precisely somebody else's poetic form that helps make everything funnier—there arise plays on quotations, allusions, parallels and other circumstantial factors.

*RL: How do you explain the prominence of versified social satire in Russian culture in recent years?*

DB: Igor' Karaulov has a great answer to that: "Lyric poetry deals with the mysterious, and the most mysterious thing today is politics."[12]

*RL: Whose occasional responses in verse to current events do you read on a regular basis?*

DB: On a regular basis—no one's. On a nearly regular basis—those by Kaganov.[13]

*RL: Can you name three recent most vivid texts in this genre?*

DB: Kaganov on Perel'man,[14] Kim on the tandem,[15] and the fourth-graders in defense of "Pussies."[16]

*RL: This last case raises the question of "network folklore" because the authorship of the text used in the video is concealed. Do you remember any other similarly vivid examples of texts without attribution? Were your own texts ever reproduced without attribution? What's your attitude to that?*

DB: I don't remember any cases when my authorship was not indicated. The more common case is when someone else's work—mostly Kaganov's—is attributed to me. But I'm so fond of him that I consider such cases a compliment.

*RL: It goes without saying that in the interim between the free press period and the emergence of the internet this kind of poetry had little chance of reaching the hearer quickly, but even then there were masterpieces of occasional lyric poetry. The question is, does it have a chance of surviving in the course of history or will its being embedded in context prevent it from doing so?*

DB: Quite honestly, whose texts come to mind more often—those by Fet, Polonskii, and Shcherbina, or those by Nekrasov? Despite all my love of Polonskii, for example, I think of myself in his words more rarely than in the words of Nekrasov's "Songs of a Free Word," especially the section titled "Be Careful," where he talks about the church. I recite those verses to myself almost daily. And it is not just because little ever changes in Russia, though that's part of the reason, too, it's because of the author's passion, bitterness, and despair that always produce good poetry and are very rarely evoked by pleasant landscapes or vicissitudes of love.

*RL: Can you identify some versified occasional responses to topical events that resonate with you? Giving a few names would be fine.*

DB: I wouldn't call such poetry "occasional responses"—it is a special synthetic genre consisting of articles and stories in verse. In this sense, I'm interested most of all in what was done by Vadim Antonov, who is practically forgotten now. There was a time in my life when I was very impressed by his "Grafoman." Generally speaking, political poetry has a no less rich tradition than lyric poetry. The most significant names for me are Byron and Nekrasov. That is to say, they were better at it than others. Interesting things were done to form by Minaev, to intonation—writing in a line—by Erenburg and his follower Shkapskaia. Both of them didn't shy away from topical issues, though they didn't stoop to the newspaper level.[17]

## *Vsevolod Emelin*

Vsevolod Olegovich Emelin (b. 1959) is a poet who became well known only in the last decade (his first collection of poetry with the characteristic title "Songs of an Outlier" came out in 2002). He is now the author of ten collections and a laureate of the Grigor'ev Poetry Prize. Responses to news in the mass media occupy a significant place in his work. Thus, in 2010–11, Emelin was a weekly contributor of social satires in verse to the internet paper *Sol'* (his verses written for *Sol'* make up his collections *Peizazh posle bitvy* and *Pesni Sol'veig*). Emelin continues the traditions of the "holy fool poets," the "seventiers," and the "self-taught intelligentsia." He says that he "works as a carpenter at a church" (cf. the apartment house boiler-rooms of the 1970s and the myth about Andrei Platonov, who supposedly worked as a street sweeper). Emelin's lyric poetry is a conglomerate of high-brow quotations, post-Soviet nostalgia, and current myths, disguising itself as pseudo-dilettantish, clunky poetry, represented in Russian literature by the continuum from the fictional Captain Lebiadkin to D.A. Prigov. In fact, Emelin's poetry is a clever exploitation of the ambiguous ontological nature of irony. On the one hand, this allows Emelin's poetry to find its readers among different strata of society adhering to different political and cultural values. On the other hand, this same poetry elicits constant criticism accusing Emelin of purposeful evasiveness and deception that conceal the absence of a point of view. Emelin's poems and journal entries can be found in his LiveJournal blog.[18]

*RL: What is the history of your relationship with this genre (as a reader and as an author)?*

*RL: How do you explain the prominence of versified social satire in Russian culture in recent years?*

*RL: Whose occasional responses in verse to current events do you read on a regular basis?*

*RL: Can you name three recent most vivid texts in this genre?*

*RL: How would you define a tradition of occasional poetry in response to topical events that is significant to you? Giving a few names would be fine.*

Vsevolod Emelin (VE): My relationship with civic-minded satirical poetry as a reader began in the distant and happy Soviet past. I think, in fourth or fifth grade. And mind you—not with the verses in the satirical magazine *Krokodil*. For some reason, I never read any verses in the Soviet-period *Krokodil*. But I learned the brown-cover (and not very thick) collection of Maiakovskii's poetry practically by heart. I don't know how it happened but I found the texts like "The Story of the Foundry Worker Ivan Kozyrev about his Moving into a New Apartment" (Maiakovskii has a whole lot of such stories) as interesting as his early poetry (which was mostly missing from the collection) and as his Soviet-propaganda, text-book material like "Left March" or "To Comrade Nette." The other thing that struck me in those years was Vysotsky's songs. Then there was a fairly long period of snobbish admiration for Mandel'shtam and Tsvetaeva, but I always treated social satire in poetic form with great respect. Then, when I realized that I'd written myself out as a tragic versifier, I turned to social satire.

It seems to me that social satire does not require an author to make a sacrificial offering of himself. It requires some skill, an understanding of the target audience (I have a problem with that, by the way), brazenness, and a big capacity for work.

I began my career writing topical satires for the "Kabare.doc" show hosted by Grigorii Zaslavskii.[19] I remember being terrified at the prospect of writing one text every month. Then I had a stint on Mostovshchikov's *Krokodil* magazine.[20] In the end, I lost all sense of decency writing for Ivan Davydov's *Sol'* portal.[21] Exploiting his good attitude to me, I sent him some incredible trash. I feel deeply ashamed when I think of it. Today I like to think that I've reached a certain average level, below which I do not descend. No big deal, but I even like some of the stuff I write myself. I write simultaneously for the *Medved'* magazine (it's a liberal publication, and I write for it twice a month), the *Zavtra* newspaper (four times a month, but less frequently recently), and the portal *Otkrytoe deistvie* (whenever they ask me to). I broke through into the literary field in my forties so getting royalties from all these places is very important for me. I think that since they pay, there are people who need my texts. Besides, do keep in mind that all the literary journals are completely closed to me.

As for the reasons why topical social satire in verse has become prominent recently, I think there are several factors. Number one, the authorities have imposed restrictions on the free press. Besides, people have grown rather tired of reading professionally written political science articles in Grani.ru or Ej.ru. Add to that the fact that the articles harp on one and the same theme. In short, it's boring. Another thing is that "relevant" "Russian" poetry has lost touch with its readers completely and shut in on itself. Meanwhile, the reader sometimes gets curious about stuff written in a column. And that is precisely where we come in. Furthermore, the appearance of the internet has made it possible to react to what's going on practically instantaneously. And the main thing, of course, was the hyped-up "Citizen Poet" project. (All the editors that have invited me to contribute have always asked me to produce something along the lines of Bykov.) As far as I can see, this is the only profit-making poetry project. Plus the events of the recent months have provided a lot of topics to respond to. I'm afraid, we'll soon begin running out of topics.

I regularly read occasional poetry by Evgenii Lesin and Ivan Davydov (it's a pity that the latter doesn't write much).

I think the three best recent texts are the two texts by Lesin[22] and "The Homeric" by Dmitrii Bykov.[23]

I have already given the main names of the tradition. But occasional poetry, in my dilettantish view, began with the odes by Lomonosov and Derzhavin. I cannot name anyone from the nineteenth century (I don't like the *iskrovtsy*—those who wrote for the *Iskra* newspaper), and I basically don't know any other poets who wrote occasional poetry (A.K. Tolstoi is not one of them).

The Silver Age doesn't provide many names, either (I don't like Sasha Chernyi and I don't think he was a social satire writer). Then, later, we have Maiakovskii, Evtushenko, Voznesenskii, Vysotsky, and Irten'ev (the early Irten'ev was very good). And finally, today, the actively writing ones are Bykov, Lesin, and Davydov. There is also Orlusha[24] and Leo Kaganov, but I hardly ever read them.

### *Ivan Davydov*

We have so far been discussing professionals writing regular poetic columns. The journalist, editor, analyst, and political consultant, Ivan Fedorovich Davydov (b. 1975) is a "dilettante poet" (the author of one small-print-run book), whose source of income is not poetry.[25] This status (alongside his lyrical nature) enables him to create his own version of occasional poetry: predominantly grotesquely fantastic ballads that contaminate, in a paradoxical manner, the themes and plotline twists recognizable from Viktor Pelevin's novels[26] and that use poetic techniques traceable to Brodsky (the author of few but outstanding occasional political verses[27]). His blog is ivand.livejournal.com. (Here one can find selections of miniatures that Davydov first published on Twitter.)

*RL: What is the history of your relationship with this genre (as a reader and as an author)?*

Ivan Davydov (ID): As a reader, I have always been interested in poetry—and in Russian poetry, the political genre is an absolute must. In a nutshell, if only because the relationship between a citizen and the state is one of the central nerves of Russian thought, where practically every statement becomes political.

As an author, I sometimes strive to make literature out of politics—"make" as in "making out with." After several attempts, which still seem successful to me, I got carried away by the process but then cooled down to it, having decided that it is not a very creative pursuit. Truth be told, I still let myself indulge in it from time to time. Watch my hands, as one cardsharp used to say.

*RL: How do you explain the prominence of versified social satire in Russian culture in recent years?*

ID: I think this has something to do with the fact that, until recently, there was no politics in Russia. As an aspect of social life, that is. It was a boring, stagnant decade. But a human being needs politics. By definition. At least as defined by Aristotle. At a minimum, as a subject of generally comprehensible conversation. Therefore, there arose a need for at least a verbal simulation of the political.

In this respect, topical social commentary in verse is in an advantageous position. Good poetry—and I firmly believe that good poetry can also be produced by versified social satire writers—is a value in and of itself. If it is good poetry, it structures reality in a new way. It is probably this added value that has created a vogue for such poetry.

*RL: Whose occasional responses in verse to current events do you read on a regular basis?*

ID: Those by Vsevolod Olegovich Emelin. And also by Andrei Rodionov, but he is a more complex case, that is, it's not clear if he's working in the same genre. Well, it's often a borderline case.

*RL: Can you name three recent most vivid texts in this genre?*

ID: "We, Russians are So Gentle" by Emelin.[28] My own, excuse my immodesty, verses on the occasion of V.V. Putin's 59th birthday.[29] That's it. The third text is hard to think of. Though, wait a minute. Iuliia Fridman[30] had a powerful text about the Russian Far Eastern partisans.[31]

*RL: Can you identify some occasional poetry that resonates with you? Giving a few names would be fine.*

ID: It would be a fairly random selection, I think. Pushkin. Nekrasov. Tolstoi, Aleksei, that is. (The last two probably don't have overtly "occasional verses," but it is clear, intuitively, why they are on this list.) Kurochkin. I like him, sin admitted. Sasha Chernyi, without a doubt. Maiakovskii. I advisedly admire even his Mossel'prom ads and verses about combatting anthrax, for example. Well, I could bring the list to a close by naming Vvedenskii, Zabolotskii, and Kharms, but it is obvious that explaining the "why" and the "how so" would take me too far.

It has to be noted that, in a situation of acute confrontation between urban intellectuals and the authorities that developed toward the end of 2011 in protest against the "imitational" character of the so-called "elections" (first, of the Duma and then, at the beginning of 2012, of the president), all four of the above authors did not side with the "authorities."[32] (The latter do not seem to have any verbal resources that would allow them to go beyond mere copying and paraphrasing crass propagandistic clichés.)

## Modern occasional poetry: examples and analysis

This section provides translations of some of the texts mentioned above, accompanied by our commentaries on their poetics (including any references to Russian poetic tradition that may significantly aid understanding) and immediate occasions for writing them.[33]

### *Dmitrii Bykov*

**The Homeric**
Insomnia. Prime Minister. Taut muscle-bound body.
He in the sea immersed himself by half
And, inspired by the United Russia Party,
With a cleaned-up pot from there arose.
The problem of choice has been resolved,
The company of bears has surrendered its positions.
While our Achilles is swimming along the coast,
His abandoned country is being ruled over by his heel.

Once, an ancient Greek, cursing his fate,
Left behind an amphora on this wild shore.
There must be in it a letter to his Russian colleague—
His counterpart—a galley slave.
Four words are in it: "Bro, beat it from the galleys!"
But the ancient wisdom wasn't heeded by the Russian leader.
Were, for an instant, Homer to see him,
A second time he would have gone all blind out of admiration.

Tell me, my Fatherland, why to this amphora
You cling with a nearly crazy fire in your eyes?
Big deal, an amphora! But for the diver,
What would you care, Russian dudes, for Phanagoria!
But if he was able to get a pot from the bottom of the sea,
For us he will be able to get oil, the World Cup, and the Summit,
And over the next twelve years he'll so get our goat
That Phanagoria will seem like our only refuge.

Solemnly holding aloft the mysterious vessel,
He's scrambling out of the water—a walking hymn to health,—
And his party members, while orating, are fellating
And, with loud slurping, are descending to the herd.

This is part of the "Citizen Poet" project, posted as a video on the website F5.ru (Bykov 2011). Immediate cause: Vladimir Putin's PR action, when he dived down to the underwater archeological excavations of the settlement of Phanagoria near Taman' in the Azov Sea and unexpectedly retrieved from the bottom some "ancient Greek" amphoras. The staged nature of the action was interpreted by the Russian opposition to Putin as a new height of indecency reached by television-oriented official propaganda.

The text is a parodic variation on O. Mandel'shtam's poem "Insomnia. Homer. Taut Sails" (1915). The other allusions are: Putin's personal contribution to Russia's winning the right to hold the 2018 soccer World Cup; and "a galley slave" is Putin's self-description referring to his second term as Prime Minister ending in 2008.

### *Ivan Davydov*

**A Royal Ballad. 59**

When the managers' "Mazdas" are still sleeping peacefully,
And the managers themselves are snorting in their IKEA beds,
Putin wakes up. He turns the stars off.
He sounds a reveille. The Russians get up, hiccupping.
In the morning, Russians are paler than the Baltic moth,
Not even remotely human—just some bog slime.
But that is where Putin comes in: by an effort of will
He makes the Russians have breakfast, wash themselves, and poop.

The Russians (seen from above, look like a collection of blurred stains)
Are hurrying to work, to the confines of their office walls.
But in actual fact, it is only Putin who works.
Not a single motor will start without him.

Without him, no flame inside a blast furnace will start to burn,
No farmer's sow will produce a litter.
No tigress in the woods will give birth to cubs without him,
Let alone a single female acrobat.

Without him the priests won't perform their rites,
Without him no poet will complete a line,
And even a thinker of conservative views
Won't caress his daughter.

Without him no souls will go to heaven and corpses into the ground,
He fills the bells of churches with the sound of ringing.
He pumps sacred oil through pipes
As if it were blood in his own veins.

But occasionally even he gets tired, being a man—not a monument.
The flood of thoughts fills his head with lead.
At that very moment a peat bog burns up somewhere in the country
Or a "Bulava" ballistic missile falls out of the sky.

But the powerful intellect overcomes the sickness.
He is already among us again, one for all . . .
And afterwards he turns the stars on for the night.

And stores the president in a secure safe.

Posted on Ivan Davydov's blog on Vladimir Putin's birthday (Davydov 2011). A purposely archaic in genre text, "dedicated to a date"—an ironic reminder of the tradition of solemnly congratulatory lyric poetry.

Allusions: Putin's predilection for being seen with large and rare animals; rumors of his affair with the athlete Alina Kabaeva; the peat bog fires in Russia (the summer of 2010); the failed launches of the "Bulava" ballistic missile in 2006–2009; and the indecent jokes about the conservative philosopher Egor Kholmogorov spread in the semi-political blogosphere.

### *Vsevolod Emelin*

**Once Again about Tenderness**

Now that tenderness over the city is so perceptible . . .
We, Russians, are very tender,
Open up on us with a traumatic weapon—and we will die.
Someone's friends will come to Manezh Square
And go on a rampage.
Because in real life
Our Russian beings
Are extremely inclined towards fascism,
As has been long established by the "Sova" center.
And persons of the Caucasian nationality,
Due to the structure of their organism,
On the contrary, are inclined towards internationality
And anti-fascism.
The moment a Russian fascist sees a person from the Caucasus,
He begins to weave a web of intrigues around him.
And if the Caucasian does not respond to the provocation,
The Russian starts throwing Hitler salutes at him.
But it's vile throwing around you Sieg Heils!
You can hit a guy in the eye.
At this point, setting its tolerance aside,
The Caucasus clenches its fists.
Anti-fascists have always beaten fascists,
Here's a Russian lying with a head gun-shot wound.
On his part, the conflict was an issue of nationality,
For the opposite side, it was an interpersonal disagreement.
The police are also for anti-fascists,
They will remember the Kursk Bulge battle,
Look at their brave, honest faces,
And let them go, with honor, back to their mountains, home.
In the meantime, far from all of the agents provocateurs
Have been neutralized.

And so Manezh Square is in turmoil,
And commentators keep saying, "Pogrom."
Here they march—the Russian fascists—
In neat rows, toward their destiny.
"F-," "C-," and "B"-high school students
From grades 10 "A" and 9 "B."
Many of them will be put in prison
Because they—fascist creeps that they are—
Have taken a dump on Manezh Square
And broken a Chinese-made silicone New Year's tree.
I congratulate you on the forthcoming New Year!
And I wish every working man, health permitting,
To be at one with their people,
Wherever his people is having a rendezvous with another people.
We are vulnerable to rubber bullets and sharp knives,
In spring, our "snow-dropped"[34] corpses come into view
In large, furtive cities.
And when our own bodies bloom, warmly light-pinkish,
On the garbage dumps,
A cavalcade of jeeps with flashing lights on the roofs
Will pass them by,
Saluting with gold pistols.

Published on 23 December 2010 on the portal *Sol'* (Emelin 2010). The epigraph is the first line of a poem that opens Andrei Rodionov's book *People of Hopelessly Antiquated Professions (Liudi beznadezhno ustarevshikh professii* 2008).

The poem addresses the ambiguity of the public's reaction to the conflicts in Moscow in December 2010 that spilled over into mass rioting involving undifferentiated and semi-organized groups of people ("soccer fans," "Caucasians," etc.), perceived to represent different ethnicities. The riots were supposedly provoked by the authorities, who, in the opinion of the rioters, had treated the killers of a Russian man, Egor Sviridov, too leniently. On 11 December, a spontaneous, unauthorized "Russian" rally gathered over 5,000 people on Manezh Square, in the course of which demonstrators beat up casual passers-by and clashed with police.

After posting in his blog another poem on the same subject, the author was summoned for questioning by the Ministry for Internal Affairs, and, as far as we know at the time of this writing, still faces the prospect of being criminally prosecuted under Article 282 of the Russian Criminal Code.

### *Iulii Kim*

I tell everyone openly:
Guys!
I like the tandem!
For their clear heads and personal appearance;

For the way they speak-and-write;

For knowing firmly
What the rights and the laws mean
And understanding like no-one else
Which way to go and what to do.
I like the tandem! And for that reason,
I VOTE FOR THEM.
Oh, how they could help the country!
But they are in prison, for now.
December 2011.

Published in the *Novaia gazeta* (Kim 2011). The epigram is stylized to resemble children's poetry. It has no connection with a specific event, but it is closely linked with the general context of the December protests. The "tandem" was a metaphor frequently used in the mass media to refer to the co-governance by the President (Dmitry Medvedev) and the Prime Minister (Vladimir Putin). The final quatrain switches the mode of narration: those familiar with Iulii Kim's work (he is a former dissident and an opponent of the Russian system of government) expect his text to be ironic, but are brought up sharp in the end by the seriousness of what preceded his final statement, realizing that the word "tandem" here actually refers to the former co-owners of the Yukos oil company, Platon Lebedev and Mikhail Khodorkovsky.

### *Iuliia Fridman*

Rumors are flying on a broken wing,
And end up overseas:
A thousand and five hundred thugs
Are holding four guerrillas under siege.

The thugs have tanks, well, just in case,
And their choppers are radio-controlled,
They wear flak jackets—but home is best,
It's dark in the taiga, and the ticks are a real pest.

The thugs are in the habit of breaking bones:
The bones of harmless teenagers, securely tied up and weaponless,
The bones of bespectacled wusses, trembling on account of their otherness,
The bones of destitute veterans and half-dead old ladies.

But this time round—the thugs whisper—
The four guerrillas are packing heat and know martial arts!
And either true or false reports
Are crawling all over the frigging internet,
And a puddle is forming between the jackboots.

A classmate of the guerrillas was captured, how could you not capture him?
They beat up on him for a day, and for another, knowing full well it was a waste of time.
But he used to share a desk at school with one of the guerrillas, the bastard.
Why flouting of the law? Just hairs standing up on the back of your neck.[35]

The special operations troops assaulted the apartment,
The oldest captured man is twenty-two (LOL),
They found a grenade and some extremist literature –
"Death to Roly-Poly," and "An Appeal to 'Squeaky-Clean' "—
Two of the men can no longer be broken on a rack or kicked in the balls.

The Primor'e government press service
Welcomes you.
The guerrillas have been killed or disarmed,
One of them is already cooperating with the investigators.
Moaning but cooperating with the investigators.
Spitting out particles of teeth, but cooperating with the investigators.
No lawlessness at all. Just cooperation with the investigators.

Songs do not shake any foundations,
They don't call for breaking the law, nor do they make for easy music.
Don't bash thugs, and in general, don't mess with cops,
Don't respond to provocations.

Posted on the author's blog (Fridman 2010) and later published with an editor's title and subtitle on the apn.ru site. The immediate cause for writing the text—the arrest of the so-called "primorskie guerrillas"—a group of six people, who, in the first half of 2010, terrorized the internal affairs departments in the Primorskii Krai. In their video addresses, the members of the group described their activities as "resistance" to the corrupt police force. One cannot fail to notice the similarity in the configuration of the pre-texts for this poem and Emelin's text quoted above. Apparently the similarity of the pre-texts has determined—to a certain extent—the pattern of the responses. Both poems are examples of ironically invective satire, i.e. an ostensible condemnation of criminals; in both cases, the opposite emotion can be clearly perceived under the thin surface of irony (this contradictory emotion is expressed more directly in the opening part of Fridman's piece and in the final section of Emelin's), and both authors employ a loosely regulated verse structure reminiscent of Maiakovskii, a classic of political sarcasm. The same can be said about Davydov's "Royal Ballad."

## Conclusion

We can describe the modern Russian occasional lyric poetry examined above from a number of standpoints. On the one hand, the flourishing of this genre is not specific to modern Russian culture. A study of the English-language segment of the internet reveals a range of experiments with the genre of the "newswire," which have shunted it out of the realm of information and into the realm of the aesthetic. In addition, there are the various examples of "spoof news," which have blatantly undermined the emphasis on the "truth" of deliberate fictionality (*The Onion* is, of course, the leading outlet of this type, but nowhere near the only example), and the subculture of minor occasional poetry (above all, the haiku[36]) that has blossomed on the internet. This sort of "aesthetic reaction" to newswires that are becoming ever more detached (from events and audiences) and impersonal is not, of course, something that has been exposed by "digital modernity." It is noteworthy, however, that specifically over the past 20 years, these forms have gained in popularity right across the world (this applies equally to the various current forms of imagelore, what Russian untranslatably terms *fotozhaba*).

On the other hand, the popularity in Russia of the type of literature we have described has, of course, a great deal to do with both the history of Russian poetry (which we briefly attempted to highlight in the first part of the chapter), and the specifics of the political situation. The "creative class," the term coined by Richard Florida which supporters and opponents alike applied to the people who took part in the protests of 2011–13, is a very effective description of the stereotypes of behavior which characterize the current opponents of the Russian authorities. The written word and poetry have traditionally been important components in the subculture of the Russian intelligentsia, to which the "creative class," no matter what they themselves may say, are genetically and typologically related. Talk of the "end of Russian literaturocentrism," so common in the 1990s, has proved to be premature.

The unprecedented success (commercial and otherwise) of Dmitrii Bykov and Mikhail Efremov's "Citizen Poet" project recalls the huge audiences that flocked to poetry evenings during another era of hopes and disappointments—the Khrushchev thaw of the late 1950s and early 1960s.

## Notes

* Translated from the original Russian by Alexander Burak.

1 For various reasons, the genre field of occasional lyric poetry has never been singled out as a separate entity. Researchers were concerned with the opposition between "non-restricted" (*vol'naia*) and official poetry. The corpus of "non-restricted" lyric poetry was first established in the collection *Russkaia potaennaia literatura XIX stoletiia* (*Concealed Russian Literature of the Nineteenth Century*) and in the Introduction to it written by Nikolai Ogarev (1861). Subsequently books with similar titles were published in the Soviet Union. The most authoritative collection of this kind is that by Okun' and Reiser (1970).

2 This process is graphically reflected in the works of prose writers in the latter part of the nineteenth century—most notably, those by Dostoevsky, Tolstoy, and Leskov.

3 "They exchanged a hooligán / For Luis Corvalán. / Is there somewhere a bitch / For a Luis-Brezhnev switch?" (*Obmeniali khuligana / Na Luisa Korvalana. / Gde b naiti takuiu bliad', / Chtob na Brezheva smeniat'?*)—Quoted from memory. (Translator's note: To preserve/create rhyme I have replaced "whore" with "bitch.")

4 "The plane is flying to the West, / Solzhenitsyn's spirits are high. / Down on the ground Böll reflects, / 'That's some real bad-ass guy'." (*Samolet letit na Zapad, / Solzhenitsyn v nem sidit. / "Ukhti-nate, khui v tomate!"—Bell', vstrechaia, govorit.*) – Quoted from memory.

5 In fact, any event could serve as an ironic cause for burlesque praises. For example,

"Spring is gone, the summer's bliss. / We have the party to thank for this!" (*Proshla vesna, nastalo leto. Spasibo Partii za eto!*) Or in a more extreme vein: "On the edge of a vast green meadow / A raven fucked a little finch. / That's a personal achievement/ Of our dear Leonid Il'ich" (*Na kraiu bol'shogo luga / Voron vyebal gracha. / V etom lichnaia zasluga Leonida Il'icha*). (Translator's note: to preserve the "bird theme" and rhyme I have replaced "rook" with "finch.")

6 For general historical background, see Gorny (2009).

7 Here I do not consider general-purpose texts (those widely quoted, copied, and discussed) by famous poets who do not generally work in the genre of occasional poetry, such as, for example, the responses to the Beslan tragedy by Aleksei Tsvetkov and Damian Kudriavtsev. Another author not discussed in this chapter is Aleksandr Smirnov, whose column "Rifma nedeli" is regularly posted on the BBC site, http://www.bbc.co.uk/blogs/russian/poeminthenews.

8 See also Tsvetkov (2012).

9 Gazeta (gazeta.ru) and Grani (grani.ru).

10 Translator's note: Itogo is a play on the name of the popular NTV news show *Itogi* that was hosted by Evgenii Kiselev.

11 *Misha* is the actor Mikhail Efremov. *Koshechka* is a comedy film by the director Grigorii Konstantinopol'skii (2009). Efremov played the role of an elderly ballerina Varechka in the first part of the film. In Dmitrii Bykov's project he impersonates the poets' variations on whose verses he recites.

12 Igor' Karaulov (b. 1972) is a poet; he is the author of the collections *Perepad napriazheniia* (2003), *Prodavtsy prianostei* (2006), and *Uporstvo man'iaka* (2010).

13 Leonid "Leo" Kaganov (b. 1972) is a poet, prose writer, journalist, television host, scriptwriter, and humorist. One of the old-timers in the network media (Fidonet OBEC. PACTET). He is also the author of the regularly-appearing poetic column on the site F5 (f5.ru/kaganov).

14 The versified text Bykov refers to was posted on 29 March, 2010 on the site F5 (Kaganov 2010). G. Perel'man is the Russian mathematician who, in March 2010, won the Clay Research Award ($1,000,000) for proving the Poincaré conjecture. The occasion (accompanied by numerous reports in the media of Perel'man's alleged unsociability) provoked numerous variations in different genres on a wide range of rhetorical themes: the "mad scientist," "from rags to riches," "the superiority of Russian science," etc. Kaganov's poem turned out to be prophetic: in June 2010, Perel'man failed to appear at the award presentation ceremony in Paris, and on June 1 declared that he refused to accept the award.

15 See Iulii Kim's poem below.

16 This refers to the poem "Bunt pionerki" *Nadia i Mariia / Chto s vami teper'?* ("The rebellion of a pioneer girl" Nadia and Maria / What has become of you?). Originally, the poem appeared as a video posting, in which it is recited by the author's under-age daughters (for the unauthorized copies see, for example, AnthemsOfRebellion [2012], Akimich [2012]).

17 The distinctive technique of writing down syllabo-tonic and tonic rhymed poetry in a line as if it were a prose text ("false prose") was not only typical of these poets of the "Silver Age." Dmitrii Bykov, who made this form of presenting text canonical, may well have been influenced in the 1970s by the memoir prose of Kataev, in which quotations were presented in this way, and also by the poetic miniatures of Feliks Krivin. Both Kataev and Krivin were very popular at the time.

18 emelind.livejournal.com.

19 Grigorii Zaslavskii is a theatre critic, who was also the host of the periodically produced entertainment show "Kabare.doc,"—a branch project of "Teatr.doc" that existed from 2004 to 2009. The show featured texts written by various Moscow poets especially for the show.

20 S. Mostovshchikov was editor-in-chief of the *Krokodil* magazine from 2005 to 2008.
21 *Sol'* was an internet portal based in Perm' that gained some popularity as a national mass media venue under the leadership of I. Davydov.
22 Evgenii Lesin (b. 1965) is a poet, journalist, and critic. He worked for *Knizhnoe obozrenie, Nezavisimaia gazeta*, and *NG-Exlibris*. See Lesin (2012a, 2012b).
23 See Bykov's poem below.
24 Orlusha is the pen name of the poet Andrei Orlov (b. 1957), who is also a journalist and the art-director of the *Krokodil* magazine.
25 Cf. the rubric "To Limber up the Fingers" in his blog, under which he often includes versified texts.
26 These recurrent in Davydov's works "post-Pelevin" motifs include: the ousting of habitual reality by virtual reality; the all-embracing circular process of exchanging things and short-changing people; the hero's striving to break out of his or her social world into the biological world of pure violence; and the scrutiny of the "masters of life," who turn out to be puppets themselves.
27 Among the features of Davydov's poetry that are reminiscent of Brodsky's techniques one can identify his trademark dissonance rhymes and his penchant for moderately non-classical meters (accentual verses with up to two [dol'nik] or three [taktovik] unstressed syllables between stressed ones).
28 See Emelin's text below.
29 See Davydov's text below.
30 Iuliia Fridman is a physicist, writer, social networking activist, and the editor of the children's magazine, *Barsuk*.
31 See Fridman's text below.
32 Dmitrii Bykov was one of the "faces" of the protest rallies; he also took an active part in organizing them. His verses, written at this time, have become a significant part of the protest subculture.
33 Translator's note: All the translations from Russian of verse passages in this section are rendered in plain, unrhymed, literal prose, designed to reproduce the meaning and imagery of the originals as closely as possible.
34 Translator's note: In Russian slang, *podsnezhnik*—a "snowdrop," means a corpse that becomes visible as the snow melts away in the spring. Other aesthetic effects apart, the poem is an extended metaphoric riff involving the assonance of the syllable *nezh-* in *nezhnyi* ("tender," "gentle") in the title and in *podsnezhnik*. The contradistinction of imagery—tender, gentle Russians as in "snowdrops" the flowers and the very real prospect of some of them turning into snow-cold corpses as in "snowdrops the dead bodies"—can only be done partial justice to in the translation.
35 Translator's note: *prosto volos dybom na kholke* is an ambiguous turn of phrase that may also conceivably mean "just a little roughing up."
36 See, for example, barack-haiku.com.

## References


Akimich. 2012. "Grazhdanin rebenok—1." Available at: http://akimich.livejournal.com/198330.html [Copy: http://tinyurl.com/bqn4nl3] (accessed 6 October 2012).

AnthemOfRebellion. 2012. "Bunt pionerki, Grazhdanin Rebenok 1—Za Pussi Riot!.flv." Available at: http://www.youtube.com/watch?v=axdsWBXCZGk (accessed 6 October 2012).

Bykov, Dmitrii. 2011. "Gomericheskoe (videoversiia)." *F5*, 15 August. Available at: http://f5.ru/pg/post/369733 (accessed 6 October 2012).

Davydov, Ivan. 2011. "Korolevskaia ballada. 59."Available at: http://ivand.livejournal.com/1532086.html (accessed 6 October 2012).

Emelin, Vsevolod. 2010. "Eshche raz pro nezhnost' " *Sol'*, 23 December. Available at: http://www.saltt.ru/node/6402 (accessed 6 October 2012).
Fridman, Iulii. 2010. "Letit molva na kryle perebitom." Available at: http://lj.rossia.org/users/aculeata/1035620.html (accessed 6 October 2012).
Gorny, Eugene. 2009. *A Creative History of the Russian Internet: Studies in Internet Creativity*. Saarbrücken: VDM Verlag.
Kaganov, Leonid. 2010. "Oda Perel'manu." *F5*, 29 March. Available at: http://f5.ru/kaganov/post/215761 (accessed 6 October 2012).
Kim, Iulii. 2011. "Za kogo golosovat': versiia Iuliia Kima." *Novaia gazeta*, 27 December. Available at: http://www.novayagazeta.ru/comments/50309.html (accessed 6 October 2012).
Lesin, Evgenii. 2012a. "The Joys of the Nearest Years." *Medved' Magazine*.
—— 2012b. "Evgenii Lesin on Political Reform Project." *Medved' Magazine*.
Ogarev, Nikolai. 1861. "Predislovie." In *Russkaia potaennaia literatura*, vol. 1, IXVI. London: Trübner & Co.
Okun', Semen, and Solomon Reiser, ed. 1970. *Vol'naia russkaia poeziia vtoroi poloviny XVIII–pervoi poloviny XIX v.* Leningrad: Sovetskii pisatel'.
Tsvetkov, Aleksei, jr. 2012. "Bol'she, chem poety. Politicheskaia karta sovremennoi russkoi poezii" *Medved'*, 26 April. Available at: http://www.medved-magazine.ru/articles/Aleksey_Tcvetkov_Politicheskaya_karta_sovremennoy_russkoy_poezii.1184.html (accessed 6 October 2012).
Zhokhova, Anastasiia. 2012. " 'Grazhdanin poet': istoriia sluchainogo biznesa na $3 mln." *Forbes*. Available at: http://www.forbes.ru/sobytiya/lyudi/84882-grazhdanin-poet-istoriya-sluchainogo-biznesa-na-3-mln.

# 12 Digitizing everything?

## Online libraries on the Runet

*Kåre Johan Mjør*

An important aspect of contemporary digital cultures and network societies is the transfer of our "cultural archive" to digital, online formats and to the language of new media (Zvereva 2012: 10). For literature, new digital, networked technology and computer-mediated communication have opened up not only various kinds of *digital* literature, or "internet literature" (cf. Chapters 10 and 11 by Schmidt and Leibov, in this volume), but also *digitized* literature, new ways of disseminating texts initially composed for pre-digital formats such as the physical book.[1] Since the internet became a public domain in the first half of the 1990s, it has made an overwhelming number of books and manuscripts accessible as electronic texts, or as "electronic representations of print literature" (Shillingsburg 2006: 40). These processes have fostered engaged discussions as to whether digitization will mean the "end of the book" (Biagini and Carnino 2009) or not (Carrière and Eco 2011). Whatever the outcome, text dissemination in new media, just like all significant media innovations in the past, will certainly have important implications for the *perception* of the archival content itself (McLuhan 1964; Carr 2010). Increasingly taking place online, contemporary cultural consumption is gradually being reshaped by the digital formats in which the cultural artifacts are disseminated.

Digitized texts present us with the phenomenon of *remediation*: the representation of one medium in another. More specifically, digitization is, in Jay David Bolter and Richard Grusin's words, a "respectful remediation," where the ambition is to present a "classic text" as unaffected as possible by this technological reworking, thereby fulfilling an "archival function without giving up its own claim to being revolutionary" (Bolter and Grusin 1999: 200–2).[2] The online publication of such texts is often organized in the form of online "libraries" or "archives," which means that they are stored within an organized virtual space on the internet.

This chapter analyzes a set of such online libraries on the Runet. I will be interested in the extent to which and different ways in which aspects of the physical book are "remediated" here. As a study of digitized literature, it focuses on the "bibliographical codes" (presentational elements, design) of a digital text, rather than its iterable "lexical codes" (letters, punctuation), which are what usually come to mind when one hears the word "text" (Shillingsburg 2006: 16). The bibliographical codes, in turn, will be related to the overall character of a library, as it appears through the selection, contextualization and not least canonization of remediated texts—fictional as well as non-fictional (philosophy, scholarly works, criticism, etc.).[3] A striking feature of the libraries analyzed below is precisely the canon-shaping power that they all possess and make use of in various ways.

Digitization and online libraries have been a prominent part of Runet digital culture since its early days.[4] In fact, the large number of digitized texts disseminated on the Runet has been seen by its chroniclers as one of its unique, defining features. "The proliferation of online libraries in Russia is a result of a specific attitude to property and especially intellectual property deeply rooted in Russian culture which tends to disregard private interests for the sake of a common cause" (Gorny 2006: 184). In a similar vein, text dissemination on the Runet is frequently interpreted as a continuation of Soviet samizdat (e.g. Kuznetsov 2004: 11) and thus situated in a national context. While my own analyses do not continue along these lines, it is important to be aware of the extent to which online libraries on the Runet have hereby also functioned as an identity marker, and to be aware that this new identity is founded not only on technological innovations, but also on a reuse of the "cultural archive." And while neither digitization as such nor its scope can be said to be unique to the Runet, the motivation behind digitization projects may at times have been culturally specific. Emerging in a period where the traditional (Soviet) distribution of print culture had collapsed and the entire library system was faced with a "degradation" in terms of human resources, financial support and indifference from the intellectual, educated society (Gudkov and Dubin 2005), online libraries became an alternative arena for disseminating Russian literature to Russians all over the world. This function has contributed to the shaping of the Runet as a particular "technoscape" (Goggin and McLelland 2009: 4), where the uses and meanings have been different when compared to other segments of the internet.

## Digitization as networking

I define an *online library* as a digital library with a certain profile and design, which is openly accessible on the internet. The term *digital library* is thus wider: it refers to organized text holdings or repositories in an electronic (digital) format as opposed to print and microfilm formats, and it may include locally stored texts, such as the seemingly obsolete CD-ROM. Hence digital libraries are not necessarily accessible online, though nowadays they often are.[5]

The first digital library ever was Project Gutenberg, created by Michael Hart in 1971.[6] Having been granted access to a computer at the University of Illinois, he came up with the idea of digitizing texts on it by typing them, and he began with the US Declaration of Independence. This was an idealist project from the start, initially powered by Hart's personal initiative and effort. According to its "mission statement" as posted on its website, the purpose of the project has been "simple": "to encourage the creation and distribution of eBooks," i.e. to preserve, share and disseminate intellectual property. The initial growth of the collection was relatively slow, the inclusion of the King James Bible in 1989 being the tenth book. Soon, however, typing was replaced by scanning, and the project now benefits from an increasing number of volunteers and an easier circulation of e-texts over the internet (Lebert 2008).

The computer in Illinois on which Project Gutenberg was created was included in the early 1970s as one of the nodes of the ARPANET, the decentralized network structure of package-switching invented some years earlier, which eventually became the internet as we know it today. Thus Project Gutenberg has been a part of the development of the internet itself. In keeping with the terminology defined above, it was a digital library that became an online library as the internet became a public domain in the first half of the 1990s. The Swedish "equivalent" to Project Gutenberg, Project Runeberg (founded in 1992), is another example of a "pre-www" project which was established before the internet as we know it today. According to the "timeline" on its website, its collections were first accessible via a Gopher protocol network, and were later transferred to the World Wide Web.[7] They have subsequently been joined by numerous other online libraries in virtually all of the internet's language segments.

The idealism behind Project Gutenberg was part of the larger grassroots "libertarian culture" of the ARPANET. Although financially supported by the US Defense Department from 1958 onwards, the network was created by students who "were permeated with the values of individual freedom, of independent thinking, and of sharing and cooperation with their peers" (Castells 2001: 24–5). Mainly a series of non-governmental individual and/or collective projects, the Runet in its initial phase (the 1990s) may be described in similar terms, however much it may have otherwise lagged behind Europe and the US in quantitative terms, and its oldest but also most famous online library, Maksim Moshkov's Library, is an illustrative example in this respect.[8] A Moscow-based computer programmer, Moshkov had started to build his collection of digital texts in 1990, either by scanning them himself or by gathering them from other collections, and, in 1994, when introduced to the World Wide Web, he decided to store his collection there.

Soon, not only did this online library start attracting many visitors; the most active of them began to send Moshkov their own digitized texts. As a result, Moshkov ceased digitizing texts himself and concentrated instead on filing and cataloguing his constantly expanding collection according to a minimalist two-level system of thematic sections and author catalogues. This became the model in accordance with which this library functioned over the next ten years or so, as described in the idiosyncratic instruction which is still present on its website, and which reflects the technological and practical challenges of the 1990s:

> If you have decided to make a contribution to this library—please do! New e-texts with books that are interesting from *your* point of view are welcome. So are corrections, remarks, proof-read and spell-checked replacements of existing e-books. In many translations here the name of the translator is missing, and this is terrible—it is very desirable to fill in these empty spaces. The structure and text quality of this library are defined by its readers; I am only standing at the reception.
>
> (Moshkov 2003. Italics in original)

Moshkov claims that he has published every text that has been sent to him, without any form of censorship. In his own words, "readers do not send bad books." The only criterion was that the text must already have been published (i.e. printed). However, the "trouble," as he puts it himself, began when authors started to send him works that had not been published elsewhere. As a result, he created the "Samizdat Journal" as a separate part of his library. Here too Moshkov has refrained from editing or censoring the texts (Vyzhutovich 2008).

The early publication history of Moshkov's library can be reconstructed via the "Recent additions" site, which dates back to 1996. Although it appears to have been open to virtually all kinds of texts, certain types soon came to receive more contributions than others. We find texts on IT and informatics, tourism, music, as well as bibliographies, photos and "primitive" computer art, humor and anecdotes, and even more current material such as news bulletins and lists of TV programs. In terms of literature, the library contains mainly fiction, and in its early years it was dominated, on the one hand, by Russian works that had not been part of the Soviet canon, or had at least only belonged to its periphery, e.g. Mikhail Bulgakov, Joseph Brodsky, Vladimir Nabokov, Mikhail Weller and the Strugatskii brothers (the latter had been one of Moshkov's own favorites, and their books were well represented in his initial, pre-www digital collection). Gradually, texts by Chekhov, Lermontov and Pushkin also appeared; still, the absence at this stage of authors such as Tolstoy, Dostoevsky, Gogol, and Turgenev is noteworthy, as observed by Moshkov himself: "My readers have a somewhat strange taste. Lev Tolstoy, for instance, is not here!" (Vasil'kov 2000). On the other hand, there has from the very beginning been a heavy presence in Moshkov's library for American science-fiction and fantasy in Russian translations (cf. Zassoursky 2004: 164–6). The taste of Runet users of the 1990s finds a parallel in the preferences of the ARPANET creators—science-fiction is apparently a globally shared interest among the "technical intelligentsia" (cf. Castells 2001: 19).

The content of Moshkov's library reflects the interests of its most active users, united by certain aesthetic preferences. In the way in which it emerged in the 1990s, it presents us with an example of how social networking in the era of web 1.0 platforms could take place. This site became a virtual meeting place for people who were interested in popular music, new technology and fantasy literature, for example, and who were therefore stimulated into contributing similar material, believed to have an appeal to their fellow users.

Since the mid-2000s, however, the character of Moshkov's library has changed, and this is for two reasons. In 2004, Moshkov was sued and fined for violating copyrights. As a result, he ceased to publish texts where there were any doubts about copyright. On the "Recent additions" page, correspondingly, the number of titles has gradually decreased since the mid-2000s.[9] Contrary to what this might suggest, however, since then the library has expanded even more rapidly. In 2005, Moshkov received financial support from the Russian Federal Agency of Press and Mass Communication, which enabled him to restructure the library.[10] In addition to several servers for self-publishing, he created a new section for classical literature (Russian and non-Russian).[11] Files in the latter are as a rule imported from other libraries, such as the Russian Virtual Library (see below). Not only has this made the structure of the library more complex; in some instances it is now functioning just as much as a portal, although the imported files have been converted to Moshkov's own format, as discussed below. The selective, eclectic library we encountered above has been replaced by a most comprehensive collection, which no longer appeals to the enthusiasts exclusively, but which instead contains "everything."

Nevertheless, the "original" Moshkov library is still discernible, not only in its "Recent additions" section and the "core library" (lib.ru) to which the former refers, but first and foremost in its bibliographical codes, which have remained unchanged since its creation in 1994. Moshkov consistently uses the monospaced font Courier and the format of txt (and not html).[12] In general, very few of the bibliographical codes characteristic of the printed book remain present with his electronic texts, which are presented as if they were "mined" from a physical object and "reincarnated" in a digital form, to use the terminology of Shillingsburg (2006: 14). While claiming to have "no interest in design," his most important reason for using this simple and minimalist format is that it will remain immune to all subsequent software and hardware changes. This was also why for a long time he declined to allow advertisements in his library, in addition to his principled non-commercial interest in the project (Vasil'kov 2000). At the time of writing this chapter, however, the library does contain moderate advertisement, on the home page as well as on the other servers.

In other words, Moshkov has arguably created a set of bibliographical codes with a character that is sufficiently minimalist for them to be ignored. However, bibliographical codes are never neutral—users have both actively identified with its aesthetics and found it outdated. Besides, Moshkov's library is founded on one fundamental distinction of print culture: the distinction between previously published and unpublished texts. The latter are consigned to the servers for self-publishing. Some editorial acts do, after all, make a difference.

Moshkov's library has for a long time ranked among the most visited websites on the Runet (Peterson 2005), and it is by far the most popular online library there (Yandex n.d.). Described as the eternal flame and the sacred cow of the Runet (Schmidt 2009: 4), it has been a source of identification, to which cultural values have been assigned. Accessing files does not necessarily mean reading, however, and we do not know to what extent these rather dense txt files (containing complete novels in one file) have actually been read. In 2000, Moshkov admitted that online texts (including his own) are challenging to read and that

> the virtual form of the book is needed first and foremost in order to trace a required quote or reference. To read it from the screen is unpleasant, to print it is expensive. When, from time to time, I have become interested in a new book on the internet, I have run out to buy a paper copy.
>
> (Vasil'kov 2000)[13]

At that time, however, computers were the only equipment available for reading these texts, and he has more recently proclaimed that he has ceased reading paper books and that they will soon become a thing of the past (Vyzhutovich 2008).

## Philosophy online

Moshkov's library began as the private collection of a bibliophile, one that became public once it was stored on the World Wide Web. A similar Runet online library is that of Iakov Krotov, founded in 1997.[14] Krotov is an Orthodox priest and an activist in the field of religious tolerance and freedom of conscience. Resident in Moscow, the city of his birth, he has since 2007 operated under the jurisdiction of the Ukrainian Autocephalous Orthodox Church.

Krotov's Library consists partly of texts written by Krotov himself (one of which is always featured on the front page), partly of texts written by others, and it is because of the extensiveness of the latter group that it deserves to be included here. The library is dominated by philosophy, theology, history and criticism. According to Krotov, the explicit purpose of this website has not been to create an online *public* library; very much like Moshkov, he began storing his own digital text collection on the internet for the sake of convenience. He describes his library as "my working archive, the archive of a historian" (Kostinskii 2000).

"Connections for Freedom," which is the subtitle of the library, refers to the catalogue system Krotov has developed (ibid.). Its collections can be browsed via five different catalogues (Author, Thematic, Systematic, Chronological, or Geographical), to which the individual text files are hyperlinked. The thematic catalogue in particular reflects Krotov's own interpretations—a text by the Slavophile Aleksei Khomiakov, for instance, is placed in the extensive thematic section on "Anti-Catholicism," and not in the far smaller one on "Slavophilism." According to Krotov, it is this cataloguing that is the most labor-intensive part of his project.

A challenge for electronic text editions is to deal with conflicting "overlapping hierarchies" (Shillingsburg 2006: 98–9). While a book is paginated, an electronic text in the form of a web page is not. The latter is organized according to title, chapters, paragraphs and sentences; the former, in addition, to pages. Krotov's Library does not provide a single, consistent solution to this problem, but in general it renders the pagination and page breaks of its non-digital sources, i.e. bibliographical codes characteristic of printed matter. His electronic texts are as a rule made up of long html text files, but in contrast to Moshkov's txt files they are often equipped with internal hyperlinks ("anchor tags"), which makes navigation within one file more convenient. Footnotes at the bottom of the web page are in some cases internally linked. As an alternative solution, this library also contains digitized images of book pages in a sequence stored in one html file, so that body text and footnote text constantly alternate as you scroll. Thus, while some of Krotov's bibliographical codes are permanent (the Times New Roman font, the light grey background color, the headings and frames), others are subject to variation (hyperlinking, author presentations, content overviews, additional materials). In the form in which it appears, this library is also a venue for testing out possible combinations of overlapping hierarchies.

The most complete collections in this library are those devoted to the thinkers Aleksandr Men and Nikolai Berdiaev. The energy invested in them reflects Krotov's own philosophical and religious preferences—these are thinkers with whom he strongly identifies (he was baptized by Men in 1974). As a "working archive," however, Krotov's library is not mainly a place where he canonizes his own favorite writers; here he has, or so it seems, stored everything he has read. Kuznetsov (2004: 336) has noted the conspicuous presence of the American Satanist Anton LaVey's *Satanic Bible*. In other words, the concept of "connections for freedom" may also be understood as referring to a liberal ideology, in keeping with which users are granted access to a highly heterogeneous and conflicting collection of texts.

Since 2000, a lasting alternative to Krotov's library for those interested in Russian philosophy has been the Landmarks Library of Russian Religious Philosophy and Fiction.[15] Named after one of the most famous publications in Russian philosophy, it is centered on Vladimir Solovyov (who figures at the top of the site) and the subsequent generation of thinkers who were deeply inspired by him (Berdiaev, Sergei Bulgakov, Pavel Florenskii and others). In historiography, Russian religious philosophy from the turn of the twentieth century is canonized as Russia's most original contribution to world philosophy, and this canonization is maintained here. The library has a simple but uniform and classic design, with the main title *Vekhi* figuring in pre-revolutionary orthography. Generally, however, the website uses not Russian or Orthodox imagery but Christian: its emblem is a ship, an ancient symbol for the Christian church, and a background image consisting of a cross, not the Orthodox one, and a Bible.

Landmarks is an anonymous library; the site contains no information as to who is responsible for the project, but the generic top domain address *net* suggests that it is maintained outside the Russian Federation. Its creators have taken care in providing text files that are convenient to work with. Footnotes are tagged, and, as in Krotov's library (but not in Moshkov's), separate book chapters are presented in separate files. On the other hand, pagination is not rendered, and in some cases it refrains even from referring to the editions it has digitized—which are nevertheless recognizable.[16]

For each of the chosen philosophers, Landmarks presents a comprehensive set of primary texts plus authoritative secondary literature. In the column on the left side of the start page, we find a series of links to other kinds of literature, apparently intended to serve as relevant contexts: "Religion," "Theology," other Russian and non-Russian philosophers, fiction, history (in particular Armenian, for some reason) and a dictionary. Also significant is the presence of a book by Galina Starovoitova, the liberal Russian politician and defender of ethnic minorities who was assassinated in 1998. She figures in the thematic section "Political Writings," where she is accompanied by Krotov, Men, their fellow Orthodox liberal Gleb Iakunin, and Aleksandr Solzhenitsyn's dissident writings.

According to the otherwise sparse information about the project, the aim is the "systematic publication of the works of Russian religious thinkers, philosophers and writers." However, judging from the dates inserted under its texts, it appears to have expanded mainly during its early years. Still, that it is continually maintained by someone was demonstrated during the Pussy Riot trial, when the start page was replaced by a photo of Artem Loskutov's "Pussy Riot Icon" and a text pleading the Russian Orthodox Church to forgive the accused, accompanied with two quotations on forgiveness from the Sermon on the Mount. The library collections were accessible, but not linked from the start page.

In general, the *Landmarks* project is less dynamic and more canon-oriented in nature than Krotov's library. Still, *Landmarks* also situates Russian religious philosophy in an overall Christian-liberal framework and not in an Orthodox-nationalist one, despite the presence of some of the founding texts of Russian nationalism, such as Nikolai Danilevskii's *Russia and Europe*, known as the "catechism of pan-Slavism." It demonstrates how an online library may create not just a canon, but also a set of contexts, by weaving together different texts from different times and places—for instance, by placing Starovoitova in the tradition of the liberal philosopher Vladimir Solovyov.

## The professionalization of libraries

Online libraries such as Moshkov's have from time to time been described as "amateurish" (Any Key 2002; Peschio, Pil'shchikov, and Vigurskii 2005: 48). Since he is a programmer by profession, the epithet is not quite deserved, but as Shillingsburg has argued, the creation of electronic editions requires not only textual critics and bibliographers, but also "librarians, typesetters, printers, publishers, book designers, programmers, web-masters, or system analysts" (Shillingsburg 2006: 94).[17] A *professional* online library, by implication, can hardly be a personal endeavor.

There exists at least one truly professional online library on the Runet: the Fundamental Electronic Library of Russian Literature and Folklore (FEB), which opened in 2002.[18] The Gorky Institute at the Academy of Sciences and the Ministry of Communication are responsible for the project, and it is led by the philologists Konstantin Vigurskii and Igor' Pilshchikov, who have computer scientists, linguists, designers, etc. at their command. By the time it went public, Pilshchikov had, together with Eugene Gorny, developed another online library, the Russian Virtual Library,[19] and common to them both is an acute digitization of texts on the basis of printed, scholarly editions. The Russian Virtual Library contains classic, avant-garde and even "unofficial" literature (samizdat texts), all of which are presented in a minimalist style described by the library as "punk design."

Like the Russian Virtual Library, the FEB is aimed first and foremost at the academic sector on the internet. Its basic unit is a so-called Digital scholarly edition, which may be an author (Pushkin), a certain work (the medieval epic the *Tale of Igor's Campaign*), a genre (Fairytales), or a reference work (dictionaries). In the case of "Pushkin," the Digital scholarly edition consists of a large body of texts—all of Pushkin's works in several different editions as well as a vast amount of commentary literature.

All material found on its pages is rendered in full accordance with already existing printed academic editions, including pagination, orthography and misprints. This library aims to reproduce the "solidity, stability, and endurance" of printed books (Shillingsburg 2006: 29), so that scholars working with the FEB editions should not need to verify the electronic texts by consulting the printed version. Yet there is one exception among the bibliographical codes: all scanned texts are converted into a uniform design provided by a consistent use of the same font (Times New Roman), while the emblem "Russian Literature and Folklore" always figures in the upper left-hand corner. The library might appear at first sight to use "image mode" (identical reproduction), but in fact it uses "text mode" (retyping).[20]

Based as it is on academic editions, this has become a highly canon-oriented project, at the center of which (so far) stand the classics of Russian literature of the nineteenth century. In addition to the actual texts that are there, its structure of filled (+) and empty virtual spaces (·) also informs us of planned publications, functioning thereby as a canon in a proper sense, i.e. as a list. The library provides a national curriculum of primary, secondary and reference texts. While its explicit purpose is pragmatic—it intends to serve the practical needs of scholars—the project also disseminates a tacit canon through the professional milieu of Russian scholars. In other words, it unites explicit pragmatism with an implicit normativity.

Another stated "fundamental principle" of the project is "historicism" (*istorizm*): "Its material is selected with reference to the historical (literary, scholarly and general cultural) context." On the one hand, this means in practice that it publishes material on the basis of printed versions, without adding, correcting or changing anything. On the other, the definition above refers not only to texts, but also to contexts, and these are provided by a small introduction, a "Description of the publication," at the front of every edition, book or article. Often, however, these tend to be canonical rather than historical, for instance, by highlighting the trans-historical qualities of Soviet dictionaries while ignoring their totalitarian context.[21] Furthermore, the library organizes its material as primary and secondary texts, itself an indication of a canonical interest (Assmann and Assmann 1987: 14). And though the notion of "secondary texts" (which are placed in the "Information Section") connotes neutrality and objectivity, at times the material turns out to be highly ideologized.[22]

In this way the FEB project presents us with the difficulty of preserving the historicity of texts online while providing them with convenient electronic formats that can accommodate advanced searches. The obvious alternative is to use "image mode" (facsimiles) to a greater extent, where the gain is historicity and bookness (cf. Shillingsburg 2006: 139–40); the loss is decreased searchability and navigability. There are, nevertheless, significant Runet libraries that have chosen this option. One is the German Runet project ImWerden, which since 2000 has published only pdf versions of books.[23] A more recent historically oriented library project is Runivers.[24] Centered on historical and philosophical works as well as various kinds of historical documents and photos, Runivers defines itself as a "electronic facsimile library" that aims to provide digital, online access to Russian "primary sources" (in the formats of pdf and djvu), of which they claim the Runet is devoid: "Russia's presence on the internet is fragmentary, limited, distorted . . .

*Figure 12.1* Scale of "bookness".

Various pseudo-scholarly works abound." In other words, alleged chaos, amateurishness and unreliability continue to be the rationale for the appearance of ever newer online libraries on the Runet.

By way of summary, I would suggest that the online libraries discussed in this chapter can be organized along a scale of bookness, where the more or less pure text mode of Moshkov's library figures at one end and the image mode of Runivers figures at the other. The FEB has developed a text mode that comes closest to image mode, Krotov with its overlapping hierarchies may be placed in the middle, while Landmarks occupies a middle ground between Moshkov and Krotov (see Figure 12.1). While the explicit purposes of Moshkov and Krotov have been storing and sharing, the FEB has given emphasis to preservation, facilitation and even cultivation of online interaction with texts (Mjør 2009: 89–90).

## Googlization and the Runet

In the West (Western Europe and the US), the question of digitization has since the mid-2000s by and large been a question of how to respond to the Google Book Search, commonly known as "Google Books."[25] Launched in 2004, this was the new digital library of a search engine that by that time had gained worldwide hegemony. What was new about Google Books was not digitization as such, but its unprecedented scale and pace, which could be achieved only by a leading brand in the new, post-industrial economy, like Google. It was indeed met with huge enthusiasm—finally the dream of global, unlimited access to knowledge was about to come true. Meanwhile, critics raised their voices. Here too, the central issue soon became that of copyrights. Agreements between Google and the publishing industry were reached in 2008, though the debate has continued since then. In the meantime, Google has announced that it intends to scan all of the world's estimated 130 million books by 2020 (Taycher 2010).

Google Books has, however, provoked other reactions as well. Jean-Nöel Jeanneney, who in the mid-2000s was the president of the French National Library, feared that the project would reinforce the Anglo-American hegemony on the internet and threaten cultural diversity. He referred both to the fact that it is based mainly on American library holdings and to the algorithm logic of its search engine, in accordance with which a search reproduces the hits that already have the highest popularity and, by implication, sources in English (Jeanneney 2007). Robert Darnton (2009: 17) likewise has warned about Google's growing monopoly in providing digital access to information.[26] This fear is supported by Siva Vaidhyanathan, who sees Google Books as part of an overall "googlization of everything," where one company increasingly determines our perspective on the world, be it through their extremely popular search engine, their email service (Gmail), YouTube (which Google bought in 2006)—or Google Books. The Western world, he argues, seems to be placing the fate of its culture in the hands of *one* commercial agent, whose main ambition, after all, is to make more money. The result is "the lack of competition, increased monopolization, and the increasing privatization of the information system" (Vaidhyanathan 2011: 152). In addition, Vaidhyanathan raises the question of whether Google Books really deserves to be called a library, since it is not organized (catalogued) on the basis of metadata (subject headings, keywords, quality indicators). Google Books is not browseable—as all the Runet libraries discussed above are, however "amateurish"—it is only searchable.

The Runet project that comes closest to Google Books in terms of ambition is certainly the FEB. The *Moscow Times* reported in 2004 (April 9) that its goal is the creation of "the world's most complete and accurate library of Russian literature online." It aims also to be a "practical antidote to the poor quality that is the inevitable by-product of decentralized information systems like the internet" (Peschio, Pil'shchikov, and Vigurskii 2005: 62). Still, in size it lags way behind Google Books, and Moshkov's library is still considered to be the largest on the Runet. Moreover, it has been developing at a relatively slow pace, dependent as it is on Russian state funding and philological expertise.

Speaking more generally, although Moshkov's library is far ahead of the other ones on quotation indexes (Yandex n.d.), there is no one particular library on the Runet that has gained a hegemony and monopoly comparable to that of Google Books. By the same token, there have been no broad cultural initiatives aimed at digitizing Russian print culture, like the French Gallica, the European Europeana and UNESCO's World Digital Library.[27] The FEB notwithstanding, digitization has mostly been the undertaking of a long chain of independent libraries of various sizes, which in the beginning were private, but which after the turn of the millennium have been joined by state-funded projects or have received support from the Russian state. And while digitization in the West has been a priority area of cultural policy, in Russia it has first and foremost been a field of cultural and technological activism.

The fact that online text repositories have been a significant part of the Runet since the beginning has led to conclusions that this makes it unique in a global perspective. Eugene Gorny (2006: 184) has proclaimed that "almost any book published in Russian can be found and freely downloaded online," while Sergei Kuznetsov believes that "the collections of books in the Russian internet are considerably larger than comparable online libraries in other countries" (quoted from Schmidt 2009: 4).[28] Both see ignorance of copyright on the Runet as a virtue, which testifies to a particular Russian attitude towards intellectual property.

However, digitization of print culture as such is above all a *global* process, and the question of ownership of intellectual property has also been central to the discussions on Google Books. Correspondingly, Russia, too, has been increasingly confronted with the problem of copyright violation, fairly similar to that faced by Google Books. Although the 1990s may have been a decade of unlimited piracy, since the turn of the millennium Russia has nevertheless gradually begun adapting to international standards of copyright (Protasov 2009). The suit against Moshkov and more generally the new Russian law on copyright (which took effect on January 1 2008) resulted not only in new online libraries outside the Russian Federation where piracy could continue, but also in new Russian e-bookstores, whose purpose was (apart from commercial interests) the legal distribution of electronic texts.[29]

Thus, I conclude by noting that, in contrast to the segments where Google Books has acquired a greater hegemony, the Runet is, after all, "unique"—not in itself because of its large number of digitized texts but because of its highly decentralized character. Although a feature of the internet as such, this increasing decentralization in the field of digitization as well is what, in my view, currently distinguishes it from Western Europe, where national libraries undertake large digitization projects, partly in order to curb the hegemony of Google. Taken together, through their canons and counter-canons, online libraries on the Runet instead make up a set of highly heterogeneous and conflicting remediations of print culture(s).

By implication, the Runet provides an example of "glocalization," where global processes foster local varieties so that globalization results in heterogenization rather than homogenization.[30] The heterogeneous technoscape that this historical co-working of dissolution and new technology produced has still been very much present after 2000. Thus, while the Runet might appear to "digitize everything," there is clearly no "googlization of everything" there yet, i.e. no hegemony of Google or the like.[31]

## Notes

1 On the terms "digitized," "digital" and "internet literature," see Schmidt (2011: 37–40).

2 Cf. also their comment on their main example, Project Gutenberg (to which I return below): "the site adds little in the way of graphic ornamentation, so as not to distract from the alphabetic texts themselves."

3 And by implication, I exclude collections and anthologies devoted to rather limited numbers of authors, genres, etc., however extensive they might otherwise be.

4 A current overview lists approximately 130 Runet online libraries (Yandex n.d.).

5 My definitions are deliberately drawn from Rudestam and Schoenholtz-Read (2002: 446), Arms (2000: 2), Earnshow and Vince (2008: xxx) and the entry for "Digital Library" on Wikipedia. The common Russian terms for "online library" are *virtual'naia biblioteka* and *elektronnaia biblioteka*, though the latter is often used for digital libraries as well (cf. Gornyi and Vigurskii 2002). My definition of online library does not include academic digital services for subscription, such as Jstor (jstor.org). In the West, "digital library" is frequently used in relation also to various digital services and archives of traditional libraries. Neither does my definition of online libraries include portals such

as the *Nauchnaia elektronnaia biblioteka* (elibrary.ru), established in 2002 with help from the Soros Foundation.

6 Project Gutenberg (gutenberg.org).

7 Project Runeberg (runeberg.org).

8 *Biblioteka Maksima Moshkova* (lib.ru).

9 In January 2012, new titles by authors such as Shakespeare, Douglas Adams, Egor Gaidar and Anatolii Chubais appeared on this page (and thus in the Library), the first "recent additions" since August 2010.

10 For details, see (or rather: listen to) Chekmaev (2007), in particular from 11:30 onwards.

11 Classical literature is placed on "Classics" (az.lib.ru), while servers for self-publishing include "Contemporary literature" (lit.lib.ru), "Russian Fantasy" (fan.lib.ru), Samizdat (zhurnal.lib.ru), and "Musical Hosting" (music.lib.ru).

12 Courier was the standard typeface of the US State Department up until 2004, when it was replaced with a "more modern" font—Times New Roman. Many are thus likely to find the Courier style "outdated."

13 Cf. also Moshkov (n.d.):

> The e-copy is difficult to read . . ., the e-version is suitable for information, reference and promotion, and, at the very least, you can print it or read the whole book from the screen if no hard copy is available at all.

Moshkov's observations find a parallel both in research on the more general characteristics of online reading (Liu 2005) and in criticism of the internet's inability to foster "deep, attentive reading" (Carr 2011).

14 *Biblioteka Iakova Krotova: Sviazi dlia svobody*, (krotov.info).

15 *Biblioteka russkoi religiozno-filosofskoi i khudozhestvennoi literatury "Vekhi"* (vehi.net).

16 An example is the first scholarly edition of Nikolai Danilevskii's *Russia and Europe* (Glagol Publishing House, 1995), which is recognizable since its scholarly apparatus is also published. Its annotated edition of Georgii Florovskii's *Ways of Russian Theology*, on the other hand, has been provided for this particular project by Bishop Aleksandr of Buenos Aires and South America. This edition bears the digital inscription "Humanitarian gift from the Holy Trinity Orthodox Mission to the Internet Library Landmarks."

17 Likewise Shillingsburg calls Project Gutenberg an "amateur" library (2006: 110).

18 *Fundamental'naia elektronnaia biblioteka: Russkaia literatura i fol'klor* (feb-web.ru).

19 *Russkaia virtual'naia biblioteka* (rvb.ru).

20 The terminology is drawn from Jeanneney (2007: 54). Image mode (pdf format) is used in some cases, but the rule is text mode. Thus its editors cannot be correct in describing their library as a "comprehensive facsimile-compilation" (Peschio, Pil'shchikov, and Vigurskii 2005: 54).

21 As an example, I quote from the presentation of the *Literary Encyclopedia* (1929–39): "This most valuable (*tsenneishii*) compendium of reference information, which has never been republished and has for a long time been a bibliographical rarity, has to a considerable degree preserved its scholarly and educational value for the present-day reader" (http://www.feb-web.ru/feb/litenc/encyclop/).

22 For further details, see Mjør (2009). As I also show here, the historical contexts have often been correspondingly ignored by its users, in particular by those accessing the material via external search engines, something that has led to misunderstandings as well as strong reactions to the ideologized (Soviet) descriptions that were assumed to be neutral.

23 *Nekommercheskaia elektronnaia biblioteka "ImWerden"* (imwerden.de). A joint project with the same features and design bears the title "The Other Literature" and is devoted to émigré books (*Nekommercheskaia elektronnaia biblioteka "Vtoraia literatura"* [vtoraya-literatura.com]). Another similar "pdf library" of Russian émigré texts is *Emigrantika* (emigrantika.ru).

24 *Runivers* (runivers.ru).
25 Google Book Search (books.google.com).
26 The historian Darnton is also the director of Harvard University Library, one of Google Books' initial partners, who in 2009 decided to stop Google's digitization of the Harvard holdings, fearing that in the long run their losses would be greater than their benefits.
27 French Gallica (gallica.bnf.fr), the European Europeana (europeana.eu) and UNESCO's World Digital Library (wdl.org).
28 Together with Vigurskii, Gorny (Gornyi and Vigurskii 2002) has likewise concluded that the number of e-texts on the Runet is larger than in the West, though this is based exclusively on a comparison of Moshkov's library and Project Gutenberg. In contrast, the FEB editors have claimed that "the growth of Russian-literature resources on the Russian internet is not keeping pace with the overall growth of the sector" (Peschio, Pil'shchikov , and Vigurskii 2005: 48).
29 Examples of the first kind include *Librusek* (lib.rus.ec, i.e. based in Ecuador); of the second: *Litres* (litres.ru). LitRes was a collaborative project of several "pirate libraries," which hereby sought to legalize their practice (Khokhlov 2007).
30 Glocalization (= globalization + localization) as a sociological term was invented by Roland Robertson (1995).
31 Correspondingly, the most popular search engines on Runet are Rambler and Yandex, not Google (Vaidhyanathan 2011: 144).

## References


Any Key. 2002. "Abonent ne nuzhen." *Ezhenedel'nyi zhurnal* 26.

Arms, William Y. 2000. *Digital Libraries.* Cambridge, MA: MIT Press.

Assmann, Aleida, and Jan Assmann, eds. 1987. *Kanon und Zensur: Archäologie der literarischen Kommunikation II.* Munich: Wilhelm Fink Verlag.

Biagini, Céderic, and Guillaume Carnino. 2009. "Le livre dans le tourbillon numérique." *Le Monde diplomatique,* September.

Bolter, Jay David, and Richard Grusin. 1999. *Remediation: Understanding New Media.* Cambridge, MA: MIT Press.

Carr, Nicholas. 2010. *The Shallows: What the Internet is Doing to Our Brains.* New York: Norton.

Carrière, Jean-Claude, and Umberto Eco. 2011. *This is Not the End of the Book: A Conversation Curated by Jean-Philippe de Tonnac.* Translated by Polly McLean. London: Harvill Secker.

Castells, Manuel. 2001. *The Internet Galaxy: Reflections on the Internet, Business and Society.* Oxford: Oxford University Press.

Chekmaev, Sergei. 2007. "Tochka otscheta. Gost v studii: Maksim Moshkov." Available at: http://www.youtube.com/watch?v=V7bmMDDJ8_s (accessed 1 April 2013).

Darnton, Robert. 2009. *The Case for Books: Past, Present, and Future.* New York: Public Affairs.

Earnshaw, Rae, and John Vince, eds. 2008. *Digital Convergence: Libraries of the Future.* London: Springer.

Goggin, Gerhard, and Mark McLelland, eds. 2009. *Internationalizing Internet Studies: Beyond Anglophone Paradigms.* New York: Routledge.

Gorny, Eugene. 2006. "A Creative History of the Russian Internet," PhD thesis, Goldsmiths College, University of London.

Gornyi, Evgenii, and Konstantin Vigurskii. 2002. "Razvitie elektronnykh bibliotek: Mirovoi i rossiiskii opyt, problem, perspektivy." In *Internet i rossiiskoe obshchestvo,* edited by Il'ia Semenov, 158–88. Moscow: Gendal'f.

Gudkov, Lev, and Boris Dubin. 2005. "Rossiiskie biblioteki v sisteme reproduktivnykh institutov: kontekst i perspektivy." *Novoe literaturnoe obozrenie* 74.

Jeanneney, Jean-Noël. 2007. *Google and the Myth of Universal Knowledge: A View from Europe.* Translated by Teresa Lavender Fagan. Chicago: University of Chicago Press.

Khokhlov, Oleg. 2007. "Chtenie s otiagchaiushchimi obstoiatel'stvami." *Kommersant" Den'gi* 48.

Kostinskii, Aleksandr. 2000. "Sedmoi kontinent." *Radio svoboda*, 7 November.

Kuznetsov, Sergei. 2004. *Oshchupyvaia slona: zametki po istorii russkogo interneta.* Moscow: Novoe Literaturnoe Obozrenie.

Lebert, Marie. 2008. "Project Gutenberg (1971–2008)." Available at: http://www.gutenberg.org/cache/epub/27045/pg27045.html (accessed 1 April 2013).

Liu, Ziming. 2005. "Reading Behavior in Digital Environment: Changes in Reading Behavior over the Past Ten Years." *Journal of Documentation* 61(6): 700–712.

McLuhan, Marshall. 1964. *Understanding Media: The Extensions of Man.* New York: McGraw-Hill.

Mjør, Kåre Johan. 2009. "The Online Library and the Classic Literary Canon: Some Observations on 'The Fundamental Electronic Library of Russian Literature and Folklore'." *Digital Icons* 2: 83–99.

Moshkov, Maksim. 2003. "Instruktsiia dlia blagodetelei i tekstodatelei." Available at: http://www.lib.ru/TXT/incoming.txt (accessed 1 April 2013).

Moshkov, Maksim. N.d. "Electronic Libraries: Future Development and Reality." Available at: http://www.docstoc.com/docs/40884242/Electronic-libraries-future-development-and-reality-Maxim-Moshkov-hard-money (accessed 1 April 2013).

Peschio, Joseph, Igor' Pil'shchikov, and Konstantin Vigurskii. 2005. "Academic Digital Libraries Russian Style: An Introduction to The Fundamental Digital Library of Russian Literature and Folklore." *Slavic & East European Information Resources* 6(2–3): 45–63.

Peterson, D.J. 2005. *Russia and the Information Revolution.* Santa Monica, CA: Rand Corporation.

Protasov, Pavel. 2009. "The Defence of Copyright on the Russian Internet." *Kultura* 1: 11–14.

Robertson, Roland. 1995. "Glocalization: Time–Space and Homogeneity–Heterogeneity." In *Global Modernities*, edited by Mike Featherstone, Scott Lash and Roland Robertson, 25–44. London: Sage.

Rudestam, Kjell Erik, and Judith Schoenholtz-Read, eds. 2002. *Handbook of Online Learning: Innovations in Higher Education and Corporate Training.* Thousand Oaks, CA: Sage Publications.

Shillingsburg, Peter. 2006. *From Gutenberg to Google: Electronic Representations of Literary Texts.* Cambridge: Cambridge University Press.

Schmidt, Henrike. 2009. "'Holy Cow' and 'Eternal Flame': Russian Online Libraries." *Kultura* 1:4–8.

—— 2011. *Russische Literatur im Internet: Zwischen digitaler Folklore und politischer Propaganda.* Bielefeld: Transcript.

Taycher, Leonid. 2010. "Books of the World, Stand up and Be Counted! All 129,864,800 of You!" Available at: http://booksearch.blogspot.no/2010/08/books-of-world-stand-up-and-be-counted.html (accessed 1 April 2013).

Vaidhyanathan, Siva. 2011. *The Googlization of Everything (and Why We Should Worry).* Berkeley: University of California Press.

Vasil'kov, Iurii. 2000. "Pochemu-to Lev Tolstoi v pisateliakh ne chislitsia. Russkii internet: sunduk s sokrovishchami ili svalka sluchainykh veshchei?" *Rossiiskaia gazeta*, 1 November.

Vyzhutovich, Valerii. 2008. "Ne shar' po polkam zhadnym vzgliadom." *Rossiiskaia gazeta*, August 21.

Yandex. N.d. "Elektronnye biblioteki." Available at: http://yaca.yandex.ru/yca/cat/Culture/Literature/Online_Libraries/ (accessed 1 April 2013).

Zassoursky, Ivan. 2004. *Media and Power in Post-Soviet Russia*. Armonk, NY: M.E. Sharpe.

Zvereva, Vera. 2012. *Setevye razgovory: kul'turnye kommunikatsii v Runete* (Slavica Bergensia 10). Bergen: Department of Foreign Languages, University of Bergen.

# Part V

# The political realm

# 13 Politicians online

## Prospects and perils of "direct internet democracy"

*Michael S. Gorham*

> We need to understand, and I emphasize this, that the majority of groups speaking out in the politicized segment of the internet today are, nevertheless, marginal.
>
> (Vladislav Surkov, cited in Leskov and Sadchikov 2010)

## Introduction: new media technology and democracy

Six months into his presidency, Dmitry Medvedev launched the presidential video blog, where, over the course of his one term in office, he published 295 posts, many of them produced exclusively for online consumption.[1] His stated rationale for the launch was "to speak about some pressing problems the world is facing today" ("Medvedev" 2009) and in later posts he elaborated on the opportunity the internet provided for enabling direct access to citizens:

> It is important that this kind of information comes directly from the original source and actually ends up on my desk, or rather in my computer. I can simply see for myself what citizens who visit the site and react to my performances in the blog are writing . . . It's a kind of direct and very effective channel of information linking the president, on the one hand, and all those who wish and who have computers on their desks, on the other.
>
> (Medvedev 2009)[2]

Medvedev took the initiative one step further in January 2010 when he prodded fellow government officials to start their own blogs as a means of improving communication and earning the trust of their constituents, warning that bureaucrats unable to use a computer or the internet could be relieved of their duties (Bilevskaia 2010). In March of that year he chastised Nizhnii Novgorod Governor, Valerii Shantsev, for not getting with the plan: "Those who can do it are modern managers; those who cannot, with all due respect, are not quite prepared" ("Medvedev potreboval" 2010). In a speech to United Russia activists in May he boldly predicted the return of an "era of direct democracy" due to the way the internet allows citizens to engage in the political process (Medvedev 2010; cf. Sidorenko 2010). Later that fall at his annual "World political forum" in Iaroslavl' he reiterated the idea with a warning to all foot-draggers: "The world is so open that no politician can hide; we are simply obligated to synchronize our watches with the people, with civil society, and first and foremost on such sensitive issues as the level of civic freedoms" (Medvedev 2011a). And in a November 2011 meeting with his "internet supporters," Medvedev reiterated the need for state authority (*vlast'*) to go digital to enhance its legitimacy, declaring that

> authorities (*vlast'*) must seek out supporters on the net in order to be up-to-date and relevant. If it does not have such supporters then it's most likely that a breach will form between authorities and a significant portion of the people.
>
> (Medvedev 2011b)

New media technologies have been widely viewed as a productive medium for the expansion of civil society and democracy. By virtue of their rhizomatic structure, the blogosphere and other social networking platforms carry the potential for breaking through traditional hierarchical models of political communication, enabling citizens and their political representatives to engage in discussion and debate directly, in a virtually unmediated manner (Lévy 2001). This poses new opportunities for political leaders, but it also poses risks. Particularly in Russia, where national television is under the relatively tight control of the state, it is the Web 2.0 agora where authoritative political discourse can fast become the object of contestation and ridicule.

So what happens when politicians themselves enter into this untamed realm in earnest, either under their own volition or at the prodding of their tech-savvy superiors? Little good, skeptics argue. Stephen Coleman claims that the politician-blogger represents something of a generic contradiction as a symbolically central authority embracing a medium that is by definition decentered and mistrusting of conventional hierarchies:

> The problem facing politicians who blog is that they are professionally implicated in the very culture that blogging seeks to transcend . . . Blogging politicians are always going to be seen as a little bit like those old Communist apparatchiks who had to sit in the front row at rock concerts and pretend to swing to the beat.
>
> (Coleman 2004)

Runet insiders confirm such concerns, fearing a devaluation of the genre as more white-collared dilettantes take it up. In an open satirical letter to Medvedev ("as one blogger to another"), Anna Vrazhina encouraged him to drop the blogging as he risked spoiling the medium by dragging the vast Russian bureaucracy in there with him: "Tell me this: have you ever actually read (former Federation Council President) Sergei Mironov's LiveJournal page?" (Vrazhina 2010). Commenting on the United Russia Party's effort to boost its social networking presence in months leading up to the December 2011 parliamentary elections, party member and active blogger Aleksandr Khinshtein buttressed the concern for form with a functional dilemma, noting that merely establishing a presence would not have much of an impact: "In order to be popular on the internet, one needs to have a certain freedom of actions. What attracts my Twitter subscribers is a free manner of expressing thought (*svobodnoe myslevyrazhenie*) that is not really cared for by the party leadership" (Tirmaste 2011).

So how do aspiring politician-bloggers who are part of the central power structure handle this underlying tension between their establishment standing, on the one hand, and the free-thinking, often anti-establishment status of Runet? One solution is to outsource the task to PR professionals more savvy about political image-making. Kirovskaia oblast' Governor and avid blogger Nikita Belykh posted a copy of a proposal he received from a PR firm (FPG-Media) which alluded to Medvedev's threat to state representatives and included the price list for its services—163,000 rubles to set up a LiveJournal blog, 84,000 to maintain it, and 199,900 to promote it to the level of a "1000-follower" or *tysiachnik* (Sal'manov 2010).

While one sees cases of official blogs that smack of canned public relations attempts, these also tend to be less successful as measured by level of attention they receive, most likely for the reasons alluded to by Khinshtein. In this chapter I look at a number of strategies politician bloggers have employed to shape a viable presence for themselves in an environment often unfriendly to those affiliated with central authority, or *vlast'*. I then examine the shifting trends in the online positioning of a new wave of recently appointed governors who, due to Vladimir Putin's return to the Kremlin, may not be as beholden to Medvedev's call for enhanced internet presences among state officials. As it turns out, despite Medvedev's declining authority, politicians continue to avail themselves to constituents through Web 2.0 platforms, but are doing so in ways that minimize the perils of truly direct online interaction and opting, instead, for a more hierarchical model of communication grounded in the discourse of "e-government."

## Mainstream margins of internet democracy

To identify more prominent government bloggers I rely in part on the website Goslyudi,[3] which ranks each politician blogger according to the frequency with which they post (*govorlivost'*), the degree to which their blogs are referenced (*upominaemost'*) and the number of readers they attract (*chitaemost'*) (Table 13.1). All of these it combines into a single rating which determines the blogger's overall rank (*svodnyi reiting*).[4] Cross-checking this rating system against that of Yandex's blog ratings shows general correlation in the order of the rank, although given that Yandex's is a ranking of all blogs, the distance between politician bloggers is considerable.[5]

Most striking even among the ostensibly pro-establishment blogs is the degree to which the top politician bloggers attempt to position themselves apart from, in contrast to, or in tension with some imagined "central" source of political power and authority. Different politicians carve out marginal space in different ways, but the tendency does appear as something of a common denominator.

Some of them are marginal by nature of their political affiliations. In part no doubt due to his national notoriety, Sergei Mironov has consistently ranked

*Table 13.1* Top-10 state-official bloggers according to Goslyudi, as of September 2011 (Yandex Runet blog rankings)

| *Blogger* | *Goslyudi* | *Yandex* |
|---|---|---|
| Leonid Volkov | 1 | 246 |
| Sergei Mironov | 2 | 75 |
| Dmitry Medvedev | 3 | 457 |
| Marat Guelman | 4 | 142 |
| Dmitrii Rogozin | 5 | 582 |
| Oleg Chirkunov | 6 | 914 |
| Nikita Belykh | 7 | 692 |
| Maksim Mishchenko | 8 | 2,012 |
| Anton Khashchenko | 9 | 3,267 |
| Oleg Shein | 10 | 1,173 |

among the top five bloggers (ranked #2), despite the negative stylistic critique noted earlier from Vrazhina. The Former Chair of the Federation Council began his LiveJournal blog in November of 2007—on the eve of parliamentary elections—as a means of developing more direct channels of communication with the population:

> I open my page on *ZheZhe* [the Russian nickname for LiveJournal—MSG] in order to be more accessible to people. I intend to the fullest extent to use the opportunities of the reverse feedback that blogs provide. If you have any ideas or suggestions that will help us, legislators, make more responsible and measured decisions, share them with me.
>
> (Mironov 2007)

Since being hung out to dry for his critical statements of Putin and United Russia, Mironov has seemed to thrive in his new self-fashioned role of prominent opposition member. His diatribes against the United Russia Party in particular brim with colloquialisms and biting invective:

> Knowing the "good traditions" (read: habits!) of the "UniRussians" [*edinorossov*—the common nickname for members of the United Russia Party—MSG], everyone understands that, in words, everything will be attractive: concern about well-being, guarantees, the defense of interests and so forth. But the true picture shows the same thing time and again—ER's desire to hold on to power (*uderzhat'sia u vlasti*) at all costs. And after the elections, when the babble of cheery speeches has died down, the "Party of Croo-,"[6] pardon me, the "Party of oligarchs and bureaucrats" will successfully forget about their promises to make our lives better. In this case, the gap between two Russias—the Russia of the poor and the Russia of the rich—will become greater.
>
> (Mironov 2011)

If one can attribute part of Mironov's success to name-recognition, the number-one ranked politician blogger, Leonid Volkov, could not make such a claim. Consistently ranked near the top of the list, how is it that a Deputy of the Ekaterinburg City Duma can go head-to-head with the likes of Mironov, Medvedev, the art director and Duma representative, Marat Guelman and Deputy Prime Minister Dmitrii Rogozin? Volkov's success depends on oppositional positioning, generous attention to civic action and local politics, and an ability to tell a good story. In a March 2011 post, for instance, he recounts the public resistance he faced handing out campaign literature in his district:

> In all honesty, it's not at all a rosy picture. It took me the entire hour to hand out a batch of twenty newspapers. Very many people refuse to talk, and the majority in word, if not in reality, couldn't give a shit (*gluboko pofig*). You get distressed by it all, of course . . .

| | |
|---|---|
| *Me*: | Hello! Permit me to lobby you for a moment! (*Pozvol'te, ia vas poagitiruiu!*) |
| *Young Couple*: | No! |
| *Me*: | Then please take a newspaper. |
| *Young Couple*: | Alright, but we're still not going to vote! |
| *Me*: | But why not? In that case, the UniRus [candidate] will definitely win. |
| *Young Couple*: | He'll win either way, whether or not you vote. |
| *Me*: | Pardon me, if you will, but I myself am a city Duma deputy, and not a UniRussian. And I won. Now I'm helping my friend. But if everyone reasons like you are, then of course we have no chance. |
| *Girl:* | You mean to say that your friend is against United Russia? |
| *Me*: | Absolutely. Here, please look at this, everything is explained here! |
| *Young Couple*: | So that's the way it is! Then we'll definitely vote for your friend! |

(Volkov 2011)

Like Volkov, former State Duma Deputy and Just Russia Party member Oleg Shein (Astrakhanskaia oblast') has consistently ranked high (currently #10) despite his presence among political elites—even prior to his nationally publicized hunger strike in March 2012 (protesting his defeat in what he believed to be a rigged Astrakhan mayoral election). Even more so than Volkov, Shein's blog serves as a primer for representative democracy and civic action. He regularly appears in the comments section of the blog, engaging directly with his mostly supportive (anti-authority) readers, at times even chastising them for their knee-jerk dismissal of all United Russia representatives—arguing at one point that the party includes "decent individuals" and that the problem rests, instead, with the corruption that comes with monopoly (Shein 2011a). He also regularly posts photos of meetings with his constituents and local civic groups. Like Volkov, Shein uses the blog to augment the physical practice of representative democracy, taking advantage of the access it provides to multimedia technologies and broader reading audiences to expand his style of democracy-in-action beyond the physical walls of the public forum (Shein 2011b).

Other top bloggers rely more on demographic than political marginality for distancing themselves from the establishment, such as in the youth-oriented posts of *Rossiia molodaia* leader and State Duma Deputy Maksim Mishchenko (currently ranked #8). Though a strong supporter of the ruling party, Mishchenko still positions himself as an outsider by virtue of his age, arguing, for instance, that the only reliable antidote to oppositional blogger Aleksei Navalny, whom he brands "the PR-man for the country of three letters" (*piarshchik strany iz trekh bukv*) is the "rejuvenation" of Russian politics (*omolozhenie rossiiskoi politiki*) (Mishchenko 2011a).[7] Mishchenko's anti-bureaucrat positioning resonates with his readers, many of whom support him even while expressing their dismay with the ruling United Russia Party:

> What a pity that a good man like Maksim supports evil in the form of a party which, in 11 years of governing hasn't done a single bit of good for common workers . . .
>
> (comment posted to Mishchenko 2011b)

> Such good and honest people like you are few and far between in UR; it's really true, I've had more than one occasion dealing with the leaders of UR responsible for various party projects: they all waved me off with all their might, directing me to ministries where they also didn't want to talk to me or help me.
>
> (comment posted to Mishchenko 2011a)

## Regional governors as outsiders

If figures such as Mishchenko can afford to stake out aggressive ideological ground, regional governors, beholden as they are to the president and more diverse constituencies, have to be more cautious in the manner in which they shape their online identity. Their marginal status often appears in a stubbornly apolitical positioning and regional focus. Astrakhanskaia oblast' Governor, Aleksandr Zhilkin, currently ranks thirteenth on the Goslyudi list and focuses exclusively on regional issues: coverage of accomplishments, foreign visits, ceremonies, and celebrations, for instance, as well as invitations to constituents to offer their opinion on issues of pending import. A post that receives one of the largest number of comments for this blog (551) invites feedback on whether or not to make fishing fee-based in the region or keep it free. The Governor calls for input and promises to show the comments to the head of the Russian Federal Fishing Agency ("Rosrybolovstvo"), when he meets with him the following week (Zhilkin 2011a).

Virtually absent from his blog during the 2011–12 Duma and presidential election season was any sign of Zhilkin's political leanings, although the headline banner at his separate website[8] contained a statement in support of the move to nominate Vladimir Putin as the presidential candidate, imploring his readers to support him.

In addition to distancing himself from national politics, Zhilkin also exemplifies another common strategy among governors—invoking anti-bureaucrat (*chinovnik*) discourse that clearly aligns them with the people, or *narod*, and creates symbolic distance from *vlast'*. In response to one reader's off-topic question in the comments to a September 2011 post, for instance—about public access to a newly constructed bridge in Astrakhan—Zhilkin not only sides with his reader but also obliquely chastises the denseness and corruptness of local bureaucrats and bemoans, more generally, *nash mentalitet* for finding ways to restrict access to commoners ("that they take 50 rubles or all sorts of bureaucrats use it, that's our mentality" [Zhilkin 2011b]).

In the wake of the protests organized in support of Oleg Shein, who launched a hunger strike to protest what he believed to be rigged voting in his unsuccessful run for mayor of Astrakhan, Zhilkin manages to enter the fray of national politics in a manner which portrays the opposition as infidels invading from Russia's urban center and himself as a spokesperson and defender of civilized, rule-abiding residents of Astrakhan:

> Navalny and his compatriots have come here in vain. They don't know the region, the people, our culture, and haven't even figured out that Astrakhanians are a hospitable people when people come to them with good intentions. But Astrakhanians do not like Varangians who start to teach them how to live.
>
> (Zhilkin 2012)

Gubernatorial blogs at the bottom end of the popularity rankings also offer insight into the phenomenon. Here one finds more examples of what *Vedomosti* reporter Elena Miazina (2010) calls "formalists"—those abiding by the president's directives half-heartedly and what *Novaia gazeta* reporter Pavel Kanygin (2010) calls "internet-losers" (*internet-lokhi*). Among other traits, bad bureaucrat blogs are infrequent in appearance and make little if any attempt to promote two-way channels of communication, such as the blog for Altiiskii Krai Governor, Aleksandr Karlin (ranked #311 out of 334),[9] or that of Vladimir Iakushev, Governor of Tiumenskaia oblast' (ranked #322). Iakushev's blog likewise suffers from a dense bureaucratic style—aligning himself stylistically with the very *chinovnik* class vilified in other blogs:

> Дорогие друзья, хочу поблагодарить всех вас за плодотворные предложения, позволившие нам оперативно внести поправки в Закон Тюменской области №128, касающийся предоставления жилищных субсидий работникам бюджетной сферы Тюмени. Надеюсь, эти изменения позволят ещё большему числу семей бюджетников присоединиться к программе. О сути внесенных поправок я рассказываю в своём видеокомментарии.
>
> (Iakushev 2011)

> Dear friends, I want to thank you all for the fruitful suggestions that have permitted us to expediently introduce amendments to the Law of Tiumenskaia oblast' No. 128 concerning the provision of living subsidies to workers of the budgeted sphere of Tiumen'. I hope that these changes allow a still

> larger number of families of budgeted workers to join the program. I will talk about the essence of the introduced amendments in my video commentary.

Ironically, given Dmitry Medvedev's recent disappearance into the shadow of newly elected President Putin, formalists such as Karlin and Iakushev may be politically better off in the long run than their Web 2.0-savvy counterparts. In a 2011 *RBK Daily* survey of the "most criticized governors," two of the highest profile governor bloggers at the time, Oleg Chirkunov (Permskaia oblast', ranked #6) and Nikita Belykh (Kirovskaia oblast', ranked #7) appeared near the top of the list, prompting Belykh to joke, "Try getting yourself on ZheZhe, Twitter, accounts in social networks after that :)" (Belykh 2011; Makunina 2011). An avid blogger since 2005, Belykh has in the year since this study faced increasing scrutiny from Vladimir Putin and his administration. In the heat of the political turmoil of January 2012 Putin admonished Belykh on national television for not resolving a controversy regarding excess utility taxes charged to residents in a Kirov neighborhood and for appearing to be slacking off on the job. Fittingly, Belykh responded to Putin point-by-point in the public forum of his blog, providing documentation that disproved both accusations (Belykh 2012). Belykh's status as a governor-non-grata has only increased since Putin's re-election: at the time of writing he finds himself under investigation by Putin's "Investigative Committee" for purported past illegal dealings with opposition leader and blogger, Aleksei Navalny. As a politically unaffiliated governor (formerly a member of the "Union of Right Forces" Party), Belykh clearly falls into the increasingly lonely category of official government blogger who is, both politically and rhetorically, located outside the symbolic domain of central authority.

Oleg Chirkunov faces no such pressure, thanks to his decision in the spring of 2012 not to run for re-election for the Permskaia oblast' governorship. Noteworthy about Chirkunov's departure from politics is his apparent attempt to improve his lot in late 2011 by extricating himself from the contentious space of LiveJournal, where he had been an active and independent-minded blogger since 2008. In October 2011, Chirkunov, the more "talkative" governor in the rankings and consistently among the top 10 overall, announced his plans to switch blogging platforms, from the now homegrown Russian *ZheZhe*, popular in Russia due in part to its robust social-networking features, to the relatively foreign and narrowly focused blog-publishing tool, Wordpress. On the surface, a relatively innocuous move, but in the context of the tension outlined above—compounded by the impending political change at the upper level of *vlast'* in Russia—it could arguably be viewed as a sign of a crisis of the genre of mainstream political blogging. Chirkunov in fact called it just that—*Krizis zhanra*—in the initial post announcing the shift, remarking that LiveJournal seemed to have lost much of its luster (with much of the action moving to Twitter) (Chirkunov 2011a). Five days later Chirkunov wrote laconically of his motivations for the shift:

> Everything has its beginning and its conclusion. And everything must have its own meaning. We have communicated on *ZheZhe* for several years now and

> it had meaning and value. But it seems to me that one format cannot live long . . . For me, the rationale for a new platform rests in the organization of a transparent process of managing the region, a real electronic government.
>
> (Chirkunov 2011b)

Underlying the purely technical reasons rests a certain disenchantment or weariness with LiveJournal as a virtual agora. It is a tension picked up on more directly by commenters to the post, many of whom see it as an act of abandonment or escape from the interactive sparring of the governor's native blogosphere:[10]

> It is your decision, but for me it is strange. Moving to an alternative platform and even a separate site, journals loose their publics. I, for instance, am too lazy to go to some sort of wordpresses also; but I will read my "friends" scroll. It's too bad, you had an interesting blog.
>
> (mishbanych, 16 October 2011, 13:55)

> I will not go to wordpress with you, naturally:)), I haven't associated you with change in a long time:)) And I won't give you anything to change, rebuild, restructure, or modernize . . . :)). There also is the life-confirming wisdom: "everything must take its own course" :)))—Without you.
>
> (perfectmixer, 16 October 2011, 14:07)

Even if Wordpress did offer the means for give-and-take in a comments section (which it does), statements of regret and defiant refusal to follow him to the alien terrain suggest that the Governor enjoyed a following only insofar as he was willing to engage with them on their own native *ZheZhe* turf. Now he is reduced to a *chinovnik* whose sole motivation for blogging was to please his boss:

> Medvedev is leaving—now all the bureaucrats can relax, shut up their blogs and sites :)
>
> (bepeck, 16 October 2011, 16:19)

Others see Chirkunov's departure from LiveJournal in just the opposite way—as a welcome sign that Chirkunov is finally getting his priorities straight:

> You're correct, Oleg Anatol'evich, to leave here. You should also leave Wordpress, and Twitter and Facebook—from everywhere, you need to get to work, return from this virtual space. The people need to see their governor in real activities, not virtual activities. Putin doesn't write anywhere [online—MSG], and the results are visible. So you, too, come back to us, Oleg Anatol'evich. Public reports to the population, meetings not with bureaucrats from municipalities, but with the population—small businesses, doctors, teachers, mine workers. Public reports and normal press conferences. Enough hiding in *ZheZhe*. They'll find you and get you.
>
> (zhukova_nata, 16 October 2011, 18:10)

This range of conflicting reactions—from LiveJournal patriots who view his departure as a sell-out to those constituents who believe his proper place as governor is making a difference in the *real* world—reflects the great difficulty establishment politicians face when attempting to engage in "direct internet democracy," particularly within the virtual walls of the Russian *ZheZhe*. Chirkunov himself seems acutely aware of this as witnessed by his reference in both posts to the move as one toward a more management-oriented platform that will enable "the organization of a transparent process of managing the region, a real electronic government." His differentiation between the two modes of electronic communication clearly goes beyond the technical specifications of the platforms. The very invocation of the notion of "genre" makes it clear that, for Chirkunov, the move is likewise one between two difference styles of communication, one (LiveJournal) less formal and more open to reflection and the critical exchange of ideas and opinions, the other (WordPress) more conducive for the day-to-day needs of a public manager keen on managing in public.

## Post-Medvedev trends

Shifting his energies away from LiveJournal wound up helping Chirkunov very little: in April 2012, he announced his plans not to run for re-election under the new open election rule, recognizing that he lacked the favor of voters and likely incoming President, Vladimir Putin. In fact, in anticipation of the new law allowing the more direct election of governors, a total of 20 sitting regional heads either resigned or were removed from their posts in the six months leading up to the new law's approval in June 2012. Given that these moves were made as a deliberate attempt by the Kremlin and United Russia to preserve their political dominance in the regions, what sort of correlation do we see between job retention and new media presence? And what trends are visible in the new media activities of those governors newly appointed by central authorities? Has the impetus for bureaucratic blogging lessened as a result of Putin's return to the presidency?

As it turns out, Medvedev's reduced status does not seem to have influenced trends in either direction. No one lost his job due to a refusal to jump on the blogging bandwagon, but neither have all bureaucrats fled the internet in the post-Medvedev era. Among the old-guard, those inclined to blog continue to do so, those disinclined have continued to remain tepid toward the medium. Many governors have lost their jobs, but there is no correlation between their job status and their ability to engage in "direct internet democracy." Instead, removal in most cases can be directly linked to: (a) ability to produce votes for United Russia; and (b) electability in a new direct voting climate.[11]

The newly appointed governors, as a subgroup of post-Medvedev politicians, embody a curious tension with regard to their inclinations to engage in new media communication. As most all of these were appointed in anticipation of a Putin presidency (in most cases well after the so-called "castling" between Putin and Medvedev had taken place), one might have expected a general disregard toward notions of "direct internet democracy." At the same time, however, a number of them are relatively young and tech-savvy and presumably comprehend that recently electoral reforms will make them more accountable to their constituents. A closer examination of their web presence reveals significant trends that suggest Medvedev's initiatives either had palpable impact, or at least were harbingers of trends to come, but that his model of politician blogger has been refined to decrease the political risk that comes with territory. Rather than total abandonment, one sees in their manner of online public self-presentation a more subtle shift away from the untamed and largely antagonistic space of Russian LiveJournal and the blogosphere in general, toward safer havens. They demonstrate a desire to enlist new technology to bring government closer to the people, but in a way—technologically and rhetorically—which obviates the awkward dynamics of the blogosphere as oppositional space.

The online presence of Vologodskaia oblast' governor, Oleg Kuvshinnikov, is emblematic of the shifting emphasis toward the more service-model of e-Government. Front and center at the main *oblast'* website[12] are links to "electronic government services," an "online reception area of the governor," and a "Citizen appeals" feature that allows users to submit comments, questions, and complaints to the Governor and other regional officials. These interactive platforms are designed around the presumption that the Governor's main job is to listen to and act on concrete problems of citizens and gives those citizens a forum for petitioning. The structure of the interaction is strictly delineated by this relationship, as is the language on both sides. Citizens engage in the language of petitioning, the governor (or his staff) relies entirely on the stock language of bureaucracy. The platform allows the governor to remain within the safe confines of bureaucratic competence and project the clear picture that he is actively listening to the population and swiftly reacting to their ideas and requests—a point which is graphically conveyed by the clearly visible presence of the green "Answer has been prepared" line listed under status across from the requests (cf. Toepfl 2012; Yagodin 2012). The Governor and his staff clearly control which requests get publicly posted to the site. Among the topics listed: "Roads of the city of Griazovets," "Payment for electricity in Ustiuzhna," "Social defense," "Mama is dying!," "The forest is our wealth," and "Sports in the village." With few if any exceptions, the language of the responses display a total mastery of neutral and emotion-less bureaucratic discourse—even in contexts highly charged with emotion:

> По информации начальника управления здравоохранения мэрии Череповца, Ваша мама находится в тяжелом состоянии. Главному врачу Городской больницы №1 поручено срочно подготовить документы для направления их в федеральную клинику.[13]

> Based on the information of the Head of the healthcare directorate of the Cherepovets Mayor's office, your mother is in critical condition. The Chief of Staff of City hospital No. 1 has been authorized to prepare documents immediately for referral to a federal clinic.

The oblast' site also features recent video addresses by Kuvshinnikov, as well as an interactive polling tool designed to gauge visitors' opinions on certain topics (e.g. "Do you approve of the switch back and forth to Daylight Savings Time?"). Two clicks away, via the Governor's own page, constituents can file applications to become part of the government's "Public Council," an initiative Kuvshinnikov promotes on his Twitter account as means of attracting "the most worthy and respected citizens of the oblast', leaders of public opinion whose voice will be heard!"[14] The page likewise features links to Facebook and VKontakte accounts listing recent activities, speeches, and writings by the Governor, as well as his Twitter and LiveJournal blog. The latter contains exclusively governance-related, public-relations posts, with little sign of the governor's own hand in the composition process. The microblogging service primarily serves the same public relations function, consisting mainly of posts that portray the Governor as an active manager or promote the region itself. "We need to more actively engage in import substitution. The majority of goods imported to our region could be produced on its own territory!" Kuvshinnikov posts on 25 October, using a declarative mode that invites little room for feedback (and indeed the post only receives a single reply—Kuvshinnikov 2012). The governor's multimedia ensemble likewise includes a YouTube account and LiveJournal blog, but these, too, singly promote the actions and views of Kuvshinnikov.[15]

Newly appointed Smolenskaia oblast' governor, Aleksei Ostrovskii, has taken a more modest approach to his public positioning in new media, limiting the interactive components of the official site to the "internet reception area" that is now a standard feature on most governors' sites, and a link to his Twitter account. In contrast to Kuvshinnikov, however, Ostrovskii appears to author tweets personally in an informal and highly interactive manner: "To everyone, everyone—a good day and good mood, good luck and faith in that things will get better! I've gone to a meeting with investors in the oblast' from the Forbes list :)))" (Ostrovskii 2012a). Even in his informality, however, Ostrovskii is careful to maintain focus on his administrative duties, project a can-do attitude, and underscore his commitment to constituents: "There is one main thing I take out of all of my meetings [with constituents—MSG]: how much I want to more rapidly increase the budget revenue of the oblast' and constantly increase expenditures on the needs of the people!" (Ostrovskii 2012b). A 24 October tweet exhibits growing confidence that his communication efforts are paying off: "I'm glad that people who reacted to my initial interactions in Twitter skeptically now thank me for my work" (Ostrovskii 2012c).

In all, six of the 20 newly appointed governors have adopted Twitter accounts and use them actively. By contrast, only two have established accounts on LiveJournal. Part of the shift may be due to more general trends away from LiveJournal and toward microblogging; for a number of years now, analysts have been predicting an end to the blogging platform. Be that as it may, there is little question the microblogging alternative represents a safer mode of "direct democracy" for elected (or appointed) officials. Rather than embracing the classic "diary" mode of the blog as a medium for public self-expression, they confine their own utterances to the less risky domain of the microblog, where, in the case of Twitter, the 140-symbol limit encourages brevity and fact, and largely restricts public interaction with "followers." Readers can only see those comments from the public that the governor-tweeter elects to reference himself (unless they happen to also follow those who post comments).

Not all governors, however, are as savvy as Ostrovskii or cautious as Kuvshinnikov at using Twitter to promote more interactive relations with their electorate. Krasnodarskii Krai Governor, Aleksandr Tkachev, learned the hard way that an invitation to an open Twitter conference can quickly go viral in ways entirely unexpected and undesired for a public official. Upon inviting followers to join him in a real-time "Twitter conference" by sending questions to the hashtag "#QuestionToTkachev" (*#VoprosTkachevu*), Tkachev was greeted with well over 20,000 questions in the course of a day, with the vast majority of them ironic and condescending in nature, zeroing in more often than not on issues of corruption and incompetency among central authorities in general and on the part of Tkachev specificially (whom many blame for the colossal mismanagement of wide-spread flooding that led to over a thousand deaths in the Black Sea town of Krymsk in July 2012):

> #QuestionToTkachev how many floods and Kushchevskii's are needed for you to go away?[16]
>
> @antkachev #QuestionToTkachev Why, according to the general prosecutor, does the fence around your dacha not exist, when Suren Gazarian has nevertheless been convicted of having damaged it?[17]
>
> @antkachev How often are you tortured by pangs of conscience? Or is it completely non-existent? #QuestionToTkachev[18]
>
> #QuestionToTkachev You are often accused of corruption and ties to criminal elements. Is it true?[19]
>
> @antkachev why is it not a custom in Russia for bureaucrats (*chinovniki*) to resign in connection with the failure to fulfill their duties? #QuestionToTkachev[20]
>
> @antkachev #QuestionToTkachev what percentage kick-back do you take from each Olympic construction project?[21]
>
> #QuestionToTkachev are you not ashamed not to be in retirement?[22]
>
> @antkachev #QuestionToTkachev Did you drink with your business-partner Tsepoviaz and congratulate him on his free and unpunished murder of children?[23]
>
> @antkachev tell us about the business successes of your niece #QuestionToTkachev[24]
>
> @antkachev—Where are we going?—#QuestionToTkachev[25]

With prominent bloggers such as Navalny directing attention to the online event, "#QuestionToTkachev" soon topped the list of trending hashtags on Runet.[26] From his side of the virtual conference table, the governor gamely ignored the barrage of negative questions, electing instead in his three hours of responses to answer 50 questions on topics ranging from education, health care, and preparations for the 2014 Olympics in Sochi to questions about his religious faith (he is a practicing Russian Orthodox), the politics of soccer, and how to land a job in the local government ("Government workers are chosen competitively. If your resume is right, then everything will work out. Leave your number. Someone will call you").[27] But with the trending hashtag attracting far more attention than the governor's Twitter feed itself, he had ostensibly lost all control of the dialogue. The narrative was now being dictated by legions of Russian-language Twitter followers antagonistic to central authority and with little-to-no geographic links to the governor's intended regional audience of Krasnodarskii Krai. Thinking he was venturing out into a virtual public square that mirrored some meeting hall or street corner in Krasnodar, he inadvertently stumbled upon a far more global and unfriendly public space that came to be defined on a virtual square over which he had no control.[28]

Particularly in the more cautious strategies seen in the example of Kuvshinnikov and the new wave of governors, recent gubernatorial forays into new media suggest that online political communication does carry great potential for enhancing government's online presence and taking advantage of more direct, multimedia tools that enable them to more efficiently provide government services. But the Tkachev debacle also underscores the dangers involved in venturing into digital environments without full understanding of their democratizing potential or their transregional, even global, scope. The internet and new media technologies have proven to be powerful tools for shaping public opinion, aggregating interest groups, and motivating them to action. They are less ideal, however, at limiting the target audience and controlling the message designated for that audience. And on Runet in particular, audiences have proven to be largely antagonistic to those perceived to be representative of central authority. Only public officials adept at establishing themselves as "outsiders"—political, demographic, or geographic—have the ability to engage with this skeptical audience in any manner approximating "direct internet democracy." The rest have found a much safer approach in the alternative model of e-government, where the boundaries of authority and constituency are clearly delineated and confined to the carefully structured, monitored, and filtered interfaces such as the online opinion polling, "internet reception area," or the sound-bite sized, centrally controlled Twitter scroll. All of these areas clearly demarcate rhetorical boundaries between citizen and *vlast'*, and do so more along the lines of petitioner and petitioned, than virtual interlocutors in the public forum of debate. In many cases, this amounts to making the bureaucracy more accessible and accountable, without necessarily exposing the bureaucrats themselves to the unpredictable *vox populi.* With the Runet still largely an oppositional space, the more modest, e-government approach may well prove to be a viable strategy for establishment governors keen on maintaining some form of positive presence online while minimizing exposure to viral attacks that often extend well beyond the physical boundaries of their regions. Local citizens may appreciate more direct means of venting frustration toward local problems and injustices, especially if they sense a concrete willingness on the part of authorities to act. While it falls considerably short of "direct internet democracy," the ability of e-government to solve concrete problems and provide real services may yet prove to be a more viable model of political communication that at least narrows the communication gap between a traditionally aloof ruling political elite and its growingly networked electorate.

## Notes

1 As opposed to excerpts from pre-recorded speeches, etc. See Yagodin (2012) for an in-depth study of Medvedev's blog.

2 For a fuller discussion of earlier precedents of Russian/Soviet rulers seeking to establish more direct links to the people—in most recent history, under the policy of glasnost, see Gorham (2014).

3 Goslyudi (goslyudi.ru).

4 The most current rankings for this "overall rating" may be found at http://www.goslyudi.ru/ratings/full/ (accessed 24 October 2012).

5 To capture the state of the political blogosphere prior to the tumultuous electoral season of 2011–12, I focus on rankings from September 2011, prior to the announcement of Vladimir Putin's intention to run for a third term as president. The most current rankings for Yandex's "top blogs" may be found at http://blogs.yandex.ru/top/ (last accessed 24 October 2012).

6 A not-so-veiled reference to "Party of Crooks and Thieves," the satirical nickname given to United Russia by blogger Aleksei Navalny and subsequently adopted by the entire opposition movement and much of the public at large.

7 The Russian equivalent to the English "f-word" is commonly referred to as a "three-letter word."

8 *Aleksandr Zhilkin* (jilkin.ru), (accessed 5 February 2013).

9 *Blog gubernatora Altaiskogo kraia* (altairegion22.ru/gov/administration/glava/blog/), (accessed 24 October 2012).

10 All of the following comments come from the comment section to Chirkunov (2011c).

11 Most of the governors forced to resign in the past six months would have been among the first to go up for re-election. Many of these were from regions that performed poorly as far as delivering votes for United Russia in December 2011; others carried baggage of scandal and corruption that translated into low popularity ratings.

12 *Ofitsial'nyi portal Vologodskoi oblasti* (vologda-oblast.ru/ru/) (accessed 6 February 2013)

13 "Mama umiraet!" (26 April 2012), http://www.vopros.vologda-oblast.ru/requests/4800.html (accessed 26 October 2012).

14 http://twitter.com/O_Kuvshinnikov/status/261408588067643392 (25 October 2012) (accessed 26 October 2012).

15 http://o-kuvshinnikov.livejournal.com. http://www.youtube.com/user/kuvshnnikovoa (accessed 26 October 2012).

16 Moshonka Medvezhonka, *@madnipple* (18 October 2012), http://twitter.com/madnipple/status/258841634555428866 (accessed 5 November 2012).

17 Andrew Eliseyev, *@andrew_eliseyev* (18 October 2012), https://twitter.com/andrew_eliseyev/status/258841932749488128 (accessed 5 November 2012).

18 Alexander Putikov, *@putikoff* (18 October 2012), https://twitter.com/putikoff/status/258841949593804800 (accessed 5 November 2012).

19 Sergey Pigida, *@jfm06* (18 October 2012), https://twitter.com/jfm06/status/258842098235756544 (accessed 5 November 2012).
20 mindalbka, *@mindalbka* (18 October 2012), https://twitter.com/mindalbka/status/258842138970836992 (accessed 5 November 2012).
21 Synthpopgirl, *@MalakhovaAnna* (18 October 2012), https://twitter.com/MalakhovaAnna/status/258842140614995968 (accessed 5 November 2012).
22 Mono Misha, *@mishamono* (18 October 2012), https://twitter.com/mishamono/status/258842206813691904 (accessed 5 November 2012).
23 Alexey Navalny, *@navalny* (18 October 2012), https://twitter.com/navalny/status/258842251969581056 (accessed 5 November 2012).
24 Vadim Lebedev, *@vadimleb* (18 October 2012), https://twitter.com/vadimleb/status/258842424921706497 (accessed 5 November 2012).
25 Shut, *@NektoNekto* (18 October 2012), https://twitter.com/NektoNekto/status/258842724931891120 (accessed 5 November 2012).
26 This capacity for popular bloggers such as Navalny to shape public debates by mobilizing and directing networked communities has of course been one of the most potent tools of the political opposition.
27 https://twitter.com/antkachev/status/258853658152820737 (accessed 5 December 2012).
28 Perhaps coincidentally—but indicative of central authorities' growing penchant for tighter internet oversight—just weeks after the Tkachev debacle reports emerged of efforts from within the Kremlin to encourage governors to exercise greater restraint in the Twitter-sphere (Rubin 2012).

## References


Belykh, Nikita. 2011. "Elektronnoe pravitel'stvo." *Belykh, Nikita Iur'evich*, 13 October. Available at: http://belyh.livejournal.com/672931.html (accessed 9 April 2012).

—— 2012. "Po kritike Predsedatelia Pravitel'stva . . ." *Belykh, Nikita Iur'evich*, 10 January. Available at: http://belyh.livejournal.com/701743.html (accessed 2 November 2012).

Bilevskaia, Elina. 2010. "On-line politika." *Nezavisimaia gazeta*, 21 January. Available at: http://www.ng.ru/politics/2010-01-21/1_online.html (accessed 23 March 2012).

Chirkunov, Oleg. 2011a. "Krizis zhanra." *Oleg Chirkunov*, 11 October. Available at: http://chirkunov.livejournal.com/382002.html (accessed 4 April 2012).

—— 2011b. "Ia zdes'." *Oleg Chirkunov*, 16 October. Available at: http://chirkunov.livejournal.com/383218.html (accessed 17 October 2011).

—— 2011c. "Al'niashinskoe sel'skoe naselenie." *Oleg Chirkunov*, 18 October. Available at: http://chirkunov.me/2011/10/18/альняшинское-сельское-поселение/ (accessed 4 April 2012).

Coleman, Stephen. 2004. "Blogs as Listening Posts Rather than Soapboxes." In *Political Blogs: Craze or Convention?* edited by Rose Ferguson and Milica Howell, 26–30. London: The Hansard Society.

Gorham, Michael S. (2014). *After Newspeak: Language, Culture and Politics from Gorbachev to Putin*. Ithaca, NY: Cornell University Press.

Iakushev, Vladimir Vladimirovich. 2011. "Kvartira dlia budzhetnika—2." *Blog Vladimira Iakusheva*, 21 April. Available at: http://gubernator.admtyumen.ru/governor_to/ru/blog.htm?postId=57@cmsVBVideoPost&mode=1 (accessed 24 October 2012).

Kanygin, Pavel. 2010. "Beregis'! Dorogu! Gubernatory vykhodiat v Internet." *Novaia gazeta*, 19 March. Available at: http://www.novayagazeta.ru/data/2010/028/01.html (accessed 24 May 2011).

Kuvshinnikov, Oleg. 2012. "Nuzhno . . ." *@O_Kuvshinnikov*, 25 October. Available at: http://twitter.com/O_Kuvshinnikov/status/261444770818301952 (accessed 5 November 2012).

Leskov, Sergei, and Aleksandr Sadchikov. 2010. "Vladislav Surkov: Genii vsegda v men'shinstve." *Izvestiia*, 16 December. Available at: http://www.izvestia.ru/politic/article3149592/ (accessed 24 May 2011).

Lévy, Pierre. 2001. *Cyberculture*. Trans. Robert Bononno. *Electronic Mediations*, Vol. 4. Minneapolis: University of Minnesota Press.

Makunina, Svetlana. 2011. "Kadyrov, Gromov, Tkachev: RBK daily predstavliaet antireiting samykh kritikuemykh gubernatorov." *RBKDaily*, 13 October. Available at: http://www.rbcdaily.ru/2011/10/13/focus/562949981716372 (accessed 30 October 2011).

Medvedev, Dmitrii 2009. "O razvitii interneta v Rossii." *Videoblog Dmitriia Medvedeva*, 22 April. Available at: http://blog.kremlin.ru/post/10 (accessed 23 March 2012).

—— 2010. "Griadet epokha vozvrashcheniia neposredstvennoi demokratii." *Videoblog Dmitriia Medvedeva*, 31 May. Available at: http://blog.kremlin.ru/post/81 (accessed 24 January 2011).

—— 2011a. "Prostranstvo priamoi demokratii budet rasshiriat'sia." *Videoblog Dmitriia Medvedeva*, 16 September. Available at: http://blog.kremlin.ru/post/106 (accessed 24 January 2011).

—— 2011b. "Dmitrii Medvedev vstretilsia so svoimi storonnikami—predstviteliami setevykh soobshchestv." *Prezident Rossii*, 9 November. Available at: http://kremlin.ru/transcripts/13443 (accessed 23 March 2012).

"Medvedev: Internet—veshch' perspektivnaia." 2009. *BaltInfo.ru*, 15 June. Available at: http://www.baltinfo.ru/2009/06/15/Medvedev-Internet--vesch'-perspektivnaya (accessed 23 March 2012).

"Medvedev potreboval ot Shantseva lichno 'kovyriat'sia' v internete." 2010. *Klub regionov*, 17 March. Available at: http://club-rf.ru/news/nijegorodskaya-oblast/medvedev_potreboval_ot_shantseva_lichno_koviryatsya_internete/ (accessed 9 April 2012).

Miazina, Elena. 2010. "Chinovniki i blogosfera." *Vedomosti*, 13 December. Available at: http://www.vedomosti.ru/politics/news/1161162/chinovniki_i_blogosfera_ot_vylazok_k_masshtabnomu_osvoeniyu (accessed 23 May 2011).

Mironov, Sergei. 2007. "Pervaia zapis' bloga." *Vesti ot Sergeia Mironova*, 29 November. Available at: http://sergey-mironov.livejournal.com/662.html (accessed 23 March 2012).

—— 2011. "'Edinaia Rossiia'—partiia oligarkhov i chinovnikov." *Vesti ot Sergeia Mironova*, 13 September. Available at: http://sergey-mironov.livejournal.com/333425.html (accessed 18 October 2011).

Mishchenko, Maksim. 2011a. "Naval'nyi—piarshchik strany iz trekh bukv." *Maksim Mishchenko*, 4 March. Available at: http://tagan.livejournal.com/495937.html (accessed 24 October 2012.

—— 2011b. "Istoricheskii s"ezd." *Maksim Mishchenko*, 27 September. Available at: http://tagan.livejournal.com/544874.html (accessed 24 October 2012).

Ostrovskii, Aleksei. 2012a. "Vsem, vsem . . ." *@a_ostrovskiy*, 25 August. Available at: https://twitter.com/a_ostrovskiy/status/239248591116439552 (accessed 5 November 2012).

—— 2012b. "So vsekh vstrech . . ." *@a_ostrovskiy*, 19 September. Available at: https://twitter.com/a_ostrovskiy/status/248629135344300033 (accessed 5 November 2012).

—— 2012c. "Rad tomu . . ." *@a_ostrovskiy*, 24 October. Available at: https://twitter.com/a_ostrovskiy/status/261090154255626242 (accessed 5 November 2012).

Rubin, Mikhail. 2012. "Kreml' zapreshchaet gubernatoram Twitter." *Izvestiia*, 7 November. Available at: http://izvestia.ru/news/539097 (accessed 6 December 2012).

Sal'manov, Oleg. 2010. "Pochem blog dlia gubernatora." *Vedomosti*, 1 February. Available at: http://www.vedomosti.ru/politics/news/2010/02/01/937123 (accessed 2 June 2011).

Shein, Oleg. 2011a. "Pro Naval'nogo: v pomoshch' konspirologam." *Oleg Shein*, 11 March. Available at: http://oleg-shein.livejournal.com/289794.html (accessed 31 October 2012).

—— 2011b. "Astrakhanskii Sotsial'nyi Forum." *Oleg Shein*, 2 July. Available at: http://oleg-shein.livejournal.com/350851.html (accessed 31 October 2012).

Sidorenko, Alexei. 2010. "Competing Models of Internet Politics." *Global Voices*, 30 November. Available at: http://globalvoicesonline.org/2010/11/30/russia-competing-models-of-internet-politics/ (accessed 14 July 2011).

Tirmaste, Maria-Luiza. 2011. "'Edinaia Rossiia' vpletaetsia v sotsial'nye seti." *Kommersant*, 6 May. Available at: http://www.kommersant.ru/doc-y/1635547 (accessed 26 May 2011).

Toepfl, Florian. 2012. "Blogging for the Sake of the President: The Online-Diaries of Russian Governors." *Europe-Asia Studies* 64(8): 1435–59.

Volkov, Leonid. 2011. "Kak ia porabotal agitatorom." *O vsiakoi vsiachine*, 9 March. Available at: http://leonwolf.livejournal.com/238492.html (accessed 9 April 2012).

Vrazhina, Anna. 2010. "Dezavuiruite eto: Pis'mo Dmitriiu Medvedevu." *Lenta*, 5 February. Available at: http://www.lenta.ru/columns/2010/02/05/blogs/ (accessed 1 June 2011).

Yagodin, Dmitry. 2012. "Blog Medvedev: Aiming for Public Consent." *Europe-Asia Studies* 64(8): 1415–34.

Zhilkin, Aleksandr. 2011a. "Platnaia ili besplatnaia rybalka, chto tselesoobraznee?" *Blog gubernatora Astrakhanskoi oblasti Aleksandra Zhilkina*, 24 March. Available at: http://alexandr-jilkin.livejournal.com/43643.html (accessed 5 December 2011).

—— 2011b. "Nevtianaia i gazovaia promyshlennost' regiona i ne tol'ko [comments]." *Blog gubernatora Astrakhanskoi oblasti Aleksandra Zhilkina*, 4 September. Available at: http://alexandr-jilkin.livejournal.com/54912.html#comments (accessed 5 October 2011).

—— 2012. "Stoliarov—legitimno izbrannyi mer. Vse ostal'noe—politicheskie insinuatsii." *Blog gubernatora Astrakhanskoi oblasti Aleksandra Zhilkina*, 10 April. Available at: http://alexandr-jilkin.livejournal.com/67908.html (accessed 24 October 2012).

# 14 Languages of memory

*Ellen Rutten*

On 5 May 2011, the comment thread of the popular Russian blog *drugoi* featured a comment by a user who called her- or himself *asurra*. This user had selected as her or his userpic an image of a rather ungraceful Simpson-like cartoon figure dressed in a bright orange bear costume. "The authorities in Russia are shit," *asurra* wrote in response to a politically tinged post by the blog host, "the police are shit. [World War II—ER] [v]eterans are heroes(I mean it) [*sic*—ER]. Oh, well and compatriots who have close connections with the West through some official documents are also heroes!"[1]

*asurra*'s comment exemplifies a specific type of Russian online language. More specifically, it is an instance of what we could call the Russian-language Internet's *language of memory*.

This chapter explores how web-mediated memory is evolving in Russia—and more specifically, how, in Russian digital realms, the *language* of memory develops. Embedding this language within the rapidly expanding transnational "digital-memories" discourse, the pages below map both the prime locations and the core features of Russia's online language of memory. In doing so, they pay special attention to online commemorations of World War II—which ranks among recent Russian history's most traumatic events—and of its veterans.[2]

## Post-Soviet memory and web wars: introduction

Starting from the early 2000s, "digital memories"—online constructions of individual, cultural or collective memory—have attracted the attention of a growing group of specialists in the fields of media and memory. Back in 2003, when speaking of the then-emerging boom in memory studies, memory expert Andreas Huyssen observed that "[w]e cannot discuss personal, generational, or public memory separately from the enormous influence of the new media as carriers of all forms of memory" (Huyssen 2003: 18). A few years later, cultural historians Astrid Erll and Ann Rigney went as far as proclaiming cultural memory's very *existence* was dependent on media. In their words, cultural memory is "always shared with the help of symbolic artifacts that mediate between individuals and, in the process, create communality across both time and space" (Erll and Rigney 2009: 1).

Formally, Huyssen and Erll and Rigney may not have framed their claims as "digital-memory" reflections, but their arguments are formative to digital-memory studies as a scholarly discipline. Thanks to their insights and those of other pioneering scholars, since the early 2000s this discipline has been providing increasingly sophisticated answers to the question: "how is memory mediated in digital media?" (see especially Van Dijck 2007; Kalay, Kvan, and Affleck 2007; Garde-Hansen, Hoskins, and Reading 2009; Arthur 2009, Neiger, Meyers, and Zandberg 2011).

Reasons to ponder this question abound. Across various world regions, digital remembering thrives, whether in the shape of online memorials for the deceased (one popular example is the website www.virtual-memorials.com), historical visualization apps (a fine example is the Museum of London's Streetmuseum app, in which users employ mobile media to superimpose historical photographs on concrete local spaces),[3] digital archives (the online September 11 Archive famously "uses electronic media to collect, preserve, and present the history of September 2001 and its aftermath"),[4] or commemorative blogs and social networking groups. In these and other digital-memory practices, existing forms of commemoration do not simply migrate to a new medium. "[D]igital technologies"—as the authors of one leading publication in the field put it—"are changing human memory discourses, practices and forms, as well as the way we conceptualise memory itself" (Garde-Hansen, Hoskins, and Reading 2009: cover text).

Digital memories are a particularly fertile object of study for readers of Russian social media. For one, Russian digital media boast unique conditions for the mediation and circulation of memories: owing to flexible copyright legislation, media piracy is much more rampant in Russia than elsewhere, and in Russian-speaking social media we find large volumes of history-related video and film footage.[5] But loose copyright laws are not the only reason for fishing Russian-speaking subjects out of the global pond of web users who actively engage with memory. Another major rationale for doing so is the high degree of politicization of Russia's rapidly growing digital communities (see Lapina-Kratasiuk et al. 2009). Blog comments, social networking discussions, guestbook entries: in Eastern Europe, even discursive spaces not devoted to history or politics proper inevitably tackle political-historical themes.

As a result, the reader of Russian digital media finds herself embedded in a world where the past is no less alive than the present. In VKontakte—the Russian answer to Facebook—and on Russian-language Twitter, alternative histories thrive and multifarious memories compete for position. Members of blog communities quarrel over the role of the country in World War II. Users of memory sites debate the role of memory in determining the geographical bounds of national sovereignty. Participants of social networks discuss Soviet repression. What unites these different groups is linguistic communication: all negotiate between and play with different *language* tools and registers to express their stance on the country's turbulent past. The word "language" here can be understood quite broadly: rather than text-only expressions, in this chapter I look at what several scholars have called *multimodal communication*. A helpful definition of this term comes from one of the pioneers in the field, Gunther Kress:

> The 21st century is awash with ever more mixed and remixed images, writing, layout, sound, gesture, speech, and 3D objects. Multimodality looks beyond language and examines these multiple modes of communication and meaning making.
>
> (Kress 2009: jacket text)

As Kress and others argue, today we are witnessing the rise of new communicative models, in which "language," "text," or "the visual" are no longer self-evident analytical categories. In our digitized age's "mashup cultures" (Sonvilla-Weiss 2010), these categories fundamentally blend and intertwine.

Below I explore the linguistic features that epitomize one specific type of multimodal discourse—digital memory discourse in Russia. As I will explain below, to this type of discourse the mixing of (audio)visual, textual and other communicative modes is a *sine qua non*. I start this analysis, however, by scrutinizing, first, the various agents who construct Russian online memory, and, second, the various digital services and media in which it can be traced.

## Voices and sources

When we talk about Russian digital memory discourse, we are talking about a set of discursive practices performed by concrete *agents*—or, to put it differently, by concrete online voices. I will not even attempt to exhaustively sketch the types of voices that take part in online memory construction. What does matter to the argument below is that the range of different social actors and the political stances and linguistic registers that they adopt are broad. Online memory "speakers" vary from xenophobes to globalization defenders, from schoolgirls to angry old men, and from the cautiously formulating *intelligent* to the barely literate. Below I focus on cross-media memory practices and online hate speech, for instance, but Russian digital spaces also accommodate text-only, conciliatorily (if critically) toned commemorations, such as this comment on a blog post by the popular Russian blogger Rustem Adagamov, aka *drugoi*:

> From each family living in Russia today, the war has taken away at least one member. In the Soviet era, warriors who fell on the battlefield were honored with monuments, poems and songs . . . In Soviet times, names were engraved on marble plates which relatives visited on Victory Day to lay flowers, and to at least touch the inscription by hand, to show the new generation that their grandfather or great-grandfather had given his life for the Motherland. How shameful that the current authorities, when they've organized lavish Victory Parades, have forgotten who it was who offered up their lives for that victory. Tell me, people, how should we remind the administration, those entrenched enemies of the people, of our deceased fellow villagers?[6]

The question of *where* we find memory discourse in Russian online space leads to no less pluralistic answers. Rather than posing this question, one should perhaps ask where we do *not* find it. The Russian-language internet is not only embedded within a public culture that is itself deeply politicized and history-oriented; it also forms a relatively autonomous alternative to the mostly top-down manipulated offline media—even if, in Russia as elsewhere, the offline and online spheres constantly overlap, intersect and (re-)shape one another.[7] Online, ordinary Russians *can* publicly express their dissenting, critical visions of the recent past that other media will only accommodate to a limited extent.

Not surprisingly, the Russian-language internet or Runet crackles with talk of the Soviet experience: even in online spaces that are not formally devoted to politics, discussions are often lushly seasoned with references to politico-historical discourse.[8]

Within these memory-devoted online media, one can discern a distinct set of prominent services and genres. What follows is a (non-exhaustive) overview of these "memory hotspots," and of the forms in which memory discourse is clustered within each individual service/genre. I do not delve into the detail of the different forms and formats here, but, for each, where possible, I do provide sources for further scholarly reading.

1 Twitter. Russian-speaking Twitter users eagerly debate the past or share individual, family and collective memories, in the form of full-fledged memory-devoted posts, but also through the use of hashtags and memory-devoted user pictures, or by setting up Twitter communities devoted to a historical event or concept.[9]
2 Facebook and its Russian counterparts. Facebook, VKontakte, Odnoklassniki and other social media are thriving as a home for Russian-language memory discourse. Some users come together in history-oriented user groups or communities, others launch individual accounts that focus on memory in particular, with user profiles revealing a clear focus on memory, and yet others post entries or comments on memory only occasionally, or only in passing, in the course of non-memory-related posts or comments.[10]
3 Blogs. A digital service that has accommodated Russian memory discourse ever since the early 2000s is the blog. The extent to which individual blogs can be labeled "memory blogs" again varies greatly: some merely feature memory-oriented user profiles and/or names, in others the recent past is discussed only when topical events prompt the author to touch upon it, and yet more blogs or blog communities have a history-exclusive focus.[11]
4 (Chat forums of) memory-devoted websites. Today the Russian web features an increasing number of websites devoted especially to Soviet (material/political/creative/consumer) culture, including but not limited to a number of websites of Soviet-focused museums. Some of them have lively chat forums, where users articulate their feelings towards the historical material on the site, engage in discussions on the recent past, and/or demonstrate their feelings on recent history via retro-oriented user pictures or usernames.
5 YouTube. YouTube is not only a treasure-trove of memory-related Russian videos, but also of (often quite lengthy) threads of comments that focus on

Soviet-era memory. These can arise in response to particular videos, but, just as often, they emerge in response to videos that, in themselves, do not touch upon Soviet memory.[12]

6 Wikipedia. In an analysis of Russian- and Ukrainian-language Wikipedia discussions, Helene Dounaevsky argues that Wikipedia's historical section is "an on-line laboratory where history is continuously being written and re-written" (Dounaevsky 2013: 130). In the so-called *talk* pages of history-related Russian Wikipedia entries, historical discussions can acquire unusually vivid dimensions. As on YouTube, history-oriented discussions also occur on the *talk* pages of entries that, at first sight, have little to do with history.

7 News sites. Both online versions of existing news sites and online news services are a platform for memory-related discussions. Apart from the sites' news sections proper, these also arise in the comment sections (once again, of both historically oriented and non-memory-related news items; it is not uncommon, for instance, to see a discussion within a "lifestyle" section turn to Soviet-era memory) (Zvereva 2012).

As this short overview demonstrates, memory debate can surface as a more or less prominent discursive component of a variety of digital services and genres. What these different services and genres share is a question to which I return below.

## Core features

Both in Russia and abroad, digital memory construction partly overlaps with and partly differs from offline memory discourse. When we focus on those features that differ between the two forms, it is helpful to rely on existing publications on digital memories. Among other conclusions:

- they have demonstrated how, online, we deal "[with memories that are] not consumed . . . but produced by the audience," and how, in digital media, "these memories are not simply shared and told . . . but creatively constructed" (Garde-Hansen, Hoskins, and Reading 2009: 12);
- they have unraveled how digital or "social-network memory" yields "a new hybrid form of public and private memory" (ibid.: 6);
- and they have convincingly argued that, online, memory generates "a new digital temporality of memory"—one where "the very condition of remembering is increasingly networked but also actively and re-actively constructed on-the-fly" (Hoskins 2009: 94).

The theoreticians in question are referring to memory practices at large—but the specific memory *language* to which web users resort takes on no less idiosyncratic forms. Despite the variety of online memory material, from Russian online discourse we can distil a set of four core features.

## Discourses of hatred

When we speak of "Soviet memory," we are referring to a highly traumatized cultural memory—and to a past whose darker dimensions remain unsettled to this day. Post-Soviet memory specialists have repeatedly touched upon the extent to which contemporary Russia, rather than sharing the recent infatuation with traumatic national memory witnessed in many Western societies, insists on a collective forgetting of the gloomier pages of Soviet history. In the words of Alexander Etkind, a historian and renowned expert in the field:

> the only certainty about the Soviet catastrophe is its scale and its uncertainty. We do not have the list of victims; we do not have the list of executioners; and we do not have adequate memorials, museums, and monuments which could stabilize the understanding of these events for generations to come.
>
> (Etkind 2011: 635–6)[13]

Given Russia's unstable memory landscape and the status of new media as a major outlet for critical public debate, it is not surprising that, in online Russian memory discourse, violent rhetoric and hateful language are thriving. Digital discussions of the recent past are marked—arguably to a greater extent than outside the Russian context—by discourses of nationalism and hostility. In the words of sociologist Adi Kuntsman, these discourses display a "choreographic" movement of "endless return to what is not resolved and not remembered" (Kuntsman 2009: 192). The comment with which this chapter opened, in which user *asurra* uses a controversy involving a war veteran to scold the incumbent Russian authorities, is a case in point. "The authorities are shit," *asurra* claims, before employing variations on the same grammatical construction, in staccato phrases: "the police are shit. Veterans are heroes."[14]

While it overlaps to some extent with its offline counterpart, this online memory discourse of hatred also has its own ingredients. First of all, web users eagerly engage in so-called *flame wars* or *holy wars*—mass-scale, long-term discussions, whose predominant tone is one of insults and mutual hatred. Their participants' aim, rather than a search for consensus, is to defend a predefined sociopolitical position.

Flame wars are not an exclusive Russian phenomenon: they have been observed and described in various local digital settings.[15] In Russian, they are mostly referred to as *kholyvory*, a Russian plural form derived from the phrase "holy war." An hour or two after *asurra* posts his or her comment on veterans and the authorities, users *lialiku* and *dronetz* use the same comment thread to launch a discussion with flame-war traits, when they debate—but fail to come to any agreement on—current attitudes in Russia to World War II. "Shame to our country, to our authorities, . . . and to all young people, who . . . remember the veterans only on 9 May [the day that Russia celebrates the victory over fascist Germany in World War II—ER]," argues *lialiku* after four ineffective attempts to convince *dronetz* that there is a lack of concern for veterans' welfare.

Having similarly tried to persuade *lialiku* in vain of the opposite, *dronetz* ends the discussion with a frustrated: "leave it, there is no use in explaining."[16]

Another component that is prevalent in hateful online memory discourse is the usage of smileys. These emoticons can be used to channel emotions in various ways: they can have a reconciliatory function, but they can also serve to legitimize an aggressive tone that the user would not otherwise have permitted him/herself.[17] An illustration of this is user *Kljaver*'s emoticon usage in derogatory comments about a war veteran who claims financial compensation from the authorities: "The old man . . . is a bad person," *Kljaver* writes. "Selling a home he had and then claiming another one. What sort of nonsense is that? :)."[18] Finally, if web users feel uncomfortable with historically sensitive comments by others, on online forums—think of YouTube comment sessions, for instance—they have the option of deleting these comments through the "mark as spam" option. In Russian online memory discourse, this option is frequently used to silence opinions whose language is not so much hatred-inciting as not to the liking of the user who deletes them. In Russian- and Ukrainian-language YouTube discussions on a war-related political incident, for instance, one Russian comment which was marked as spam said: "HOW DARE YOU OPEN YOUR MOUTH AND ACCUSE WESTERN UKRAINE OF FASCISM!!! HAVE YOU EVEN SO MUCH AS ONCE IN YOUR LIFE PLACED FLOWERS FOR THOSE SAME VETERANS????"[19] Although voiced somewhat crudely, this comment is a non-violent, thematically relevant response, and the motivation for deleting it is unlikely to be anything other than political.

Deleting posts, the use of emoticons as legitimizers for aggression, and *kholyvory*: these and related linguistic and rhetoric devices demonstrate just to what extent digital media serve as platforms for the "circulation of affect" (Kuntsman 2012). Where many print sources on memory present themselves as neutral documents on the past, digital debaters foreground and openly express emotions—emotions among which, in any case in Russia, hatred occupies a particularly prominent space.

## Ritualized language

Cultural historian (and contributor to this volume) Vera Zvereva has shown that in online discussions of the Soviet past, Russian web users often have little interest in actual historical commemoration. Frequently, their insistence on "unearthing the facts" is quasi-historical: it is oriented on political or social identity construction, rather than memory proper (Zvereva 2011, 2012). Participants show one another who they are by defining their position in the region's ongoing memory wars; what factually happened in the past hundred years is of secondary concern to them. This is true for my *asurra* example, too: in his or her comment, a view on a historical event (World War II and its civilian participants) is squeezed in between—and instrumentalized in—a critique of the current Russian authorities.

By implication, the language that Russia's online memory debaters use contains a high degree of standardized/ritualized political phrasings. Users borrow phrases from official Soviet discourse—"Glory to the USSR!," "Glory to our fallen heroes!," for instance—and embed them within their own (personal, family or more general political/historical) narratives of the Soviet past. In her work on these linguistic practices, Zvereva cites, among others, the following examples from Russian-language online communities:

> Mariia Zelentsova: My great-grandfather exploded on a mine on 9 MAY '45, *fame and honor to those who fell for us!!!* [Capitals original—ER]
>
> Nikita Sergeevich: My great-great-uncle was a military pilot, according to some reports he went missing without trace . . . on May 9 1945. *Eternal honor to the heroes.*[20]

If these citations couple official rhetoric to relatively neutral descriptive language, online we also witness more ironic blends of official and manifestly non-standard, slang registers. Perhaps the most famous example of this provocative "linguistic mashup" is the slogan with which blogger *kcooss* welcomes readers of his online journal.[21] In a pun on a popular pejorative name for Putin's party, *kcooss* writes: "Lenin is alive, Putin is/has a Party of Crooks and Thieves" (*Lenin zhiv, Putin PzhiV*).[22] That *kcooss* bases his historical parallel on more than wordplay alone illustrates the explanatory phrase that follows: "Russia has one longstanding tradition: once every 200 years the occupants are chased from the Kremlin: 1612—1812—2012."[23]

Artem, Mariia, Nikita and others all mingle ideologized "formulas of glorification and commemoration" with less official, colloquial writings and slang phrases. Together, they engage in the ongoing creation of a language of remembering that one could call idiosyncratic for digital spaces. When contrasted with offline equivalents, this online language of remembering is emphatically hybrid and eclectic: it flexibly accommodates contrasting language registers and styles within one single discursive statement. In short, it epitomizes the "mashup" and "remix" practices—the blending of existing cultural artifacts into new creative fusions—that mark online cultures in general (see above). As computer-mediated discourse experts have argued, remix is "one aspect of the new discourse practices that digital media and participatory platforms . . . make possible"—one that "can be used as a resource for engaging with and resisting dominant discourses" (Androutsopoulos 2013: 49, see also Androutsopoulos 2010). In the Russian context, the standardized formulas of Soviet rhetoric are a particularly beloved object of discursive "remix resistance." This infatuation with "Soviet talk" is not surprising: ever since the early Soviet period, Russians have eagerly played on its official slogans, standard phrases and abbreviations.[24]

## Cursory discourses

Online memory discourse is less polished than that of printed texts. On the one hand, many scholars have argued that online language is much more cautiously polished than is commonly acknowledged (among others, see Tavosanis 2006).

On the other hand, experts of digital communication have documented a (sometimes conscious) playful flouting of linguistic, orthographic, grammatical or punctual perfection in many online languages, including Swedish, German, French, Chinese—and Russian (among others, see Durscheid 2002; Segerstad 2005; Anis 2007, and Guseinov 2009). One digital-writing manual even advises against linguistic correctness specifically in digital writing: the authors implore readers to "[t]hink blunt bursts" and to "[a]ppreciate unruliness" (Hale and Scanlon 1996: 15).

In the memory discourse which this chapter explores, the dominance of non-polished language translates itself into a sometimes deliberately cursory discourse: when Russian-speaking web users discuss their recent past, the language that they use has little in common with the cautiously edited language of top-down or official historiographical sources. Many a user defines his or her view on the past in hastily written, brief entries or comments, whose interpunction, spelling and grammar are not always in tune with official norms. The short comment by *asurra* with which this chapter opened contained only one such "cursory mistake"—that is, the omission of the blank space between "heroes" and "I mean it." More radical is the deviation from standard writing norms in the same discussion by user *stanislavbel*, who argues:

> Instead of giving a respectable pension . . . they give people an apartment! ofcourse provocating relatives or the veterans themselves, knowing the eternal accommodation problems in russia.give them a pension not of 12 thous rubles but 1000 thous. or more, I don't know . . . but so that others(who did not fight [in the war—ER) are not envious. . . . GIVE THE PENSION and don't make a foool of yourselves. [*sic*—ER][25]

Missing blank spaces (between "russia." and "Give," between "others" and "(who)"), a lack of capitalization (of "russia,"), typos ("foool"): *stanislavbel's* text brims over with the playfully "erratic" language that marks online writing—a language whose users do not necessarily *intend* to defy linguistic norms, but whose markedly amateur linguistic aesthetics is often part of a deliberately home-crafted, quasi-amateur "aesthetics of imperfection" that, in online circles, ranks as an asset rather than a taboo.[26]

Similar deviations from normative language can be observed in digital-memory discourse outside Russia, too—but within Russia, they provide an especially radical break with non-digital memory writings. In Russia, after all, until perestroika, a highly normative linguistic culture reigned.[27]

As with the other features mentioned, the cursory memory discourse in which users like *stanislavbel* engage constitutes more than a formal change from print memory discourse: their deviating interpunction, grammar and spelling illustrate one of the key findings of digital memory experts to date. Above I cited Andrew Hoskins, who claims that online, the very condition of remembering is "actively and re-actively constructed on-the-fly" (Hoskins 2009: 94). With its (sometimes quasi-)hastily crafted and remixed statements and comments, Russian online memory discourse is emblematic of this new model of continually updated, revised and expanded remembering.

## Multimodal language

Online memory language is no rigidly textual language. It is significantly more (audio)visually oriented than non-digital memory language. Admittedly, different digital services and genres can be more or less (audio)visually or textually inclined—think of the primarily visually oriented World-War-II-era photo blog, as opposed to the text-only Wikipedia entry. As a rule, however, online the line between strictly linguistic and other forms of communication is largely blurred.

The multimodal orientation of (Russian) online communication means that, if post-Soviet digital-memory discourse includes the text-oriented samples I have discussed so far, users can also express their attitude towards the Soviet past through (audio)visual components. In fact, the bloggers, YouTube commentators and SNS community members whom I have cited above rarely express their views on Russian history through text only. They also do so through retro-styled user pictures or memory-related user profile data, or by posting Soviet-related pictures of film clips.

The *asurra* fragment with which this chapter opened is, once again, exemplary: it is impossible for us to read the comment that *asurra* makes about veterans without being reminded of the (ironic-clumsy version of a) national icon that (s)he has selected as a user picture: the bear. It is similarly impossible to grasp the full breadth of the YouTube discussion from which I cited above—on a political incident relating to World War II commemorations—without taking into account its (audio-)visual components. Not only are its participants responding to a video, they are also visually representing themselves through user pictures of national flags, coats of arms, armed knights and other highly politicized images. These visual ingredients provide indispensable clues to their position in the debate.

In these and other online commemorations of the Soviet experience, multimodal language dominates and colors the process of remembering. This is not to say that (audio-)visual practices are a rarity in offline memory cultures: commemorative monuments, films or museum installations are but a few examples of (audio-)visual memory genres that predate digital communication. What does set the "multimodal" dynamics of online remembering apart from offline variants is a feature that I discussed earlier in this analysis: its infatuation with mashing up cultural heritage. Online, commemorative acts are, to a substantially greater extent than elsewhere, acts of a continual mixing and remixing of existing textual, visual and audiovisual cultural artifacts. Remix is especially relevant to digital discourse in Russia, with its sparse copyright legislation and thriving media-piracy practices.

## Conclusion

Russian digital media boast their own online Russian memory language. Certain qualifications must be made when discussing this language: first, in many respects,

Russian digital-memory discourse constantly interacts and overlaps both with *offline* memory discourse and with *non-Russian* digital commemorative debates; and, second, at this stage scholarly explorations of the vast amount of empirical material are limited. Once we take these reservations into account, however, we *can* cautiously speak of a Runet-based "language of memory." Surfacing in digital services that range from Wikipedia via social media to museum websites, this Runet memory language is marked by the set of core features that I outlined above: the persistent use of discourses of hatred; the frequent occurrence of ritualized Soviet-style phrasings; an omnipresence of unpolished orthography, grammar and punctuation; and, finally, a strong visual component.

At first glance, the four dimensions that I single out here—or some of them, at least—may strike one as strictly formalist features. Upon closer inspection, however, it is not hard to see that their relevance extends far beyond the rigidly formal. They point to digitization's profound impact on the ways in which we remember. Together, these linguistic features demonstrate that online, cultural remembering is—to a substantially greater extent than its print counterpart—an act of intense trans-media creativity, spontaneity and emotional engagement.[28]

That this online act of remembering acquires idiosyncratic traits in the Russian context is beyond doubt. Russian copyright legislation, as we saw, facilitates an especially eager celebration of "multimodal" memory practices—that is, commemorative narratives in which textual and (audio-)visual components blend. Toying with the ideologically burdened formulas of Soviet-speak, this is a type of historical language play that we rarely find in online environments outside Russophone spheres. One could also argue that the ardent affective investment that we witness across Russia's digital memory spaces is unique to those post-socialist societies that lack a fully fleshed-out public memory culture—though a comparative transnational study of online discourses of hatred is still outstanding.[29] At the same time, the memory practices of *asurra* and others exemplify a social structure that transcends national and geopolitical boundaries. This is, to borrow new media critic Geert Lovink's words, the "deep underlying social architecture" that permeates the internet as a whole, and that we are only now beginning to fathom (Lovink 2007: 111).

## Notes

1 Fragment from comment by user *asurra*, from discussion on drugoi.livejournal.com, 5 May 2011. http://drugoi.livejournal.com/3549532.html?page=2#comments (accessed 6 April 2012).

2 I am grateful to the editors of this volume, as well as the participants of the Future of Russian 4 conference, for helpful suggestions in crafting this chapter; special thanks to Michael Gorham and Alexei Yurchak for feedback that was as detailed as it was fruitful. Needless to say, responsibility for any remaining errors is mine alone.

3 See museumoflondon.org.uk/Resources/app/you-are-here-app/home.html for a description.

4 Citation taken from the project's homepage: 911digitalarchive.org (accessed 20 December 2012).

5 For a recent report on piracy software usage in Russia, see "Unlicensed Software" (2012).

6 В каждой семье ныне живущих в России, война забрала хоть одного родственника. В советские времена войнам павшим на полях сражения воздвигались памятники, слагались стихи и песни … В советские времена, были высечены имена на мраморных плитах, к которым приходили родственники в День Победы возложить цветы, и хотя бы притронуться к надписи рукой, показать подрастающему поколению, что их дед, прадед сложил голову за Родину. Прискорбно, что нынешняя власть, устраивая пышные парады победы, забыла, кто за эту победу отдал свою жизнь. Люди подскажите, как напомнить засевшим врагам народа в лице администрации, о погибших односельчанах. *liborte*, Comment posted on 5 June 2011 at http://drugoi.livejournal.com/3549532.html?thread=418299484#t418299484 (accessed 20 December 2012).

7 For a helpful study of the post-Soviet Russian mediascape, see Beumers, Hutchings, and Rulyova (2008).

8 The trend to turn to political and memory-related themes even in markedly non-political or non-historical Runet discussions has been discussed in Vera Zvereva's chapter "'Kto-nibud' etomu verit???": Praktiki chteniia i obsuzhdeniia novostei v Runete" (Does Anyone Believe This??? New Commenting on Mail.ru) in Zvereva (2012).

9 To date, there have been few elaborate studies of memory talk on Russian Twitter; an exception, still in print as this volume was written, is Paulsen (2013).

10 Vera Zvereva discusses memory and identity construction on these platforms in detail in Zvereva (2011, 2012).

11 For helpful discussions of memory discourse in Russian blogs, see Kukulin (2013) and Trubina (2010).

12 For two analyses that include insights on memory discourse on Russian-language YouTube and/or Rutube, see Chapter 8 by Ingunn Lunde, in this volume and Rutten (forthcoming, a).

13 Among others, for more on the problems of post-Soviet memory culture, see Etkind (2004) and Nowak (2008).

14 *asurra*, http://drugoi.livejournal.com/3549532.html?page=2#comments.

15 On the phenomenon of flaming see, for instance, Oegema et al. (2008).

16 Fragment from comments by user *lialiku* and *dronetz*: http://drugoi.livejournal.com/3549532.html?page=2#comments (accessed 21 December 2012).

17 Adi Kuntsman discusses the aggressive potential of smileys and other emoticons in Kuntsman (2009: 196–7).

18 Fragment from comment by user *Kljaver*: http://drugoi.livejournal.com/3549532.html?page=5 (accessed 21 December 2012).

19 *Myanarch*, "U VAS ESHCHE . . .," http://www.youtube.com/all_comments?v=gp8e-m4Akg8 (accessed 6 April 2012) (capitals original—ER).

20 Cited from Vera Zvereva, "The Language of Memory in Digital Ru.net Communities," paper presented at *Virtual Russia* conference, 19–22 October 2011; italics Zvereva's.

21 I thank Roman Leibov for directing me to this blog and its opening slogan.

22 *kcooss*, homepage: http://kcooss.livejournal.com (accessed 7 January 2013).

23 The juxtaposition of 2012 with two historical milestones is thriving in (online) discussions of contemporary Russian politics and political memory. For a more elaborate discussion of the parallels between the three "12 years," see Grigor'ev (2012).

24 Among others, for more on this historical trend, see Sarnov (2002), Kupina (1999), on its contemporary online variations, in addition to Zvereva (2012), see Lunde (2013).

25 *stanislavbel*, "Vmesto togo . . .," http://drugoi.livejournal.com/3549532.html?page=7#comments (accessed April 6, 2012).

26 For a more elaborate discussion of this aesthetics of imperfection, see Rutten (forthcoming, b).

27 On the "landslide of the norm" and on its digital manifestations in post-Soviet Russia, see Lunde and Roesen (2006) and Lunde and Paulsen (2009).
28 With this insistence on the creative, the spontaneous and the emotional, online memory could well be a useful guide to understanding what happens in our brains when we remember—perhaps more than offline memory. I thank Ingunn Lunde for this suggestion on a link between online and cerebral commemoration.
29 Such a study would need to reckon not only with historical backgrounds, but also with such pragmatic factors as the extent to which different legal cultures recognize hate speech as a formal crime (I thank Vlad Strukov for this helpful observation).

## References

Androutsopoulos, Jannis. 2010. "Localizing the Global on the Participatory Web." In *The Handbook of Language and Globalization*, edited by Nikolas Coupland, 203–31. Malden, MA: Wiley-Blackwell.

—— 2013. "Participatory Culture and Metalinguistic Discourse: Performing and Negotiating German Dialects on YouTube." In *Discourse 2.0: Language and New Media*, edited by Deborah Tannen and Anna Marie Trester, 47–72. Washington, DC: Georgetown University Press.

Anis, Jacques. 2007. "Neography: Unconventional Spelling in French SMS Text Messages." In *The Multilingual Internet: Language, Culture, and Communication Online*, edited by Brenda Danet and Susan Herring, 87–116. Oxford: Oxford University Press.

Arthur, Paul. 2009. "Trauma Online: Public Exposure of Personal Grief and Suffering." *Traumatology* 15(4): 65–75.

Beumers, Birgit, Stephen Hutchings, and Natalia Rulyova. 2008. *The Post-Soviet Russian Media: Conflicting Signals*. New York: Routledge.

Dounaevsky, Helene. 2013. "Building Wiki-History: Between Consensus and Edit Warring." In *Memory, Conflict and New Media: Web Wars in Post-Socialist States*, edited by Ellen Rutten, Julie Fedor, and Vera Zvereva, 130–42. New York: Routledge.

Durscheid, Christa. 2002. "Spelling of Electronic Texts." *Muttersprache* 110(1): 52–62.

Erll, Astrid, and Ann Rigney, eds. 2009. *Mediation, Remediation, and the Dynamics of Cultural Memory*. Berlin: De Gruyter.

Etkind, Alexander. 2004. "Hard and Soft in Cultural Memory: Political Mourning in Russia and Germany." *Grey Room* 16: 36–59.

——. 2011. "Stories of the Undead in the Land of the Unburied: Magical Historicism in Contemporary Russian Fiction." *Slavic Review* 68(3): 631–58.

Garde-Hansen, Joanne, Andrew Hoskins, and Anna Reading, eds. 2009. *Save As ... Digital Memories*. Basingstoke: Palgrave Macmillan.

Grigor'ev, Leonid. 2012. "1612-1812-2012: Chto bylo? Chto znaem? Chto dumaem?" *Diletant* 1. Available at: http://www.diletant.ru/journal/327/article_24053/ (accessed 7 January 2013).

Guseinov, Gasan. 2009. "Instrumenty opisaniia nepolnoi kommunikatsii v blogosfere." In *From Poets to Padonki: Linguistic Authority and Norm Negotiation in Modern Russian Culture* (Slavica Bergensia 9), edited by Ingunn Lunde and Martin Paulsen, 275–87. Bergen: Department of Foreign Languages, University of Bergen.

Hale, Constance, and Jessie Scanlon. 1996. *Wired Style: Principles of English Usage in the Digital Age*. San Francisco: West Group Publishers.

Hoskins, Andrew. 2009. "Digital Network Memory." In *Mediation, Remediation, and the Dynamics of Cultural Memory*, edited by Astrid Erll and Ann Rigney, 91–106. Berlin: De Gruyter.

Huyssen, Andreas. 2003. *Present Pasts: Urban Palimpsests and the Politics of Memory*. Stanford, CA: Stanford University Press.

Kalay, Yehuda, Thomas Kvan, and Janice Affleck, eds. 2007. *New Heritage: New Media and Cultural Heritage*. New York: Routledge.

Kress, Gunther. 2009. *Multimodality: A Social Semiotic Approach to Contemporary Communication*. New York: Routledge.

Kukulin, Ilya. 2013. "Memory and Self-Legitimization in the Russian Blogosphere: Argumentative Practices in Historical and Political Discussions in Russian-Language Blogs of the 2000s." In *Memory, Conflict and New Media: Web Wars in Post-Socialist States*, edited by Ellen Rutten, Julie Fedor, and Vera Zvereva, 112–29. New York: Routledge.

Kuntsman, Adi. 2009. *Figurations of Belonging: Queerness, Migranthood and Nationalism in Cyberspace and Beyond*. Oxford: Peter Lang.

—— 2012. "Introduction: Affective Fabrics of Digital Cultures." In *Digital Cultures and the Politics of Emotion: Feelings, Affect and Technological Change*, edited by Athina Karatzogianni and Adi Kuntsman. Basingstoke: Palgrave Macmillan. Kindle edition.

Kupina, Nataliia. 1999. *Iazykovoe soprotivlenie v kontekste totalitarnoi kul'tury*. Ekaterinburg: Izdatel'stvo Ural'skogo universiteta.

Lapina-Kratasiuk, Ekaterina, Robert Saunders, Ellen Rutten, Henrike Schmidt, and Vlad Strukov, eds. 2009. *The Russian Cyberspace Journal* 1 (*Virtual Power: Russian Politics and the Internet*). Available at: http://www.digitalicons.org/issue01/ (accessed 16 April 2013).

Lovink, Geert. 2007. *Zero Comments: Blogging and Critical Internet Culture*. New York: Routledge.

Lunde, Ingunn. 2013. "'A Stroll through the Keywords of My Memory': Digitally Mediated Commemoration of the Soviet Linguistic Heritage." In *Memory, Conflict and New Media: Web Wars in Post-Socialist States*, edited by Ellen Rutten, Julie Fedor, and Vera Zvereva, 101–11. New York: Routledge.

Lunde, Ingunn, and Martin Paulsen, eds. 2009. *From Poets to Padonki: Linguistic Authority and Norm Negotiation in Modern Russian Culture* (Slavica Bergensia 9). Bergen: Department of Foreign Languages, University of Bergen.

Lunde, Ingunn, and Tine Roesen, eds. 2006. *Landslide of the Norm: Language Culture in Post-Soviet Russia* (Slavica Bergensia 6). Bergen: Department of Foreign Languages, University of Bergen.

Neiger, Motti, Oren Meyers, and Eyal Zandberg, eds. 2011. *On Media Memory*. Basingstoke: Palgrave Macmillan.

Nowak, Andrzej. 2008. *History and Geopolitics: A Contest for Eastern Europe*. Warsaw: Polish Institute of International Affairs.

Oegema, Dirk, Jan Kleinnijenhuis, Koos Anderson, and Anita van Hoof. 2008. "Flaming and Blaming: The Influence of Mass Media Content on Interactions in On-line Discussions." In *Mediated Interpersonal Communication*, edited by Elly Konijn, Martin Tanis, Susan Barnes, and Sonia Utz. New York: Routledge.

Paulsen, Martin. 2013. "#Holodomor: Twitter and Public Discourse in Ukraine." In *Memory, Conflict and New Media: Web Wars in Post-Socialist States*, edited by Ellen Rutten, Julie Fedor, and Vera Zvereva, 82–97. New York: Routledge.

Rutten, Ellen. Forthcoming, a. "Why Digital Memory Studies Should Not Overlook Eastern Europe's Memory Wars." In *Memory and Theory in Eastern Europe*, edited by Uilleam Blacker, Alexander Etkind, and Julie Fedor. Basingstoke: Palgrave Macmillan.

—— Forthcoming, b. "(Russian) Writer-Bloggers: Digital Perfection and the Aesthetics of Imperfection." *Journal of Computer-Mediated Communication*.

Sarnov, Benedikt. 2002. *Nash sovetskii novoiaz: malen'kaia entsiklopediia real'nogo sotsializma*. Moscow: Materik.

Segerstad, Ylva Hård af. 2005. "Language Use in Swedish Mobile Text Messaging." In *Mobile Communications: Renegotiation of the Social Sphere*, edited by Rich Ling and Per E. Pedersen, 313–34. London: Springer.

Sonvilla-Weiss, Stefan, ed. 2010. *Mashup Cultures*. Vienna: Springer.

Tavosanis, Mirko. 2006. *Are Blogs Edited? A Linguistic Survey of Italian Blogs Using Search Engines.* Available at: http://uni-leipzig.de/~burr/CorpusLing/pdf/aaai-caaw_AreBlogsEdited_M_Tavosanis.pdf (accessed 1 December 2011).

Trubina, Elena. 2010. "Past Wars in the Russian Blogosphere: on the Emergence of Cosmopolitan Memory." *Digital Icons* 4. Available at: http://www.digitalicons.org/issue04/files/2010/11/Trubina-4.4.pdf (accessed 21 December 2012).

"Unlicensed Software" 2012. "Unlicensed Software: Still Widespread in Russian Companies, but Repression Intensifies." *East-West Digital News*, 24 October. Available at: http://www.ewdn.com/2012/10/24/unlicensed-software-still-widespread-in-russian-companies-but-repression-intensifies/ (accessed 9 November 2012).

Van Dijck, José. 2007. *Mediated Memories in the Digital Age*. Stanford, CA: Stanford University Press.

Zvereva, Vera. 2011. "Historical Events and the Social Network 'V Kontakte'." *East European Memory Studies* 7. Available at: http://www.memoryatwar.org/resources-newsletter (accessed 21 December 2012).

—— 2012. *Setevye razgovory: kul'turnye kommunikatsii v Runete* (Slavica Bergensia 10). Bergen: Department of Foreign Languages, University of Bergen.

# 15 Is there a Russian cyber empire?

*Dirk Uffelmann*

The concept of Empire is characterized by a lack of boundaries: Empire's rule has no limits.

(Hardt and Negri 2000: xiv)

## Introduction: the Runet—a pioneer?

Is the Russian internet (Runet) and—in a broader sense—the internet in the Commonwealth of Independent States (CIS), a pioneer in the field of internet technology?[1] One might form this counter-intuitive impression from reading Deibert and Rohozinski's statement: "while the countries of the CIS are often seen as lagging behind Europe, North America, and the technological tigers of Asia, they may be leaders in the development of next-generation [internet] controls" (Deibert and Rohozinski 2010a: 7).

Historically speaking, the Soviet Union and early post-Soviet Russia were in anything but a pioneering position when it came to internet development. Even if the research consensus that the ARPANET was originally designed as a military defense strategy *against* the Soviet Union (see, for example, Gunkel 2001: 83–4) has been challenged (Naughton 2000: 83–5), it remains undisputed that the embargo against the COMECON countries heavily affected the development of internet technology in the Soviet Union and its successor states. At least until the late 1990s, their internet communities lagged behind those in the US and Western Europe.

However, as Deibert and Rohozinski (2010a: 7) stress,

> Some of the first, and most elaborate, forms of just-in-time blocking, terms-of-usage policies, surveillance, and legal takedown notices occurred among the countries of the CIS over the last several years. Examining that region in detail may give us insight into the future of information controls elsewhere.

They go on to describe the Runet as a kind of unifying factor for CIS countries' internet communities, "completely separate" from the rest of the online world.[2] They even go as far as to speak of the "rise of the Internet to the center of Russian culture and politics," and to state that Russians, both in the homeland and in the

Russian-speaking diaspora, which they calculate to be 27-million-strong worldwide, "tend to live *online* in the RUNET" (Deibert and Rohozinski 2010b: 18–19, italics in the original).

Whereas Deibert and Rohozinski focus on the control of *imports* into a country's national internet zone, including the import of related control technologies and doctrines from Russia to other CIS countries, I propose to view attempts at controlling imports as symptoms of an (actual or alleged) *external influence.* My interest is focused on *perceptions of export* and on the power implications ascribed to this export: is the export of information and technology via the Runet to internet users in other countries viewed as expansive cyberimperialism, or cybercolonialism, or the welcome purveyance of virtual liberty?

This question concerns various disciplines in social sciences and humanities: it can be addressed from the point of view of political science, of Internet Studies and—thanks to the Russian language as a national marker of the goods of export in question—of sociolinguistics. Coming from Slavic Studies, my approach is rooted in language culture studies, rather than in political science. I will rely both on quantitative data on internet usage and on a hermeneutic reading of power implications in statements by Russian and non-Russian actors. Referring to the concept of "cyberimperialism" as defined in Ebo (2001), this chapter investigates whether the Russian internet has the potential to serve as a "fifth column" in an expansive foreign cultural policy pursued by the Russian Federation and/or by performative Russian speech acts online.

I will distinguish between three perspectives: (1) the online presentation of Russia's foreign cultural policy, especially that of the Russkiy Mir Foundation; (2) the reactions of the governments of countries with large Russian-speaking minorities to Russian new media; and (3) the attractiveness of technologically advanced Runet sites such as Russian LiveJournal, Mail.ru, VKontakte, YouTube, Rutracker.org and other Russian-language-based new media to users outside the Russian Federation (RF).[3] This will eventually lead me to a terminological distinction of various modes of cyberpower and cyberhegemony by means of language and to a specific understanding of empire.

## Theories of linguistic and cyberimperialism

What remained of the former Russian political domination and cultural hegemony in Eurasia after the fall of the Soviet territorial empire in 1991? A conglomerate of post-imperial, post-colonial states? I clearly cannot engage in discussions among historians and political scientists about what an empire *is* in general and what the specific features of the Soviet Empire actually *were.* For my purpose it is sufficient to draw attention to the fact, acknowledged by Burbank and Cooper (2010: 455), that under Vladimir Putin's presidency the "Russian empire has reappeared in yet another transmutation on its Eurasian space." The new old president's plans for a Eurasian Union seem to confirm this interpretation (Torbakov 2012). If it can be justified to speak of some sort of contemporary Russian post- or neo-empire, a combined quantitative and sociolinguistic analysis such as the one proposed here can provide insight into the nature of the possible corresponding Russian post- or neo-imperialism. Focusing on the actual discourse around the Russian internet as a means of such an attitude or strategy, I will concentrate on cultural, linguistic and technological facets of what could be *perceived* as imperialism by those facing disadvantages.

Linguistic imperialism was defined by Phillipson (1992: 307) with regard to English: "The dominance of English is asserted and maintained by the establishment and continuous reconstitution of structural and cultural inequalities between English and other languages." Especially productive is Phillipson's distinction of intrinsic, extrinsic and functional arguments in favor of a hegemonic language (ibid.: 273). My hypothesis is that, when it comes to the argumentation of Russian linguistic neo-imperialists, the alleged intrinsic values of the Russian language[4] are less prominent than extrinsic (a large number of speakers, the availability of teaching materials and dictionaries) and functional arguments (like the "bridge to the world" topos; cf. Bowden 2009). I argue here that there is a facet of a re-appearing Russian empire which is closely connected with the Russian language, but only distantly with Putin and in some respects even contrary to his neo-imperialism. What I—*cum grano salis*—call a Russian-language-based "cyber empire" is, however, in no way contradictory to power but consists of an amalgam of free information and hegemonic strategies.

We cannot get rid of the paradox that, in the Runet, the civilizational mission of information freedom has implications of colonial hegemony, since it is performed in a language which is also used and promoted by representatives of a former colonial power. The Runet can therefore be suspected of a "neohegemony of cybercolonialism" (Tong 2001: 66)—a paradox which is reflected in the term *cyber*imperialism. In Internet Studies the early enthusiasm for an entirely uncontrolled distinct cyberspace (Barlow 1996; cf. Paasonen 2009: 21–2), combined with illusions of democratization, turned towards explorations of repression (see Goldsmith and Wu 2006; Morozov 2011). I adhere to the term *cyberimperialism* as put forward in Ebo's volume in 2001, which might have been the actual turning point in the political axiology of the internet, exactly because of its paradoxical capacity, encompassing both freedom and repression (cf. Chun 2006: 37–76), because a specific form of overlap between these dimensions is exactly what I aim to describe with regard to the Runet.

Most of the contributors to Ebo's volume take the US, with the technological advancement of its internet industry, as their point of departure. When we look at post-Soviet Eurasia, this situation is partly reflected in the relative Russian advancement in internet industry today, if compared to all the other CIS states. The second, more important factor is the impact which a large linguistic cyber-community like English or Russian has on other national communities which *nolens volens* must make use of the resources available in these languages if they do not want to fall even further back in technological respects. As Vehovar (2001: 135) has shown, small countries face challenges in the age of cyberglobalization: they experience stronger negative than positive effects for their economies.

So, is there a Russian cyberimperialism directed towards Russia's smaller neighbors? Rusciano (2001: 15, 24) provides a generally critical answer about the mere possibility of cyberimperialism because of the decentralized structure of the internet and of its potential to be used by grassroots organizations. He nevertheless acknowledges the existence of what he calls "hegemonic discourse imperialism," where representatives of "core nations consciously or unconsciously define and disseminate language and linguistic constructs for understanding the world through the media of cyberspace" (ibid.: 11). When it comes to Russia, even more drastic associations with the internet as a means of cyber war come to mind: the attacks by (most likely Russian) hackers on Estonia and Georgia (cf. Klimburg 2011: 48–51). These countries, which after 1991 tried to distance themselves as much as possible from Russia, seem to have been "punished" for their policy with cyberattacks, whose actual perpetrators have not been identified. The same goes for an attack on the Kyrgyz internet service providers (ISPs) Elcat and AsiaInfo (ONI 2005) and Kyrgyz news sites in 2005. The political background and agenda of the hacker(s), who called himself/themselves "the shadow team," remain unclear. What is alarming is that the hacker(s) interfered with Kyrgyz sovereignty. The attacks seem, however, to have been launched from infected computers which were situated not in Russia, but in Ukraine (ONI 2005). Independently of the actual perpetrators' origin, countries that rely on communication technology imported from the RF (for example, Mail.ru) have reasons to view themselves as being especially vulnerable to *Russian* hackers.

In all the cases mentioned above, we are dealing with the political and/or military dimensions of "hard power within cyberspace" (Nye 2011: 126), not with cultural and linguistic soft power.[5] Russian as a *language* did not play a role. Is it symptomatic of the more robust nature of Russian neo-imperialism that cultural and linguistic dimensions are secondary?

## Deliberate Russian linguistic (cyber) imperialism

One might believe this if one acknowledges the deterioration of the Russian language in the post-Soviet independent states, which have downgraded the status of Russian in administration and education, and from which the "beached diaspora" of ethnic Russians have migrated in their hundreds of thousands to the Russian Federation (Laitin 1998: 29). In a way, however, Russia (and Russian) "returned" to Central Asia during the 2000s (Matveeva 2007). Russophonia has been promoted since the Putin administration's "international turn," with the declaration of the "Year of the Russian Language" in 2007. Since some of the Kremlin's political strategists are internet savvy (cf. Carr 2011), Michael Gorham (2011: 24) has argued that the Runet can be viewed by them as a tool of soft power. The Russian Federation's foreign cultural policy is coordinated by "Fond Russkiy mir" (The Russian World Foundation). The website of this state organization, founded in 2007, explicitly says of its target group:

> *Russkii mir* is not just Russians, not just citizens of the Russian Federation, not just compatriots in the countries of the near and far abroad, emigrants, natives of Russian and their descendants. It is also foreign citizens who speak Russian, who study or teach it, all those who are sincerely interested in Russian and who are concerned about its future.
>
> (O fonde 2007)

The diasporas are a special goal of the foundation, which merited a separate subcategory in the presidential edict (O fonde 2007). The fact that this particularly envisages the diasporas in the so-called "Near Abroad," including Central Asia, is highlighted by the conference *Do the New Independent States Need the Russian Language?* (cf. Ibragimova 2008), held on behalf of Russkiy Mir in Moscow on 29 February 2008. On 9 April 2010 "Russkiy Mir" hosted another conference in Moscow focusing exclusively on *Russian Speakers in Central Asia* (Press-sluzhba 2010). At the conference, the foundation presented the results of quantitative and qualitative research in four Central Asian countries. The respondents (described as "Russian compatriots" (*rossiiskie sootechestvenniki*), 1,000 in Kazakhstan and 900 in Kyrgyzstan) were asked how they view their linguistic situation in their Central Asian home country: "A comparison between the results from 2006 and 2009 in Kazakhstan and Kyrgyzstan shows an increase in the number of optimists who are convinced that 'Russia does everything it can,' and a decrease in the number of those who do not feel any support" (Press-sluzhba 2010).

The website also reports successful institutionalization in Central Asia, noting that "the Russian World Foundation has opened nine Russian centers in the countries of Central Asia: three in Kazakhstan—in Astana, Aktoba and Ust'-Kamenogorsk; three in Kyrgyzstan—in Bishkek, Kant and Osh . . ." (ibid.).

In a press release of 8 October 2011, Ivan Krylov, a press officer at Russkiy Mir, makes a normative statement about the function of the Russian-speaking diaspora in Central Asia: "For the Russian Diaspora, the most important task is to preserve and develop the Russian *civilizational* space in Central Asia" (Krylov 2011, italics mine—DU). Not only does Krylov use the imperial topos of bringing civilization to the subjects, he also expresses an overt desire for "Russian influence" via information when quoting Stanislav Epifantsev, the head of the Orthodox charity organization "Vladimirskoe obshchestvo":

> In our present world, he who controls the media is the one who is in charge . . . The Russian language in Central Asia is a key position in the countries of the region, which affects the situation of the Russian population and at the same time the not insignificant factor of Russia's influence.
>
> (Krylov 2011)

Although, on its website, Russkiy Mir reflects on the development of the Russian internet, the connection to Central Asia is not given much prominence here. When Russkiy Mir opened a center in Tajikistan, however, the foundation's website quoted the rector of the Tajik National University, Nuriddin Saidov, who praised the center because its computer infrastructure made the Runet accessible to Tajik students: "The Russian Centre, N. Saidov said, will give the university's students the opportunity to improve their proficiency in Russian, to get acquainted with contemporary Russian research and literature and to use the Runet" (Russkii tsentr 2010).

Obviously, cultural institutes from other countries also teach and promote their countries' languages and use the internet for this purpose. What is particular about the Russo-Eurasian case is that, with Russkiy Mir in Central Asia, this is happening in a post-imperial space where Soviet nostalgia and revisionism are still very much alive. Reacting to post-colonial anxieties in the Near Abroad (cf. Uffelmann 2011a), the argumentation used by Russkiy Mir officials often betrays the interests of the Russian Federation (and of the organization itself), but tries to hide this behind external functional arguments; the target group itself is said to be calling for the foundation's activities.[6] The aforementioned Stanislav Epifantsev serves once again as a mouthpiece: "The Russian language is a sort of bridge which links Kyrgyzstan to the whole world and makes it competitive in the world labor market" (Zakharova 2006).

Soviet (and colonialist) reminiscences are palpable in diasporic Russians' use of the Runet: "The internet is used by cyber-Russians as an instrument for the revival of the kind of universalism which served as the basis of the Soviet state," (Sonders 2004: 189), a sentiment that is reflected in Iatsenko's praise for the Runet and the "Geopolitical Potential of Russian World": "The Runet is an 'impersonal' but highly effective carrier of the language, the very .ru-zone which gives all users the opportunity to obtain information and communicate irrespective of citizenship, and, in so doing, to broaden the Russian-speaking space" (Iatsenko 2007). Practical proof of this is the fact that the Russian Ministry of Telecommunications and Mass Communications (Minkomsviaz') actively supports Russian-language-based sites abroad by funding the RUnet Award subcategory for non-RF-based websites.[7]

There is, however, no consensus about the real future significance of Russian-language-based usage of the internet in Central Asia. At a round table of Russian online journalists held on 24 February 2011, the positions diverged dramatically: will the demand for Russian internet offers in Central Asian countries be stable? Or will the Runet share the fate of, as formulated in the header, its offline predecessor—the Soviet Union? Among the most skeptical was Ivan Preobrazhenskii:

> I do not want to say that the Runet is dead, but in the sense of a communicative Soviet Union [kommunikativnyi SSSR] it is coming to an end . . . We are losing Central Asia as Central Asia is losing the Russian language . . . When this generation of Russophones vanishes, the Russian-language internet will vanish as well.
>
> (Batyrshin et al. 2011)

The opposite opinion was held by Radik Batyrshin, who pointed to the attractiveness of the Russian news website Fergana to Central Asian users,[8] and by Ivan

Zassoursky (Batyrshin et al. 2011), who made a functional (and clearly anti-authoritarian) argument: "In my view there is a great deal of propaganda and nonsense, including commercial nonsense, in the Russian-language Runet, but this is the very place where the truth is told about what is happening in all these countries [of Central Asia]."

## The status of Russian in Kazakhstan and Kyrgyzstan

For the sake of economy, this chapter cannot cover all Central Asian countries and so must select two examples. On the one hand, it might be productive to compare cases that are as different as possible, say, Kazakhstan and Turkmenistan (cf. Schäfer and Uffelmann 2012). Here instead I will focus on Kazakhstan and Kyrgyzstan, countries which appeared to be targets both of Russian hackers and of the RF's foreign cultural policy. An additional reason for this selection is that we are dealing with two cases which are historically rather similar, and culturally and linguistically close, but which display strong differences in recent politics and economics. It can be hypothesized that these differences also amount to divergent constellations in language culture online.

Both Kazakh and Kyrgyz territories experienced Russian colonial rule in the nineteenth century and achieved civilizational progress thanks to Soviet modernization. As a legacy of this (or even of earlier periods), the political culture in the entire region is fixated on strong leader personalities. The relatively stable authoritarian regime in Kazakhstan stands in stark contrast, however, to the periodic revolutionary turmoil (accompanied by interethnic clashes) which Kyrgyzstan suffered during the 2000s.[9]

The Russian language also spread as a colonial legacy across Eurasia, even if this occurred with huge regional differences. Among the Central Asian countries, it is Kazakhstan and Kyrgyzstan which nowadays have the largest "linguistically russified" minorities (Russians, Ukrainians, Belarusians, Tatars, Germans, Koreans and others, cf. Smagulova 2008: 446, 459). Their numbers shrank as a result of remigration to Russia, which in Kazakhstan happened mostly because of early post-Soviet ethnicization (Peyrouse 2007: 492–4), while in Kyrgyzstan these people were lured away by the better economic prospects available outside the country (Koenig 2000: 67; Wright 2000: 89). Yet the size of the Russian-speaking groups and that of the titular population in Kazakhstan are still roughly equal (Landau and Kellner-Heinkele 2001: 23–5). In Kyrgyzstan today, after the wave of emigration, the number of people with Russian as their first native language is estimated to be 9 percent, but 39.3 percent say they have a command of Russian as a second language, and 78 percent use it actively (Kyrgyzskaia Republika 2009). According to official Kazakhstani data, in 2004, some 75 percent of Kazakhs were fluent in Russian (Pavlenko 2008: 289). In both countries the majority of the mass media still publish or broadcast in Russian (Shaibakova 2005: 51).

For both former Soviet republics, independence started with "a deliberate 'removal' of the 'colonial' language from the public sphere" (Pavlenko 2008: 282). Soon, however, the respective post-colonial nationalisms displayed a rather defensive quality (Adams, Centeno, and Varner 2007: 84), which led to paradoxical approaches: "Kazakhstan and Kyrgyzstan have attempted to perpetuate the Soviet idea of fraternal coexistence and cooperation between their respective national groups while quietly supporting the indigenization of the bureaucratic ranks" (Saunders 2006: 54).

Since the mid-1990s, Kazakhstan's presidential administration has tackled the "Russian problem" with an inclusive strategy. It tries to avoid direct opposition between Kazakh and Russian and to "appease both the Russian-speakers and Russophone Kazakhs" (Dave 2007: 166). A comparable turn towards "balance" and bilingualism was observed in the language politics of Kyrgyz President Askar Akaev during the 1990s (Wright 2000: 90; Landau and Kellner-Heinkele 2001: 27, 94).

Against this backdrop, the constitutional status of Russian in Kazakhstan and Kyrgyzstan underwent an analogous development: in 1989, in both Soviet republics, Kazakh and Kyrgyz respectively were declared the sole state languages. In response to Russian protests and the peak of the remigration wave, this was corrected in § 7 (2) of the Kazakhstani Constitution of 1995: "In state institutions and local self-administrative bodies the Russian language shall be officially used on equal grounds along with the Kazak language" (Constitution 2012).

The Kyrgyz law of 2000, "On the official (Russian) language of the Kyrgyz Republic" similarly enshrined almost equal status for Russian. The legislation of both countries privileges Russian as the language of "interethnic communication" (Bohr 2010: 225), while remaining vague in determining the juridical status of languages (Kuzhabekova 2008: 168–9).

In Kazakhstan's practical language policy, the role of Russian in both administration and education was downgraded (Laruelle and Peyrouse 2004: 126–9, 146–50). In Kyrgyzstan, Russian native speakers were removed from posts in administration in a similar way to what happened in Kazakhstan. On the other hand, in Kyrgyzstan, Russian still maintained its role in education (Landau and Kellner-Heinkele 2001: 186–8). This especially applies to the capital city, Bishkek, where Kyrgyzstan's Russians are concentrated and where a programmatic Russian-Kyrgyz (Slavonic) University was founded in 1992 (Kolstoe 1995: 231–2, 241–2). Teaching Russian is regarded as a product Kyrgyzstan can sell to foreigners coming to the country (Ibragimova 2008: 69).[10] But on 18 June 2011, the acting president, Roza Otunbaeva, proposed shifting from Russian to Kyrgyz in education.

## The status of the internet in Kazakhstan and Kyrgyzstan

With the last update of its survey of 30 June 2012, Internet World Stats counted 7.884m internet users in Kazakhstan and 2.194m in Kyrgyzstan, which corresponds to penetration of 45.0 percent and 39.3 percent respectively (Internet World Stats 2012). In both countries, an oligopoly of internet service providers dominates the internet market. Strong differences, however, exist in the role of the former monopoly. Access to the Kaznet[11] is controlled by five licensed "first-tier" internet service providers (ISPs), with Kazakhtelekom in an almost monopoly position. The former monopoly is being accused of hindering competing companies by resorting to technical interference and monitoring (Deibert et al. 2010: 185). Most of the 100 second-tier ISPs depend on telecommunications infrastructure controlled by Kazakhtelekom, which means that many of them automatically reaffirm the pre-filtering carried out by Kazakhtelekom.

To some extent, the pre-filtering carried out by Kazakhtelekom has also affected Kyrgyz ISPs who have relied on data sent through Kazakhtelekom's connections. This has made the Russian LiveJournal platform unavailable in Kyrgyzstan on several occasions. In Kyrgyzstan, the former state company Kyrgyztelekom transferred a significantly larger segment of the market to private companies than Kazakhtelekom did (Budde 2010). Kyrgyztelekom also does not pre-filter content sold to "second-tier" operators (Deibert et al. 2010: 193–5).

Both countries share a similarly huge digital divide between urban and rural areas. This is even more drastic in Kyrgyzstan, where only Bishkek (77 percent) and, to a much lesser degree, Osh (10 percent), are well connected, whereas in Kazakhstan internet penetration in cities like Pavlodar or Ust'-Kamenogorsk is not that much worse than in Almaty and Astana.

The picture differs significantly when it comes to filtering and control: during the 2000s the Kazakhstani state established centralized control over the Kaznet by transferring responsibility for the domain *.kz* to the State Agency of the Republic of Kazakhstan for Informatization and Communications in 2004 and by merging this agency with the Ministry of Culture and Information into the Ministry of Communications and Informatization in 2010. The Kyrgyz top-level domain *.kg* used to be administered by a private company (Deibert et al. 2010: 194), but was also transferred to a state body by presidential decree in April 2009 (Mambetalieva and Kim 2009: 153–4).

Since 2009 private blogs have been subject to the same juridical liability as mass media in Kazakhstan (Zakon 2009) which, even if it does not result in concrete allegations, compels users to self-censor. As far as internet control is concerned, Kazakhstan adopted the Russian model of registration software obligatory for all internet providers (Deibert et al. 2008: 181). Most likely the state also makes additional informal requests to Kazakhtelekom to filter particular sites for political reasons (Deibert et al. 2010: 187). This affects both sites from outside the *.kz*-zone (predominantly Russian sites) and Kazakhstani opposition groups' webpages.

Kazakhstan's internet controls became more internationally visible in 2005 when Kazakhtelekom blocked borat.kz (Saunders 2007: 236). The censoring strategy was subsequently questioned by (younger) Kazakhstani officials (ibid.: 242, cf. Uffelmann 2011b), but the practice was revived when Kazakhtelekom banned Russian LiveJournal in 2009 because of a post to the blog maintained by Nazarbaev's former son-in-law Rakhat Aliev that contained compromising materials directed against the Kazakhstani president (Taratuta and Zygar' 2010). Access to Russian LiveJournal was reopened just before the OSCE summit in

2010, but blocked again along with 12 other foreign webpages on 20 August 2011 (Baidauletov 2011).

The most recent instance of blocking affected all cellphone and internet traffic in Zhanaozen in December 2011 after riots in the western Kazakh city. While journalists from Russian news sites such as Lenta's Il'ia Azar were arrested (Na zapade 2011), government-friendly bloggers were brought into the city by the prime minister's press service, which advertised a *goszakaz* [state order] for blogging on Twitter (PM.kz 2012), in order to broadcast a positive image of a situation that was normalizing.

Kazakhstan's strategy of " 'event-based' information control," which—in contrast to China's permanent firewall—only "temporally 'shapes' internet access," was viewed by Deibert et al. (2008: 183) as characteristic of many countries in the Commonwealth of Independent States, whereas the tactic recently applied in Zhanaozen already belongs to what the ONI researchers call second- and third-generation internet control (Deibert and Rohozinski 2010a). Yet fresh ground was broken when Kazakhstan proposed the introduction of a joint cyber police force during the summit of the Shanghai Cooperation Organization held in Almaty on 24 April 2012 (Kazakhstan 2012).

In this respect, the situation in Kyrgyzstan is drastically better: attempts to impose political control over internet content failed in 2005 and 2006 (Deibert et al. 2010: 196). Occasional blocking and distributed denial-of-service (DDoS) attacks, especially in 2005 (ONI 2005) and 2009 (Mambetalieva and Kim 2009: 154–5), have no clear connection to Kyrgyz state officials, but were instead instigated from outside Kyrgyzstan. In 2010 and 2011, the political map of Kyrgyzstan saw a surge of competing parties who also publicized themselves on the internet, extensively using Russian online[12] and relying on Social Network Sites (SNS), whose technical infrastructure originates in Russia, for this purpose (the party Ata Meken uses VKontakte: http://vk.com/edinyi_kyrgyzstan2). In April 2012, in the aftermath of the elections, a Kyrgyz civil-society initiative launched the Russian-language Facebook group "Molodezh'—za novuiu kadrovuiu politiku," which managed to attract some 3,500 members within its first two weeks (Molodezh' 2012).

## Perceptions of Russian cyberimperialism

Can the Runet, viewed against the backdrop of Kazakhstani attempts to filter information from Russian web resources and of online Kyrgyz democratic competition, be regarded as an "Empire of Liberty" (Jefferson), a provider of freedom of information? Deibert and Rohozinski argue that, "across the CIS, especially in the increasingly authoritarian countries of Uzbekistan, Belarus, and Kazakhstan, the RUNET has become the last and only refuge of public debate" (Deibert and Rohozinski 2010b: 20). They point to specialized Russian-language news sites such as Fergana or Neweurasia, video portals such as Stan, and also to mainstream news providers such as Lenta or News.mail.ru.[13] Neweurasia uses "bridge-bloggers," i.e. locals in Central Asia, to provide information which is forwarded to a kind of digital "tamizdat" outside Central Asia—intended to be accessible from Central Asia (Wilkinson and Jetpyspayeva 2012: 1400–1). Also telling are the national ranking figures for fergananews.com, which, in January 2012, three months after the Kyrgyz presidential elections, ranked 42,304th on Alexa Traffic, 1,598th in Kazakhstan, but 96th in Kyrgyzstan (Alexa "fergananews.com" 2012).

Whereas Kazakhstan occasionally blocks sites providing political information, in Kyrgyzstan, the only reported case concerned the local news site centralasia.ru, along with the websites of two Kyrgyz newspapers respublica.kg and msn.kg. When they were attacked from computers in Ukraine in 2005, the hacker attacks "constituted de facto censorship" (ONI 2005).

As can be seen from these examples, foreign influence can obviously be detrimental. What interests me is whether there is a tendency to ascribe such interferences to Russia (or something Russian) and to perceive this as cyberimperialism. A similar reflex is obvious in Dan Goodin's coverage of DDoS attacks on virtually all Kyrgyz ISPs on 18 January 2009, which continued for approximately one week. The San Francisco-based author of the article "DDoS attack boots Kyrgyzstan from net" adds a subtitle full of prejudice and stereotype: "Russian bears blamed." Goodin (2009) speaks of some "Russian cybermilitia," claiming that "geopolitical disputes [are] spilling into cyberspace."

Some of the aforementioned Central Asian, mostly Kazakhstani media strategies, such as filtering or blocking, can also be regarded as reactions to perceptions of a Russian cyberimperialist threat (Schäfer and Uffelmann 2012). What the "national zones," created by some Kazakh ISPs (Deibert and Rohozinski 2010b: 27), will exclude is, for the most part, Runet content.

## Performative russophonia

Since blocking and filtering appear "inconsistent," even in Kazakhstan (Deibert et al. 2010: 188), the occasional occurrence is not yet sufficient proof of an all-encompassing fear of Russian cyberimperialism on a political level. We need to look into other factors: beyond Russian state intentions and Central Asian state perceptions lies the performative significance of Russian language usage online.[14] Many people in Central Asia obviously choose to use Russian online when visiting Runet resources such as Mail.ru or VKontakte.

Davies (1996: 488), in his review of Phillipson's *Linguistic Imperialism*, asked the rhetorical question: "What if the dominated . . . wanted to adopt [the hegemonic language]?" On the one hand, one might regard this sort of voluntary decision as testimony to a user's "colonized" mind (cf. Memmi 1957), which must yet be "decolonized" by the "rediscovery and the resumption of [his own] language" (Ngũgĩ 1986: 108). On the other hand, one could also argue with reference to Spivak (1996: 292) that the use of the hegemonic language allows the subaltern to be heard (or, in our case, to be read online), and it is only by doing this in Russian that they can draw attention to violations of human rights in their countries. Either way, essential to an analysis of the power implications of the usage of cultural webpages and SNS are aspects of language performance. The actual political intentions of users of Russian language online can—from this point of view—be regarded as secondary; neither a subject of power nor her/his intention can be clearly identified. It is the "objects," the users, who are central to understanding the scale and possible implications of an imperial "imbalance" which, in this case, "is not imposed from without but from within" (Davies 1996: 490).

The motivations for using Russian online can easily be discerned: both the Kaznet and the Kyrgyz internet have not only a quantitative but also a qualitative problem (Dmitrienko 2006; Kurgannikov 2009). This expels about 80 percent of Kaznet-users to non-Kazakhstani sites (Bekirova 2010), whereas the Runet offers access to elaborated and nuanced resources from contemporary culture (music downloads and video-sharing, for example, from RuTube).[15] As one Kyrgyz user puts it:

> the problem is. that our country is for the most part Russian-speaking, and we really do not need an internet of our own. and as a consequence there is also no particular incentive to develop our own (informational, social) resources. i.e. kyrgnet is in any case an appendix of the russian one.
>
> (Chainek 2009; punctuation *sic*)

As a result, it is Russian that is almost exclusively used on the internet in Kazakhstan (94.1 percent). Only 4.5 percent of webpages in the .kz-zone are written in Kazakh (and 1.4 percent in English). If one combines these figures with Bekirova's estimation that 80 percent of internet traffic from Kazakhstan leaves the .kz zone, the actual usage of webpages in Kazakh is reduced to roughly 1 percent. This constellation may also "account for the high percentage of Kazakh[stani] Web sites hosted in Russia (including those on the country-code domain name '.kz')" (Deibert et al. 2010: 185). The language distribution in the Kyrgyz internet is quite similar: sites in Russian account for 90 percent, webpages in Kyrgyz for 8 percent and websites in English for 2 percent (ibid.: 193). It is clear from this that Russian resources are much more popular than English ones: Kazakhs and Kyrgyz use VKontakte rather than Facebook (which has only 362,420 users out of 5.3m internet users in Kazakhstan and 64,620 out of 2.194m in Kyrgyzstan respectively; Internet World Stats 2011). The most popular website in Kazakhstan is Mail.ru (Alexa "mail.ru" 2012), while VKontakte is in fifth and Odnoklassniki in eighth place (Alexa "KZ" 2012).[16] Odnoklassniki is the most frequently used social network site in Kyrgyzstan (Alexa "odnoklassniki.ru" 2012, rank 5). As one of the residues of the anarchic nature of the early internet, the Runet possesses a very specific attraction, not only to users in Central Asia but across the world, because there is so much illegal copyrighted material on the Runet which cannot be found in other national zones.

In the market for entertainment, the vast resources of the Runet are the top choice. If this "voluntary communication dependency" (Lee 1988: 80) is the choice of non-Russian citizens in Kazakhstan or Kyrgyzstan, one can agree with Rusciano that "cultural imperialism is an unplanned by-product of the market" (Rusciano 2001: 15). Tong acknowledges the need for language skills: "Members of LDCs [less developed countries] who wish to participate or work on the Net must be 'fortunate' enough to be bilingual" (Tong 2001: 72). If English is not accessible to them, another major web language such as Russian will inevitably come in. This observation compels us to include Central Asian Runet users within the Runet community itself. They do not just enter Russian words into browsers but actively contribute to SNS, news sites, etc.

When approaching cultural identity as a performative category, Russian as a medium of communication (online and offline) turns out to be relevant not only to cultural Russians (Pavlenko 2008: 298) or the continuously "Russian speaking-population" (Laitin 1998: 263–4), but to all people who at least occasionally communicate in Russian or consume Russian cultural and commercial offers.[17] I suggested calling them *virtual Russians*, giving preference to this term over "cyber-Russians" (*kiberrusskie*) (Sonders 2004: 189) because the notion of *virtual habits* better reflects the potential of coexistence with other situational identities (see Uffelmann 2011a: 177; cf. Schatz 2000). This observation encompasses a re-linguistification of the spatial turn. Due to the decentralized nature of the web, this communicative, cyberlinguistic space can only be vaguely circumscribed, because its concrete localities are extremely difficult to grasp, given that virtual Russophonia may well coexist with *multiple linguistic habits*.

What is more, one cannot presuppose stability: if Saunders in 2009 included Uzbekistan in his list of "elapsed cultural Russians," communicating in Russian online (Saunders 2009: 18), the picture in 2012 looks different. As the round table of Russian web journalists demonstrated, it is extremely hard to project present data into the future. At present, users from Kazakhstan and Kyrgyzstan contribute significantly to the Runet, but if the newly elected Kyrgyz president Almazbek Atambaev heeds Otunbaeva's call to switch Kyrgyz education to the titular language,[18] it may change there over time, as it has in Uzbekistan.

## Conclusion: in what sense is there a Russian cyber empire?

What follows from this diagnosis of instability in the virtual Russophone community, in terms of the initial question regarding the existence of a Russian cyber empire? Does not the very term *empire* suggest both stability and the exercise of power along the top-down axis? Can we really speak of cyberimperialism if both features cannot be taken for granted? We obviously have to add more concretely defining epithets if we want to preserve the term: facets of *deliberate cyberimperialism* can be found in statements by some advocates of a "Russian world"; *perceived cyber-imperialism* can be deduced from the blocking and filtering of information from the Runet in countries outside the RF; *performative linguistic cyberhegemony*—the most relevant finding—is accomplished by ordinary users or by the existing communication structures in the Eurasian internet: "traces of linguistic imperialism are currently manifest in the very texture of on-line interaction" (Gunkel 2001: 87). If the notion of a cyber empire were to be preserved, one would have to make clear that, in the era of post-sovereignty in international relations, this "empire" is not identical to deliberate imperialism. The most relevant agents of this "empire" are the "colonized" who, at the same time, can hardly be called victims, but must be regarded as performers.

The instability and fluidity of this not properly imperialistic "empire," combined with the non-encompassing spread of Runet usage, echo the way in which Hardt and Negri circumscribe their capitalized "Empire":

> In contrast to imperialism, Empire establishes no territorial center of power and does not rely on fixed boundaries or barriers. It is a decentered and deterritorializing apparatus of rule that progressively incorporates the entire global realm within its open, expanding frontiers. Empire manages hybrid identities, flexible hierarchies, and plural exchanges through modulating networks of command. The distinct national colors of the imperialist map of the world have merged and blended in the imperial global rainbow.
>
> (Hardt and Negri 2000: xii–xiii)

The reapplication of this notion of empire to the Runet and to the Russian cyber-linguistic isles in Eurasia's landmass leads me to a counter-intuitive thesis: in contrast to the traditional Russian and Soviet territorial empire, this reminds more of a sea-power's selective control over several ports, some coasts and isles: *the Runet functions as a Russian post-imperial thalassocracy.*

## Notes

1 The writing of this chapter was supported by a Visiting Fellowship at CRASSH, University of Cambridge. A first draft was presented at Harvard's working seminar "Informing Eurasia: Informational Approaches to Eurasian Cultures, Politics and Societies" in February 2012. I am especially grateful to Ai Abo, who served as discussant at Harvard, for her advice, and to Stephen Hutchings, who commented upon an earlier version of this chapter in Bergen in June 2012.

2 This claim is only partially correct: Yandex (yandex.ru), Mail.ru (mail.ru) and VKontakte (vkontakte.ru) are the top websites by reach in Russia, but Google (google.com) and Microsoft (microsoft.com) rank among the top ten as well (Gemius 2010: 193).

3 LiveJournal (livejournal.com), YouTube (youtube.ru), Rutracker.ru (rutracker.ru).

4 In the spirit of Ivan Turgenev's notorious formula "great, powerful, righteous, and free Russian language."

5 With regard to the soft power exerted by contemporary Russia, it would be worth mentioning the TV news channel Russia Today or the Russian Orthodox Church.

6 "The overwhelming majority (90 per cent and more) are convinced that Russia has to develop its connections with compatriots. They expect support, above all in the field of culture, in learning the Russian language and in youth work" (Press-sluzhba 2010).

7 In 2006, out of 37 contenders, this award was given to Germany.ru (germany.ru) (Premiia 2006).

8 Fergana (fergana.ru).

9 For an overview of the key political and economic features of both countries, see Cummings and Nørgaard (2010: 72).

10 Implicitly Kazakh educational institutions pursue a comparable goal. This is clear from the fact that most Kazakhstani universities are bilingual (Landau and Kellner-Heinkele 2001: 183–4).

11 Whereas it has become common to use *Kaznet* as an analogue to *Runet*, there is no similar consensus about *Kyrnet, Kirnet, Kirgnet* or *Kyrgnet* (a Yandex Blogs search (blogs. yandex.ru) on 15 October 2012, produced 546 hits for *кирнет*, 153 for *кырнет*, 4 for *киргнет* and 2 for *кыргнет*).
12 For example, the party of the elected president Almazbek Atambaev has an active Russian blog on its webpage: (sdpk.kg/blog). The unsuccessful presidential candidate Kamchybek Tashiev has been much more active on Twitter in Russian (@Tashiev_Kamchy) than his rivals Almazbek Atambaev (@AtambaevKG) and Adakhan Madumarov (@AdahanMadumarov).
13 Neweurasia (neweurasia.net or neweurasia.ru), Stan (stan.tv), Lenta (lenta.ru), News. mail.ru (news.mail.ru)
14 For the significance of performativity in Runet research, see also Chapter 8 by Ingunn Lunde, in this volume.
15 RuTube (rutube.ru).
16 Odnoklassniki (odnoklassniki.ru).
17 In contrast to Russkiy Mir's understanding of "sootechestvenniki," virtual Russians as I see them need in no way sympathize with the RF or the Putin regime. Russophonia can also be overtly Russophobic (cf. Kavkaz Center, kavkazcenter.com/russ/).
18 First hints in this direction came on 28 December 2011, when Atambaev argued for the compulsory teaching of Kyrgyz to children as early as at kindergarten.

## References

Adams, Laura, Miguel Centeno, and Charles Varner. 2007. "Resistance to Cultural Globalization—A Comparative Analysis," In *Conflicts and Tensions*, edited by Helmut K. Anheier and Yudhishthir R. Isar, 80–9. London: SAGE.

Alexa "fergananews" 2012. Available at: http://www.alexa.com/siteinfo/fergananews. com (accessed 20 January 2012).

Alexa "KG" 2012. Available at: http://www.alexa.com/topsites/countries/KG (accessed 18 October 2012).

Alexa "KZ" 2012. Available at: http://www.alexa.com/topsites/countries/KZ (accessed 18 October 2012).

Alexa "mail.ru" 2012. Available at: http://www.alexa.com/siteinfo/mail.ru (accessed 18 October 2012).

Baidauletov, Serik. 2011. "Kazakhstan predlozhil LiveJournal pokaiat'sia." Available at: http://iwpr.net/node/54674 (accessed 15 October 2012).

Barlow, John Perry. 1996. "A Declaration of Independence of Cyberspace." Available at: http://projects.eff.org/□barlow/Declaration-Final.html (accessed 15 October 2012).

Batyrshin, Radik et al. 2011. "Kogda razvalitsia Runet? Polnaia versiia." *Mir24.TV*. Available at: http://mir24.tv/news/community/69935 (accessed 15 October 2012).

Bekirova, Alina. 2010. "Glavnaia problema Kazneta—nizkoe kachestvo ego soderzhaniia." *TsentrAziia*. Available at: http://www.centrasia.ru/newsA.php?st=1273126920 (accessed 15 October 2012).

Bohr, Annette. 2010. "The Central Asian States as Nationalising Regimes." In *Politics of Modern Central Asia: Critical Issues in Modern Politics*, edited by Bhavna Dave, vol. II, *State-Society Relations: Stability and Transformation*, 215–43. New York: Routledge.

Bowden, Brett 2009, *The Empire of Civilisation: The Evolution of an Imperial Idea*, Chicago: University of Chicago Press.

Budde. 2010. "Kyrgyzstan—Telecoms, Mobile and Internet." Available at: http://www. budde.com.au/Research/Kyrgyzstan-Telecoms-Mobile-and-Internet.html (accessed 15 October 2012).

Burbank, Jane and Frederick Cooper. 2010. *Empires in World History: Power and the Politics of Difference*, Princeton, NJ: Princeton University Press.

Carr, Jeffrey. 2011. "The Geopolitical Strategy of Russian Investment in Facebook and Other Social Networks." *Georgetown Journal of International Affairs*. Special Issue 2011: *International Engagement on Cyber*. 209–15. Available at: http://journal.georgetown.edu/special-issue-cyber-2/special-issue-cyber/ (accessed 15 October 2012).

Chainek. 2009. "Svoenravnyi_Chainek." Available at: http://diesel.elcat/kg/lofiversion/index.php?t1794460-100.html (accessed 20 January 2012).

Chun, Wendy Hui Kyong. 2006. *Control and Freedom: Power and Paranoia in the Age of Fiber Optics*, Cambridge, MA: MIT Press.

Constitution. 2012. "The Constitution." Available at: http://www.kazakhstan.orexca.com/kazakhstan_constitution.shtml (accessed 15 October 2012).

Cummings, Sally N., and Ole Nørgaard. 2010. "Conceptualising State Capacity." In *Politics of Modern Central Asia: Critical Issues in Modern Politics*, edited by Bhavna Dave, vol. II, *State-Society Relations: Stability and Transformation*, 65–90. New York: Routledge.

Dave, Bhavna. 2007. *Kazakhstan: Ethnicity, Language and Power*. London: Routledge.

Davies, Alan. 1996. "Review Article: Ironising the Myth of Linguicism." *Journal of Multilingual and Multicultural Development* 17(6): 485–96.

Deibert, Ronald, and Rafal Rohozinski. 2010a. "Beyond Denial: Introducing Next-Generation Information Access Controls." In *Access Controlled: The Shaping of Power, Rights, and Rule in Cyberspace*, edited by Ronald Deibert, John Palfrey, Rafal Rohozinski, and Jonathan Zittrain, 3–13. Cambridge, MA: MIT Press.

Deibert, Ronald, and Rafal Rohozinski. 2010b. "Control and Subversion in Russian Cyberspace." In *Access Controlled: The Shaping of Power, Rights, and Rule in Cyberspace*, edited by Ronald Deibert, John Palfrey, Rafal Rohozinski and Jonathan Zittrain, 15–34. Cambridge, MA: MIT Press.

Deibert, Ronald, John Palfrey, Rafal Rohozinski, and Jonathan Zittrain, eds. 2008. *Access Denied: The Practice and Policy of Global Internet Filtering*. Cambridge, MA: MIT Press.

——, eds. 2010. *Access Controlled: The Shaping of Power, Rights, and Rule in Cyberspace*. Cambridge, MA: MIT Press.

Dmitrienko, M. 2006. "Dai lapu, Kaznet—mnenie riadovogo iuzera." Available at: http://www.wasp.kz/net/day-lapu-kz.htm (accessed 19 May 2010).

Ebo, Bosah L., ed. 2001. *Cyberimperialism? Global Relations in the New Electronic Frontier*. Westport, CT: Praeger Publishers.

Gemius. 2010. "Do you CEE? The Internet Market of Central and Eastern Europe in 2010." Available at: http://www.slideshare.net/mroczekm/iab-gemius-do-you-cee-8662674 (accessed 15 October 2012).

Goldsmith, Jack and Tim Wu. 2006. *Who Controls the Internet? Illusions of a Borderless World*. Oxford: Oxford University Press.

Goodin, Dan. 2009. "DDoS Attack Boots Kyrgyzstan from Net: Russian Bears Blamed." Available at: http://www.theregister.co.uk/2009/01/28/kyrgyzstan_knocked_offline/ (accessed 15 October 2012).

Gorham, Michael. 2011. "Virtual Rusophonia: Language Policy as 'Soft Power' in the New Media Age." *Digital Icons: Studies in Russian, Eurasian and Central European New Media* 5(2): 23–48. Available at: http://www.digitalicons.org/issue05/files/2011/05/Gorham-5.2.pdf (accessed 15 October 2012).

Gunkel, David J. 2001. "The Empire Strikes Back Again: The Cultural Politics of the Internet." In *Cyberimperialism? Global Relations in the New Electronic Frontier*, edited by Bosah L. Ebo, 83–91. Westport, CT: Praeger Publishers.

Hardt, Michael, and Antonio Negri. 2000. *Empire*. Cambridge, MA: Harvard University Press.

Iatsenko, Elena. 2007. "Geopoliticheskii potentsial Russkogo mira: pochemu iazyk snova stanovitsia nadezhdoi i oporoi." *Nezavisimaia gazeta* 29 May. Available at: http://www.ng.ru/scenario/2007-05-29/11_hope.html (accessed 15 October 2012).

Ibragimova, G.D. 2008. "Aktual'nye podkhody k formirovaniiu russkoiazychnoi sredy v Kirgizii." In *Nuzhen li russkii iazyk novym nezavisimym gosudarstvam? Materialy konferentsii. Moskva, 29 fevralia 2008 goda*, edited by Russkiy Mir, 68–71. Moscow: Avanti Izdat. i. Tip.

Internet World Stats. 2012. "Asia Internet Usage Stats: Facebook and Population Statistics." Available at: http://www.internetworldstats.com/stats3.htm (accessed 25 January 2013).

Kazakhstan. 2012. "Kazakhstan: V ramkakh ShOS budet sozdana kiberpolitsiia." novosti@mail.ru. Available at: http://news.mail.ru/politics/8758241/ (accessed 15 October 2012).

Klimburg, Alexander. 2011. "Mobilising Cyber Power." *Survival* 53(1): 41–60.

Koenig, Matthias. 2000. "Social Conditions for the Implementation of Linguistic Human Rights Through Multicultural Policies: The Case of the Kyrgyz Republic." In *Language Policy and Language Issues in the Successor States of the Former USSR*, edited by Sue Wright, 57–84. Clevedon: Multilingual Matters Ltd.

Kolstoe, Paul. 1995. *Russians in the Former Soviet Republics*. London: Hurst.

Krylov, Ivan. 2011. "Russkim sootechestvennikam v Tsentral'noi Azii neobkhodimy svoi sredstva massovoi informatsii." Available at: http://www.russkiymir.ru/russkiymir/ru/news/common/news23199.html (accessed 15 October 2012).

Kurgannikov, D. 2009. "Sviazannye odnoi sviaz'iu." *info-TSES*. Available at: http://www.info-tses.kz/red/article.php?article=66421 (accessed 15 October 2012).

Kuzhabekova, Aliya. 2008. "Language Policies in Independent Kazakhstan: The Kazakh Russian Dilemma." *Linguistic Changes in Post-Communist Eastern Europe and Eurasia*, edited by Ernest Andrews, 161–84. Boulder, CO: East European Monographs.

Kyrgyzskaia Respublika. 2009. "Kyrgyzskaia Republika: Perepis' naseleniia i zhilishchnogo fonda." Available at: http://212.42.101.100:8088/nacstat/node/23 (accessed 15 October 2012).

Laitin, David D. 1998. *Identity in Formation: The Russian-Speaking Populations in the Near Abroad*, Ithaca, NY: Cornell University Press.

Landau, Jacob M., and Barbara Kellner-Heinkele. 2001. *Politics of Language in the Ex-Soviet Muslim States*. London: Hurst.

Laruelle, Marlène, and Sébastien Peyrouse. 2004. *Les Russes du Kazakhstan: Identités nationales et nouveaux États dans l'espace post-soviétique*. Paris: Maisonneuve et Larose.

Lee, Paul Siu-Nam. 1988. "Communication Imperialism and Dependency: A Conceptual Clarification." *Gazette* 41: 69–83.

Mambetalieva, Tattu, and Oksana Kim. 2009. "Kyrgyzstan." 153–4. Available at: http://www.giswatch.org/sites/default/files/Kyrgyzstan.pdf (accessed 15 October 2012).

Matveeva, Anna. 2007. "Traditionen, Kalküle, Funktionen: Russlands Rückkehr nach Zentralasien." In *Machtmosaik Zentralasien. Traditionen, Restriktionen, Aspirationen* (= *Osteuropa* 8/9): 277–94.

Memmi, Albert. 1957. *Portrait du colonisé, précédé de portrait du colonisateur*. Corrêa: Buchet/Chastel.

Molodezh'. 2012. "Molodezh'—za novuiu kadrovuiu politiku." Available at: http://www.facebook.com/groups/201596076617262/?ref=ts&fref=ts (accessed 15 October 2012).

Morozov, Evgeny. 2011. *The Net Delusion: How Not to Liberate the World*. London: Allen Lane.

Na zapade. 2011. "Na zapade Kazakhstana po-prezhnemu nespokoino ... V Zhanaozene zaderzhany rossiiskie zhurnalisty." RussiansKz.Info. Available at: http://www.russianskz.info/society/2605-na-zapade-kazahstana-po-prezhnemu-nespokoyno-v-zhanaozene-zaderzhany-rossiyskie-zhurnalisty.html (accessed 15 October 2012).

Naughton, John. 2000. *A Brief History of the Future: The Origins of the Internet*. London: Phoenix.

Ngũgĩ, wa Thiong'o 1986. *Decolonising the Mind: The Politics of Language in African Literature*. London: James Currey.

Nye, Joseph S. Jr. 2011. *The Future of Power*. New York: Public Affairs.

O fonde. 2007. "O fonde. Fond 'Russkii Mir' byl sozdan ukazom Prezidenta RF V.V. Putina 21 iiunia 2007 goda." Available at: http://www.russkiymir.ru/russkiymir/ru/fund/about (accessed 15 October 2012).

ONI 2005. "Special Report: Kyrgyzstan: Election Monitoring in Kyrgyzstan." Available at: http://opennet.net/special/kg/ (accessed 15 October 2012).

Paasonen, Susanna. 2009. "What Cyberspace? Travelling Concepts in Internet Research." In *Internationalizing Internet Studies: Beyond Anglophone Paradigms*, edited by Gerard Goggin and Mark McLelland, 18–31. New York: Routledge.

Pavlenko, Aneta. 2008. "Multilingualism in Post-Soviet Countries: Language Revival, Language Removal, and Sociolinguistic Theory." *International Journal of Bilingual Education and Bilingualism* 11(3/4): 275–314.

Peyrouse, Sébastien. 2007. "Nationhood and the Minority Question in Central Asia: The Russians in Kazakhstan." *Europe-Asia Studies* 59(3): 481–501.

Phillipson, Robert. 1992. *Linguistic Imperialism*. Oxford: Oxford University Press.

PM.kz. 2012. "Segodnia po priglasheniiu press-sluzhby Prem'er-Ministra RK gruppa naibolee izvestnykh bloggerov Kazakhstana vyletaet v Akatau." Available at: http://scribe.twitter.com/#!/pm_kz/status/150519235733495809 (accessed 15 October 2011).

Premiia. 2006. "Runet za predelami .RU." Available at: http://oldpermiaruneta.ru/archive/premia-2006/allnom/full/ (accessed 20 January 2012).

Press-sluzhba. 2010. "Russkoiazychnye v Tsentral'noi Azii." Available at: http://www.russkiymir.ru/russkiymir/ru/fund/activity/action0064.html (accessed 15 October 2012).

Rusciano, Frank L. 2001. "The Three Faces of Cyberimperialism." In *Cyberimperialism? Global Relations in the New Electronic Frontier*, edited by Bosah L. Ebo, 9–25. Westport, CT: Praeger Publishers.

Russkii tsentr. 2010. "Russkii tsentr otkrylsia v Tadzhikskom natsional'nom universitete." 16 October. Available at: http://www.russkiymir.ru/russkiymir/ru/fund/activity/action0075.html (accessed 15 October 2012).

Saunders, Robert. 2006. "Denationalized Digerati in the Virtual Near Abroad: The Internet's Paradoxical Impact on National Identity among Minority Russians." *Global Media and Communication* 2(1): 43–69.

—— 2007. "In Defence of Kazakshilik: Kazakhstan's War on Sacha Baron Cohen." *Identities: Global Studies in Culture and Power* 14: 225–55.

—— 2009. "Wiring the Second World: The Geopolitics of Information and Communications Technology in Post Totalitarian Eurasia." *Russian Cyberspace* 1(1): 1–24. Available at: http://www.digitalicons.org/issue01/pdf/issue1/Wiring-the-Second-World_R-A-Saunders.pdf (accessed 15 October 2012).

Schäfer, Zarifa, and Dirk Uffelmann. 2012. "Gibt es einen russischen Cyberimperialismus gegenüber dem Nahen Ausland? Bemerkungen mit Blick auf Kasachstan und Turkmenistan." *Von der digitalen zur interkulturellen Revolution?*, edited by Ursula Reutner, 413–33. Baden-Baden: Nomos.

Schatz, Edward. 2000. "The Politics of Multiple Identities: Lineage and Ethnicity in Kazakhstan." *Europe-Asia Studies* 52(3): 489–506.

Shaibakova, Damina D. 2005. *Funktsionirovanie russkogo iazyka v Kazakhstane: vchera, segodnia, zavtra*. Almaty: KazUMOiMJa.

Smagulova, Juldyz. 2008. "Language Policies of Kazakhization and Their Influence on Language Attitudes and Use." *The International Journal of Bilingual Education and Bilingualism* 11(3/4): 440–75.

Sonders [Saunders], Robert. 2004. "Natsional'nost': kiberrusskii." *Rossiia v global'nom kontekste* 4(2): 182–92.

Spivak, Gayatri Chakravorty. 1996. *The Spivak Reader: Selected Works*, edited by Donna Landry and Gerald MacLean. London: Routledge.

Taratuta, Juliia, and Michail Zygar'. 2010. "Kreml' nachinaet ogranichivat' runet." *newsland; informatsionno-diskussionyi portal* 26 April. Available at: http://www.newsland.ru/News/Detail/id/494436/ (accessed 18 May 2010).

Tong, Deborah. 2001. "Cybercolonialism: Speeding Along the Superhighway or Stalling on a Beaten Track?" In *Cyberimperialism? Global Relations in the New Electronic Frontier*, edited by Bosah L. Ebo, 65–79. Westport, CT: Praeger Publishers.

Torbakov, Igor. 2012. "Russia: Putin's Tsar Paul Complex." *EurasiaNet*. Available at: http://www.eurasianet.org/node/65144 (accessed 18 October 2011).

Uffelmann, Dirk. 2011a. "Post-Russian Eurasia and the Proto-Eurasian Usage of the Runet in Kazakhstan: A Plea for a Cyberlinguistic Turn in Area Studies." *Journal of Eurasian Studies* 2(2): 172–83.

—— 2011b. "Umriss einer crossmedialen und grenzüberschreitenden Slavistik." In *Medien und Wandel*, Passauer Studien zur interdisziplinären Medienforschung 1, edited by Christoph Barmeyer et al., 161–83. Berlin: Logos Berlin.

Vehovar, Vasja. 2001. "Prospects of Small Countries in the Age of the Internet." In *Cyberimperialism? Global Relations in the New Electronic Frontier*, edited by Bosah L. Ebo, 123–37. Westport, CT: Praeger Publishers.

Wilkinson, Cai, and Yelena Jetpyspayeva. 2012. "From Blogging Central Asia to Citizen Media: A Practitioner's Perspective on the Evolution of the *neweurasia* Blog Project." *Europe-Asia Studies* 64(8): 1395–414.

Wright, Sue. 2000. "Kyrgyzstan: The Political and Linguistic Context." In *Language Policy and Language Issues in the Successor States of the Former USSR*, edited by Sue Wright, 85–91. Clevedon: Multilingual Matters Ltd.

Zakharova, E. 2006. "Russkii iazyk v Kyrgyzstane teriaet status ofitsial'nogo: soglasny li s etim zhiteli strany?" http://www.fergananews.com/article.php?id=4659 (accessed 15 October 2012).

Zakon. 2009. "Zakon 178-4 ot 10.07.2009 'O vnesenii izmenenii i dopolnenii v nekotorye zakonodatel'nye akty Respubliki Kazakhstan po voprosam informatsionnokommunikatsionnykh setei'." http://www.pavlodar.com/zakon/?dok=04418&all=all (accessed 15 October 2012).

# Index

Locators shown in *italics* refer to figures and tables.

For Product Safety Concerns and Information please contact our EU
representative GPSR@taylorandfrancis.com
Taylor & Francis Verlag GmbH, Kaufingerstraße 24, 80331 München, Germany

www.ingramcontent.com/pod-product-compliance
Lightning Source LLC
Chambersburg PA
CBHW071923080326
R17960300001B/R179603PG40689CBX00007B/1
*9781138206007*